THE 8085A MICROPROCESSOR:
Software, Programming, and Architecture

BARRY B. BREY

DeVRY Institute of Technology
Columbus, Ohio

PRENTICE-HALL, Englewood Cliffs, New Jersey 07632

Library of Congress Cataloging-in-Publication Data

Brey, Barry B.
    The 8085A microprocessor.

    Includes index.
    1. Intel 8085A (Microprocessor)   I. Title.
QA76.8.I2913B74   1986   005.265   85-25602
ISBN 0-13-246711-9

Editorial/production supervision and
    interior design: Eileen M. O'Sullivan
Cover design: Wanda Lubelska
Manufacturing buyer: Gordon Osbourne

Printed in the United States of America

10   9   8   7   6   5   4

ISBN   0-13-246711-9   025

Prentice-Hall International (UK) Limited, *London*
Prentice-Hall of Australia Pty. Limited, *Sydney*
Prentice-Hall Canada Inc., *Toronto*
Prentice-Hall Hispanoamericana, S.A., *Mexico*
Prentice-Hall of India Private Limited, *New Delhi*
Prentice-Hall of Japan, Inc., *Tokyo*
Prentice-Hall of Southeast Asia Pte. Ltd., *Singapore*
Editora Prentice-Hall do Brasil, Ltda., *Rio de Janeiro*
Whitehall Books Limited, *Wellington, New Zealand*

To my mother

CONTENTS

No-op, STC, CMC

PREFACE

It is important for students of computer science, electronic technology, and electronic technician programs to understand how to program a microprocessor. Programming not only requires an understanding of high-level languages, but also how to manipulate data at the assembly or machine language level. Today the microprocessor is used to control many different processes in almost all industries. It has replaced the mainframe computer, and in many instances the minicomputer, for process control. It is therefore essential for future and present success that low-level control software be fully understood by students in any of the aforementioned disciplines.

This text presents not only the instruction set for a very common microprocessor, the Intel 8085A, but also provides a sound foundation in structured programming at the assembly or machine level. You will learn all the basic machine language building blocks that are used to construct modern process control systems.

In Chapters 1 to 3 we discuss in detail the fundamentals required to program and understand the application of the microprocessor. We also introduce some of the programming techniques used in modern programming.

After the basic principles have been introduced, in Chapters 4 to 6 we describe the operation of each 8085A instruction.

Once the instruction set of the 8085A has been introduced, in Chapter 7 we study the assembler and Chapter 8 the structured program flowcharting. This is an important step that is often neglected.

The remainder of the text is devoted to developing some of the most important programming building blocks: data manipulation, fixed-point arithmetic, floating-point arithmetic, conversion algorithms, table-lookup techniques, sorting, and diagnostic software.

Once programming and most of the major building blocks of microprocessor system software design have been studied, in Chapter 16 we introduce the architecture of the Intel 8085A microprocessor.

After completing this text the student is prepared to study microprocessor hardware and interfacing in a subsequent course. This text has fully prepared the student for this endeavor.

chapter one

INTRODUCTION TO MICROPROCESSORS

This chapter introduces you to the microprocessor—the ninth wonder of the modern world. It is absolutely critical that the programming of the microprocessor be understood to compete successfully in today's complex job market. It is to this end that this first chapter introduces you to this intricate modern electronic marvel. Imagine, an entire book devoted to a single integrated circuit that occupies less than 2 square inches of space! Just a few decades ago a device of this complexity would have occupied at least a 2-square-yard area.

1-1 OBJECTIVES

Upon completion of this chapter, you will be able to:

1. Trace the history of the microprocessor from its meager beginnings to the present day
2. Identify some of the major microprocessor manufacturers and the microprocessors they produce
3. Define what a microprocessor is and describe the function of the main components in a microprocessor-based computer system
4. Describe the basic operations performed by the microprocessor
5. List some commonly found microprocessor input/output equipment
6. Name some of the more common 8085A-based microprocessor training aids

1-2 HISTORY OF THE MICROPROCESSOR

The microprocessor was conceived by Intel Corporation in California in 1971 as a 4-bit microcontroller designed for use in an electronic calculator. It did not take long before other applications for this device were dreamed up by inventive minds at such companies as Balley Corporation. One of the early applications of this device was a video arcade game.

The Intel 4004

This early computer on a chip was the Intel 4004 microprocessor, which could add two 4-bit binary numbers and perform many other operations. (A bit is a binary digit capable of storing a 1 or a 0.) You might think that a 4-bit microprocessor has very limited application today, but believe it or not, it still has wide application. If you were to buy a microwave oven or similar device, you would probably find that it contained a 4-bit microprocessor. Two of the most common microprocessors used in applications such as microwave ovens are the TMS-1000, which is manufactured by Texas Instruments, and the Intel 4040, which is an updated version of the original 4004.

   The 4004 was a fairly primitive device by today's standards, capable of addressing 4096 different memory locations. For many applications this is not enough memory. In addition to memory size, the word size of the 4004 proved to be too restrictive in many cases. A 4-bit number can store only 16 possible codes. For the many applications that handle alphabetic information, 4 bits proves to be too limiting because there are 26 letters in the alphabet plus a variety of special characters and numbers. It normally takes at least a 6-bit and often a 7-bit binary number to encode all of these different characters. To solve this problem Intel introduced an 8-bit microprocessor, the 8008.

The Intel 8008

The Intel 8008 could handle 8-bit numbers (bytes), which was a great improvement over the 4004. (A byte is usually equal to 8 bits.) In addition to the increase in word size, the memory size was increased from 4096 four-bit words in the 4004, to 16K eight-bit words in the 8008. (A computer K is equal to 1024.) The 4004 and the 8008 could both add numbers at the rate of 20,000 per second, which at the time was fast enough for many of the early applications. With engineers dreaming up new tasks for the microprocessor every day, this speed eventually began to limit the application of these early microprocessors. The main reason these early devices were so slow is that they were constructed from the then state-of-the-art PMOS logic circuitry. (PMOS is an acronym for P-channel metal-oxide semiconductor.) PMOS logic is inherently slow, and in addition to being slow, it is fairly difficult to interface to standard TTL logic because it uses a negative power supply.

Then, at about this same period of time, there was a breakthrough in the fabrication of NMOS logic circuitry. (NMOS is an acronym for N-channel metal-oxide semiconductor.) NMOS logic is much faster than PMOS logic and it also uses a positive power supply, which makes it more readily adaptable to be connected to TTL logic. This is important because many of the ancillary integrated circuits connected to a microprocessor are TTL circuits. NMOS allowed speeds to be increased by a factor of about 25 times, which is significant. This new technology was used in the construction of the now famous Intel 8080 microprocessor.

The Intel 8080

The Intel 8080 was introduced in 1973 and its introduction is responsible for catapulting the world into the age of microprocessors. The 8080 was a greatly enhanced 8008 that could perform 500,000 operations per second and address 64K bytes of memory space. This device was also responsible for ushering in the age of the home computer, which was first introduced by MITS in 1974. This first hobby or home computer was the Altair 8800, which generated keen interest in microprocessing.

Although the Altair 8800 computer is no longer manufactured, it did represent a change in the way people viewed the computer. A computer was no longer viewed as a mystical device suited only for large corporations or the military. It was a device that would, in a few short years, begin to populate American homes in the form of Apples, Ataris, Commodores, IBMs, and various other microprocessor-based systems.

Other Early Microprocessors

Up until 1973, Intel was the major producer of microprocessors; then other manufacturers began to see that this new device had a future and started to manufacture their own modified versions of the Intel 8080 microprocessor. Many of the early microprocessors are no longer actively produced because of the popularity exhibited by the Intel 8080 microprocessor. Some of these microprocessors, together with their manufacturers, are listed in Table 1-1. You many notice from the list of microprocessors in Table 1-1 that not all of these microprocessors are in production today, and in fact some of these companies no longer make new microprocessors.

TABLE 1-1 EARLY 8-BIT MICROPROCESSORS

Manufacturer	Part number
Fairchild	F-8
Intel	8080
MOS Technology	6502
Motorola	MC6800
National Semiconductor	IMP-8
Rockwell International	PPS-8

Microprocessors of Today

The thrust in recent microprocessor development seems to come from three different manufacturers: Intel, Motorola, and Zilog. Each continues to market new and improved versions every year or two. Microprocessors today vary in size from 4 bits all the way up to 32-bit versions. Table 1–2 lists many of the microprocessors being manufactured by these three companies, together with their basic word size.

TABLE 1-2 MICROPROCESSORS MANUFACTURED BY INTEL, MOTOROLA, AND ZILOG

Manufacturer	Part number	Word width
Intel	8048	8
	8051	8
	8085A	8
	8086	16
	8088	16
	8096	16
	Iapx-186	16
	Iapx-188	16
	Iapx-286	16
	Iapx-386	32
	Iapx-432	32
Motorola	6800	8
	6805	8
	6809	8/16
	68000	16/32
	68008	16/32
	68010	16/32
	68020	32
Zilog	Z8	8
	Z80	8
	Z8001	16
	Z80000	32

1-3 THE MICROPROCESSOR

What is a microprocessor? The microprocessor is a device that can be commanded to perform a variety of various functions—it is a programmable controller. All microprocessors perform the same three basic functions in a system: data transfer, arithmetic and logic, and decision making. These are the same three tasks that can be performed by any microprocessor, minicomputer, or mainframe computer system.

Figure 1–1 illustrates a typical block diagram of a computer system with the micro-processor at the center. The microprocessor is pictured at the center because it con-trols the memory and input/output (I/O) blocks. The interconnections are data, address, and control paths (buses) between the microprocessor and these ancillary devices.

Figure 1-1   The block diagram of a microprocessor based computer system.

Buses

The address bus connections are used to supply a memory address or an I/O address to the memory and I/O blocks. The address, which is a binary number, is used to point to a unique memory location or I/O device. Memory can be envisioned as a series of numbered (addressed) boxes that hold an 8-bit binary number in an 8-bit microcomputer.

The data bus connections, which would be 8 bits wide for an 8-bit micro-processor, are used to carry the information to or from the memory and I/O. Data bus lines are, in most cases, bidirectional lines capable of transmitting information in either direction.

The control bus connections are used to control both the memory and I/O sys-tems. The control bus consists of three general signals: $\overline{RD}$ (read), $\overline{WR}$ (write), and $IO/\overline{M}$ (input/output or memory). $\overline{RD}$ is used to control the reading of data from memory or I/O, $\overline{WR}$ is used to control the writing of data to memory or I/O, and $IO/\overline{M}$ is used to select I/O or memory.

Data Transfer

The microprocessor spends a great deal of its time transferring data to and from the memory and I/O. About 50 percent of its time is spent fetching instructions from the memory and preparing to execute them. Computers today store the commands or instructions in their memory so that they can be executed at a very high rate of speed.

Arithmetic and Logic

A small portion of the microprocessor's time is spent performing arithmetic or logic operations. These operations can be executed in 1 to 2 microseconds (μs) in most microprocessors. Table 1–3 illustrates the typical arithmetic and logic operations that most microprocessors can perform. Notice that multiplication and division have been omitted from the listing. This was done because not all of the currently manufactured microprocessors are capable of performing these two operations.

TABLE 1-3 ARITHMETIC AND LOGIC OPERATIONS
FOUND IN MANY MICROPROCESSORS

Operation	Notes
Addition	—
Subtraction	Two's-complement addition
AND	Logical multiplication
OR	Logical addition
XOR	Exclusive-OR
NOT	Inversion
Shift	Either arithmetic or logical
Rotate	—

Decisions

The ability of the microprocessor to make decisions allows it to process information more efficiently. It also allows the programmer to develop software that can choose different paths through a program. This ability has made the computer system the powerful device that it is today.

Microprocessors make decisions based on numerical facts. Table 1-4 illustrates some testable conditions that microprocessors use to make decisions.

TABLE 1-4 COMMON TESTABLE CONDITIONS
USED BY MICROPROCESSORS TO MAKE DECISIONS

Numeric condition	Testable conditions
Zero	Equal to zero
	Not equal to zero
Sign	Positive
	Negative
Parity	Odd parity
	Even parity
Carry	Carry equal to one
	Carry equal to zero

1-4 THE MEMORY SYSTEM

The memory system in a computer performs two very important tasks: (1) memory is used to store the instructions of a program, and (2) memory is used to store data for use by the program. In most systems the program is stored in a read-only memory (ROM) and the data are stored in a random access memory (RAM), the term used for a read and write memory.

The Program

The program in a computer system is made up of various instructions that direct the operation of the microprocessor. Instructions are binary numbers that are interpreted by the microprocessor as various operations that are to be executed by the microprocessor. A grouping of these instructions is called a program. Programs vary in length from a few hundred instructions in simple systems to thousands of instructions in complex systems.

A simple example of a program is adding the numbers 3 and 2 together. To direct the computer to perform this addition, a series of instructions are stored in the memory as a program. The first instruction fetches the 3 from the memory. This is comparable to writing it down on a piece of paper. The second instruction gets the 2 out of the memory and adds it to the 3. This is comparable to writing the 2 beneath the 3 and adding them together in your mind. Finally, a third instruction is required to store, or save, the answer in the memory—the same thing that you do when you write the answer down on a piece of paper. Notice how the simple task of adding two numbers together seems more difficult than normal. This is because each step must be thought of and written down as a separate instruction in a program.

Types of Memory

As mentioned earlier, the ROM, or some form of ROM such as an EPROM (erasable programmable read-only memory), is used to store the program and the RAM is used to store the data. This is not always true, of course, but it is in many cases.

The ROM memory that is commonly found associated with the microprocessor

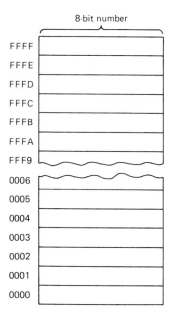

Figure 1-2 A symbolic representation of a computer system memory. Each box (memory location) contains a binary number and each location is addressable by a number (memory address).

is typically either a factory- or mask-programmed ROM or a field-programmable EPROM. The EPROM is programmable in the field by a device called an EPROM programmer. In addition to being programmable, the EPROM is constructed using a process that allows it to be erased if a mistake is detected.

The RAM memory is most often some form of NMOS or CMOS memory device. In small systems, memory is often constructed from static RAM (SRAM) and large memory systems are often constructed from dynamic RAM (DRAM).

Figure 1–2 pictures a symbolic memory that illustrates the address and also some binary data stored in each address or memory location. It makes programming much easier if you think of the memory as a row of mailboxes that can each hold a number. Each mailbox also has an address that is used to locate the data stored in it.

1-5 INPUT/OUTPUT DEVICES

The input/output block in a computer system is the microprocessor's connection to the outside world. The microprocessor communicates to human beings and/or machines through this block. Without this communications path, the computer would truly be a worthless device.

I/O devices are defined as devices that can either accept an electrical signal for processing or generate an electrical signal to accomplish work. Just about any device in use by today's modern society could be, and often is, interfaced to a microprocessor as an I/O device. This has largely been made possible since analog-to-digital (ADC) and digital-to-analog (DAC) converters are available. Some of the more common I/O devices are listed in Table 1–5.

TABLE 1-5 COMMON INPUT/OUTPUT DEVICES

Device	Type	Common usage
Switch	Input	Used to sense events such as key depressions on a keyboard, limits in certain mechanical systems, etc.
ADC	Input	Used to convert any analog voltage into a digital signal that can be sensed by the microprocessor
Indicator	Output	An LED or similar device that can indicate a single condition or, in some cases, display a numeric or alphabetic character
Motor	Output	Used to position external mechanical devices; may be a stepper motor or an ac or dc motor
Solenoid relay	Output	Used to control electrical or contacts or physically move an external device
DAC	Output	Used to convert the digital output of the microprocessor into an analog voltage

1-6 MICROPROCESSOR TRAINING AIDS

Microprocessor training aids (trainers) are devices that contain a keyboard, a set of numeric displays, and usually a method of connecting the trainer to an outside circuit. A typical microprocessor training aid is pictured in Fig. 1–3. This device, the SDK-85, is manufactured by Intel to train people on the 8085A microprocessor. Trainers are probably one of the most inexpensive methods of learning the operation of a microprocessor. Most training aids, such as this one, cost less then $500 and are fairly easy to operate. Figure 1–4 pictures the Micromodule-85 training aid from DeVRY INC, which owns and operates the DeVRY Institutes of Technology. These aids, which are both 8085A based, are used in the laboratory to introduce and train students in programming the microprocessor.

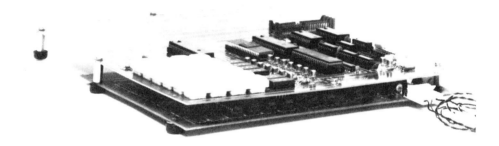

Figure 1-3   The Intel SDK 85 microprocessor trainer. (Photograph courtesy of Intel Corporation.)

Figure 1-4   The Micromodule 85, 8085A based microprocessor trainer (Courtesy of DeVRY Inc.)

Trainer Functions

The trainer normally contains a hexadecimal keypad for data entry plus additional keys for control. The control keys control:

1. The reading of data from the memory
2. The writing of data to memory
3. The displaying and modifying of the contents of the microprocessor's registers
4. The execution of a program stored in the memory
5. The debugging of a faulty program by the use of a single-instruction execution mode of operation
6. The reseting of the microprocessor if the program becomes entangled in an infinite loop

The trainer also contains a set of numeric displays that are capable of displaying hexadecimal data as a two-digit number and a four-digit number. The displays normally indicate any one of the following:

1. A sign-on message such as 8085, which is displayed when the unit is first turned on or reset
2. An address and data from any memory location
3. The contents of an internal register and its letter designation
4. Some indication that a user program is being executed, such as the letter E
5. Breakpoint addresses during programming

In addition to the keyboard and displays, the trainers also have an area that can be used to expand the circuitry. For example, suppose that you wished to add an analog-to-digital converter to the trainer for an experiment. This is accomplished by wiring up the circuit on the breadboard area of the SDK-85 or on an external breadboard for the Micromodule-85.

1-7 SUMMARY

1. Intel Corporation developed the first microprocessor, the 4004, a 4-bit machine that could directly address 4K nibbles of memory.
2. Four-bit microprocessors still find wide application in such systems as microwave ovens, dishwashers, and even in automobiles.
3. Eight-bit microprocessors are much more useful in many applications because alphabetic data requires at least a 6-bit binary code for representation and more often a 7-bit code.
4. PMOS logic, which was used in early microprocessors, proved to be too slow. This led to the development of NMOS logic and the modern gender of the microprocessor.

5. As early as 1974, the home computer began to appear on the scene in the form of the Altair 8800 computer system.

6. Today microprocessors are available in 4-, 8-, 16-, and 32-bit versions.

7. The microprocessor is a device that performs arithmetic and logic, data transfer, and makes some rudimentary decisions based on numerical facts.

8. Buses are used to control the system connected to a microprocessor. All microprocessors contain an address bus, a data bus, and a control bus.

9. The memory in a microprocessor-based system is used to store the instructions of a program and the data used by a program.

10. A program is a collection of instructions that are used to perform a useful task in a computer.

11. RAM (random access memory) is used to store temporary data, and ROM (read-only memory) is used to store programs and more permanent data.

12. An input/output device is a device that will either accept an electrical signal or generate one.

13. A microprocessor trainer is a device that is used to learn how to program the microprocessor. Most trainers allow the user to enter data or commands, view the data from the memory or internal registers, and execute or single-step through a program.

1-8 GLOSSARY

Address bus   A set of connections that are used to provide the memory and I/O with an address.

Bit   One binary digit (0 or 1) or position in a binary number. Also a contraction for *binary* digi*t*.

Buses   Common paths that are used to interconnect the many components in a system.

Byte   Generally, an 8-bit binary number. A contraction formed from *binary* (B) and *eight* (YTE).

CMOS   Complementary metal-oxide semiconductor technology.

Control bus   A common set of connections that is used to control both the I/O and the memory.

Data bus   A common set of connections that is used to transfer all the information in a computer system.

DRAM   Dynamic random access memory.

EPROM   An erasable programmable read-only memory is a device that can be erased with an ultraviolet lamp and reprogrammed electrically.

Input device   A device, such as a keyboard, that sends data to the microprocessor.

I/O   The input/output equipment provides the microprocessor with its interface to the outside world.

K   In computer terminology a K is generally equal to 1024 decimal.

Mainframe computer   A mainframe computer system is a large computer designed to handle extremely large jobs. The term *mainframe* comes from the fact that the machine is often mounted in one or more rack panels or frames.

Memory   A device that stores binary information for the microprocessor.

Microcomputer   A computer system constructed around a microprocessor.

Microprocessor   A device that can be programmed to control just about any situation. It is a programmable controller.

Microprocessor trainer   A device used to learn the operation and programming of a particular microprocessor.

Minicomputer   A scaled-down version of a mainframe computer that is today losing definition because of the microprocessor-based microcomputer.

NMOS   N-channel metal-oxide semiconductor technology.

Output device   A device, such as a printer, that accepts data from the microprocessor.

PMOS   P-channel metal-oxide semiconductor technology.

Program   A collection of instructions that direct a computer to perform a task.

RAM   Random access memory is memory that can be written into as well as read out.

ROM   Read-only memory is memory that has been permanently programmed with information that can only be read from the memory.

SRAM   Static random access memory.

TTL   Transistor-transistor logic is a bipolar transistor technology.

Word size   Generally, the word size is determined by the width of the microprocessor's internal arithmetic circuitry.

QUESTIONS AND PROBLEMS

1-1. What corporation developed the first microprocessor?

1-2. What are some of the early applications of the microprocessor?

1-3. What led to the development of the 8-bit microprocessor?

1-4. One byte is equal to how many bits?

1-5. A 4K memory device contains how many decimal memory locations?

1-6. What breakthrough ushered in a faster and more versatile microprocessor?

1-7. List three different 8-bit microprocessors.

1-8. List three different 16-bit microprocessors.

1-9. Give a brief definition of the microprocessor.

1-10. What three main blocks comprise the block diagram of a typical microprocessor-based computer system?

1-11. What three main operations are performed by the microprocessor?

1-12. What buses interconnect the blocks in a microprocessor-based computer system?

1-13. List four common arithmetic and logic operations performed by the microprocessor.

1-14. List three common factors that the microprocessor uses to make a decision.

1-15. In what type of memory is the program in a microprocessor-based computer system stored?

1-16. Data of a transitory nature are stored in what type of memory?

1-17. Define the term *program*.

1-18. What types of RAM read and write memory are found in various computer systems?

1-19. Define the term input/output.

1-20. List four commonly found I/O devices.

1-21. What hardware features are usually found in a microprocessor trainer?

1-22. What functions are most often found in a typical microprocessor trainer?

_____ chapter two _____

SOFTWARE DEVELOPMENT

Before a detailed study of the programming of the 8085A microprocessor can be conducted, it is important to develop an understanding of the programming task. (Programs are often called software.) In this chapter we approach this by introducing the systems most often used to develop software, the development task, various programming approaches, and software design, and discuss assemblers, interpreters, and compilers. Once these areas are fully understood, it is much easier to learn how a particular microprocessor functions and finally, to write efficient, well-documented software.

2-1 OBJECTIVES

Upon completion of this chapter, you will able to:

1. Describe the essential components of a software development system
2. List common software tools used within the software development system
3. Define the problems so that a program can be written
4. Detail the program development task
5. Describe programming approaches, such as top-down, modular, and structured
6. List the steps most often used in software design
7. Describe the following software systems: assembler, interpreter, and compiler

2-2 SOFTWARE DEVELOPMENT SYSTEMS

What is a software development system? A software development system is a machine that has specifically been designed to make software development as efficient as possible. A software development system, as the system pictured in Fig. 2–1, should have the following essential component parts:

1. A video display terminal for data entry and display
2. An editor for entering the source program into the system
3. An assembler for developing bit manipulation and I/O software
4. A high-level programming language such as PL/M or Pascal for developing the intricate portions of the software, which most often use complicated arithmetic
5. A linker, which is used to connect software modules together to form the software system
6. A disk memory system for saving the software for latter use
7. An I/O port that can connect a printer to the system for printing a hard copy of the software
8. An EPROM programmer for storing the completed software on an EPROM

Figure 2–1   The Intel Personal Development System (iPDS). This system is used to develop software, test the software and hardware as a unit, and program ROMs. (Photograph courtesy of Intel Corporation.)

The Video Display Terminal

The video display terminal (VDT) portion of the software development system should have a standard typewriter keyboard, including additional cursor positioning keys. It is also desirable to have some programmable function keys or other mechanism for entering often used keying sequences. A numeric keypad can also be helpful at times, especially if the software development task requires the entry of long series of numeric data. For operator convenience the positon and angle of the keyboard should be adjustable.

The Editor

The software development system's editor is extremely important because it is used not only to enter the source program into the system, but also to modify it. (The source program is a program written in BASIC or assembly language.) The editor should be capable of deleting unwanted lines of the program, moving entire lines or blocks of lines from one point to another, replacing labels with other labels, finding any line or label, and repeating lines of software. An editor without these minimum features is very hard to use and makes the software development task more difficult. Most modern word processing software can function as an editor because most and usually all of the features are provided.

An Assembler

The assembler is a program that converts the symbolic source program into the binary machine language object program for the desired microprocessor. It should at least be capable of indicating simple syntax errors as they appear in the source program. (A syntax error is an error in form: for example, a missing or misplaced comma or variable.)

The assembler is used to develop the software required to control I/O devices because I/O control software usually requires a considerable amount of bit manipulation. Bit manipulation is difficult to accomplish efficiently with a high-level programming language. The assembler is also used where the time required to execute the software is critical. For most other software functions a high-level programming language is often more expedient at generating software.

Pascal or PL/M

Pascal and PL/M are two examples of high-level programming languages that are quite useful in developing software for a microprocessor-based system. They are commonly used to develop portions of the software that require extensive arithmetic manipulation of complicated data structures. A high-level language's advantage is not software efficiency, because the software it generates is not nearly as efficient as that developed by an experienced assembly language programmer. A high-level language's advantage lies in the fact that it can generate complicated code at a tremendous rate of speed compared to that needed by an experienced programmer using an assembler.

The Linker

The linker is used to build the final machine language system by linking together (connecting) all the software modules. Software modules may consist of assembly language programs, high-level-language programs, and subroutines from one or more system software libraries.

The EPROM Programmer

The EPROM programmer is an important part of the system because it is the place the final system software is sent after the development task. The EPROM holds the program so that it can be plugged into the hardware system for testing. Whenever software is stored on an EPROM it is called firmware.

The EPROM programmer should be able to program a wide variety of different EPROMs. Today, EPROMs vary in size from 1K by 8 (2708) to 64K by 8 (27512).

2-3 THE DEVELOPMENT TASK

Where does one start when developing a software system? The first thing not to do is to start writing a program. Writing a program in a minimal amount of time, efficiently, requires a considerable amount of forethought. The thinking process is the first step in software development. This section details the proper steps required to develop software in the shortest possible time and at the lowest cost.

Problem Definition

Before a program can be written to solve a task, the task must be fully understood and properly defined. This is the step most often skipped by an inexperienced programmer (hacker)—a programmer who may never complete a program.

After the task is understood, the input and output data must be defined. The following questions about the input and output data should be listed so that there is no confusion at a later time.

1. What is the form of the input data? (ASCII string, ASCII character, binary byte, binary word, packed BCD, unpacked BCD, etc.)
2. What is the required form of the output data? (ASCII string, ASCII character, binary byte, binary word, packed BCD, unpacked BCD, etc.)
3. Do the input data require a buffer?
4. Do the output data require a buffer?
5. Is there any change required in the form of data between the input and the remainder of the program?
6. Do the output data need to be conditioned before they are sent out of the program?

Suppose that a system uses a simple decimal keyboard for input data and a six-digit display for output data. The data from the keyboard are in BCD code; the output data are also BCD. This means that the data must be in BCD form to enter and exit the software. An output buffer is probably required because there are six digits of output data. These questions are designed to make you think about the problem before the software is actually written.

Once the input and output specifications are made, the program itself can be defined. This section will vary from program to program, but a few steps can be followed for every program, which are listed below.

1. Is there any need to store temporary data? If so, how much space will be required?
2. Are any portions of the program repeated many times? If so, these portions should be developed and debugged and written as subroutines.
3. Can the program be broken into separate areas so that several programmers can develop the software simultaneously?
4. Can a portion of the software be developed with a high-level language such as Pascal or PL/M?
5. How much memory space is required for the entire program?

Program Development

Once all of this information is gathered, the programmer or team of programmers can begin developing the software. If the program is rather large, a software manager may break the task into individual assignments for members of a programming team. Teamwork on a large program reduces the total development time considerably if the work is assigned to the most qualified individual programmers.

Each section of the software is developed and fully tested. The testing of the software is usually accomplished by using a software driver. The software driver is a program that is written to test every possible input and output condition of the section of software under test. Suppose that you are assigned the task of developing a section of software that is to divide any number by a 12. A software driver to test your part of the software must provide all possible numbers so that your divide program can be fully tested. It must also be able to determine if the outputs obtained are correct.

Once all the software for a large program is fully tested in sections, it is linked together and tested as a unit. The final test usually points out that there has been some error in passing information from one section of the software to another. This would be corrected by respecifying a portion of the software.

The Final Test

The last step in developing system software is to burn an EPROM and test the software in the finished hardware system. If all goes well, the final system will work correctly. If not, either the hardware is at fault and it must be corrected or an unforeseen software error has occurred. This must be corrected by returning to the software development stage.

Hardware testing is accomplished by another device, called an in-circuit emulator. The emulator is a device that replaces the microprocessor in the hardware system. Once the microprocessor is replaced, the emulator can completely control the hardware. Functions that emulators commonly perform are: single-step, register and memory displays, and traces. Each of these functions allows the test engineer to find bugs in software and hardware.

2-4 PROGRAMMING APPROACHES

Three basic programming techniques are discussed in this chapter: top-down, modular, and structured programming. Each technique has its merits, but today it seems that the most efficient technique is a combination of all three techniques. The idea of this combination will be introduced after each technique has been fully described.

Top-Down Programming

When developing software using the top-down approach, a shell of the entire system is created using dummy calls to lower-level software modules. Suppose that a program is required to read a character from the keyboard and display it on a VDT screen. This process is to continue until the carriage return (enter) key is pressed on the keyboard. Figure 2–2 illustrates the flow of this type of system. Notice that there are three places where lower-level software is used by the program shell: read key, display character, and check for a carriage return. Once the outer shell is constructed, the lower-level software is designed for each of the three tasks. In many cases the lower-level software will form its own shell, which may require that even lower-level software is constructed.

This technique is useful for the system design manager because it allows the entire system to be designed without undue detail to the low-level software required to implement the design. The software is designed in a top-down fashion: from the top (outer shell) to the bottom (lower-level software) or inner shell.

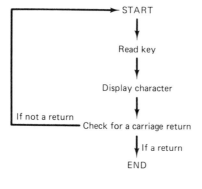

Figure 2-2 A flow diagram for inputing data from a keyboard, displaying the keyboard data, and continuing this procedure until a carriage return is entered.

Modular Programming

This approach is not unlike the top-down approach in that the program is broken down into parts. A module by definition is a program that implements just one function. This technique is very helpful to a software manager because the manager can assign portions of a system by choosing and assigning the modules to various programmers. The problems involved with this approach are that it is sometimes difficult to determine the length of a module before it is written and it is often difficult to interface modules. If you look at Fig. 2–2 again you will see that there are three modules that can be assigned to three different programmers. The read key statement, the display character statement, and the check for a carriage return are the modules that are assignable in this example.

Structured Programming

Structured programming has become a very popular topic in the past few years, but it is never clearly defined. It has recently been associated with a standard set of rules that apply to most programs in general. The rules set the structure of the program. The top-down and modular approaches both fit one of the rules: develop programs in a stepwise fashion (as in Fig. 2–2), and push details lower and lower into simpler software modules.

Another rule, which is often implied with structured programming, is never use a GOTO (BASIC or Pascal language). Instead, use a well-structured sequence like the DO WHILE, REPEAT UNTIL, or IF-THEN-ELSE. GOTO statements can cause a lot of confusion at a later date when the software may require a modification.

This text will develop structures in assembly language that are useful in developing software. These structures, together with a programming methodology for their use, are presented in later chapters together with the software.

The Programming Approach

As can be seen from the prior discussion of various programming approaches, there is no correct approach. The correct approach is actually a combination of top-down, modular, and structured programming. In fact, it is extremely difficult to separate one approach from another. We will see in later chapters that the structured programming technique aids in developing software because it teaches certain design algorithms (constructs) that can be applied to a wide variety of problems without much modification. These algorithms are the structure in structured programming.

2-5 SOFTWARE DESIGN

As presented in Section 2–4, the major programming techniques are used to develop software, as are the techniques presented in Section 2–3. In this section we attempt to connect all this information into a software design methodology—a methodology that can be applied to developing any software system, from the simplest program to the most complex system.

Steps Used to Design Software

The following steps are most often used to develop a software system:

1. Define the system as clearly as possible.
2. Design the overall system using the top-down approach to develop the outer shell.
3. Determine which modules are to be broken out of the outer shell for assignment to individual programmers (the modular approach).
4. Individual modules are designed using structured programming techniques.
5. The modules are tested using software drivers or other appropriate techniques.
6. The modules are linked together and tested as a system.
7. Based on the outcome of step 6, the system is either redesigned or it is complete and it goes into production.

These steps provide a general method for obtaining the final software product. They are a suggested sequence of events that the author has found to be effective in managing software products over the years. These steps apply to microprocessor-based systems using assembler or high-level languages as well as to systems for much larger mainframe computer systems.

Overall system design.   This is the most important step in the entire development process. If the system is not fully understood and clearly defined, it is doubtful that the remaining steps in the process can be completed. The more information placed in this specification, the easier it will be to design the overall system. Information for the specification is gathered from the future users of the completed system and their managers. Often, experts in a particular area are called in and consulted on details that are not familiar to the programming team.

Once the specification is completed, it should be examined by all persons involved with the operation of the system. If the users can understand your specification, it probably can readily be converted into the design.

System design.   In this step, the specifications are used to create the shell of the program. The shell is most often created using the top-down techniques covered in Section 2–4.

Module specification.   This step is used to locate modules in the shell of the program for assignment to individual programmers. Not only are the modules selected, but the skill level required to develop the software for each module is also decided. The most qualified programmers are then selected to develop or code the modules using structured programming techniques.

Module design.   It is at this stage that the most cooperation is required from each team member. Each person developing each module must communicate with each other programmer so that the data will flow properly from module to module. This is very important. In addition to communications between programmers, each module must be documented in great detail so that in the future another programmer can modify or debug a faulty module.

Module testing.   As mentioned, modules are tested using special programs called software drivers. In addition to testing modules with a software driver, it is extremely important that the programmer go through each step of the software on paper. This can often save a great deal of time in debugging faulty modules later. It also saves time on the software development system, which can be utilized by other programmers.

System testing.   The last phase, or at least it should be, is final system testing. This stage is where the actual modules are linked together and the entire system is tested as a unit. (This type of testing can take many months for a large and complicated system.) Based on the outcome of this test, either the faulty module or modules are redesigned or the system is placed into operation in the field. (It is rare that the system is 100 percent functional on the first pass of this design technique.)

Once a system has been placed into service in the field, it is often necessary to modify the system. This happens because if it is a large system, it cannot be fully tested in the laboratory. In fact, very large systems may never be completely debugged.

2-6 ASSEMBLERS, INTERPRETERS, AND COMPILERS

This section of the text introduces the assembler used to develop I/O and bit manipulation software, the interpreter used for testing high-level-language programs, and the compiler as a software development tool. These three software development tools are used extensively in the field.

The Assembler

As mentioned earlier, an assembler is a program that converts symbolic machine code (source code), sometimes called assembly language, into binary machine code (object code). Symbolic machine code is a language that is much easier to understand than binary machine code. It is constructed using mnemonic codes that are easily recognizable by human beings. An example mnemonic code is ADD, which is easy for us to recognize as addition. If the binary machine code for an addition is written (0100 0111, for example), it is virtually impossible for a beginner or often an experienced programmer to decipher the function.

Binary machine code is the actual language of the microprocessor. The microprocessor does not understand mnemonic code; it only understands binary machine code. For human beings to be able to easily write a program for a microprocessor, a device called an assembler is used to convert symbolic machine language into binary machine language.

In addition to converting symbolic machine code into binary machine code, many assemblers also allow the programmer to call up prewritten sequences of instructions called macros. A macro is a sequence of predefined steps that are invoked by using a special command that the programmer has written.

An example is division. The 8085A cannot divide. To circumvent this problem, a macro can be written and labeled DIV. Every time a division is required in a program, the programmer can invoke the division macro by using DIV.

For an assembler to be truly effective, one more addition is generally provided, the pseudo operation. Pseudo operations are special commands that may or may not generate machine code. One such example is the EQU pseudo operation. EQU is used to equate a label with a value or another label. It is much more readable if your program is written so that the number 7 is equated to the word SEVEN. This is accomplished by using the equate mnemonic as follows:

SEVEN   EQU   7

Interpreters

Most of us are familiar with the interpreter in the form of the BASIC language. In a machine that contains a BASIC interpreter, a program is entered and as it is executed, any error that occurs is indicated at the exact time of the error. This makes debugging a very simple task because in many cases you know exactly which line is in error. The interpreter is capable of doing this because it executes a line at a time. It does not convert the entire program into machine code, as the assembler, and execute it. If it did, it would be very difficult to locate the line or lines of code that are in error.

Interpreters are not used directly in system software development for microprocessors. They can be used to precheck a program written in a high-level language before it is compiled (converted into binary machine language).

Compilers

If a high-level language is used in program development, it will probably be in the form of a compiler. A compiler is a device that converts a high-level-language program into binary machine code. This makes the program fairly efficient because it usually takes less room than if it were in an interpretive form and it also executes at a much higher rate of speed.

As mentioned before, high-level-language compilers are extremely useful when developing systems that require a lot of complicated arithmetic. They are not suitable for all program development because it is difficult to use them to control I/O devices and to manipulate binary data.

2-7 SUMMARY

1. The major components of a software development system are: a VDT, an editor, an assembler, a high-level programming language, a linker, a disk memory system, a printer, and an EPROM programmer.

2. Assemblers are used for developing bit manipulation and I/O control software and compilers are used for developing intricate arithmetic.

3. The linker connects or links software modules together to form the complete software system.

4. The EPROM programmer is used to store the final software system onto an EPROM.

5. The first thing not to do when developing a software system is to write the program.

6. To define the software problem completely, a lot of thought and information gathering must occur.

7. Three programming techniques are commonly used in software development: top-down, modular, and structured.

8. The top-down programming technique requires that a shell of the program be constructed without any detail to lower-level software.

9. Modular programming is a technique that separates the software into modules which are then assigned to individual programmers.

10. Structured programming requires the use of a strict set of predefined structures, such as DO WHILE and REPEAT UNTIL, when developing software.

11. A good software design methodology requires that the system is defined, top-down techniques are used to design the program shell, modules are broken out of the shell, programmers use structured programming to develop the modules, and extensive testing of all the software, both the modules and the entire system.

12. The assembler is a program that converts mnemonic code, in the source program, into the binary machine code of the object program.

13. Interpreters are high-level-language systems that are excellent for error checking because they execute the software a line at a time.

14. The compiler is a program that converts a high-level language into binary machine language.

2-8 GLOSSARY

Assembler   A program that converts symbolic source code into binary object code.

Assembly language   The symbolic source program is often referred to as an assembly language program.

Binary machine code   The actual binary commands that the microprocessor understands as instructions.

Compiler   A program that converts a high-level language into binary machine language.

EPROM programmer   A device that is used to program EPROMs.

Hacker   An inexperienced programmer who writes software in a random pattern.

Interpreter   A program that accepts high-level-language commands and executes them one at a time.

Linker   A program that connects or links together software modules.

Macro   A sequence of events in symbolic machine code that can be invoked by using a single user-created mnemonic code.

Mnemonic code   An abbreviated command for a computer system, such as ADD for addition and SUB for subtraction.

Module   A section of software that performs one task.

Pseudo operation   A special assembly language command that is used to control the assembler. Pseudo operations may or may not generate machine code.

Shell   The outer portion of a program developed using top-down programming techniques.

Software development system   A system that is used to develop programs that includes a VDT, assembler, high-level language, linker, printer, disk memory, and EPROM programmer.

Software driver   A program that completely tests software.

Symbolic machine code   A program that uses mnemonic codes instead of binary machine codes.

Syntax error   A mistake in the normal form of a statement in an assembler, interpreter, or compiler.

VDT   The video display terminal contains a video screen and a keyboard.

QUESTIONS AND PROBLEMS

2–1. What is the purpose of a software development system?

2–2. List four of the essential components of a software development system.

2–3. Why is it desirable to have a numeric keypad on a VDT?

2–4. List three of the operations that an editor can perform.

2–5. The source program is converted to what type of program by an assembler?

2–6. What is a syntax error?

2–7. Where would a high-level language such as Pascal or PL/M be useful when developing software?

2–8. List two types of software modules linked together by a linker.

2–9. What is the first thing not to do when writing software?

2–10. Why is teamwork important when developing software for a large system?

2–11. What is a software driver, and how is it used in software development?

2–12. Name the three programming approaches most often used for software development.

2–13. Which programming approach uses a shell?

2–14. A software module is used in which programming approach?

2–15. Which programming approach is associated with a standard set of rules?

2–16. List the seven steps used for proper software design.

2–17. Should experts always be called in when developing a software system? Explain your answer.

2–18. Is communications an important part of software development? Explain your answer.

2–19. Is it normal for a software system to function perfectly at the end of the development cycle?

2–20. Define the term *mnemonic code.*

2–21. Briefly explain the structure of symbolic machine code.

2–22. What is the difference between symbolic machine code and binary machine code?

2–23. Explain how the pseudo operation EQU functions.

2–24. What feature makes the interpreter an excellent high-level-language debugging tool?

2–25. Describe the difference between a high-level-language interpreter and a compiler.

chapter three

8085A ARCHITECTURE

Before the 8085A can be programmed, it must be understood. The key to understanding this microprocessor is its architecture. In this chapter we explain the 8085A's internal operation, programming model, memory and I/O structure, data and command words, and present an overview of the instruction set.

3-1 OBJECTIVES

Upon completion of this chapter, you will be able to:

1. Draw the 8085A programming model and explain the purpose of each register
2. Describe the purpose of each flag bit and explain what its contents indicate
3. Draw the memory and I/O maps of the 8085A and explain the purpose of any special memory locations
4. Convert decimal numbers into binary integers, binary fractions, binary-coded decimal, and binary floating-point numbers
5. Convert binary integers, binary fractions, binary-coded decimal, and binary floating-point numbers into decimal numbers
6. Encode and decode ASCII-coded alphanumeric characters
7. List the three basic types of 8085A instructions

3-2 THE 8085A ARCHITECTURE

The 8085A is an 8-bit general-purpose microprocessor that is ideally suited to many applications. In this section we introduce the internal architecture of the 8085A microprocessor.

The 8085A Block Diagram

Figure 3-1 illustrates the internal block diagram of the 8085A microprocessor. Although a detailed understanding of the internal operation of the 8085A is not required for programming, it does help to explain why some of the instructions operate in a particular fashion.

The 8085A contains a register array, a timing and control section, an arithmetic and logic unit (ALU), an instruction register and decoder, and bus connections to the outside world. Notice that there are 16 address bus connections, A_{8-15}, and a shared (multiplexed) address/data bus containing the least significant 8 bits of the memory address, A_{0-7} and the data bus D_{0-7}. A 16-bit memory address allows the 8085A to directly address 64K different memory locations. The address/data bus also allows the 8085A to access 8 bits of data at a time, which means that each memory location or I/O device attached to the address/data bus contains 8 bits of data.

The registers.   The 8085A contains a variety of internal registers that are used to hold temporary data, memory addresses, instructions, and information about the status of the 8085A. The function of some of these registers will be explained here and the remainder will be explained in Section 3-3 together with the programming model of the 8085A.

Instruction register: This register is used to hold the instruction that the 8085A is currently executing. Its outputs are connected to the instruction decoder, which decodes the instruction and controls the rest of the processor, memory, and I/O through the timing and control block and external pins to the outside world.

Temporary register: The temporary register is used to hold information from the memory or the register array for the ALU. The other input to the ALU comes from the accumulator. The result, available at the output of the ALU, is fed to the internal 8-bit data bus for distribution to the accumulator, register array, or memory.

Incrementer/decrementer address latch: This block is used to hold the address of data to be accessed in the memory or I/O. It is also used to add one or subtract one from any of the other registers in the register array.

Miscellaneous sections.   The interrupt control section is used to determine the priority of the interrupt control inputs and also to supply, in some cases, an interrupt instruction to the instruction register. An interrupt is an operation where the external circuitry interrupts a program. When the program is interrupted, the microprocessor executes another program that responds to the external interrupt.

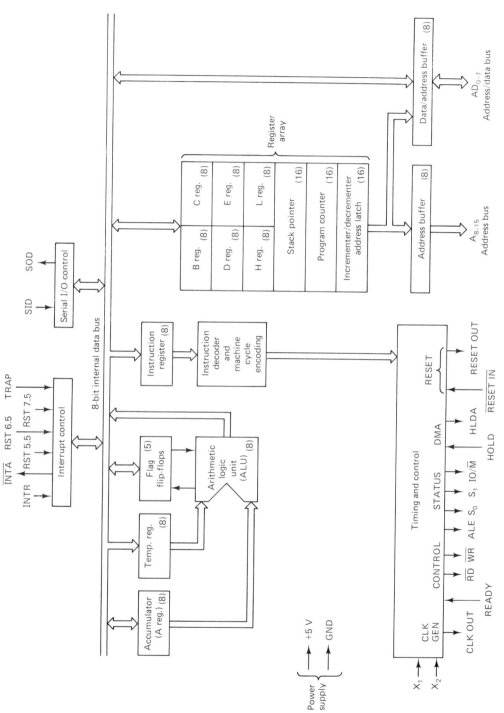

Figure 3-1 The functional block diagram of the Intel 8085A microprocessor. (Diagram courtesy of Intel Corporation.)

The serial I/O control section is used to control the two serial I/O data pins: SID (serial input data) for reading a bit of external data and SOD (serial output data) for writing a bit of external data.

The timing and control section provides the basic control bus signals $\overline{\text{RD}}$, $\overline{\text{WR}}$, and IO/$\overline{\text{M}}$. In addition to these basic control signals, other signals are supplied to control the external hardware and also accepted to control some internal functions. More detail on these control signals and the system architecture are provided in Chapter 16, which covers the 8085A system architecture from a hardware point of view.

3–3 THE PROGRAMMING MODEL

Before an instruction can be explained or a program written, the structure of the internal register set must be fully understood. This section details the programming model—the set of available registers that can be affected by a program.

Figure 3–2 illustrates the internal register set of the 8085A. The register set can be broken into two discrete portions: general-purpose registers and special-purpose registers.

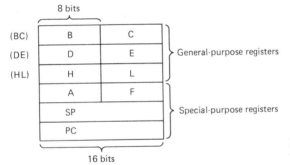

Figure 3–2 The programming model of the 8085A microprocessor.

General-Purpose Registers

The 8085A contains a set of six general-purpose registers: B, C, D, E, H, and L. These registers are called *general purpose* because they can be used in any manner by the person programming the microprocessor. The general-purpose registers can be used to hold numeric data, BCD data, ASCII data, and in fact, any type of information that may be required. They are flexible enough so that they can be used as six 8-bit registers or as three 16-bit register pairs.

The valid register pairs are BC, DE, and HL. Registers pairs can be used to hold 16-bit numeric data or any other 16-bit coded information. In addition to being able to hold 16 bits of data, register pairs can also be used to address data in memory. If a memory address is placed into a register pair, certain instructions allow the contents of the location addressed by the register pair to be manipulated.

Special-Purpose Registers

The special-purpose registers—A, F, SP, and PC— are used for accumulating results from arithmetic and logic instructions and also for housekeeping. The term *housekeeping* is used to refer to tasks that are required but normally occur without the intervention of the programmer.

The accumulator register (A).   The accumulator is a very important register in the 8085A microprocessor because it is used to accumulate the answer after almost every arithmetic and all logic operations. You might call the A register the answer register because the answer is normally found here.

The flag register (F).   The flag register contains 5 bits that are used as flags or indicators for the ALU. Any time the 8085A executes most arithmetic or logic instruction, the flags will change. (Refer to Fig. 3-1 for the placement of the flag register.) The results reflected by the flag bits indicate the condition of the outcome of the answer from the ALU. Figure 3-3 illustrates the contents of the flag byte. The 5 flag bits include:

1. The sign flag bit (S) is used to indicate whether the result of an arithmetic or logic operation is positive or negative. A logic 1 in this bit indicates a negative outcome and a logic 0 a positive outcome.
2. The zero flag bit (Z) indicates whether the outcome of an ALU operation is zero or not zero. A logic 1 in this bit indicates a zero result and a logic 0 indicates a not-zero result.
3. The auxiliary carry flag bit (AC) holds the carry that occurs between the least significant and most significant halves of the result from the ALU. (This flag is normally used only by the DAA command.)
4. The parity flag bit (P) indicates the parity of the result from the ALU. A logic 1 in this bit indicates even parity and a logic 0 indicates odd parity. (Parity is a count of the number of 1's in a number expressed as even or odd.)
5. The carry flag bit (CY) holds the carry that occurs from the most significant bit of the accumulator after an addition, the borrow after a subtraction, or a logic zero after all logic operations.

The program counter (PC).   The program counter does not count programs. The program counter is used by the 8085A to locate the next instruction to be executed. Why is it called a counter? It is called a counter because it is a counter. It

F_7	F_6	F_5	F_4	F_3	F_2	F_1	F_0
S	Z		AC		P		CY

Figure 3-3   The 8085A flag register.

counts up through the memory, allowing the microprocessor to sequentially execute the next instruction from the memory. The importance of this register and a greater discussion of its operation appears in Chapter 6.

The stack pointer (SP).   The stack pointer allows the 8085A to track its last-in, first-out (LIFO) stack. The stack in the 8085A processes data so that the first data into the stack are the last data out of the stack. For example, if a 2, a 3, and a 4 are placed on the stack, they come off the stack in reverse order, as a 4, a 3, and a 2. You might think that this is a strange way of storing information. It is, unless subroutine nesting is important. Subroutines, and the importance of this type of stack, are described in Chapter 6.

3-4 MEMORY AND I/O

As mentioned earlier, the memory is used to store programs and data, and the I/O system is used to allow human beings and machines to communicate with the microprocessor. Both areas are very important and it is critical that they are understood before a program is written.

The 8085A Memory Map

The memory map of the 8085A is depicted in Fig. 3–4. Notice that the memory locations are numbered in hexadecimal from 0000 through location FFFF. This means that the capacity of the memory is 64K locations. Each memory location holds one byte of information, which can be an instruction or any form of data.

In addition to the numbered memory locations, there are also some RST locations listed at certain memory locations. RST is an acronym for restart. The restart is an instruction that is discussed in Chapter 6. (Trap is a special type of restart.)

The memory of the 8085A is most often broken into two areas. One area of memory is devoted to the system program and is most often populated with ROMs. The other area of memory is used to store data and also programs, in microprocessor-based training systems, and is usually populated with semiconductor RAMs.

The reset location is a very important memory location in the 8085A memory map. The reset location (0000) is where the 8085A will begin to execute a program after the reset button, or input, of the 8085A is activated. If you are developing the system software for an 8085A, you must start the program at location 0000. If you are using a microprocessor trainer, its system program begins at location 0000. This means that your program must begin in some location in the trainer's RAM. This varies from trainer to trainer, of course. The Intel SDK-85 has its RAM at location 2000 through 20FF and the DEVRY Micromodule-85 has its RAM at location 1400 through 17FF.

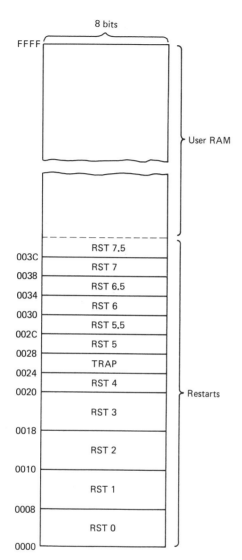

8 bits

FFFF

User RAM

003C — RST 7.5
0038 — RST 7
0034 — RST 6.5
0030 — RST 6
002C — RST 5.5
0028 — RST 5
0024 — TRAP
0020 — RST 4
0018 — RST 3
0010 — RST 2
0008 — RST 1
0000 — RST 0

Restarts

Figure 3-4 The memory map of the 8085A microprocessor showing the RST locations and the user RAM area.

The 8085A I/O Map

The 8085A can directly address 256 different input and 256 different output devices. External I/O devices are called I/O ports in an 8085A-based system. An input port is an external device that passes information to the microprocessor and an output port is an external device that accepts information from the microprocessor. The port number is like a memory address because it is used to address an external I/O device and it is often called the port address.

Figure 3–5 depicts the I/O map for the 8085A microprocessor. The I/O ports are numbered from 00 to FF and all ports are available to the user unless a microprocessor-based trainer is in use. A complete discussion of the two I/O commands, IN and OUT, is presented in Chapter 4.

FF

8-Bit
user
I/O ports

00

Figure 3–5 The I/O port map of the 8085A microprocessor showing the I/O port numbers.

3-5 DATA WORD FORMATS

There are many different data word formats that must be understood before a program can be written. This section covers unsigned integers, signed integers, ASCII-coded alphanumeric data, BCD-coded data, binary fractions, and floating-point numbers.

The Unsigned Integer

Unsigned integers, in the 8085A microprocessor, are most often either 8 or 16 bits in width, but they could be any multiple of 8 bits in width. The 8-bit unsigned integers are found in the memory system and also in any single register. The 16-bit unsigned integers are found in two contiguous bytes of memory and in register pairs.

8-bit unsigned integer. Figure 3–6 shows the binary format of an 8-bit unsigned integer stored in either the memory or a register. All 8 bits are used to hold the value of a number with the binary weights as indicated in the illustration.

2^7	2^6	2^5	2^4	2^3	2^2	2^1	2^0
(128)	(64)	(32)	(16)	(8)	(4)	(2)	(1)

Note: Weights are in parentheses.

Figure 3–6 The format of an 8-bit unsigned integer in a register or a memory location.

Some examples of 8-bit unsigned integers include $0000\ 0001_2$ (01H) = 1, $1000\ 0000_2$ (80H) = 128_{10}, $1100\ 0000_2$ (C0H) = 192_{10}, and $1111\ 1111_2$ (FFH) = 255_{10}. The allowable range of 8-bit unsigned integers is 0–255_{10}. *(Note: Hexadecimal quantities are always denoted with the letter H following the hexadecimal number. For example, 67H is equal to 67 hexadecimal.)*

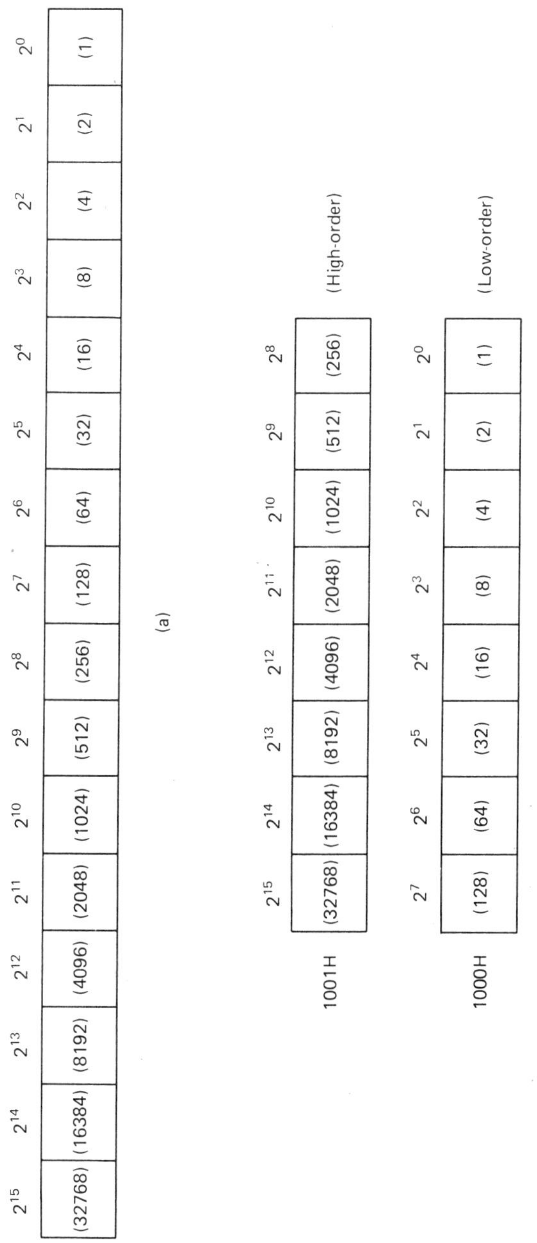

Figure 3-7 Sixteen bit unsigned integer word formats. (a) in a register; (b) in the memory.

Note: Weights are in parentheses.

16-bit unsigned integer.   Figure 3–7 shows the format of the 16-bit unsigned integer in a register pair and also in the memory. Notice that when a 16-bit integer is stored in the memory it is always stored with the least significant 8 bits in the lowest-numbered memory location and with the most significant 8 bits in the next contiguous memory location. The least significant portion is called the low-order part and the most significant portion is called the high-order part.

Some examples of 16-bit unsigned integers include $0000\ 0000\ 0010\ 0000_2$ (0020H) = 32_{10}, $0010\ 0000\ 1000\ 1110_2$ (208EH) = 8334_{10}, and $1111\ 1010\ 0000\ 1011_2$ (FA0BH) = $64,011_{10}$. The allowable range of 16-bit unsigned integers is 0–65,535. *Note:* When this text uses binary numbers they are always presented in BCH (binary-coded hexadecimal). A BCH number is a binary number that is grouped in 4-bit segments: for example, $0000\ 1100_2$ = 0CH.

Signed Integers

Single-byte signed integers are 7-bit numbers plus a sign bit. Positive numbers are stored with a 0 in the sign bit followed by a 7-bit magnitude, and negative numbers are stored with a 1 in the sign bit followed by a 7-bit two's complement of the magnitude. Both the positive and negative 8-bit integers are illustrated in Fig. 3–8.

Figure 3-8   Signed 8-bit integers formats. (a) positive integer; (b) a negative integer.

Positive numbers range in value from 0 to 127 and negative numbers range in value −1 to −128. Some examples of positive signed 8-bit numbers are $0000\ 1000_2$ = 8, $0111\ 1111_2$ = 127_{10}, and $0101\ 0000_2$ = 80_{10}. Negative numbers are not quite as easy to calculate, so it may pay to become familiar with Fig. 3–9, which can be used to determine the value of a positive or a negative number. The weight (value) of the sign bit is −128. If a 1 appears in this position, it is equal to −128, and if a 0 appears, it is equal to 0. The remaining bit positions are numbered +64, +32, +16, +8, +4, +2, and +1. If a number such as $1000\ 0011_2$ is converted to decimal using Fig. 3–9, a −128, +2, and +1 are added together to arrive at a value of −125. If a number such as $0001\ 0101_2$ is converted to decimal, a +16, +4, and +1 are added together to arrive at +21.

D_7	D_6	D_5	D_4	D_3	D_2	D_1	D_0
(−128)	(+64)	(+32)	(+16)	(+8)	(+4)	(+2)	(+1)

Note: Weights are in parentheses.

Figure 3-9   The binary weights of each bit position in a signed 8-bit integer.

Sixteen-bit signed numbers are treated in the same manner as 8-bit signed numbers. The extreme left-hand bit is the sign bit and the remaining bits contain the magnitude for a positive number and the two's complement of the magnitude for a negative number. Figure 3–10 depicts the weights of each position for conversions.

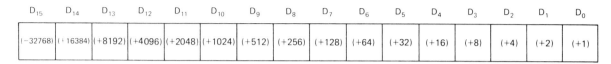

Note: Weights are in parentheses.

Figure 3–10   The binary weights of each bin position in a signed 16-bit integer.

ASCII Data Format

Refer to Appendix C for a complete listing of ASCII-coded characters. ASCII is an acronym for American Standard Code for Information Interchange. This code is used by virtually all manufacturers of computer peripheral equipment, and it is therefore an excellent idea to become familiar with it.

The first 32 codes are used for control codes and are numbered from 00H to 1FH. To obtain any of these codes, on most computer keyboards hold the control key down and type a letter A for 01H, a letter B for 02H, and so on. The 00H code is most often obtained by holding the control and shift keys down while typing the letter P.

It is important to notice that ASCII code is a 7-bit code. The eighth bit is used to hold the parity bit in a data communications system. In computer systems this bit is often a logic 0. In some printers a 0 in the eighth bit causes the printer to print ASCII characters and a 1 causes it to print graphics characters.

BCD Data Format

In the many systems that do not contain an ASCII keyboard, data are entered on a numeric keyboard and encoded by the keyboard circuitry as a binary-coded-decimal (BCD) number. This number is usually processed as an unpacked BCD number. An unpacked BCD number is a number that is stored one digit per byte. In other words, to store a 76 in unpacked BCD code would take two bytes of memory. The first byte contains a 0000 0111 (7) and the second byte a 0000 0110 (6). (Refer to Table 3–1 for a list of valid BCD codes.)

In certain cases it is desirable to conserve memory space. When this is the case, BCD numbers are usually packed two BCD codes per byte. A packed BCD number is stored as a two-digit BCD number per byte. To store a 76 in packed BCD code would take one byte of memory (0111 0110).

TABLE 3-1 BCD CODES FOR THE
NUMBERS 0 THROUGH 9.

Decimal	Unpacked BCD
0	0000 0000
1	0000 0001
2	0000 0010
3	0000 0011
4	0000 0100
5	0000 0101
6	0000 0110
7	0000 0111
8	0000 1000
9	0000 1001

Signed BCD numbers are not nearly as common as unsigned BCD numbers. If they are used, the negative numbers are stored in ten's-complement form. For example, a − 14 is stored as a 1000 0110 (86), which is the ten's complement of a 14. To form a ten's-complement number, first subtract the number to be converted from a 99 and then add a 1 to the result.

Binary Fractions

Binary fractions can also be stored in either byte or two-byte form for use by the 8085A, although they are not very commonly found. Usually, they are unsigned numbers that use the leftmost bit position, which has a weight of 2^{-1}. For example, if the binary number 1100 0000 is found in a memory location and it is known that it is an unsigned fraction, its value is 0.75_{10}.

Floating Point Data

How are numbers that are not integers or fractions (mixed numbers) stored in a computer system's memory? The floating-point format is used to store noninteger as well as integer data in many computer systems. Floating-point numbers are similar to scientific notation in base 10. They have a mantissa and an exponent. The mantissa is a normalized number between 1 and less than 2. The exponent is a power of 2 that represents the position of the binary point in the original number. Examples 3–1 through 3–3 illustrate a few binary numbers converted to normalized floating-point numbers.

(Example 3–1) $1110010 = 1.110010 \times 2^6$

(Example 3–2) $11.10001 = 1.1110001 \times 2^1$

(Example 3–3) $0.001101 = 1.101 \times 2^{-3}$

Floating-point numbers are often stored in four bytes of memory. Figure 3-11 illustrates the format for a four-byte (single-precision) floating-point number. The left-hand bit position is used to indicate the sign of the mantissa; the next eight bit positions are used for the exponent, which is stored in excess 127 notation; and the last 23 bits are used to store the magnitude of the mantissa.

Figure 3-11   The format of the four byte single precision floating point number.

The excess 127 notation exponent is an unsigned integer that is equal to the exponent plus 127. For example, if the value of the exponent is determined to be a 6, the number coded for the excess 127 notation exponent is 133. If the exponent is determined to be a -2, the excess 127 notation exponent is 125.

The mantissa is a 23-bit number with a hidden or implied twenty-fourth bit position. Notice that when a number is normalized, the left-hand bit is always a logic 1. Because this 1 is always present, we do not need to store it in the memory. (A zero is the only case where an implied 1 is missing. In this case all four bytes of the number are zero, to indicate a zero number.) Examples 3–4 through 3–7 illustrate some decimal numbers that have been converted to floating-point numbers.

(Example 3–4)

$$100_{10} = 1100100_2$$
$$1100100_2 = 1.1001 \times 2^6$$

S Exponent   Mantissa

0 10000101   10010000000000000000000

(Example 3-5)

$$-12.75_{10} = -1100.11_2$$
$$-1100.11_2 = 1.10011 \times 2^3$$

S Exponent   Mantissa

1 10000010   10011000000000000000000

(Example 3-6)

$$2.1_{10} = 10.0001100110011001100110$$
$$1.0001100110011001100110 \times 2^1$$

S Exponent   Mantissa

0 10000000   0000110011001100110110

(Example 3-7)

$$0 = 0$$
$$0 = 0 \times 2^0$$

S Exponent   Mantissa

0 00000000   00000000000000000000000

3-6 COMMAND WORD FORMATS

There are basically three different command word formats used by the 8085A: one-byte-, two-byte-, and three-byte-long commands. The one-byte commands represent 204 instructions; the two-byte commands represent 18 instructions; and the three-byte commands represent 24 instructions. The 8085A has 246 of its 256 possible commands implemented. The remaining instructions are not implemented in all versions of the 8085A. Appendix D contains a listing of these hidden instructions together with a description of the operation of each. Again, be aware that not all versions of the 8085A will respond to these instructions.

One-Byte Commands

The one-byte commands, which are the most numerous, are used for most of the commands in a program. They are used for moving numbers from a register to a register, from a register to memory, from memory to a register, and also to accomplish most of the arithmetic and logic operations. The first byte of any command is always the op-code. The op-code tells the 8085A microprocessor which operation to execute.

Two-Byte Commands

The two-byte commands, all 18 of them, are used for immediate data instructions or for the input/output commands, IN and OUT. Figure 3–12 illustrates the form of both the immediate and input/output commands.

Figure 3–12   The two byte command format. (a) a two-byte instruction using immediate data; (b) a two-byte I/O instruction using an I/O port address.

Figure 3–12(a) shows how the op-code is followed by immediate data for a two-byte-long immediate command. The operation specified by the op-code is performed using the data in the byte immediately following the op-code. If the operation indicated by the op-code is addition, the data in the next byte would be added.

Figure 3–12 (b) shows a two-byte input/output command. Here the byte that immediately follows the op-code does not contain data; it contains the address of the external I/O device. For IN or OUT the data are always transferred to or from the accumulator register, with the second byte of the command used to address the I/O port number.

Three-Byte Commands

The 24 three-byte commands are used either to specify an op-code and two bytes of immediate data or an op-code and a 16-bit binary address. Figure 3–13 illustrates both forms of three-byte-long commands.

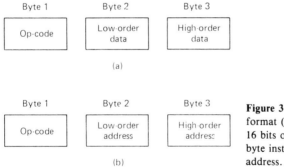

Figure 3–13   The three-byte command format (a) a three-byte instruction using 16 bits of immediate data; (b) a three-byte instruction using a 16-bit memory address.

Refer to Fig. 3–13(a) for a three-byte-long instruction that uses data for an operand. (The operand is the data used by an op-code). Notice that the data are encoded so that the least significant 8 bits (low-order data) follows the opcode and the most significant 8-bits (high-order data) follow the low-order byte. It may take some time to get used to this, because this is different from the way that a number is normally written. Some examples of 16-bit hexadecimal data broken into low- and high-order parts are illustrated in Table 3–2.

TABLE 3-2 HEXADECIMAL DATA OR ADDRESSES
CONVERTED TO LOW- AND HIGH-ORDER FORM FOR A
THREE-BYTE-LONG INSTRUCTION.

Hexadecimal data	Low-order	High-order
0023	23	00
1000	00	10
1234	34	12
ABCD	CD	AB
10EC	EC	10

Figure 3–13(b) shows a three-byte command that requires a memory address in place of the data. Just as with the data, a memory address must also be coded with the low-order portion first followed by the high-order portion.

3-7 THE INSTRUCTION SET

The instruction set of the 8085A microprocessor can be broken into three main categories: data transfer instructions, arithmetic and logic instructions, and program control instructions. This section introduces these three forms of instructions; they are covered in complete detail in Chapters 4, 5 and 6.

Data Transfer Instructions

Data transfer instructions represent a lot of processing time in most software systems. For this reason it is important that these instructions are understood. There are actually five types of data transfer instructions available for use in the 8085A instruction set. These types are: register-to-register moves, move immediates, indexed moves, direct moves, and input/output. (None of these instructions affect the flag register.)

Arithmetic and Logic Instructions

Another common operation in a microprocessor-based system is some simple arithmetic or logic operation. The 8085A is capable of a wide assortment of arithmetic and logic operations. Instructions that the 8085A is capable of executing are: addition, subtraction, AND, OR, NOT, exclusive-OR, and various forms of rotation. These operations can be used to address any internal register or the contents of any memory location. They can even be performed using immediate data. (Most of these instructions affect the flag register.)

Program Control Instructions

The 8085A microprocessor can execute four different types of program control instructions. These four types are: unconditional and conditional jumps, indirect jumps, unconditional and conditional subroutine calls, and unconditional and conditional subroutine returns. The conditional instructions are used to test the flag bits. If the condition under test is true, a jump occurs to some other instruction in the program, and if the condition is false, the program continues with the next sequential step.

3-8 SUMMARY

1. The 8085A microprocessor is a general-purpose 8-bit microprocessor that is ideally suited to many control applications.

2. The 8085A microprocessor contains a register array, timing and control section, an arithmetic and logic unit (ALU), and bus connections to the outside world.

3. The 8085A microprocessor is capable of addressing 64K bytes of memory through an 8-bit data bus via a 16-bit address bus.

4. The timing and control section generates the major system control signals: $\overline{RD}$, $\overline{WR}$, and IO/$\overline{M}$.

5. The programming model of the 8085A contains two sections: a general-purpose section and a special-purpose section. The general-purpose section consists of six registers (B, C, D, E, H, and L), which are used as 8-bit registers or in pairs as 16-bit register pairs (BC, DE, and HL). The special-purpose registers include the accumulator (A), the stack pointer (SP), the flag register (F), and the program counter (PC).

6. The accumulator is used to hold an operand before and the result after an arithmetic and logic operation.

7. The stack pointer is used by the 8085A to address the LIFO stack.

8. The flag register is used to hold information about the result of an arithmetic and logic operation. The flag bits are: zero (Z), sign (S), parity (P), carry (CY) and auxiliary carry (AC).

9. The program counter (PC) addresses the next instruction to be executed by the 8085A. It always points to the next instruction in the program.

10. The 8085A is capable of directly addressing 256 different input and 256 different output devices. External I/O devices are often called I/O ports in an 8085A-based system.

11. Data to be used by the 8085A can take many forms: unsigned and signed binary integers, binary fractions, packed and unpacked BCD, ASCII, and floating point.

12. Instructions for the 8085A are one, two, or three bytes in length.

13. Instructions types are: data transfer, arithmetic, and logic or program control.

3-9 GLOSSARY

Accumulator register   The accumulator register is used to hold an operand before an arithmetic or logic operation and the result after the operation.

Address/data bus   A common set of connections that are used to convey half of the address (A_{0-7}) to the memory of I/O and to transfer the data (D_{0-7}).

ASCII code   ASCII data consist of an alphanumeric code used in many computer systems.

BCD   Binary-decimal code are data stored in groups of 4 bits that represent the decimal numbers 0 through 9.

Exponent   The binary power of 2 in a floating-point number that is used to reference the position of the binary point in the mantissa.

Flag register   A register that holds the condition of the ALU after an arithmetic or logic operation.

Floating-point number   A number that is used to store very large or very small integers, fractions, or mixed numbers.

General-purpose registers   A set of registers that can be used in any way that the programmer sees fit.

Housekeeping   Tasks that are normally processed by the microprocessor without intervention from the programmer.

Instruction register   A register that is used to hold the instruction so that the microprocessor can decode it.

IO/$\overline{M}$ The IO/$\overline{M}$ (input/output or memory) signal indicates whether a transfer is via memory or I/O.

LIFO   A LIFO (last-in, first-out) stack memory is used to store data and return addresses in the memory.

Mantissa   The part of a floating-point number that is equal to 1 through less than 2.

Op-code   The op-code is the part of an instruction that specifies the operation for the microprocessor.

Operand   The data used by the op-code.

Parity   A count of the number of 1's in a number expressed as even or odd.

Port, I/O   An external I/O device.

Program counter   A register that holds the address of the next instruction to be executed.

Programming model   A model of the internal user-affectable registers in a microprocessor.

$\overline{RD}$ The $\overline{RD}$ (read) signal is used to cause the memory or I/O to read or send data to the microprocessor.

SID   The serial input data pin is used to allow the microprocessor to accept serial data.

Signed integer   A whole number that can be either positive or negative.

SOD   The serial output data pin is used to allow the microprocessor to send serial data.

Special-purpose registers   A group of registers that are used for processor housekeeping.

Stack   *See* LIFO.

Stack pointer   A register that is used to address the LIFO stack.

Unsigned integer   A whole number that has no arithmetic sign.

$\overline{WR}$ The $\overline{WR}$ (write) signal is used to enable the memory or I/O to accept data from the microprocessor.

QUESTIONS AND PROBLEMS ━━━━━━━━━━━

3-1. The 8085A address bus contains how many bits?

3-2. The 8085A can directly address how many different memory locations?

3-3. What is the purpose of the instruction register that is pictured in Fig. 3-1?

3-4. The SID and SOD pins on the 8085A microprocessor are used for what purpose?

3-5. List the three main 8085A control signals.

3-6. Draw the programming model of the 8085A microprocessor.

3-7. List at least three types of data normally held in the general-purpose registers.

3-8. When two general-purpose registers are connected together to form a 16-bit register, what is this new register called?

3-9. What is the answer register?

3-10. List each of the flag bits and briefly describe their function.

3-11. Why is the program counter called a counter?

3-12. The stack pointer (SP) is used to reference what type of stack memory?

3-13. Describe the memory of the 8085A microprocessor.

3-14. Where would the ROM in an 8085A-based system probably be found?

3-15. How many different external input devices can be accessed by the 8085A microprocessor?

3-16. What is an I/O port?

3-17. Convert the following decimal numbers to 8-bit unsigned integers: 12, 33, 55, 100, 155, 196, and 212.

3-18. Convert the following decimal numbers to 16-bit unsigned integers: 156, 522, 1000, 2009, and 10,000.

3-19. Convert the following 8-bit signed integers to decimal numbers: 1111 1111, 1000 0111, 0110 1000, and 0111 0000.

3-20. Convert the following decimal numbers to 8-bit signed integers: 12, -12, 32, -63, and -100.

3-21. Using the ASCII coding chart in Appendix C convert your name to ASCII code.

3-22. How is an ASCII BS (backspace) obtained on many keyboards? (Not by using the backspace button!)

3-23. Write the following decimal numbers as both packed and unpacked BCD numbers: 12, 3, 10, 99, 13, and 712.

3-24. Convert the following decimal numbers to four-byte binary floating-point form: 12, -22, 10.5, 0.002, and -4.25.

3-25. Convert the following three four-byte binary floating-point numbers into decimal numbers:

$$0100\ 0001\ 0100\ 0000\ 0000\ 0000\ 0000\ 0000$$

$$1011\ 1111\ 1000\ 0000\ 0000\ 0000\ 0000\ 0000$$

$$0100\ 1000\ 1110\ 1000\ 0000\ 0000\ 0000\ 0000$$

3-26. How many different commands are implemented in the 8085A microprocessor's instruction set?

3-27. What is an op-code?

3-28. What is an operand?

3-29. Explain the order of the data in a three-byte command.

3-30. Convert the following hexadecimal numbers to the correct form for data storage in the second and third bytes of a three-byte-long command: 1234H, ACDCH, 87FFH, 3443H, and 9080H.

3-31. What three main categories of instructions comprise the 8085A instruction set?

3-32. Which types of instructions do not affect the flags?

3-33. What type of instruction will affect the flags?

_____ chapter four _____

DATA TRANSFER INSTRUCTIONS

One of the most common types of instructions in the 8085A microprocessor's instruction set is the data transfer instruction. Data transfer instructions come in many forms: register to register, register to memory, memory to register, and stack operations.

In this chapter we present the various addressing modes available for all instructions and also all the data transfer instructions, including the machine language and assembly language versions.

4-1 OBJECTIVES

Upon completion of this chapter, you will be able to:

1. Explain how the 8085A responds to each of the following addressing modes: direct, register, register indirect, and immediate
2. Use the MVI and LXI instructions to place immediate data into any internal register or any external memory location
3. Use LDA, STA, LHLD, and SHLD to load or store the accumulator and HL register pair from or to the memory
4. Explain the operation of the BC, DE, and HL register pairs for the register indirect mode of addressing instructions LDAX, STAX, and the operand M
5. Select a MOV instruction to transfer data from any register to any register or memory

6. Explain the operation of the stack when used by the PUSH, POP, and XTHL instructions

7. Briefly describe the operation of the IN, OUT, SPHL, and XCHG instructions

4-2 ADDRESSING MODES

The 8085A microprocessor uses four different addressing modes for most instructions: direct, register, register indirect, and immediate. Before a particular instruction is examined, it is essential that each of these addressing modes is completely understood. In this section we detail the addressing modes so that the subsequently explained instructions can be completely understood.

Direct Addressing

Instructions that directly address the memory always include the memory address of the data. This address is stored following the op-code in the program. The form of each instruction that uses direct addressing is illustrated in Fig. 4-1.

Byte 1	Byte 2	Byte 3
Op-code	Low-order address	High-order address

Figure 4-1 A direct addressed instruction showing the op-code, low and high order addresses.

Notice that this type of addressing requires that the instruction contains an op-code followed by a 16-bit memory address stored in two additional bytes of memory following the op-code. (All instructions that use direct addressing are three bytes in length.) It is also important to note that the address of the data is stored so that the least significant byte follows the op-code and the most significant byte follows the least significant byte. This was discussed in Chapter 3 for storing 16-bit data in the memory. Table 4-1 shows how various addresses are stored following an op-code

TABLE 4-1 VARIOUS ADDRESSES CONVERTED TO MACHINE CODE FOR THE DIRECT ADDRESSING MODE OF OPERATION

Hexadecimal address	Machine-coded form B1–B2–B3
1234H	XX–34–12
1000H	XX–00–10
4BCDH	XX–CD–4B

Notes: XX is any op-code that allows direct addressing; minus signs are used to separate bytes of data in the machine-coded form.

in machine language. If this form of addressing is used by a particular instruction, an a16 is found in the assembly language listing provided in Appendix B and also throughout this and the next two chapters.

Register Addressing

Register addressing is one of the more common forms of addressing used by the 8085A microprocessor. The instruction specifies the register (B, C, D, E, H, L, or A) or the register pair (BC, DE, HL, or SP) used with the instruction. All register addressed instructions are one byte in length. This mode of addressing will be heavily illustrated when the MOV data transfer instructions are discussed later in this chapter.

Register Indirect Addressing

With register indirect addressing, a register pair holds the address of the memory location accessed by the instruction—the memory location is indirectly addressed by the register pair. If the HL register pair is used to indirectly address memory, the letter M is used in place of a register. For example, suppose that the HL pair contains a 1000H and the letter M is used as a register. An instruction using the M will access memory location 1000H because the HL register pair points to that memory location.

There are also a few instructions that allow memory to be addressed indirectly through the DE and BC register pairs. These are also discussed later in this chapter. The SP (stack pointer) is also used to indirectly address the stack memory through a few commands—the stack operations—which are also discussed later in this chapter.

Immediate Addressing

The immediate addressing mode is used when constant data are used in a program. The data are encoded immediately following the op-code in the program memory (see Fig. 4–2). The 8085A microprocessor has two forms of immediate addressing: 8- and 16-bit immediate addressing. The 8-bit form uses the notation d8 in Appendix B and the instruction lists in this and the next two chapters and the 16-bit form uses d16. Table 4–2 illustrates some 8- and 16-bit immediate data instructions. The 8-bit immediate instructions are always two bytes in length and the 16-bit immediate data instructions are always three bytes in length. Notice from Table 4–2 that if 16-bit data are used, the data are stored in the same form as an address, as discussed earlier in the section on direct addressing.

Byte 1   Byte 2

| Op-code | Immediate data |

Figure 4–2   A MVI instruction showing the placement of the 8-bits of immediate data.

TABLE 4-2 EIGHT- AND 16-BIT
IMMEDIATE DATA ENCODED IN
HEXADECIMAL MACHINE LANGUAGE

Hexadecimal immediate data	Machine Code B1–B2–B3
66H	XX–66
9FH	XX–9F
100H	XX–00–01
1000H	XX–00–10
1234H	XX–34–12

Notes: XX is any op-code that allows immediate addressing; minus signs are used to separate bytes of data in the machine-coded form.

4-3 IMMEDIATE DATA TRANSFER INSTRUCTIONS

The 8085A microprocessor has two basic forms of the immediate data transfer instruction. One form, MVI (move immediate), is used to transfer an 8-bit number into a register or memory location indirectly addressed by the HL register pair, and the other form, LXI (load immediate), is used to load a pair of registers with a 16-bit number. Table 4–3 illustrates all of the immediate data transfer instructions, together with their assembly language and machine language forms. The term *immediate* is used to indicate that the data immediately follow the op-code in the program.

TABLE 4-3 IMMEDIATE DATA TRANSFER INSTRUCTIONS

Assembly	Machine	Comment
MVI B,d8	06–d8	d8 is moved into B
MVI C,d8	0E–d8	d8 is moved into C
MVI D,d8	16–d8	d8 is moved into D
MVI E,d8	1E–d8	d8 is moved into E
MVI H,d8	26–d8	d8 is moved into H
MVI L,d8	2E–d8	d8 is moved into L
MVI M,d8	36–d8	d8 is moved into M
MVI A,d8	3E–d8	d8 is moved into A
LXI B,d16	01–ll–hh	d16 is moved into BC
LXI D,d16	11–ll–hh	d16 is moved into DE
LXI H,d16	21–ll–hh	d16 is moved into HL
LXI SP,d16	31–ll–hh	d16 is moved into SP

Notes: d8, 8 bits of data; d16, 16 bits of data; hh, high-order data byte; ll, low-order data byte; M, memory location indirectly addressed by the HL register pair.

The Move Immediate Instruction (MVI)

This instruction is used to place an 8-bit number into any register or memory location indirectly addressed by the HL register pair. Each MVI instruction is two bytes in length: the first byte contains the op-code and the second byte contains the data—an 8-bit number. Example 4–1 shows how a 12H is placed into the B register in both hexadecimal machine language (06–12) and symbolic assembly language (MVI B, 12H).

```
(EXAMPLE 4-1)

06-12    MVI B,12H    ;moves 12H into B
```

Just as a number can be moved into the B register (see Example 4–1), a number can be moved into an internal 8085A register. Example 4–2 shows some additional move immediate instructions with comments that explain what each accomplishes. The MVI M,d8 instruction is used to store a byte of data in the memory. This instruction uses the HL register pair to refer to (point to) a location in the memory. (Refer to Section 4–1 on indirect addressing.) M always refers to the memory location indirectly addressed by the HL register pair.

```
(EXAMPLE 4-2)

1E-64    MVI E,64H    ;moves a 64H into E
1E-64    MVI E,100    ;moves a 100 into E
3E-FF    MVI A,-1     ;moves a -1 into A
```

Suppose that the HL register pair contains a 1000H and the MVI M, 11H instruction is executed. This instruction moves the immediate byte of data (11H) into the memory location indirectly addressed by the HL register pair (1000H). In other words, an 11H is stored in memory location 1000H. Example 4–3 illustrates how this instruction is stored in the memory together with the instructions required to place a 1000H in the HL register pair.

```
(EXAMPLE 4-3)

26-10    MVI H,10H    ;moves a 10H into H
2E-00    MVI L,00H    ;moves a 00H into L
36-11    MVI M,11H    ;moves a 11H into location 1000H
```

The Load Immediate Instruction (LXI)

Load immediate is used to load a 16-bit number into any register pair (BC, DE, and HL) or the stack pointer register (SP). Each LXI instruction is three bytes in length: the first byte contains the op-code and the second and third bytes contain the 16 bits of immediate data. The data are always stored with the low-order portion (ll) following the op-code and the high-order portion (hh) following the low-order portion. Example 4–4 shows how a 10CDH is placed in the HL register pair with a LXI instruction. Notice how the least significant byte (CD) immediately follows the op-code (21) and the most significant byte (10) follows the least significant byte. Of course, in symbolic assembly language, the number appears as a 10CDH.

```
(EXAMPLE 4-4)

21-CD-10  LXI H,10CDH  ;moves a 10CDH into HL
```

If Example 4-3 is redone using the LXI instruction in place of the two MVI instructions used to load the HL register pair, the resulting program (see Example 4-5) is a simplified version.

```
(EXAMPLE 4-5)

21-00-10  LXI H,1000H  ;point to location 1000H
36-11     MVI M,11H    ;moves a 11H to 1000H
```

4-4 DIRECT DATA TRANSFER INSTRUCTIONS

Direct data transfer instructions are useful if only one byte or word of data is to be transferred to or from the memory. If more than one byte or word is transferred, it is more efficient if the indirectly addressed instructions are chosen for the transfer. The 8085A has two forms of the direct addressed instruction: the load and store accumulator and the load and store HL register pair instructions. These instructions are listed in both machine and symbolic assembly language in Table 4-4. All directly addressed instructions are three bytes in length: the first byte is the op-code and the second and third bytes contain the memory address of the operand.

TABLE 4-4   DIRECT LOAD AND STORE INSTRUCTIONS

Assembly	Machine	Comment
LDA a16	3A–ll–hh	A is loaded from a16
STA a16	32–ll–hh	A is stored at a16
LHLD a16	2A–ll–hh	HL is loaded from a16
SHLD a16	22–ll–hh	HL is stored at a16

Notes: a16, 16-bit memory address; ll, low-order address; hh, high-order address.

The Load/Store Accumulator Instructions (LDA/STA)

Two instructions that directly address memory are available to load and store the contents of the accumulator. In both cases the op-code is followed by a 16-bit memory address. In the LDA instruction, the address (a16) is used by the microprocessor to locate the location of the data to be moved into the accumulator from the memory.

The STA instruction uses the address to point to the memory location where a copy of the accumulator is to be stored.

Example 4–6 shows how a number stored in memory location 1000H is copied into location 1200H by using a LDA and a STA instruction.

```
(EXAMPLE 4-6)

3A-00-10   LDA 1000H ;A loaded from 1000H
32-00-12   STA 1200H ;A stored at 1200H
```

The Load/Store HL Register Pair Instructions (LHLD/SHLD)

The LHLD and SHLD instructions are similiar to the LDA and STA instructions except that instead of transferring the contents of the accumulator to and from the memory, they transfer the contents of the HL register pair. Example 4–7 illustrates these two commands used to transfer the contents of memory locations 1000H and 1001H into locations 1200H and 1201H. In this example LHLD 1000H copies the contents of location 1000H into the L register and the contents of location 1001H into the H register. The SHLD instruction then stores the L register at memory location 1200H and the H register at location 1201H. Notice that the data in HL are stored in the standard Intel format: low-order byte at the lowest-numbered memory location and the high-order byte at the highest-numbered memory location. This form of storage is true anytime that 16-bit data are stored in the memory.

```
(EXAMPLE 4-7)

2A-00-10   LHLD 1000H ;load HL from 1000H
22-00-12   SHLD 1200H ;store HL at 1200H
```

4-5 INDIRECT DATA TRANSFER INSTRUCTIONS

Although the letter M is used to indirectly address memory, there are other ways to indirectly address memory. In this section we will not cover the M operand, which is presented in Section 4–3 and later sections; it will cover the LDAX and STAX instructions, which also indirectly address memory.

TABLE 4-5   INDIRECTLY ADDRESSED INSTRUCTIONS

Assembly	Machine	Comment
LDAX B	0A	Loads A from location BC
LDAX D	1A	Loads A from location DE
STAX B	02	Stores A at location BC
STAX D	12	Stores A at location DE

Table 4-5 lists the different forms of the LDAX and STAX instructions. Notice that each instruction is only one byte in length because the address of the data is stored in a register pair rather than with the op-code, as in the direct addressing instructions.

To illustrate the operation of the LDAX and STAX instructions, Example 4-6 will be repeated using the BC and DE register pairs to indirectly address memory location 1000H and 1200H. Example 4-8 illustrates how the register pairs are loaded with the memory addresses and then uses the LDAX B instruction to load the accumulator from memory location 1000H and the STAX D instruction to store the accumulator at memory location 1200H.

```
(EXAMPLE 4-8)

01-00-10   LXI   B,1000H ;load BC with 1000H
11-00-12   LXI   D,1200H ;load DE with 1200H
02         LDAX  B       ;load A from location 1000H
1A         STAX  D       ;store A at location 1200H
```

4-6 REGISTER DATA TRANSFER INSTRUCTIONS

The largest group of data transfer instructions is the register data transfer group. This group contains 63 different instructions called moves (MOV). The basic form of the MOV instruction is listed in Fig. 4-3. The rightmost register is called the source register and the leftmost register is called the destination register. The MOV instruction transfers a copy of the data in the source register to the destination register. Note that the destination register changes and the source register does not change. This is indicated by the arrow in Fig. 4-3.

MOV rd , rs

rd = destination register
rs = source register

Figure 4-3 The MOV instruction illustrating both the source and destination registers and also the direct of the data transfer.

A complete list of all the MOV instructions is located in Table 4-6 together with a comment on what each accomplishes. Notice that some of these instructions use indirect addressing as well as register addressing. Also, not all of the instructions have a useful function—MOV B,B, for example, will actually copy the contents of the B register into the B register, but this does not serve any useful function.

Example 4-9 shows how a number in the accumulator is moved into both the D and the E registers. The first instruction copies the contents of the accumulator into the D register and the second copies the accumulator into the E register.

```
(EXAMPLE 4-9)

57   MOV D,A  ;A copied into D
5F   MOV E,A  ;A copied into E
```

TABLE 4-6. MOVE (MOV) DATA TRANSFER
INSTRUCTIONS

Assembly	Machine	Comment
MOV B,B	40	Copies B into B
MOV B,C	41	Copies C into B
MOV B,D	42	Copies D into B
MOV B,E	43	Copies E into B
MOV B,H	44	Copies H into B
MOV B,L	45	Copies L into B
MOV B,M	46	Copies M into B
MOV B,A	47	Copies A into B
MOV C,B	48	Copies B into C
MOV C,C	49	Copies C into C
MOV C,D	4A	Copies D into C
MOV C,E	4B	Copies E into C
MOV C,H	4C	Copies H into C
MOV C,L	4D	Copies L into C
MOV C,M	4E	Copies M into C
MOV C,A	4F	Copies A into C
MOV D,B	50	Copies B into D
MOV D,C	51	Copies C into D
MOV D,D	52	Copies D into D
MOV D,E	53	Copies E into D
MOV D,H	54	Copies H into D
MOV D,L	55	Copies L into D
MOV D,M	56	Copies M into D
MOV D,A	57	Copies A into D
MOV E,B	58	Copies B into E
MOV E,C	59	Copies C into E
MOV E,D	5A	Copies D into E
MOV E,E	5B	Copies E into E
MOV E,H	5C	Copies H into E
MOV E,L	5D	Copies L into E
MOV E,M	5E	Copies M into E
MOV E,A	5F	Copies A into E
MOV H,B	60	Copies B into H
MOV H,C	61	Copies C into H
MOV H,D	62	Copies D into H
MOV H,E	63	Copies E into H
MOV H,H	64	Copies H into H
MOV H,L	65	Copies L into H
MOV H,M	66	Copies M into H

TABLE 4-6   (Continued)

Assembly	Machine	Comment
MOV H,A	67	Copies A into H
MOV L,B	68	Copies B into L
MOV L,C	69	Copies C into L
MOV L,D	6A	Copies D into L
MOV L,E	6B	Copies E into L
MOV L,H	6C	Copies H into L
MOV L,L	6D	Copies L into L
MOV L,M	6E	Copies M into L
MOV L,A	6F	Copies A into L
MOV M,B	70	Copies B into M
MOV M,C	71	Copies C into M
MOV M,D	72	Copies D into M
MOV M,E	73	Copies E into M
MOV M,H	74	Copies H into M
MOV M,L	75	Copies L into M
MOV M,M	—	Invalid instruction
MOV M,A	77	Copies A into M
MOV A,B	78	Copies B into A
MOV A,C	79	Copies C into A
MOV A,D	7A	Copies D into A
MOV A,E	7B	Copies E into A
MOV A,H	7C	Copies H into A
MOV A,L	7D	Copies L into A
MOV A,M	7E	Copies M into A
MOV A,A	7F	Copies A into A

Note: M, location indirectly addressed by the HL register pair.

Another example (Example 4–10) using MOV instructions is to clear the contents of all the internal registers. Here the accumulator is first cleared to zero with a MVI instruction and then moves are used to clear the remaining internal registers.

```
(EXAMPLE 4-10)

3E-00   MVI A,0   ;clear A
47      MOV B,A   ;clear B
4F      MOV C,A   ;clear C
57      MOV D,A   ;clear D
5F      MOV E,A   ;clear E
67      MOV H,A   ;clear H
6F      MOV L,A   ;clear A
```

Indirectly Addressing Memory Using M

Suppose that Example 4-8 is again repeated, but in this case the MOV command will be used rather than the LDA and STA instructions. Refer to Example 4-11 for the program that moves the number from location 1000H into location 1200H via the address stored in the HL register pair (M).

```
(EXAMPLE 4-11)

21-00-10   LXI H,1000H  ;point to 1000H
7E         MOV A,M      ;copy A from 1000H
26-12      MVI H,12H    ;point to 1200H
77         MOV M,A      ;store A at 1000H
```

4-7 STACK DATA TRANSFER INSTRUCTIONS

As mentioned in Chapter 3, the Intel 8085A microprocessor has a LIFO (last-in, first-out) stack memory that is used to store both return addresses from subroutines and data temporarily. This section of the text deals with the latter purpose. Table 4-7 lists the stack data transfer functions available in the 8085A microprocessor's instruction set. This set of instructions consists of PUSHes, POPs, and an XTHL instruction.

TABLE 4-7   STACK DATA TRANSFER INSTRUCTIONS

Assembly	Machine	Comment
POP B	C1	Data retrieved from the stack to BC
POP D	D1	Data retrieved from the stack to DE
POP H	E1	Data retrieved from the stack to HL
POP PSW	F1	Data retrieved from the stack to PSW
PUSH B	C5	Data stored from BC on the stack
PUSH D	D5	Data stored from DE on the stack
PUSH H	E5	Data stored from HL on the stack
PUSH PSW	F5	Data stored from PSW on the stack
XTHL	E3	HL exchanged with stack data

Note: PSW, processor status word (accumulator and flags).

Stack Memory Operation

Before the stack data transfer instructions can be covered, it is important that the operation of the LIFO stack be understood. The microprocessor does not know where the stack memory is located when power is first applied to the system; it must be told. This is normally accomplished by first loading the SP (stack pointer) register with an address in the memory. (Loading the stack pointer at the beginning of a program is essential if any of the stack operations are used!) The programmer decides what portion of the read/write memory is to function as a stack and then loads the SP with the top location plus one. The stack pointer always points to the current exit point. (Refer to Fig. 4-4 for a pictorial view of the stack and the stack pointer.)

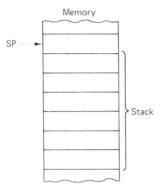

Figure 4-4 The stack memory which begins at one memory location below the SP address.

Operation of Push and Pop

The stack in the 8085A memory is a LIFO stack or more descriptively a push down–pop up stack. The name push down–pop up describes how the stack functions. If data are pushed (placed) on the stack, they move into the memory locations SP–1 and SP–2. (Note that data are stored in pairs.) The high-order register is stored first (SP–1), followed by the low-order register (SP–2). The SP is then decremented by two so that the next push occurs below the first.

Suppose that the SP is loaded with 1000H and BC contains a 1234H. A PUSH B instruction places the 12H from B in memory location 0FFFH (SP–1) and the 34H from C in memory location 0FFEH (SP–2). The SP is then decremented by 2 to 0FFEH. If this is followed by a POP PSW (POP A and flags), data from location

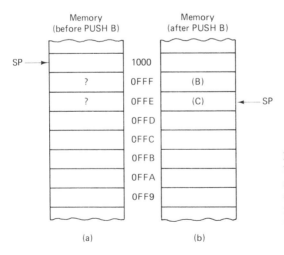

Figure 4-5 (a) The stack and SP before the execution of a PUSH B instruction. (B) the stack and SP after the execution of a PUSH B instruction illustrating the placement of the contents of both the B and C registers on the stack.

(SP) 0FFEH are moved into the flags and data from (SP + 1) 0FFFH are moved into the accumulator. The SP is then incremented by 2 to 1000H. Figure 4–5 illustrates the foregoing sequence of events.

(EXAMPLE 4–12)

```
C5    PUSH B ;store BC on stack
D5    PUSH D ;store DE on stack
C1    POP  B ;stack data to BC
D1    POP  D ;stack data to DE
```

Example 4–12 illustrates how the stack can be used to exchange the contents of the DE and BC register pairs. First BC is pushed on the stack followed by DE. Because DE was the last information placed on the stack, it is the first to come off the stack. A POP B will remove previous contents of DE from the stack and place it into BC. If this is followed by a POP D, the prior contents of BC are removed from the stack and placed into DE. The contents of the two registers have been swapped. Notice that the SP would be back at its original value, which means that the same area of memory can be reused by the next PUSH-POP sequence. It is also important to note that PUSHes and POPs must occur in pairs: one PUSH, one POP, two PUSHes, two POPs, and so on. If not, the stack pointer will eventually fill or read every memory location in the computer system.

Exchange HL with Stack Data (XTHL)

This instruction exchanges the contents of the HL pair with the most recent data on the stack. For example, if a 1000H is pushed on the stack and HL contains a 2000H, an XTHL command will exchange these two values so that HL equals 1000H and the stack data equal 2000H. This instruction and its application are illustrated in later chapters on programming.

4-8 MISCELLANEOUS DATA TRANSFER INSTRUCTIONS

In previous sections in this chapter we have explained the operation of most of the data transfer instructions except for the I/O instructions and some of the special instructions. Table 4–8 lists the remaining data transfer instructions together with a brief description of their operation.

TABLE 4-8 MISCELLANEOUS DATA TRANSFER
INSTRUCTIONS

Assembly	Machine	Comment
IN p8	DB–p8	Inputs data to A
OUT p8	D3–p8	Outputs data from A
SPHL	F9	HL is copied to SP
XCHG	EB	HL is swapped with DE

Note: p8, an 8-bit I/O port address.

Input/Output Data Transfer Instructions

As mentioned in Chapter 3, a computer system contains memory and I/O in addition to the CPU or MPU. To allow data transfers between the microprocessor and I/O, the 8085A instruction set contains two I/O instructions: IN and OUT. The IN instruction inputs data from an I/O device into the accumulator and the OUT instruction sends accumulator data out to an I/O device.

The I/O system for the 8085A microprocessor consists of 256 unique device addresses or port numbers. A port number is an address for an I/O device, just as a memory address is an address for the memory. The port number is used to select a particular I/O device. Both the IN and the OUT instructions are two bytes in length: the first byte is the op-code and the second is the I/O port number (p8).

Load SP from HL (SPHL)

The SPHL instruction is a one-byte instruction that copies the contents of the HL register pair into the stack pointer (SP). This instruction is used in some systems to initialize the stack pointer, and in other systems the LXI SP,d16 instruction is used to load the stack pointer. In any case it is probably one of the least used 8085A instructions.

Exchange DE with HL (XCHG)

The XCHG instruction exchanges the contents of the HL register pair with the contents of the DE register pair. Suppose that this instruction is used in a program to move a number from memory location 1000H into 1200H (refer to Example 4-8). This task is accomplished by pointing to location 1200H with DE and location 1000H with HL. The MOV commands and an XCHG can then be used to transfer the data, as illustrated in Example 4-13.

```
(EXAMPLE 4-13)

11-00-12  LXI   D,1200H ;point to 1200H
21-00-10  LXI   H,1000H ;point to 1000H
7E        MOV   A,M     ;get data from 1000H
EB        XCHG          ;switch pointers
77        MOV   M,A     ;save data at 1200H
```

4-9 SUMMARY

1. Data transfer instructions are used to transfer information from register to register, from register to memory, from memory to register, to and from the stack, and to and from the I/O devices in a system.
2. Four different addressing modes are used in the Intel 8085A microprocessor: direct, register, register indirect, and immediate.

3. Direct addressing is used whenever a memory location is accessed by storing the address of the memory location with the instruction.

4. Register addressing is used to address either a single 8-bit register (B, C, D, E, H, L, or A) or a 16-bit register pair (BC, DE, HL, and SP).

5. Register indirect addressing allows the instruction to address memory through the address held in a register pair.

6. Immediate addressing is used whenever the data (8 or 16 bits) are a constant. Immediate data immediately follow the op-code in the program.

7. MVI and LXI are the two immediate data transfer instructions in the 8085A instruction set. MVI is an 8-bit immediate instruction and LXI is a 16-bit.

8. The M register or operand is used to indirectly address memory through the HL register pair.

9. Only the accumulator and the HL register pair can be directly stored in the memory. LDA and STA are used for accumulator direct storage, and LHLD and SHLD are used for the HL register pair.

10. In addition to M for indirectly addressing the memory, the DE and BC register pairs are also available. LDAX and STAX allow the accumulator to be indirectly stored or loaded from the memory using the BC or DE register pairs.

11. Register data transfer instructions are the most numerous form of data transfer—63 instructions.

12. The stack memory in the 8085A microprocessor is a LIFO (last-in, first-out) memory used to store data and return addresses from subroutines.

13. The stack pointer (SP) register is used to indirectly address the stack for the stack data transfer instructions PUSH, POP, and XTHL.

14. The PSW is the processor status word which contains both the accumulator, as the high-order register, and the flag byte, as the low-order register.

15. IN and OUT are used to effect data transfer to and from the external I/O devices, often called I/O ports.

4-10 GLOSSARY

Destination register   The register that receives a copy of the data in an instruction.

Direct addressing   If memory data are directly addressed, the memory address is stored with the instruction in a program. The address is stored so that the second and third bytes of the instruction contain the memory location of the operand.

Immediate addressing   An immediate instruction contains the data used with the instruction in the form of the byte (8-bit data) or bytes (16-bit data) of data immediately following the op-code in the program.

Immediate data   8- or 16-bit data that immediately follow the op-code.

M register   The M register is the memory location indirectly addressed by the HL register pair.

Port   An I/O device in the 8085A system is called an I/O port.

Port address   An 8-bit number used to address a unique external I/O device.

Register addressing   A register-addressed instruction specifies the register or register pair where the data are located.

Register indirect addressing   Register indirect addressing is used to address memory through a register pair. The register pair holds the address of the memory data.

Source register   The register that supplies the data in an instruction. This register is never changed by an instruction.

QUESTIONS AND PROBLEMS

4-1. What four addressing modes are available for use in the 8085A microprocessor instruction set?

4-2. Direct addressed instructions are _____ bytes in length.

4-3. Where is the memory address of a direct-addressed instruction located?

4-4. Convert the following 16-bit memory addresses into the form required when stored with a direct addressed instruction: 1000H, 234AH, ABCDH, 5000H, and 456FH.

4-5. What 8-bit registers are available for use with a register addressed instruction? What register pairs are available?

4-6. When using register indirect addressing, to what does the letter M refer?

4-7. Which immediate instruction is two bytes in length, and why?

4-8. Convert the following symbolic assembly language instructions into hexadecimal machine language instructions: LXI D,1200H, MVI C, 90H, LXI SP,1234H, MVI M,10, and MVI M, 10H.

4-9. Write a sequence of immediate instructions that will place a 0000 into BC and a 12H into the accumulator.

4-10. Write a sequence of immediate instructions that will store a 16H in memory location 1200H and a 17H in memory location 1202H.

4-11. Explain how the LDA 1000H instruction functions.

4-12. Explain what answer is found in memory location 1200H and 1201H in the following sequence of instructions.

```
26-22       MVI H,22H
2E-44       MVI L,44H
22-00-12    SHLD 1200H
```

4-13. Which register indirect instruction is used to store the contents of the accumulator into the memory location indirectly addressed by the BC register pair?

4-14. Explain what answer is found in memory location 1200H in the following sequence of instructions.

```
06-12    MVI B, 12H
0E-00    MVI C, 00H
3E-77    MVI A, 77H
12       STAX B
```

4-15. Write a sequence of instructions that will use register indirect addressing to transfer the number stored in memory location 1300H into memory location 1301H.

4-16. Why is it rare to find the MOV B,B instruction in use in a program?

4-17. Explain what the MOV M,C instruction does if HL = 1233H and C = 34H.

4-18. Write a sequence of instruction that use MOV instructions to swap the contents of the BC register pair with the DE register pair.

4-19. Write a sequence of instructions that will store a zero in memory location 1000H through 1003H.

4-20. If a 1000H is pushed on the stack followed by a 2000H, which number is the first to come off the stack?

4-21. The push instruction is used to place the contents of any _____ on the stack.

4-22. What is the PSW?

4-23. What number appears in the BC register pair after the following sequence of instructions?

```
21-00-30     LXI H,3000H
11-00-20     LXI D,2500H
E5           PUSH H
D5           PUSH D
E1           POP H
C1           POP B
```

4-24. If a PUSH PSW is immediately followed by a POP B, in which register do the flag data appear?

4-25. Explain what the OUT 12H instruction accomplishes.

4-26. Which two instructions from this chapter can be used to place a number into the SP?

chapter five

ARITHMETIC AND LOGIC INSTRUCTIONS

The 8085A arithmetic and logic instructions described in this chapter include the following operations: addition, addition with carry, subtraction, subtraction with borrow, inversion, AND, OR, exclusive-OR, and rotation. In addition to the arithmetic and logic operations, in this chapter we present a detailed view of the operation of the flag bits with each instruction. None of the instructions described in Chapter 4 affected the flags, whereas all the instructions in this chapter affect the flags.

5-1 OBJECTIVES

Upon completion of this chapter, you will be able to:

1. Explain the operation of the 8085A arithmetic and logic instructions and indicate their effect on the flag bits
2. Write short programs using the arithmetic and logic operations
3. Use the logic instructions to clear, set, and complement bits
4. Test the accumulator using the ANA A or ORA A instruction
5. Explain the operation of the shift and rotate instructions and their effect on the flag bits

5-2 ADDITION

Addition takes several forms in the 8085A microprocessor: 8-bit binary, 16-bit binary, and two-digit binary-coded-decimal (BCD) addition. In binary addition either signed or unsigned numbers are added, and in BCD addition only unsigned numbers are added. The instruction set supports additions using register addressing, register indirect addressing, and immediate addressing, but not direct addressing.

8-Bit Binary Addition

Because the 8085A is an 8-bit microprocessor, most of the addition instructions are 8-bit additions. Table 5-1 illustrates all the possible 8-bit addition commands. Notice that all the addressing modes are represented except for direct addressing. It is also critically important to recognize that the flag bits will always be affected by any of these instructions. Any addition instruction will always add the operand to the accumulator.

TABLE 5-1 EIGHT-BIT BINARY ADDITION INSTRUCTIONS

Assembly	*Machine*	*Comments*
ADI dB	C6–dB	A = d8 + A
ADD B	80	A = A + B
ADD C	81	A = A + C
ADD D	82	A = A + D
ADD E	83	A = A + E
ADD H	84	A = A + H
ADD L	85	A = A + L
ADD M	86	A = A + M
ADD A	87	A = A + A
		(A = A × 2)

Notes: d8, 8-bits of data; and M, memory location indirectly addressed by the HL register pair.

Example 5-1 illustrates a short sequence of instructions that add a 12H to the contents of the accumulator, which initially contains a 55H. After the 8085A adds

```
(EXAMPLE 5-1)


3E-55    MVI A,55H ;place 55H in A
C6-12    ADI 12H   ;add 12H to A
```

the 12H and the 55H together, the result (67H) is placed into the accumulator. The flags change as follows:

    Z = 0   The result is not zero.
    P = 0   The parity of the result is odd.
  CY = 0   No carry occurred for this addition.
  AC = 0   No half-carry occurred.
    S = 0   The result is positive.

Suppose that it is desirable to add the number in the B register to the number in the A register. This is accomplished by using the ADD B instruction, which adds the contents of the B register to the contents of the A register and places the sum in the A register. This sequence, together with the loading of both the A and B registers, is illustrated in Example 5-2. In this example a 40H and an EEH are added together, resulting in a sum of 2EH. The carry out of the accumulator is held in the carry flag. The flags are changed to the following conditions:

    Z = 0   The result is not zero.
    P = 1   The parity of the result is even.
  CY = 1   A carry occurred for this addition.
  AC = 0   No half-carry occurred.
    S = 0   The answer is positive.

```
(EXAMPLE 5-2)

3E-40      MVI A,40H   ;load A with 40H
06-EE      MVI B,0EEH  ;load B with EEH
80         ADD B       ;A = A + B
```

Suppose that it is desirable to add the number in the B register to the number in the C register and place the sum in the D register. This addition is accomplished by using the ADD B instruction, which adds the contents of the B register to the contents of the A register. Before the addition takes place, the number in C must be moved to A, and after the addition, the answer, in A, must be moved into D. Example 5-3 illustrates this sequence and also the instruction required to load both B and C. A 2FH is added to an 8 to generate a result of 37H. Notice the extra instructions required to position C before the addition and also position the result D after the addition. The flags change as indicated:

    Z = 0   The result is not zero.
    P = 0   The parity of the result is odd.
  CY = 0   No carry occurred for this addition.
  AC = 1   A half-carry occurred.
    S = 0   The answer is positive.

(EXAMPLE 5-3)

```
06-2F     MVI B,2FH  ;place 2FH into B
0E-08     MVI C,8    ;place 8 into C
79        MOV A,C    ;position C
80        ADD B      ;add B to C
57        MOV D,A    ;move sum to D
```

Addition with Carry

Whenever large numbers, numbers with more than 8 bits, or multiple-byte numbers are added together, the carry must be propagated from one 8-bit segment to the next. Propagation from one byte to another is illustrated in Fig. 5–1. To accomplish a carry in multiple-byte addition, the add with carry instruction is used to propagate the carry from one byte to the next. Table 5–2 lists all the add with carry instructions.

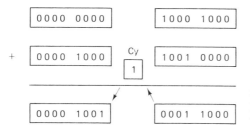

Figure 5-1 Multiple byte addition illustrating the carry propagation through the carry bit.

TABLE 5-2 ADD WITH CARRY INSTRUCTIONS

Assembly	Machine	Comment
ACI d8	CE–d8	A = A + d8 + CY
ADC B	88	A = A + B + CY
ADC C	89	A = A + C + CY
ADC D	8A	A = A + D + CY
ADC E	8B	A = A + E + CY
ADC H	8C	A = A + H + CY
ADC L	8D	A = A + L + CY
ADC M	8E	A = A + M + CY
ADC A	8F	A = A + A + CY

Notes: CY, carry; d8, 8 bits of data; M, memory location indirectly addressed by the HL register pair.

Suppose that the DE register pair contains a 16-bit number that is to be added to the number in the BC pair. To accomplish this multiple-byte addition, it is necessary to add E and C together and then add D and B together with the carry from the addition of E and C. The sequence of instructions required to accomplish this addition is listed in Example 5–4. Notice that the ADD E instruction generates a carry

(EXAMPLE 5-4)

```
01-10-01   LXI B,110H   ;load BC with 110H
11-FF-01   LXI D,1FFH   ;load DE with 1FFH
79         MOV A,C      ;C = C + E
83         ADD E
4F         MOV C,A
78         MOV A,B      ;B = B + D + Cy
8A         ADC D
47         MOV B,A
```

which is added into the most significant byte of the answer with the ADC D instruction. The answer, which is found in the BC register pair, is 30FH.

16-Bit Addition

Although Example 5-4 illustrates 16-bit addition, the 8085A instruction set contains special instructions (DAD) that also accomplish a 16-bit addition. Table 5-3 lists these 16-bit addition instructions.

TABLE 5-3 SIXTEEN-BIT DAD (DOUBLE-ADD) ADDITION INSTRUCTIONS

Assembly	Machine	Comment
DAD B	09	HL = HL + BC
DAD D	19	HL = HL + DE
DAD H	29	HL = HL + HL
		(HL = 2 × HL)
DAD SP	39	HL = HL + SP

Suppose that Example 5-4 is modified so that the number in the BC pair and the number in the HL pair are added. Example 5-5 illustrates the new sequence of events required to accomplish this 16-bit addition. Unlike other addition instructions, which affect all the flags, the DAD instruction affects only the CY flag.

(EXAMPLE 5-5)

```
01-10-01   LXI  B,110H   ;load BC with 110H
21-FF-01   LXI  H,1FFH   ;load HL with 1FFH
09         DAD  B        ;HL = HL + BC
```

BCD Addition

BCD addition is like binary addition except that the numbers that are added together can only range in value from 0 through 9. In the 8085A a special instruction is provided that allows BCD addition to be accomplished by using the binary addition instructions. The DAA instruction is used after a BCD addition (with a binary add instruction) in order to correct the BCD result. Example 5-6 illustrates the summa-

```
(EXAMPLE 5-6)

3E-11    MVI  A,11H  ;place 11 BCD in A
C6-19    ADI  19H    ;add 19 BCD
27       DAA          ;correct result
```

tion of the packed BCD numbers 11 and a 19. After the addition, the accumulator contains a 2AH, which is not a valid BCD number—the answer should be a 30_{BCD}. DAA corrects the answer and provides a 30H after the instruction is executed. (Note that 30H and 30_{BCD} are exactly the same when coded in the memory.) The DAA instruction changes the result through the two tests listed by adding a 00H, 06H, 60H, or 66H to the accumulator.

1. If the least significant half-byte is greater than 9 or if the AC flag bit is set, a 06H is added to the accumulator.
2. If the most significant half-byte is greater than 9 or if the CY flag bit is set, a 60H is added to the accumulator.

Increment

The last form of addition available is to increment or add 1. The increment command is either an 8-bit (INR) increment or a 16-bit (INX) increment instruction (see Table 5-4). The INR instructions affect all the flags except CY, and the INX instructions affect no flags. Although there is no example of these instructions at this point in the text, the increment instruction is extremely useful, as we shall discover in later chapters on programming.

TABLE 5-4 INCREMENT INSTRUCTIONS

Assembly	Machine	Comment
INR B	04	B = B + 1
INR C	0C	C = C + 1
INR D	14	D = D + 1
INR E	1C	E = E + 1
INR H	24	H = H + 1
INR L	2C	L = L + 1
INR M	34	M = M + 1
INR A	3C	A = A + 1
INX B	03	BC = BC + 1
INX D	13	DE = DE + 1
INX H	23	HL = HL + 1
INX SP	33	SP = SP + 1

Notes: None of these instructions affects the accumulator except for INR A; M, memory location indirectly addressed by the HL register pair.

5-3 SUBTRACTION

The 8085A supports 8-bit binary subtraction and decrement. It also supports a subtraction instruction which allows a borrow, if it occurs, to be propagated through additional bytes of a number. This instruction—subtract with borrow—is often used for multiple-byte subtraction. If 16-bit or BCD subtraction is required, a program must be written to accomplish it, as illustrated in Chapter 10.

8-Bit Subtraction

Table 5-5 lists all the various subtraction instructions, which include register, register indirect, and immediate addressing, but not direct addressing. Each of these instructions affects the flag bits so that they reflect various conditions about the difference after a subtraction.

TABLE 5-5 EIGHT-BIT SUBTRACTION INSTRUCTIONS

Assembly	Machine	Comment
SUI d8	D6–d8	A = A − d8
SUB B	90	A = A − B
SUB C	91	A = A − C
SUB D	92	A = A − D
SUB E	93	A = A − E
SUB H	94	A = A − H
SUB L	95	A = A − L
SUB M	96	A = A − M
SUB A	97	A = A − A (A = 0)

Notes: d8, 8 bits of data; M, memory location indirectly addressed by the HL register pair.

Example 5-7 illustrates a simple sequence of instructions that find the difference between 2EH and 3FH. The accumulator equals an EFH after the subtraction and the flags change as indicated:

Z = 0   The result is not zero.

P = 1   The parity of the result is even.

CY = 1   A borrow occurred for this subtraction.

AC = 1   A half-borrow occurred.

S = 1   The answer is negative.

```
(EXAMPLE 5-7)

3E-2E    MVI A,2EH ;place 2EH in A
D6-3F    SUI 3FH    ;subtract 3FH
```

Notice that the borrow is held in the carry flag and the half-borrow is held in the AC flag after a subtraction. Borrows that occur for 8-bit subtraction are most often ignored, but borrows that occur for multiple-byte subtractions are cascaded through the more significant bytes of the difference.

Subtract with Borrow

Whenever multiple-byte numbers are subtracted, the borrow must be propagated from one 8-bit segment into another. Borrow propagation is illustrated in Fig. 5-2 for a multiple-byte subtraction. To develop a program that propagates the borrow, a new instruction is required. The subtract-with-borrow instructions are listed in Table 5-6.

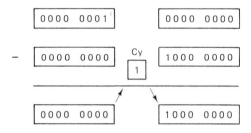

Figure 5-2 Multiple byte subtraction illustrating the borrow propagation through the carry flag.

TABLE 5-6 SUBTRACT-WITH-BORROW
INSTRUCTIONS

Assembly	Machine	Comment
SBI d8	DE–d8	A = A – d8 – CY
SBB B	98	A = A – B – CY
SBB C	99	A = A – C – CY
SBB D	9A	A = A – D – CY
SBB E	9B	A = A – E – CY
SBB H	9C	A = A – H – CY
SBB L	9D	A = A – L – CY
SBB M	9E	A = A – M – CY
SBB A	9F	A = A – A – CY

Notes: d8, 8 bits of data; M, memory location indirectly addressed by the HL register pair.

Suppose that the number in the DE pair is subtracted from the BC pair. Just as with addition, the least significant byte is operated on first. Once the difference of C and E is determined, the D register is subtracted from the B register with a borrow. This effectively propagates the borrow through the most significant byte of the result. Example 5-8 illustrates the sequence of instructions required for this subtraction.

(EXAMPLE 5-8)

```
01-00-01    LXI B,100H    ;place 100H in BC
11-01-00    LXI D,1       ;place 1 in DE
79          MOV A,C       ;C = C - E
93          SUB E
4F          MOV C,A
78          MOV A,B       ;B = B - D - Cy
9A          SBB D
47          MOV B,A
```

In this example the 01H in E is subtracted from the 00H in C. This generates a result in C of FFH and also a borrow, which is held in the CY flag. When the 00H in D is subtracted from the 01H in B with borrow, the result is 00H. The borrow is subtracted from B as well as the 00H in the D register. The difference after this sequence is a 00FFH, and it is found in the BC register pair.

Decrement

The final form of subtraction available in the 8085A is decrement or subtract 1. The decrement command is either an 8-bit (DCR) decrement or a 16-bit (DCX) decrement instruction (see Table 5-7).

TABLE 5-7 DECREMENT INSTRUCTIONS

Assembly	Machine	Comment
DCR B	05	B = B - 1
DCR C	0D	C = C - 1
DCR D	15	D = D - 1
DCR E	1D	E = E - 1
DCR H	25	H = H - 1
DCR L	2D	L = L - 1
DCR M	35	M = M - 1
DCR A	3D	A = A - 1
DCX B	0B	BC = BC - 1
DCX D	1B	DE = DE - 1
DCX H	2B	HL = HL - 1
DCX SP	33	SP = SP - 1

Notes: None of these instructions affects the accumulator except for DCR A; M, memory location indirectly addressed by the HL register pair.

The DCR instructions affect all the flags except CY and the DCX instructions affect no flags. Although there is no example of these instructions at this point in the text, the decrement instruction, as well as the increment instruction, are extremely useful, as we shall discover in later chapters on programming.

Compare

The compare instruction is a modified subtraction instruction. It performs 8-bit binary subtraction with one unique modification—the difference is not routed into the accumulator. This instruction changes only the flag bits so that they reflect the difference. You might wonder why. Suppose that you were required to determine if the number in the accumulator is a 12H. You could subtract 12H from the accumulator and look at the zero flag bit. The problem with this is that the original number in the accumulator is destroyed (lost). The compare allows this comparison without the loss of the number in the accumulator.

The compare instructions are available with the same addressing modes as the subtract instructions, as illustrated in Table 5–8. As programming is learned in later chapters, this instruction will become indispensable.

TABLE 5-8 COMPARE INSTRUCTIONS

Assembly	Machine	Comment
CPI d8	FE–d8	* = A – d8
CMP B	B8	* = A – B
CMP C	B9	* = A – C
CMP D	BA	* = A – D
CMP E	BB	* = A – E
CMP H	BC	* = A – H
CMP L	BD	* = A – L
CMP M	BE	* = A – M
CMP A	BF	* = A – A

Notes: d8, 8 bits of data; *, result affects only the flags; M, memory location indirectly addressed by the HL register pair.

5-4 LOGIC INSTRUCTIONS

The 8085A microprocessor is capable of executing four basic logic functions: invert, AND, OR, and exclusive-OR. Why does a microprocessor instruction set contain logic instructions? One reason is that logic instructions are sometimes used to replace discrete logic gates. Today, program storage costs about $\frac{1}{20}$ of a cent per byte. If an instruction can be used to replace an external logic circuit, imagine the amount of money saved by programmed logic! Another reason is that system control software usually requires bit manipulation—a logic operation.

Inversion

The CMA instruction, 2FH in machine language, is used to one's complement or invert the contents of the accumulator. This operation, which affects no flag bits, causes each bit of the accumulator to be inverted (changed from 1 to 0 or 0 to 1). CMA causes the accumulator to appear as eight inverters. This means that this one-byte instruction can be used to replace eight discrete inverters provided that the speed is not too great. The amount of circuitry replaced by the CMA instruction is $1\frac{1}{3}$ of 7404 TTL hex inverter. Cost advantage: software = \$0.0005 versus hardware = \$0.40, a saving of 80,000 percent.

In addition to inverting the accumulator (often called NOT), this instruction together with an INR A is used to form the two's complement of the accumulator. Whenever a number is two's complemented, its arithmetic sign is changed. Example 5-9 illustrates two sequences of instructions that will two's-complement the contents of the accumulator.

```
(EXAMPLE 5-9)

2F      CMA     ;ones complement A
3C      INR A   ;form twos complement of A


    or


3D      DCR A   ;decrement A
2F      CMA     ;form twos complement of A
```

The AND Operation

The AND instruction, whose operation is represented as a $\wedge$, actually has two separate functions in a microprocessor-based system: selectively clearing bits of the accumulator and replacing discrete AND gates.

The binary multiplication, or AND instruction, functions as eight independent two-input AND gates, as illustrated in Fig. 5-3. This instruction is used to replace two 7408 quad two-input AND gates. The cost advantage: software = \$0.0005 ver-

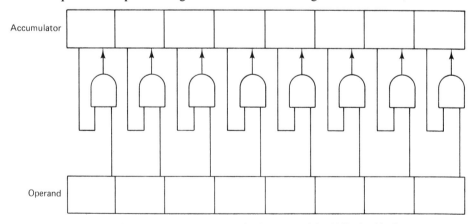

Figure 5-3 Notice how the 8-bit number in the operand is ANDed with the accumulator bit position by bit position.

sus hardware = $0.80, a saving of 160,000 percent. The effect on the flag bits is as follows: Z, S, and P are set or reset depending on the outcome of the AND operation, CY is always cleared, and AC is always set.

In addition to replacing external logic circuitry, the AND function can also be used to selectively clear (mask) any number of bit positions in the accumulator. This command will, in other words, turn off individual bits in the accumulator. The 8 bits of the accumulator are available to use as eight switches for controlling external hardware.

Figure 5-4 illustrates this effect by using ×'s (don't cares) to represent each bit of the accumulator and 00001111 as a test bit pattern ANDed with the accumulator. The outcome clearly indicates that the 0's in the test bit pattern force the corresponding bit positions to 0 and the 1's in the test pattern allow the corresponding bit positions to pass through to the result unchanged. All the possible AND instructions are listed in Table 5-9.

```
    X X X X   X X X X      Accumulator
∧   0 0 0 0   1 1 1 1      Operand
    ─────────────────
    0 0 0 0   X X X X      Result
```

Figure 5-4 The AND operation illustrating the effect on the result. A 0 ANDed with anything results in a 0. A 1 ANDed with anything results in no change.

TABLE 5-9 AND INSTRUCTIONS

Assembly	Machine	Comment
ANI d8	E6–d8	A = A ∧ d8
ANA B	A0	A = A ∧ B
ANA C	A1	A = A ∧ C
ANA D	A2	A = A ∧ D
ANA E	A3	A = A ∧ E
ANA H	A4	A = A ∧ H
ANA L	A5	A = A ∧ L
ANA M	A6	M = A ∧ M
ANA A	A7	A = A ∧ A

Notes: d8, 8 bits of data; ∧, symbol for the AND operation; M memory location indirectly addressed by the HL register pair.

The ANA A instruction has a special function. With ANA A, the accumulator is ANDed with the accumulator and as a result the value of the accumulator does not change. This instruction does change the flags, so that a number in the accumulator can be tested for a zero–not zero, positive–negative, or an even–odd parity condition. For this reason the ANA A instruction should be thought of as a TEST A instruction.

The OR Operation

The inclusive-OR instruction, whose operation is represented as a V, actually has two separate functions in a microprocessor-based system: selectively setting bits of the accumulator and replacing discrete OR gates.

The binary addition or inclusive-OR instruction functions as eight independent two input OR gates, as illustrated in Fig. 5–5. This instruction is used to replace two 7432 quad two-input OR gates. The cost advantage: software = $0.0005 versus hardware = 0.80, a saving of 160,000 percent. The effect on the flag bits is as follows: Z, S, and P are set or reset depending on the outcome of the OR operation; CY and AC are always cleared.

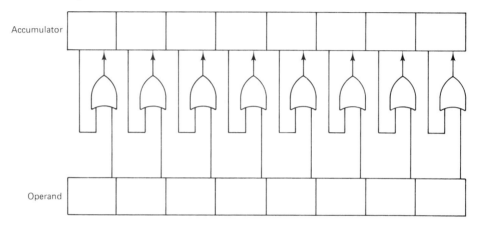

Figure 5–5   The OR operation showing how the 8-bit number in the operand is ORed with the accumulator bit position by bit position.

In addition to replacing external logic circuitry, the OR function can also be used to selectively set any number of bit positions in the accumulator. This command will, in other words, turn on individual bits in the accumulator. The 8 bits of the accumulator are available to use as eight switches for controlling external hardware. The AND operation is used to turn bits off, and the OR operation is used to turn bits on.

Figure 5–6 illustrates this effect by using ×'s (don't cares) to represent each bit of the accumulator and 00001111 as a test bit pattern ORed with the accumulator. The outcome clearly indicates that the 1's in the test bit pattern force the corresponding bit positions to 1, and the 0's in the test pattern allow the corresponding bit posi-

	X X X X X X X X	Accumulator
V	0 0 0 0 1 1 1 1	Operand
	X X X X 1 1 1 1	Result

Figure 5–6   The OR operation illustrating the effect on the result. A 1 ORed with anything results in a 1. A 0 ORed with anything results in no change.

tions to pass through to the result unchanged. All the possible OR instructions are listed in Table 5–10.

TABLE 5-10 OR INSTRUCTIONS

Assembly	Machine	Comment
ORI d8	F6–d8	A = A V d8
ORA B	B0	A = A V B
ORA C	B1	A = A V C
ORA D	B2	A = A V D
ORA E	B3	A = A V E
ORA H	B4	A = A V H
ORA L	B5	A = A V L
ORA M	B6	A = A V M
ORA A	B7	A = A V A

Notes: d8, 8 bits of data; V, symbol for the OR operation; M, memory location indirectly addressed by the HL register pair.

The ORA A instruction, as the ANA A instruction, has a special function. With the ORA A instruction, the accumulator is ORed with the accumulator and the value of the result does not change. This instruction does change the flags so that a number in the accumulator can be tested for a zero–not zero, positive–negative or even–odd parity condition. For this reason, the ORA A and the ANA A instructions should both be thought of as TEST A instructions.

The Exclusive-OR Operation

The exclusive-OR instruction, whose operation is represented as a V̶, actually has two separate functions in a microprocessor-based system: selectively inverting bits of the accumulator and replacing discrete exclusive-OR gates.

The exclusive-OR instruction functions as eight independent two-input exclusive-OR gates, as illustrated in Fig. 5–7. This instruction is used to replace two 7486 quad two-input exclusive-OR gates. The cost advantage: software = $0.0005 versus hardware = $0.80, a saving of 160,000 percent. The effect on the flag bits is as follows: Z, S, and P are set or reset depending on the outcome of the exclusive-OR operation; CY and AC are always cleared.

In addition to replacing external logic circuitry, the exclusive-OR function can also be used to selectively invert any number of the bit positions in the accumulator. This command will, in other words, complement individual bits in the accumulator. The 8 bits of the accumulator are available to use as eight switches for controlling external hardware. The AND operation is used to turn bits off, the OR operation is used to turn bits on, and the exclusive-OR operation inverts bits.

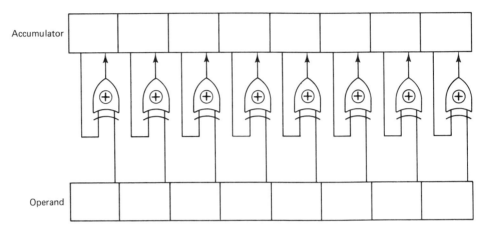

Figure 5-7   The exclusive-OR operation showing how the 8-bit number in the operand is exclusive-ORed with the accumulator bit position by bit position.

Figure 5-8 illustrates this effect by using ×'s (don't cares) to represent each bit of the accumulator and 00001111 as a test bit pattern exclusive-ORed with the accumulator. The outcome clearly indicates that the 1's in the test bit pattern force the corresponding bit positions to invert, and the 0's in the test pattern allow the corresponding bit positions to pass through to the result unchanged. All the possible exclusive-OR instructions are listed in Table 5-11. An added bonus is the XRA A instruction, which always clears the accumulator to zero. This command should be thought of as a CLEAR A instruction.

TABLE 5-11   EXCLUSIVE-OR INSTRUCTIONS

Assembly	Machine	Comment
XRI d8	EE–d8	A = A ⊻ d8
XRA B	A8	A = A ⊻ B
XRA C	A9	A = A ⊻ C
XRA D	AA	A = A ⊻ D
XRA E	AB	A = A ⊻ E
XRA H	AC	A = A ⊻ H
XRA L	AD	A = A ⊻ L
XRA M	AE	A = A ⊻ M
XRA A	AF	A = A ⊻ A

Notes: d8, 8 bits of data; ⊻, symbol for the exclusive-OR operation; M, memory location indirectly addressed by the HL register pair.

```
         XXXX  XXXX    Accumulator
    ∀    0000  1111    Operand
    ─────────────────
         XXXX  X̄X̄X̄X̄    Result
```

Figure 5-8 The exclusive-OR operation illustrating the effect on the result. A 1 exclusive-ORed with anything results in inversion. A O exclusive-ORed with anything results in no change.

5-5 SHIFT AND ROTATE INSTRUCTIONS

In certain applications it is desirable that information be shifted or rotated. The 8085A microprocessor is capable of all types of logical rotation and certain forms of shifting.

The Rotate Instructions

There are four instructions that allow the contents of the accumulator to be rotated left or right. Each rotate instruction affects the contents of the accumulator and the Cy flag bit.

Figure 5-9 illustrates the operation of the four rotate instructions: RRC and RLC, 8-bit rotates, and RAR and RAL, 9-bit rotates. Table 5-12 lists each instruction and its machine and assembly language forms.

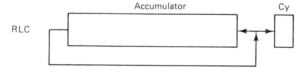

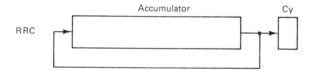

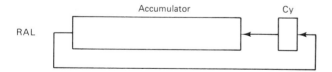

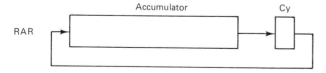

Figure 5-9 The operation of the rotate instructions. Notice that RLC and RRC are 8-bit rotates and RAL and RAR are 9-bit rotates.

Suppose that the accumulator contains two 4-bit BCD digits and software is required to reposition them so that the most significant digit and least significant digit exchange places. This is easily accomplished by using any of the 8-bit rotate instructions listed in Table 5–12. Example 5–10 illustrates the RRC instruction used four times to rotate the accumulator four places. The RLC instruction is also able to accomplish the same result by rotating the number left instead of right.

TABLE 5-12   EIGHT- AND 9-BIT ROTATE INSTRUCTIONS

Assembly	Machine	Comment
RLC	07	Rotate A left
RRC	OF	Rotate A right
RAL	17	Rotate A left through carry
RAR	IF	Rotate A right through carry

Note: RLC and RRC are 8-bit rotates and RAL and RAR are 9-bit rotates.

```
(EXAMPLE 5-10)

OF   RRC   ;rotate right 4 bit positions
OF   RRC
OF   RRC
OF   RRC
```

The Shift Instructions

Although there are no shift instructions in the instruction set, some of the instructions described earlier in this chapter are used for shifting. The ADD A instruction will shift the accumulator left one bit position, and the DAD H instruction will shift the HL register pair left one bit position.

The shift-right operation must be synthesized from the rotate instructions. Two right shifts are normally used in practice: logic and arithmetic. The logical shift right requires that a zero be placed in the leftmost bit position, and the arithmetic shift right requires that the sign bit be copied through the number. Figure 5–10 illustrates

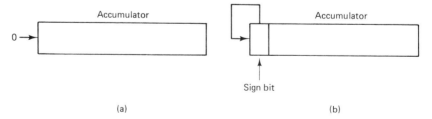

Figure 5-10   (a) The logical shift right. Notice a logic zero is shifted into the left end of the accumulator; (b) The arithmetic shift right. Notice that the sign bit, which does not change, is copied into the accumulator.

each type of shift-right operation graphically. These shifts are synthesized in Example 5–11 (logical shift right) and Example 5–12 (arithmetic shift right).

```
(EXAMPLE 5-11)

B7   ORA A   ;clear carry
1F   RAR     ;logical right shift


(EXAMPLE 5-12)

07   RLC     ;capture sign bit in carry
OF   RRC
1F   RAR     ;arithmetic right shift
```

5-6 SUMMARY

1. The arithmetic and logic instructions affect the flag bits, whereas the data transfer instructions of Chapter 4 did not affect the flags.

2. Most of the arithmetic and logic instructions gate the result into the accumulator.

3. Most arithmetic and logic instructions use register, immediate, and register indirect addressing.

4. Addition is available as add 1 to any register or register pair, 8- and 16-bit binary, 8-bit binary with carry, and binary-coded decimal (BCD).

5. Subtraction is available as subtract 1 from any register or register pair, 8-bit binary, 8-bit binary with borrow, and as a compare, which is a form of subtraction.

6. The logic operations are AND, OR, exclusive-OR, and invert.

7. The logic instructions are ideal for control because AND is used to clear bits, OR is used to set bits, and exclusive-OR is used to complement bits. This gives the programmer complete control over each bit of a number.

8. Programmed logic is used to replace discrete logic circuits at a tremendous cost advantage.

9. Some of the 8085A instructions have hidden functions: ADD A is used as a shift the accumulator left, DAD H is used as a shift HL left, ANA A and ORA A are used to test the accumulator, and SUB A and XRA A are used to clear the accumulator.

10. The rotate commands are used to create the shift-right functions: logical and arithmetic shift right.

5-7 GLOSSARY

Accumulator adjust   The act of correcting the result of a BCD addition. The result of each BCD digit is corrected by adding a 6 if a carry occurred or the result exceeded 9.

AND   The logical multiplication operation (AND) is: $0 \cdot 0 = 0$, $0 \cdot 1 = 0$, $1 \cdot 0 = 0$, and $1 \cdot 1 = 1$.

Arithmetic right shift   Whenever a number is shifted to the right, the sign bit is copied through the number for an arithmetic right shift.

Borrow   A borrow out of the most significant bit of the result after a subtraction is held in the carry flag. $CY = 1$ for a borrow and $CY = 0$ for no borrow.

Compare   A special form of subtraction where the value of the difference is lost but the flag bits reflect the difference.

Decrement   To decrement is to subtract 1 from a register, register pair, or memory location.

Don't cares   A don't care ($\times$) is a bit that contains either a 1 or a 0.

Exclusive-OR   The exclusive-OR operation is: $0 \oplus 0 = 0$, $0 \oplus 1 = 1$, $1 \oplus 0 = 1$, and $1 \oplus 1 = 0$.

Increment   To increment is to add 1 to a register, register pair, or memory location.

Inversion   Whenever a bit is inverted, it is changed from a 1 to a 0 or from a 0 to a 1.

Logical shift   When a number is shifted, a zero is moved into the left- or rightmost bit for a logical shift.

Mask   The act of removing part of a number, usually through the AND instruction. The portion that is removed becomes 0.

Multiple-byte number   A number that is more than one byte in width.

OR   The logical addition operation (OR) is: $0 + 0 = 0$, $0 + 1 = 1$, $1 + 0 = 1$, and $1 + 1 = 1$.

Programmed logic   Software that is used to replace the function of hardware circuitry.

Rotate   Whenever a number is shifted to the right or left, a bit drops off the end of a register. If this bit is recirculated through the register, the number is said to be rotated.

QUESTIONS AND PROBLEMS

5-1. What forms of addressing are used with most of the arithmetic and logic instructions?

5-2. List all the flag bits and indicate their contents after the following additions: 12H + 33H, F0H + 33H, 0FH + 40H, and 3FH + ABH.

5-3. Develop a sequence of instructions in both machine and assembly language that will add a 55H to the number in the B register.

5-4. Develop a sequence of instructions in both machine and assembly language that will add the number in the H register to the number in the L register.

5-5. Where would the add-with-carry instruction find most of its application?

5-6. Develop the sequence of instructions, in both machine and assembly language, that will add the number in the DE register pair to the number in the HL register pair. (You may not use DAD D.)

5-7. Explain what the DAD D instruction accomplishes.

5-8. The DAD instructions affect which flag bits?

5-9. The 8085A has a special command for BCD addition. Does this command precede or follow the BCD addition?

5-10. Develop a program in both machine and assembly language that will add the BCD number in the B register to the BCD number in the L register.

5-11. What instruction is used to add a 1 to the HL register pair? Which flag bits are affected by this instruction?

5-12. List all the flag bits and indicate their contents after the following subtractions: 12H − 33H, F0H − 33H, 0FH − 40H, and 3FH − ABH.

5-13. Where is the borrow found after a subtraction, and what does it indicate?

5-14. What instruction is used to subtract the contents of the memory location pointed to by the HL pair from the accumulator?

5-15. Develop a sequence of instructions, in both machine and assembly language, that will subtract the number in the D register from the number in the E register.

5-16. Develop a sequence of instructions, in both machine and assembly language, that will subtract the number in the DE register pair from the number in the HL register pair.

5-17. True or false: If the DCR B instruction is executed, all the flags will change.

5-18. What is the main difference between a compare and a subtract instruction?

5-19. Why is the compare instruction useful?

5-20. What 8085A instruction is used to invert the contents of the accumulator?

5-21. Write a sequence of instructions in both machine and assembly language that will one's-complement the contents of the DE register pair.

5-22. The AND operation is used to _____ bits in the accumulator.

5-23. The OR operation is used to_____ bits in the accumulator.

5-24. The exclusive-OR operation is used to _____ bits in the accumulator.

5-25. If NAND is NOT AND, is it possible to replace a NAND gate with programmed logic?

5-26. What special function is provided by the ANA A instruction?

5-27. Explain the difference between an RRC instruction and an RAR instruction.

5-28. Why can the RLC instruction be used in place of the RRC instruction of Example 5-10?

5-29. What is the difference between an arithmetic and a logic shift right?

5-30. Develop a sequence of instructions in both machine and assembly language that will shift the number in the BC register pair to the left one bit position.

_____ chapter six _____

PROGRAM CONTROL INSTRUCTIONS

The 8085A has a variety of program control instructions which allow the flow of a program to be altered. This ability is one of the main reasons that computer systems are so powerful. Program control instructions allow the computer to make decisions and modify the flow of the program in accordance with the outcome of the decision.

There are two basic forms of program control instructions available: jump and call. The jump instructions allow the program to jump to any location in the memory to continue a program. The call instructions allow a group of instructions (subroutine) to be reused by the program in many different places.

6-1 OBJECTIVES

Upon completion of this chapter, you will be able to:

1. Explain the operation of the unconditional and conditional jump instructions
2. Describe which flags are tested by each conditional jump instruction
3. Explain the operation of the unconditional and conditional call and return instructions
4. Indicate how the stack functions when used by the call and return instructions
5. Define the term *subroutine* and describe its importance in software development
6. Use most of the instructions in short programs
7. Describe the operation of such instructions as NOP, RST, STC, CMC, RIM, SIM, and HLT

6-2 UNCONDITIONAL JUMP INSTRUCTIONS

The unconditional jump instruction is a three-byte instruction that allows the programmer to jump over unused portions of the memory to any other memory location in the system. Before these instructions are used, some additional detail must be given to both the machine and assembly language versions of a program. Example 6-1 illustrates how the jump instruction is to be coded in the memory in both machine and assembly language forms. Notice that a new component, the address, exists for both versions. The address of the instruction appears at the left in machine language (1000 and 2000), and a label takes the place of the address in the assembly language (WILD and NEXT) form.

```
(EXAMPLE 6-1)

1000 C3-00-20   WILD: JMP NEXT ;go to location NEXT

    .   .   .   .    .   .

2000 C3-00-10   NEXT: JMP WILD ;go to location WILD
```

The first instruction jumps to memory location NEXT for the next instruction, and then the instruction at memory location NEXT jumps to location WILD. This sequence is repeated without interruption—an infinite loop. A label is used as a symbolic memory address and a hexadecimal number (memory location) is used as the actual memory address. The importance of the jump is that a task can be repeated over and over without reprogramming the computer.

Table 6-1 illustrates the two unconditional jump instructions available in the 8085A instruction set: JMP and PCHL.

TABLE 6-1 UNCONDITIONAL JUMP INSTRUCTIONS

Assembly	Machine	Comment
JMP a16	C3–ll–hh	Program continues at a16
PCHL	E9	Program continues at address HL

Notes: a16, 16-bit memory address; 11, low-order byte of the address; hh, high-order byte of the address.

The JMP instruction uses direct addressing, and the PCHL instruction uses register indirect addressing. JMP places the address, in bytes 2 and 3, into the program counter so that the next program instruction is located at the address stored with the JMP instruction. The PCHL instruction transfers the contents of the HL register pair into the program counter, causing the microprocessor to jump to the memory location addressed by the HL register pair. It could be stated that the PCHL instruction is a JMP M instruction.

Example 6-2 illustrates how the PCHL instruction is used in a program. Here the PCHL instruction causes the program execution to continue at memory location LOOP—an infinite loop.

```
(EXAMPLE 6-2)

1000 21-00-10  LOOP: LXI H,LOOP  ;load HL with LOOP
1003 E9              PCHL        ;jump to LOOP
```

6-3 CONDITIONAL JUMP INSTRUCTIONS

The conditional jump instructions are in many respects the same as unconditional jumps except that they allow the programmer to make a choice. A condition can be tested by the microprocessor to determine whether or not a jump occurs. The conditions that are tested by the conditional jumps are the same conditions held in the flag bits. Each flag bit, except for AC, has a pair of conditional jump instructions that are used to test the flag bit. The conditional jump instructions and the conditions tested by them are listed in Table 6-2.

TABLE 6-2 CONDITION JUMP INSTRUCTIONS

Assembly	Machine	Comment
JZ a16	CA–ll–hh	Jump if zero
JNZ a16	C2–ll–hh	Jump if not zero
JC a16	DA–ll–hh	Jump if carry set
JNC a16	D2–ll–hh	Jump if carry cleared
JM a16	FA–ll–hh	Jump if minus
JP a16	F2–ll–hh	Jump if positive
JPE a16	EA–ll–hh	Jump if parity even
JPO a16	E2–ll–hh	Jump if parity odd

Notes: a16, 16-bit memory address; ll, low-order byte of the address; hh, high-order byte of the address.

Testing the Zero Flag Bit

The zero flag bit is tested by the JNZ and JZ instructions. The JNZ instruction will jump to the address stored with the instruction if the zero flag indicates a nonzero result. The program continues with the next sequential instruction if the zero flag bit indicates a zero result. If the condition is true, a jump occurs, and if the condition is false, the next sequential instruction is executed. The JZ instruction jumps if zero and continues with the next sequential instruction if not zero.

Example 6-3 illustrates how the JNZ instruction can be used to repeat the shift-left instruction (DAD H) 10 times. Notice that the B register is used to hold a count of 10. This program continues to shift the HL register pair to the left until B be-

```
(EXAMPLE 6-3)

2000  06-0A      START:  MVI  B,10  ;load B with 10
2002  29         LOOP:   DAD  H     ;shift HL left 1 bit
2003  05                 DCR  B     ;decrement B
2004  C2-02-20           JNZ  LOOP  ;LOOP if B not 0
2007  C3-07-20   END:    JMP  END   ;infinite loop
```

comes a zero. As long as B is not a zero, the program continues to jump to memory location LOOP because the JNZ instruction checks the zero flag bit. The zero flag bit is set or cleared by the DCR B instruction, causing the JNZ instruction to jump to LOOP as long as B is not zero. In addition to illustrating the first program in this text, this sequence also serves to show a programmed loop and a wait loop. The wait loop uses the unconditional jump instruction so that the microprocessor stops executing new instructions at the end of the program.

Testing the Carry Flag Bit

The carry flag bit is tested by the JC and JNC instructions. JC jumps to the address stored with the instruction if the carry is set and JNC jumps if the carry is cleared. In both cases, if the condition being tested is false, no jump will occur.

The carry is most often tested after a comparison. If the magnitude of the accumulator is greater than or equal to the number being compared with it, no carry is generated. This conditional test is illustrated in programming Example 6-4. In this partial program the accumulator is tested to see if its contents are greater than or equal to 50H, and if the accumulator is greater than or equal to 50H, a jump to memory location 3000H occurs. Otherwise, the instruction stored at location 2005H is executed. The JC instruction is used to test if the accumulator is less than the number being compared with it.

```
(EXAMPLE 6-4)

2000  FE-50      CPI  50H    ;compare A with 50H
2002  D2-00-30   JNC  3000H  ;jump if A >= 50H
```

Testing the Sign Flag Bit

The sign flag bit is tested with the JM and JP instructions. JM is used to test a number for a minus condition and JP tests for a positive condition. Suppose that the number stored at memory location 0100H is to be tested for its arithmetic sign. Example 6-5 illustrates the sequence of instructions required to accomplish this test. Notice in this program that the number is moved into the accumulator and then tested. Merely moving a number into the accumulator does not change the flags; the flags change only for an arithmetic or logic instruction. Here the ORA A instruction, which does not change the contents of the accumulator, is used to modify the flags so that the number in the accumulator can be tested for a positive or a negative condition. If test is negative, the program continues with the next sequential instruction, and if positive, the program jumps to location 3000H for the next instruction.

```
(EXAMPLE 6-5)

2000 3A-00-01  LDA 100H  ;get data
2003 B7        ORA A     ;test A
2004 F2-00-30  JP  3000H ;jump if A +
```

Testing the Parity Flag Bit

The parity flag bit is tested by the JPO and JPE instructions. The parity flag bit
indicates how many 1's are contained in the accumulator expressed as even or odd.
For example, if the accumulator contains two 1's, parity is even. If the accumulator
contains no 1's, it is also considered to have even parity. Parity is most often used
in a data communications environment for testing the validity of received data. The
JPO or JPE instruction is used in this situation to test received data for the correct
parity.

Suppose that the data stored at memory location 0110H must be tested for even
parity. The program to do this looks similar to the program illustrated in Example
6-5 except that the jump instruction is different. (see Example 6-6). Here the number
is loaded into the accumulator and then tested by the ORA A instruction, just as
in Example 6-5. This time the test is followed by the JPO instruction. If the data
at 0110H have odd parity, a jump to an error-handling routine (ERROR—location
unknown) occurs, and if the parity is even, the program continues with the next sequential instruction.

```
(EXAMPLE 6-6)

2000 3A-10-01  LDA 110H  ;get data
2003 B7        ORA A     ;test data
2004 E2-XX-XX  JPO ERROR ;jump if parity odd
```

6-4 SUBROUTINES

One of the most important programming features of any microprocessor is the
subroutine. A subroutine is a short sequence of instructions that performs a single
task. Subroutines are special because they are used as many times as necessary without
being stored more than one time in a program. The advantages afforded by subroutines are a significant savings of memory space, and the task of writing a program
is simplified because subroutines are written once and used many times.

Linking to a Subroutine

A group of instructions are provided that allow the programmer to use a subroutine
from any point in a program. These instructions are named CALL instructions. Table
6-3 lists all the possible conditional and unconditional CALL instructions.

When the 8085A executes a CALL instruction, two things occur: (1) the contents of the program counter are pushed onto the stack, and (2) the program con-

tinues at the address stored with the CALL instruction. The CALL instruction is a combination of the PUSH and the JMP instructions.

TABLE 6-3 CALL INSTRUCTIONS

Assembly	Machine	Comment
CALL a16	CD–ll–hh	Calls the subroutine at a16
CC a16	DC–ll–hh	Calls the subroutine on a carry
CNC a16	D4–ll–hh	Calls the subroutine on no carry
CZ a16	CC–ll–hh	Calls the subroutine on zero
CNZ a16	C4–ll–hh	Calls the subroutine on not zero
CM a16	FC–ll–hh	Calls the subroutine on minus
CP a16	F4–ll–hh	Calls the subroutine on positive
CPE a16	EC–ll–hh	Calls the subroutine on even parity
COP a16	E4–ll–hh	Calls the subroutine on odd parity

Notes: a16, 16-bit memory address; ll, low-order byte of the memory address; hh, high-order byte of the memory address.

Why is the CALL instruction different from a JMP? The main difference is the PUSH that occurs before the jump. The PUSH stores the contents of the program counter on the stack. Because the program counter always contains the address of the next step in the program, the stack now contains what is often called the return address. The return address is used by the subroutine to return to the point of interruption in the main program. It is for this reason that subroutines must be called rather than jumped to in a program. A JMP to a subroutine would afford no method of returning to the main program at the proper point.

Notice that Table 6-3 contains both unconditional and conditional CALL instructions. The conditional CALL instructions test the flag bit indicated by the instruction, and if true, the call occurs; if not true, the next sequential instruction is executed. Suppose that the Z flag contains a 1. This indicates that the outcome of an arithmetic or logic operation was zero. If the CNZ command is executed, the program continues with the next instruction. If the CZ command is executed, the program continues at the subroutine addressed by the CZ instruction.

Returning from a Subroutine

As mentioned, the CALL instruction places a copy of the contents of the program counter on the stack (the return address). The RET (return) instruction is used to return to the main program at the instruction that follows the CALL. This can be accomplished because the address of this instruction is stored on the stack—the call placed it there. The return is affected by removing the return address from the stack and placing it back into the program counter. The RET command POPs a number from the stack and places it into the program counter. A list of the available return instruction is located in Table 6-4. As with the CALL instructions, there are both conditional and unconditional returns. If the condition is true, the conditional return instruction removes a number from the stack and places it into the program counter. If the condition is false, the return instruction has no effect and the program continues with the next sequential instruction.

TABLE 6-4 RETURN INSTRUCTIONS

Assembly	Machine	Comment
RET	C9	Return from subroutine
RC	D8	Return if carry set
RNC	D0	Return if carry cleared
RZ	C8	Return if zero
RNZ	C0	Return if not zero
RM	F8	Return if minus
RP	F0	Return if positive
RPE	E8	Return if parity even
RPO	E0	Return if parity odd

Using the Call and Return Instructions

To truly understand the operation of the CALL and return instructions, an example is required. Suppose that a subroutine is written that will two's-complement the accumulator. (Although this is a trivial task, it can be coded as a subroutine.) Example 6-7 illustrates this subroutine, which is stored at memory address 2040H. The one's complement is formed by inverting all the bits of the accumulator with the CMA instruction and then the result is incremented to obtain the two's complement. The RET instruction changes this task from a sequence of instructions, in a program, into a subroutine. Therefore, all subroutines must terminate execution with one of the return instructions.

```
(EXAMPLE 6-7)

2040 2F    COMP: CMA    ;ones complement accumulator
2041 3C          INR A  ;form the twos complement
2042 C9          RET    ;return from the subroutine
```

Example 6-8 shows how the subroutine of Example 6-7 is used in a program. Here the accumulator is loaded with a plus one followed by the CALL COMP instruction, which calls the subroutine and changes the sign of the accumulator. Although this program has no real application, it does illustrate how the CALL instruction is used to link to a subroutine. The first CALL COMP instruction places a 2005H on the stack. Remember that the CALL pushes the program counter on the stack and the program counter always points to the next instruction in the program. Next, the first CALL COMP jumps to memory location 2040H (COMP). The

8085A executes the CMA and INR A instructions, and when it executes RET, it removes the 2005H from the stack and places it into the program counter so that the next instruction executed is at 2005H. This is the second CALL COMP instruction.

```
(EXAMPLE 6-8)

2000 3E-01      START: MVI  A,1   ;load 1 into accumulator
2002 CD-40-20          CALL COMP  ;change sign
2005 CD-40-20          CALL COMP  ;change sign
2008 C3-08-20   END:   JMP  END   ;end program
```

When the second CALL COMP is executed, the program counter contains 2008H—the address of the instruction following the CALL. This becomes the address returned to after the subroutine is called the second time. Notice that the same group of instructions (subroutine) is used from two different locations in the program. Transfer to and from this subroutine is illustrated in Fig. 6-1.

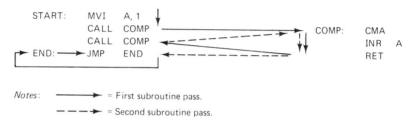

Notes: ———————▶ = First subroutine pass.

          — — — —▶ = Second subroutine pass.

Figure 6-1   Program flow diagram illustrating the path of this program as a subroutine is called twice by the main program.

Subroutines are critically important in developing software that is efficient and easy to write. Suppose that a sequence of instructions, 50 bytes long, is required to print data on a printer. A program must print data 15 times. If the program does not use a subroutine for printing, it takes 15 times 50 or 750 bytes of memory to print 15 times. If, on the other hand, a subroutine is used for printing, it takes 51 bytes of memory for the subroutine (RET must be added) and 45 bytes for the 15 CALL instructions, for a total of 96 bytes. Programs utilizing subroutines are considerably shorter and take much less time to code.

The Restart Instructions

The restart instructions, as listed in Table 6-5, are actually special unconditional CALL instructions. The reason is that they call a subroutine at a fixed location in the memory of the 8085A microprocessor instead of a variable location as addressed by the CALL instruction. For example (see Example 6-9), if the RST 2 instruction is executed, it calls the subroutine that begins at memory location 0010H. RST 2 is equivalent to a CALL 0010H instruction. The main difference is that the CALL 0010H instruction requires three bytes of memory for storage, whereas the RST 2 instruction requires only one byte.

TABLE 6-5 RESTART INSTRUCTIONS

Assembly	Machine	Comment
RST 0	C7	Calls the subroutine at 0000H
RST 1	CF	Calls the subroutine at 0008H
RST 2	D7	Calls the subroutine at 0010H
RST 3	DF	Calls the subroutine at 0018H
RST 4	E7	Calls the subroutine at 0020H
RST 5	EF	Calls the subroutine at 0028H
RST 6	F7	Calls the subroutine at 0030H
RST 7	FF	Calls the subroutine at 0038H

```
(EXAMPLE 6-9)

RST N = CALL  N x 8
RST 2 = CALL  2 x 8 or CALL 0010H
```

Notice that the restart address can be determined by multiplying 8 times the restart number. A RST 6 instruction calls the subroutine that begins at memory address 48_{10} or 30H.

RST instructions are used for system subroutines because of the reduced amount of memory required for their storage in a program. Remember that every time that a RST is used in place of a call, two bytes of memory are saved. It is also important to remember that since most system software is stored in ROM, these RST instructions are not always available to the user. This is true on many of the microprocessor trainers that are available.

One other important fact about the RST instructions is they are spaced eight bytes apart in the memory. This means that a RST subroutine must normally contain a JMP if the subroutine is more than eight bytes in length so that it can be continued elsewhere in the memory.

6-5 MISCELLANEOUS INSTRUCTIONS

The last types of instructions to be discussed control either the microprocessor directly or the hardware interrupt structure of the microprocessor. A list of these instructions and a brief comment about their functions are provided in Table 6-6.

Microprocessor Control Instructions

The first four instructions in Table 6-6 are used to control the microprocessor's operation or to modify the carry flag bit.

The NOP instruction. NOP is the symbolic op-code for no operation. What is a no operation instruction? This instruction is used to waste time (about 2 μs) in

TABLE 6-6 MISCELLANEOUS CONTROL INSTRUCTIONS

Assembly	Machine	Comment
NOP	00	Performs no operation
STC	37	Set carry flag
CMC	3F	Complement carry flag
HLT	76	Halt until reset or interrupt
EI	FB	Enable interrupts
DI	F3	Disable interrupts
RIM	20	Read interrupt mask
SIM	30	Set interrupt mask

programs that require time delays. (It takes this amount of time to execute a no operation.) NOPs are also used when writing machine language programs in order that room can be left within the program for future additions. Today the NOP is of little use because most software is written in assembly language.

The STC and CMC instructions.   STC and CMC are used to control the carry flag bit. STC sets carry and CMC complements carry. If the carry needs to be cleared, an STC followed by a CMC is used, or in most cases the ANA A or ORA A instruction is found. ANA A and ORA A both clear the carry flag. Why is it important to be able to modify the carry flag? Carry is used for multiple-byte addition and subtraction, which both require that it be cleared before these operations begin. In addition to multiple-byte arithmetic, the carry flag is sometimes used to indicate an error condition at a return from a subroutine.

The HLT instruction.   The HLT (halt) instruction is used to stop program execution. The only way that execution can continue after a HLT is to reset the microprocessor or have an interrupt occur. Both the reset and the interrupt must come from the external hardware. It is for this reason that the use of this command must be reserved for special purposes such as catastrophic system failure.

The Interrupt Control Instructions

The last four instructions in Table 6–6 are used to control the hardware interrupt structure of the 8085A microprocessor. An interrupt is a hardware-initiated subroutine call that interrupts the currently executing program. In other words, whenever the hardware interrupts the microprocessor, a subroutine is called which services the interrupt. This special subroutine is called an interrupt service subroutine.

Figure 6–2 illustrates the input pins to the 8085A microprocessor and two special serial data pins (SID and SOD) that are controlled or read by the interrupt control instructions RIM and SIM. The TRAP input is a maskable input that cannot be affected by the interrupt control instructions, while the remaining four inputs (RST 7.5, RST 6.5, RST 5.5, and INTR) are affected by the interrupt control instructions.

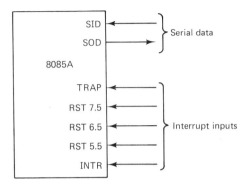

Figure 6-2 The serial data (SID and SOD) and interrupt request (TRAP, RST 7.5, RST 6.5, RST 5.5 and INTR) connections of the Intel 8085A microprocessor.

Table 6-7 illustrates these interrupt inputs, their subroutine locations, and the logic level required to trigger them. Notice that the TRAP input is both level and edge sensitive. This means that a positive edge must occur followed by a steady logic 1 level in order for the subroutine, which begins at location 0024H, to be called.

TABLE 6-7 8085A INTERRUPT INPUTS

Input pin	Subroutine location	Sensitivity
TRAP	0024H	Positive edge and level
RST 7.5	003CH	Positive edge
RST 6.5	0034H	Positive level
RST 5.5	002CH	Positive level
INTR	Provided by user	Positive level

Whenever an interrupt service subroutine takes effect, all future interrupts are disabled (except for TRAP). This is why a special instruction (EI) is needed to reenable the interrupt inputs. EI enables INTR and all the interrupt inputs that are unmasked, and DI disables all the interrupt inputs except the TRAP. (Note: TRAP will disable other interrupts when it is accepted.)

The SIM Instruction

The SIM instruction (set interrupt masks) is used to enable or disable the RST 7.5, RST 6.5, and RST 5.5 pins. This instruction is also used to control the SOD (serial output data) pin on the 8085A and to reset the edge-triggered RST 7.5 input. Table 6-8 lists the bits of the accumulator before a SIM and their effect on the operation of the machine. To change the SOD pin on the 8085A, a 1 is placed in SOE and the data for the SOD pin are placed in the SOD bit. This is followed by the execution of the SIM instruction. To mask the RST pins of the 8085A, a 1 is placed in the MSE bit and then 0 or 1 in each of the mask bits M. A mask of 1 turns the corresponding interrupt input off and a mask of 0 turns it on. The two instructions in

TABLE 6-8 ACCUMULATOR CONTROL BIT PATTERN BEFORE A SIM INSTRUCTION IS EXECUTED

			Accumulator before a SIM				
7	6	5	4	3	2	1	0
SOD	SOE	X	R7.5	MSE	M7.5	M6.5	M5.5

Notes: SOD, serial output data; SOE, when active, data are transferred from the SOD bit to the SOD pin; R7.5, resets the RST 7.5 input; MSE, must be active for mask bits M7.7, M6.5, and M5.5 to take effect; M7.5, masks RST 7.5 off when 1; M6.5, masks RST 6.5 off when 1; M5.5, masks RST 5.5 off when 1.

Example 6–10 illustrate how SOD is set: RST 6.5 is enabled and pins RST 7.5 and RST 5.5 are disabled.

```
(EXAMPLE 6-10)

3E-CD    MVI A,OCDH    ;set up bit pattern
30       SIM           ;change masks and SOD
```

The RIM Instruction

The RIM instruction (read interrupt mask) is used to read the SID pin (serial input data), the masks, interrupt pins, and the interrupt enable status. The RIM instructions will read the information listed in Table 6–9 into the accumulator after the RIM is executed. The SID bit position of the accumulator indicates the logic level of the SID pin at the time of the RIM. The 17.5, 16.5, and 15.5 bits indicate the logic level present on the RST pins at the time of the RIM instruction. The IE bit of the accumulator indicates whether EI or DI has been executed most recently. This bit is also affected whenever an interrupt takes effect because interrupts always clear IE disabling future interrupts. The M7.5, M6.5, and M5.5 bits indicate the current condition of the interrupt masks.

TABLE 6-9 CONTENTS OF THE ACCUMULATOR AFTER EXECUTION OF THE RIM INSTRUCTION

			Accumulator after a RIM				
7	6	5	4	3	2	1	0
SID	17.5	16.5	17.5	IE	M7.5	M6.5	M5.5

Notes: SID, data from the SID pin; 17.5, logic level at the RST 7.5 pin; 16.5, logic level at the RST 6.5 pin; 15.5, logic level at the RST 5.5 pin; IE, indicates that interrupts are enabled; M7.5, logic level of the M7.5 mask bit; M6.5, logic level of the M6.5 mask bit; M5.5, logic level of the M5.5 mask bit.

6-6 SUMMARY

1. Program control instructions allow a program to jump around unused sections of the memory and also allow the program to test the flag bits in order to make decisions.

2. The unconditional jump (JMP) is a three-byte instruction that causes program execution to continue at the memory address stored with the instruction.

3. The conditional jump instructions allow the flags (Z, CY, S, and P) to be tested. If the outcome of the test is true, a jump occurs, and if the outcome is false, the next sequential instruction in the program is executed.

4. Subroutines are short programs that perform one task, are ended with a return instruction, and can be used many times from another program.

5. The CALL instruction is used to link to a subroutine. It does this by pushing the contents of the program counter onto the stack and jumping to the memory location stored in bytes 2 and 3 of the instruction.

6. The return address is the contents of the program counter that are placed on the stack by a CALL instruction. The return address is removed from the stack by the return (RET) instruction, which places it back into the program counter from the stack.

7. Conditional call and return instructions work like the conditional jump instruction. If the condition being tested is true, the call or return occurs, and if false, the next sequential instruction is executed.

8. Restarts (RST) are special one-byte call instructions. The location called by a RST can be determined by multiplying the restart number times 8. For example, RST 5 is equivalent to a CALL 0028H, which is 8 times 5.

9. The NOP instruction performs no operation and is sometimes used in time-delay software because it takes about 2 μs to do nothing.

10. STC and CMC are used to set carry and complement carry, respectively.

11. The HLT (halt) instruction is used to halt execution until either a system reset or an interrupt.

12. The 8085A contains five interrupt inputs (TRAP, RST 7.5, RST 6.5, RST 5.5, and INTR) and two serial data pins (SID and SOD).

13. The RIM (read interrupt masks) and SIM (set interrupt masks) instructions are used to control the interrupt structure of the 8085A and also the serial data pins.

14. EI (enable interrupts) and DI (disable interrupts) are used to turn all the interrupts on and off except for TRAP, which can never be disabled.

6-7 GLOSSARY

CALL instructions CALL instructions are special instructions that perform two tasks: (1) the contents of the program counter are pushed onto the stack, and (2) a jump to the subroutine occurs.

Conditional jump   An instruction that tests a flag bit to determine whether or not to jump to another part of a program. If the condition under test is true, the jump occurs, and if not true, the next sequential step in the program is executed.

Halt   A condition arising from the execution of the HLT instruction. The only way to exit a halt condition is via an interrupt or a reset.

Infinite loop   A programmed loop that has no ending which is often used to terminate the execution of a program in microprocessor trainers.

Interrupt   A hardware-initiated subroutine call that interrupts the currently executing program.

Interrupt masks   Bits in a special interrupt register that allow the programmer to individually enable or disable the RST 7.5, RST 6.5, and RST 5.5 pins.

Interrupt service subroutine   A subroutine that is called by a hardware interrupt. The subroutine services the interrupt.

Restart instruction   A restart instruction is a one-byte CALL instruction.

Return address   The return address is the contents of the program counter which is saved on the stack by a call and removed from the stack by a return.

Return instructions   A special instruction that is used to terminate a subroutine. The return instruction removes a number from the stack and places it into the program counter.

Subroutine   A group of instructions that perform a single task which can be called from any location in a program. Subroutines are always terminated by the return instruction.

Unconditional jump   An unconditional jump is an instruction that will always jump to the memory location stored in bytes 2 and 3 for continuation of the program.

QUESTIONS AND PROBLEMS ▬▬▬▬▬▬▬▬▬▬

6-1. Explain what an unconditional jump instruction accomplishes.

6-2. What is the difference between the JMP instruction and the PCHL instruction?

6-3. Why is the short program illustrated in Example 6-2 called an infinite loop?

6-4. The conditional jump instructions are used to test which four flag bits?

6-5. If two numbers are compared and it is desired to determine whether they are equal, which conditional jump is used, and why?

6-6. Why is the carry flag tested with conditional jump instructions?

6-7. Why is the ORA A instruction called a test accumulator instruction in Example 6-5?

6-8. When is it normal to test the parity flag?

6-9. What is a subroutine?

6-10. Which instruction is used to link to a subroutine?

6-11. Explain what two operations are performed by the CALL instruction.

6-12. What is a return address?

6-13. The CZ instruction will call a subroutine if the outcome of an arithmetic and logic operation is _____ .

6-14. The return instruction removes data from the stack and places them into which register?

6-15. Write a short subroutine that will triple the contents of the accumulator.

6-16. Use the subroutine that was written in Question 6-15 to multiply the accumulator by 9.

6-17. If the 8085A had an RST 9 instruction, what hexadecimal memory address would be called by this instruction?

6-18. Just exactly what does the NOP instruction accomplish?

6-19. Show how the carry flag is cleared using two different techniques.

6-20. What two ways are used to exit a halt condition?

6-21. What is an interrupt?

6-22. What is an interrupt service subroutine?

6-23. How are the SID and SOD pins controlled on the 8085A microprocessor?

6-24. A logic 1 in a mask bit after the SIM instruction will turn the corresponding interrupt pin _____ .

6-25. What is the MSE bit position of the accumulator used for before a SIM instruction?

6-26. Write a subroutine to place a logic 1 on the SOD pin followed by a logic 0. (This subroutine may not affect the interrupt masks.)

6-27. Write a subroutine that will not return until the SID pin contains a logic 0. If it contains a logic 1, your subroutine must loop.

chapter seven

ASSEMBLY LANGUAGE

Assembly language is used for most programming today because it is extremely difficult to program a microprocessor in its native hexadecimal machine language. The assembly language program or assembler is a program that takes the input (the source program) coded in mnemonic or symbolic machine language and converts it into a hexadecimal machine language program (object program).

The main reason that software is not written in hexadecimal machine language directly is that whenever a program is modified in machine language, the addresses must be relocated. For example, if a JMP 1000H appears in the program and a two-byte instruction is added prior to the JMP 1000H, address 1000H must probably be incremented by 2. Imagine a program that contains 10 or 15 JMP instructions and the amount of work required to relocate them. The assembler does this work automatically for the user.

7-1 OBJECTIVES

Upon completion of this chapter, you will be able to:

1. Define the terms *assembler, assembly language, source program, object program*
2. Briefly describe the operation of a two-pass assembler
3. Define the purpose of each field in an assembly language statement and indicate the type of information typically found in each field
4. Explain the purpose of the following assembly language pseudo operations: DB, DW, DS, ORG, and EQU

5. Identify common assembly language errors so that you do not make them

6. Describe the purpose of a macro assembler and explain the directives common-ly found with an 8085A macro assembler

7-2 THE ASSEMBLER

As mentioned in the introduction to this chapter, an assembler is a program that converts software written in symbolic machine language into hexadecimal machine language. The symbolic version of the software is called a source program because it is the source of the information provided to the assembler program. The output from the assembler program is called the object program because it is the object of the assembler process (see Fig. 7-1).

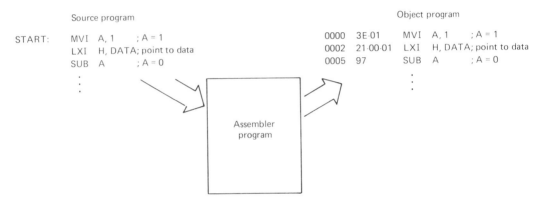

Source program				Object program			
START:	MVI	A, 1	; A = 1	0000	3E-01	MVI	A, 1 ; A = 1
	LXI	H, DATA; point to data		0002	21-00-01	LXI	H, DATA; point to data
	SUB	A	; A = 0	0005	97	SUB	A ; A = 0

Assembler
program

Figure 7-1   The assembler program shown converting a source program into an object program.

The Two-Pass Assembler

Most assemblers convert the source code into object code by passing or scanning the source code twice. This type of assembler is called a two-pass assembler. Early in the development of the assembler program, some computer systems were supplied with a one-pass assembler, but its use had many limitations. The most notable limita-tion of the one-pass assembler is that it does not allow forward addressing. This means that the software cannot jump ahead to an instruction in a program, which makes programming difficult at times and sometimes virtually impossible. The reason a for-ward reference is difficult with the one-pass assembler is that the assembler does not know where the memory location for the forward reference is located. The two-pass assembler corrects this problem by adding an extra pass to the process to correct the problem of forward addressing.

Pass one.   During the first pass of the assembly process, the source program is scanned, and a table of labels used within the program is constructed by the assembler. Figure 7–2 illustrates a short source program and the label table generated by the assembler for the program. Each entry in the table contains the label and the address at which the label appears in the program. The assembler always assumes that the first instruction of the program is stored at memory address 0000H unless it is otherwise directed with the ORG command. (ORG is discussed in Section 7–4.)

	Source program	
START:	LXI	H, DATA; point to data
	XRA	A ; clear A
	MVI	B, 5 ; load counter
LOOP:	ADD	M ; add data
	INX	H ; point to next datum
	DCR	B ; decrement count
	JNZ	LOOP ; if count not zero
ENDP:	JMP	ENDP ; end program
DATA:	DB	1, 2, 3 ; define data
	DB	4, 5

Label table

Label	Address
START	0000
LOOP	0006
ENDP	000C
DATA	000F

Figure 7-2   The source program and the Label Table that is generated by the assembler.

During the first pass the assembler determines the length of each instruction by updating an internal program counter. This internal program counter allows the assembler to complete the label table by equating each label with the counter. Once the label table is complete, the second pass begins.

Pass two.   During the second pass of the source program by the assembler, an object program is formed by referring to the label table for any labels that appear in the program and also to an instruction table. The instruction table contains all the valid op-codes allowed by the assembler in both symbolic and machine language forms. These tables are used to convert the source program into the object program. Example 7–1 illustrates the final version of the object program that is presented in Fig. 7–2.

```
(EXAMPLE 7-1)

   (OBJECT)                      (SOURCE)
ADDR B1 B2 B3

0000 21-0F-00    START: LXI H,DATA  ;point to data
0003 AF                 XRA A       ;clear A
0004 06-05              MVI B,5      ;load counter
0006 86          LOOP:  ADD M        ;add data
0007 23                 INX H        ;point to next datum
0008 05                 DCR B        ;decrement count
0009 C2-06-00           JNZ LOOP     ;if count not zero
000C C3-0C-00    ENDP:  JMP ENDP     ;end program
000F 01-02-03    DATA:  DB  1,2,3    ;define data
0012 04-05              DB  4,5
```

In addition to building the object program, the second pass also lists the program in both source and object forms on the printer or CRT terminal. If any errors are detected—such as invalid op-codes—the asembler also lists them so that they can be corrected by the programmer. A list of the error codes and a discussion of each type appears in Section 7–5. The assembler does not write the program for you, but it does make it a lot easier to write and debug a program.

7-3 THE ASSEMBLY LANGUAGE STATEMENT

Before it is possible to write assembly language source programs, the basic assembly language statement must be thoroughly understood. This statement contains four distinct fields or portions—label, op-code, operand, and comment—that are meant to contain certain types of information (see Example 7–2). Each of these fields must contain either a space or some alphanumeric characters, and each field must be separated by at least one space.

```
(EXAMPLE 7-2)

LABEL     OP-CODE    OPERAND    COMMENT

START:    CALL       SUBR       ;call subroutine
```

The Label Field

The label field contains a symbolic memory address that is used to refer to the statement in a program. Labels are optional and must end with a colon in some Intel 8085A assemblers. Labels are constructed from alphanumeric characters and must begin with the letter of the alphabet. The remaining digits can be numbers or letters, and in some systems a limited number of special characters may also be used. Table 7–1 illustrates a number of valid and invalid labels. A comment can also be specified with the label field in many 8085A assemblers. If the first character of the label is

TABLE 7-1   VALID AND INVALID LABELS

Label	Valid/invalid	Comment
DOGGY:	Valid	All alphabetic characters
DOG12:	Valid	All alphanumeric characters
SUB:	Invalid	An op-code
D:	Invalid	A register
DOG6.5:	Invalid	A special character (.)
4DOG:	Invalid	Begins with a number
DOG_HOUSE:	Valid	The underscore is often valid
*WATER:	Valid	This is a valid comment
;WELL	Valid	This is a valid comment

an asterisk (*) or a semicolon (;), the entire statement is a comment. This is useful when documenting a program because the program can be broken into sections by using the asterisk character. Example 7-3 illustrates some comment lines that are used to identify a segment of a program.

```
(EXAMPLE 7-3)

****************************************************
******** The system software begins here **********
****************************************************
*
START: LXI  H,DATA
       JMP  START    ;loop to START
```

It is also important to remember that most assemblers do not allow the use of op-codes and registers as labels. For example, if an ADD is used as a label, most systems will indicate a label error. Similarly, if the letter A, B, or any other valid 8085A register is used as a label, an error will occur.

The Op-Code Field

This field must always contain a valid op-code. If it does not, the assembler will indicate an error. The op-codes for the 8085A have been covered in previous chapters and are listed in Appendix A. Any other entry in this field will result in an error.

The Operand Field

The operand field may contain register names, data, or labels. If more than one of these is present, they must be separated by a comma. Data must be encoded as decimal, binary, octal, hexidecimal, or ASCII. Table 7-2 illustrates the different forms of data allowed in the operand field. When using hexadecimal data it is important to include

TABLE 7-2   VALID FORMS OF OPERAND DATA

Operand	Type	Comment
100	Decimal	8- or 16-bit quantity
1000	Decimal	16-bit quantity
50D	Decimal	8- or 16-bit quantity
10H	Hexadecimal	8- or 16-bit quantity
23AFH	Hexadecimal	16-bit quantity
OFFH	Hexadecimal	8- or 16-bit quantity
120	Octal	8- or 16-bit quantity
11001111B	Binary	8- or 16-bit quantity
'A'	ASCII	8-bit quantity
'AB'	ASCII	16-bit quantity
'HELLO'	ASCII	Multiple-byte quantity

an extra zero in front of any hexadecimal numbers that begin with a letter. If you do not, the assembler will indicate an error in most cases. ASCII data may at times appear as one or more letters surrounded by apostrophies.

In addition to specifying the number system of the operand data, the assembler is also capable of performing some arithmetic on the operand data. Table 7–3 illustrates the types of arithmetic operations available and some examples.

TABLE 7–3. OPERAND ARITHMETIC OPERATIONS

Operation	Example	Comment
+	LABEL + 2	This points to address LABEL plus two bytes
–	LABEL – 1	This points to address LABEL minus one byte
*	DOG*3	This equates to the value of DOG times 3
/	SEVEN/2	This equates to the value of SEVEN divided by 2; if SEVEN equals 7, it equates to 3, the unrounded integer portion of the result
NOT	NOT TRUE	NOT generates the one's complement of TRUE
AND	DI AND FI	AND generates the logical product of DI and FI
OR	DD OR FF	OR generates the logical sum of DD and FF
XOR	TG XOR HU	XOR exclusive-ORs TG and HU together
MOD	COW MOD 8	Cow is divided by 8 and the remainder of the result is generated; for example, if COW equals 9, the result is 1

The Comment Field

The comment field must begin with the semicolon in most 8085A assemblers and may continue to the end of the line only. If it is to be continued into the next line, the line must begin with an asterisk or a semicolon. Example 7–4 illustrates some example comments.

```
(EXAMPLE 7-4)

;this is a comment
START: LXI D,DATA   ;comment
*this is a comment
;
;
;the above are comments except for START: ....
```

7-4 ASSEMBLER PSEUDO OPERATIONS

The assembler pseudo operations are directives to the assembler program that may or may not generate machine code. For example, the END pseudo operation indicates that the end of the program has been reached. Other pseudo operations include: DB, DW, DS, ORG, EQU, IF, ENDIF, SET, GLB, EXT, TITLE, and SPC. All pseudo operations are placed in the op-code field of a statement.

Define Byte (DB)

The DB (define byte) pseudo operation is used to define 8-bit memory data for a program. Example 7–5 illustrates many examples of the use of this statement.

```
(EXAMPLE 7-5)

DATA:    DB   1,2,3,4  ;define DATA as four bytes
DATA1:   DB   100      ;define DATA1 as 100 decimal
DATA2:   DB   0A0H     ;define DATA2 as A0 hexadecimal
DATA3:   DB   1111B    ;define DATA3 as 1111 binary
DATA4:   DB   'D'      ;define DATA4 as ASCII D
DATA5:   DB   'HELLO'  :define DATA5 as 10 ASCII bytes
         DB   'THERE'
DATA6:   DB   ''''     ;define DATA6 as an ASCII '
```

Define Word (DW)

The DW (define word) pseudo operation is used to store a 16-bit number in the memory for use by a program. Example 7–6 illustrates many examples of the usage of the DW directive.

```
(EXAMPLE 7-6)

DATA:    DW   1000H    ;define DATA as 1000H
DATA1:   DW   10H      ;define DATA1 as 0010H
DATA2:   DW   10101B   ;define DATA2 as 10101 binary
DATA3:   DW   'AB'     ;define DATA3 as ASCII BA
DATA4:   DW   START    ;define DATA4 as label start
```

Define Storage (DS)

The DS (define storage) directive is used to reserve space in a program for variable data. Some examples of this are listed in Example 7-7. This example shows how 10 bytes of memory can be reserved between DATA and DATA1.

```
(EXAMPLE 7-7)

DATA:    DB   10   ;define DATA as 10 decimal
         DS   10   ;reserve 10 bytes of memory
DATA1:   DB   0DH  ;define DATA1 as 13
```

Origin (ORG)

The ORG (origin) pseudo operation is used to change the starting location of the program to some other address besides 0000H. In fact, it can be used at any place in a program to change the location of the assembled machine language instructions. Some examples of the ORG directive and its application are listed in Example 7–8.

```
(EXAMPLE 7-8)

                         ORG   1000H      ;set origin to 1000H
1000 3E-01       START:  MVI   A,1        ;set A to 1
1002 C3-00-10            JMP   START      ;jump to START
;
;new origin
;
;
                         ORG   2000H      ;set origin to 2000H
2000 01-02-03    DATA:   DB    1,2,3      ;define DATA
2003 41-42-43    DATA1:  DB    'ABC'      ;define DATA1
```

Equate (EQU)

The EQU (equate) directive is used to equate a label to another label or value. This is used in a program to make the program more readable. An example of the equate directive is illustrated in Example 7–9.

```
(EXAMPLE 7-9)

                         ORG 100
0064 3E-01               MVI A,ONE   ;A = 1
0066 21-00-01            LXI H,DATA  ;point to DATA
0069 C3-64-00            JMP START
006C 01-00      ONE:     EQU 1
006C 00-01      DATA:    EQU 100H
006C 64-00      START:   EQU 100
```

IF and ENDIF

The IF and ENDIF directives allow the programmer to conditionally assemble portions of a program. The IF statement evaluates the argument included in the IF statement to determine if it is true or false. True and false conditions are determined by the value of the least-significant-bit position of the argument (true = 1 and false = 0). If the argument is true (LSB = 1), the assembler generates the object code for the statements between the IF and the ENDIF statements. If the argument is false (0), the assembler does not generate object code for the statements between the IF and ENDIF statements.

A useful application of these pseudo operations is in certain types of setup programs. For example, suppose that a computer system will output either 80 or 132 columns to a printer. The setup program allows the programmer to change the setup information by answering some simple true-and-false questions as the one listed in

```
(EXAMPLE 7-10)

***** Setup program *****
*****
FALSE:     EQU   0
TRUE:      EQU   1
*****
***** PRINTER PAGE WIDTH *****
***** C80 = TRUE for 80 columns C80 = FALSE for 132 columns
*****
C80:       EQU   TRUE
```

the source program of Example 7-10. Example 7-11 illustrates the portion of the
setup program that uses the IF and ENDIF statements to set the width of the printer
to either 80 or 132 columns. Notice how the IF C80 is used for true (1) and the IF
NOT C80 is used to cause the false condition. The information in PWIDE causes
the printer to print either 80 or 132 columns.

```
    (EXAMPLE 7-11)

              IF    C80        ;(true) for 80 columns
    PWIDE:    DB    1BH,11H    ;PWIDE = 1BH, 11H
              ENDIF
              IF    NOT C80    ;(false) for 132 columns
    PWIDE:    DB    1BH,21H    ;PWIDE = 1BH, 21H
              ENDIF
```

SET

The SET direct is used in the same manner as the EQU directive except that the SET
directive is temporary. A label may be equated to a value only once during assembly,
whereas the SET directive may be used to reset the same label to a different value
later in the assembly process. In most cases SET is used only for special cases in an
assembly language program.

Global (GLB) and External (EXT)

Global (GLB) and external (EXT) are used in a programming environment that contains a linker program to link software modules together. The linker is a program
that is used to connect (link) different assembly language program segments (modules)
together. One problem that arises when modules are linked together is that the variables in each module are defined only in the module. This prevents other modules
from using the same variables.

  The GLB statement is used to allow a software module to make local variables
available to other software modules. Example 7-12 shows how the variables DOG
and CAT and the subroutine name DOGCAT are made available to other software
modules.

  If module DOGCAT is used in another module, the EXT statement is used so
that the linker knows that DOGCAT is external to the module. This allows the linker

```
(EXAMPLE 7-12)

*
***** Define global labels *****
*
            GLB   DOGCAT ;make DOGCAT global
            GLB   DOG    ;make DOG global
            GLB   CAT    ;make CAT global
*
***** DOG times two plus CAT subroutine *****
*
DOGCAT:     LDA   DOG    ;Double DOG
            ADD   A
            MOV   B,A
            LDA   CAT
            ADD   B        ;double DOG plus CAT
            RET            ;end subroutine
DOG:        DB    0
CAT:        DB    0
```

to search other modules for labels that are defined as global. If a label is external, it must always be defined as a global label in another module. An example of a module that uses DOGCAT and its variables DOG and CAT, which are defined as global labels in Example 7-12, is listed in Example 7-13.

```
(EXAMPLE 7-13)

*
***** Make MODULE1 global *****
*
            GLB   MODULE1   ;make module1 global
*
***** Define DOGCAT, DOG and CAT as external *****
*
            EXT   DOGCAT   ;make DOGCAT external
            EXT   DOG      ;make DOG external
            EXT   CAT      ;make CAT external
*
***** Subroutine MODULE1 *****
*
MODULE1:    MVI   A,12H
            STA   DOG      ;set DOG = 12H
            MVI   A,2
            STA   CAT      ;set CAT = 2
            CALL  DOGCAT   ;do subroutine
            RET
```

TITLE and SPC

In addition to all the previous pseudo operations, some assemblers also contain the listing control directives TITLE and SPC.

The TITLE directive allows the programmer to (1) feed to the top of a new page, (2) place a title at the top of the new printed page, and (3) continue to print the title at the top of each subsequent page until another TITLE directive appears in the program.

The SPC directive allows the programmer to insert blank lines of paper between sections of a program. The number of blank lines is specified by the argument of the SPC directive. Example 7–14 illustrates the TITLE and SPC directives.

```
(EXAMPLE 7-14)

TITLE   'THIS IS THE TITLE'
SPC     7
```

7-5 ASSEMBLER ERROR DETECTION

Most 8085A assembler programs are capable of detecting errors in certain portions of the assembly language statement. Unfortunately, assemblers cannot detect errors in the order of the statements in a program. If this were possible, programmers would not be needed because the assembler could automatically correct any errors in the program.

Table 7–4 lists the error codes detected by the assembler and a brief description of each type of error. When an error is detected by the assembler, it is printed together with the source and object programs in the listing. Example 7–15 illustrates some statements that contain errors.

TABLE 7-4 ERROR CODES FOR THE 8085A ASSEMBLER

Code	Name	Comment
D	Duplicate label error	This label appears at some other point in the program in the label field
E	Expression error	The expression (argument) is too complex to compute
L	Label error	The label is incorrectly used or inconsistently used in a program
N	Not implemented	The expression applies to a different version of the assembler
O	Overflow error	The expression is too complicated
P	Phase error	The value of the label changes between passes 1 and 2 of the assembler
R	Register error	You specified a nonexistent register
S	Syntax error	This occurs most often for a typographical error in a program
U	Undefined label error	Occurs if a label is referenced but does not appear in the label field
V	Value error	Occurs when the operand is larger than 16 bits or 8 bits for 8-bit instructions

(EXAMPLE 7-15)

```
0000 00-00-00 U  START:   LXI  H,DATA
0003 00-00-00 0           MVO  A,B
0006 80                   ADD  B
0007 3E-00    V           MVI  A,1000
0009 00-00-00 E           ADD  A,B
000C C6-10    D  START:   ADI  10H
000E 00-00-00 N           IF   TRUE
0011 01          TRUE:    DB   1
```

7-6 MACRO ASSEMBLERS

A macro assembler is a special form of the standard assembler that allows the programmer to define new op-codes. For example, the 8085A cannot switch the contents of the HL register pair directly with the BC register pair. It may be common in a particular program to require this task. The task can be programmed as a subroutine or as a macro. With the subroutine (see Example 7-16) a CALL SWITCH instruction is inserted in the main program each time the HL and BC register pairs are switched. If the same task is developed as a macro, the program contains the op-code SWITCH for each time that switch is used by the program.

(EXAMPLE 7-16)

```
SWITCH:     PUSH H    ;stack HL
            PUSH B    ;stack BC
            POP  H    ;BC to HL
            POP  B    ;HL to BC
            RET
```

Macros

To convert the subroutine listed in Example 7-16 into a macro,* the macro is first defined and then all the steps of the subroutine except RET follow the macro definition statement (see Example 7-17). The MEND statement is used to end the macro. From this point forward the assembler automatically inserts the macro coding into the program each time that this new op-code SWITCH is found in a program. Example 7-18 illustrates the SWITCH macro used in a short assembled program. Notice from this example that the assembler inserts the steps between MACRO and MEND

(EXAMPLE 7-17)

```
SWITCH:     MACRO     ;define new op-code SWITCH
            PUSH H    ;stack HL
            PUSH B    ;stack BC
            POP  H    ;BC to HL
            POP  B    ;HL to BC
            MEND      ;end new op-code SWITCH
```

*The macros defined here are used in the Hewlett-Packard HP64000 logic development system. Other systems may use slightly different definitions.

of the original macro into the program. The assembler precedes each step of the macro with a plus sign (+) so that it can be identified in the listing.

```
(EXAMPLE 7-18)

;               (SOURCE PROGRAM)
;
START: LXI      B,1000H ;load BC
       LXI      H,2000H ;load HL
       SWITCH           ;envoke macro
       JMP      START   ;repeat
;
;
;               (ASSEMBLED VERSION)
;
0000 01-00-10   START: LXI      B,1000H ;load BC
0003 21-00-20          LXI      H,2000H ;load HL
0006                   SWITCH
0006 E5              +  PUSH     H          ;stack HL
0007 C5              +  PUSH     B          ;stack BC
0008 E1              +  POP      H          ;BC to HL
0009 C1              +  POP      B          ;HL to BC
000A C3-00-00          JMP      START
```

Macros with Parameters

One of the more useful features of the macro is its ability to pass parameters to the macro from a program. Suppose that a program is required to add two 16-bit numbers located in the memory and store the sum in the memory. A macro can be written that will allow these data to be added and defined in the macro calling sequence. Variable macro data must be defined in the operand field and each variable must be preceded by an ampersand (&). This macro is illustrated in Example 7–19.

```
(EXAMPLE 7-19)

DADD:    MACRO   &VAR1,&VAR2,&VAR3
         PUSH    PSW        ;save registers
         PUSH    H
         PUSH    D
         LHLD    &VAR1      ;get first variable
         XCHG
         LHLD    &VAR2      ;get second variable
         DAD     D          ;generate sum
         SHLD    &VAR3      ;save sum
         POP     D          ;restore registers
         POP     H
         POP     PSW
         MEND
```

In this example the new op-code (macro) is DADD for double addition. Associated with this op-code are three variables that are used within the macro to define the memory locations where the data are stored and where the sum is stored. The 16-bit number stored at memory location &VAR1 and &VAR2 are added and the result is stored at location &VAR3. Example 7–20 shows how this macro is used in a short program. As you can see from this example, the macro assembler can provide the programmer with a new set of options. It is even possible to write a simple high-level language using macro instructions.

```
(EXAMPLE 7-20)

;              (SOURCE PROGRAM)
;
START:     DADD    ONE,TWO,THREE
           JMP     START
ONE:       DW      9
TWO:       DW      4
THREE:     DW      0
;
;              (ASSEMBLED VERSION)
;
0000                 START:   DADD    ONE,TWO,THREE
0000 F5          +            PUSH    PSW       ;save registers
0001 E5          +            PUSH    H
0002 D5          +            PUSH    D
0003 2A-14-00    +            LHLD    ONE       ;get first variable
0006 EB          +            XCHG
0007 2A-16-00    +            LHLD    TWO       ;get second variable
000A 19          +            DAD     D         ;generate sum
000B 22-18-00    +            SHLD    THREE     ;save sum
000E D1          +            POP     D         ;restore registers
000F E1          +            POP     H
0010 F1          +            POP     PSW
0011 C3-00-00                 JMP     START
0014 09-00           ONE:     DW      9
0016 04-00           TWO:     DW      4
0018 00-00           THREE:   DW      0
```

7-7 SUMMARY

1. Assemblers are programs that convert symbolic machine language into hexadecimal machine language.

2. The source program, which is the input to the assembler, is a program written in symbolic machine language, and the object program, which is the output of the assembler, is in hexadecimal machine language.

3. Most assemblers are two-pass, which means that they look at the source program twice. The first time to generate a label table and the second time to develop the assembled hexadecimal version of the source program.

4. An assembly language statement is composed of four fields: label, op-code, operand, and comment. The label field is used to address a statement, the op-code field holds the symbolic op-code, the operand field holds the address or object of the op-code, and the comment field is for comments by the programmer.

5. Assembler labels must begin with an alphabetic character and may be followed by any combination of alphabetic or numeric characters. The last position of a label must be a colon in most 8085A-based assemblers.

6. The operand may contain labels or numbers. If numbers are contained in the label field, they may be decimal, binary, octal, hexadecimal, or ASCII.

7. The assembler has some additional directives called pseudo operations. The most common pseudo operations are: DB, DW, DS, ORG, EQU, IF, ENDIF, SET, GLB, EXT, TITLE, and SPC.

8. The assembler is capable of detecting errors in form. The most common errors include: duplicate labels, expression, label, overflow, register, syntax, and undefined label.

9. A macro assembler is a standard assembler that allows the user to specify new op-codes. This is done by defining the new op-code with the MACRO statement and ending the definition with the MEND statement.

10. Macros can be written to pass parameters through to the code contained between the MACRO and MEND statements. All the parameters must begin with the ampersand (&), which is used to distinguish a parameter from a label.

7-8 GLOSSARY

Assembler   A program that converts symbolic machine language (sometimes called assembly language) into hexadecimal machine language.

Comment   A portion of an assembler statement that starts with a semicolon (;) or an asterisk (*) that is used by the programmer to comment about a program.

Conditional assembly   A factor in the assembler that allows code to be generated if a particular condition is true.

Directive   *See* Pseudo operation.

External variable   In modular programming, labels that do not exist in the current module are considered external to the module.

Global variable   In modular programming, labels that exist in the current module that will be used in other modules are declared global.

Label   A symbolic address that is used in an assembly language program to address statements. If it appears in the label field, it is most often followed by a colon(:).

Label table   A table of labels that is generated during pass one in a two-pass assembler containing each label and its relative address in the program.

Linker   A program that takes assembly language or high-level-language modules and connects or links them together. The linker is an important tool in modular programming.

Macro assembler   A special form of the assembler that allows the user to define new op-codes.

MOD   Specifies the remainder after a division. MOD 10, for example, divides by 10 and yields the remainder after the division.

Object program   The output of the assembler which is listed and stored in the memory in hexadecimal machine language.

Operand   The data acted on by the op-code.

Origin   The starting point or address of a program that is defined to the assembler using the ORG directive.

Pseudo operation   A directive that commands the assembler to perform certain special functions. Pseudo operations may or may not generate machine code.

Source program   The input to the assembler written in symbolic machine language and often called the assembly language program.

Syntax error   An error in form, usually a typographical error.

Two-pass assembler   An assembler that looks at the program twice: the first time to generate a label table and the second time to generate the object program.

QUESTIONS AND PROBLEMS

7-1. Why is software written in assembly language instead of machine language?

7-2. A symbolic program is called a _____ program and the machine-coded version is called the _____ program.

7-3. What occurs during each pass of a two-pass assembler?

7-4. Why is it rare to find a two-pass assembler?

7-5. What are the four fields found in each assembly language statement?

7-6. From the following list of labels, determine which are valid and which are invalid. For all invalid labels, give the reason that it is invalid.
   (a) DOGGY.3:
   (b) COW33
   (c) 33WATER:
   (d) WINTER_SNOW:
   (e) MELLOW YELLOW:

7-7. If the first character of a label is an asterisk, the entire statement becomes a _____ .

7-8. Code a 12 as a decimal, octal, and hexadecimal operand.

7-9. Write your name as an ASCII operand.

7-10. Where is a semicolon found in a statement?

7-11. The operand 19 MOD 8 evaluates to _____ .

7-12. What pseudo operation is used to store an ASCII-coded name such as WATERLOO in memory using the assembler?

7-13. What does the DS directive accomplish?

7-14. Form an assembly language statement that will start to assemble a program at memory location 0800H.

7-15. Explain the difference between the EQU and SET statements.

7-16. True or false: The IF statement checks the variable in the operand field to determine if it is even or odd. If even, the statements between IF and ENDIF are assembled.

7-17. GLB and EXT are used in a moduler programming environment for what reason?

7-18. What is a linker?

7-19. Where are the error codes listed in the output of the assembler?

7-20. Given the following statements, determine which error code is listed if each statement is assembled by the assembler.

    (a) MVI A,666

    (b) POP X

    (c) MOV A.B

    (d) JMP START.5

7-21. What is the difference between a macro and a subroutine?

7-22. What is a macro assembler?

7-23. The _____ statement defines the macro and the _____ statement ends the definition.

7-24. What appears in the output listing of the assembler to distinguish macro instructions?

7-25. How can parameters be passed through to a macro?

_____ chapter eight _____

STRUCTURED ASSEMBLY LANGUAGE PROGRAMMING

What is structured assembly language programming? It is a programming methodology that aids in the development of complicated software with a minimum amount of effort. In this chapter we present the basic structures, programming techniques, and the basic approaches required to solve problems through software. We also develop an understanding of flowcharting, which aids in the development and documentation of complex programs.

8–1 OBJECTIVES

Upon completion of this chapter, you will be able to:

1. Describe the purpose of each common flowcharting symbol
2. List the basic structured programming constructs and briefly describe each construct
3. Explain how the programmed loop functions
4. Convert a word problem into a flowchart using the basic constructs of structured programming

8–2 FLOWCHARTING

Flowcharts are used to design the control flow of a software-based system and are always included in program documentation so that future software modifications can be made with minimal effort. Before flowcharting can be used to solve software control structures, the flowcharting symbols must be understood.

Flowcharting Symbols

Figure 8-1 depicts the most common flowcharting symbols that are used in flowcharts of assembly language programs: process, predefined process, input/output, decision, connector, and terminal. Although this is not a complete list of all the possible flowcharting symbols, it is generally understood to be the most pragmatic subset for structured assembly language programming.

Symbol	Name	Function
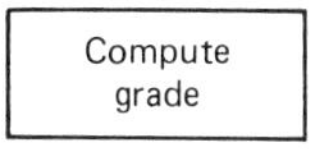 Compute grade	Process	Used to indicate any type of arithmetic or procedural operation
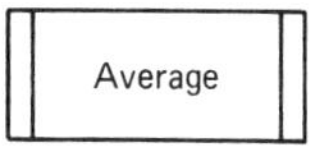 Average	Predefined process	Used to invoke a subroutine which is normally used as a predefined process in assembly language
 Read score	Input/output	Used for any input or output operation
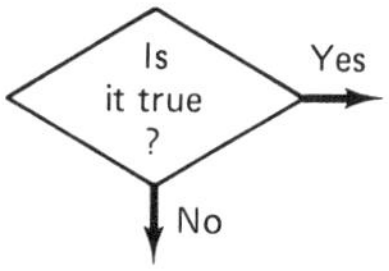 Is it true ? Yes / No	Decision	Used to ask a question in a program with either two or three outcomes
3	Connector	Allows the flowchart to be drawn without crisscrossed flow lines
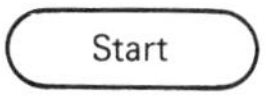 Start	Terminal	Indicates the starting or ending point of the program or predefined process

Figure 8-1 The commonly used flowcharting symbols.

The process symbol.   The process flowcharting symbol is used to indicate any type of process in a program. The process depicted by this symbol can be either arithmetic or procedural in nature and is always written inside the symbol as an equation or a simple phrase in English describing the process. Do not write assembly language coding in the process or any of the other flowcharting symbols. Each block in a flowchart should represent many assembly language instructions. If the flowchart is understandable by a nonprogrammer, it has all the requirements of being capable of documenting the program and making the flowchart easier to code into assembly language.

The predefined process.   This block is very important when writing software because it allows the programmer to indicate the need for subroutines in the completed program. The predefined process block usually contains the name of the subroutine. Remember that a subroutine is a grouping of instructions that is used many times in a program but stored only once in the memory. This reduces coding time and makes software maintenance much easier.

The input/output symbol.   Whenever data are input to the program or output from the program, the input/output symbol is used. This specially shaped symbol makes it easier to identify an input or output operation in the flowchart. Usually, the type of data and the direction of data flow is indicated within the symbol. Some examples include: input character, output character, output line, send data, and receive data.

The decision symbol.   Because a computer system's power comes from its ability to make decisions, the decision flowcharting symbol is indeed very important. In most cases this symbol is used to answer a question about the flow of a program. The question is written inside the decision symbol. The symbol itself has one input point and up to three output points. In most cases two outputs are used to answer yes–no, true–false, 1–0, and similar questions, and three outputs are used to answer questions, such as $+$, $-$, or 0.

The connector.   The connector symbol is used to eliminate crisscrossed connecting lines in a complicated flowchart. Its use is optional, but using it makes the flowchart more readable, which is very important. Connectors usually contain numbers or letters and come in pairs. One of the connectors in the pair has a flow arrow into it and the other has a flow arrow out of it.

The terminal symbol.   Programs all start somewhere and require a symbol to indicate where they start. The terminal symbol is used to indicate the start of a program and also the starting and ending points of a predefined process (subroutine) flowchart. This symbol usually contains the word START, END, RETURN, or the name of a subroutine.

An Example Flowchart

Figure 8–2 illustrates the flowchart that might be used to compute the class average grade on a test. Notice that this simple program contains every type of flowcharting symbol listed in Fig. 8–1.

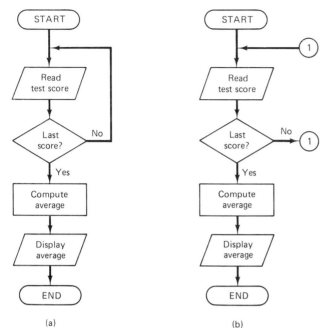

Figure 8-2   A sample flowchart of a program which illustrates how a test average is computed for a class group.

In addition, the operations performed by each symbol are written in clear and concise English so that anyone can understand the sequence of events in this flowchart. Notice that the flowchart flows from the top to the bottom, a technique that is often called top-down programming. Also notice that the flow of the program is illustrated with arrows that move from symbol to symbol. This allows the programmer to more easily construct the assembly language version of this program. How easy is it to find the beginning and ending point of this flowchart? Easy, because the terminal symbols clearly show the starting and ending points of this simple program's flowchart.

Figure 8-2 is provided so that the connector symbol can be illustrated. In this example it is probably better not to use the connector symbol because the flow lines do not cross. Again as mentioned previously, the connector is normally used only to prevent flow lines from crossing.

8-3 BASIC CONSTRUCTS

A construct is a sequence of steps that has one input or entrance point and one output or exit point. There is a group of basic constructs or structures that is used to solve virtually all programming problems. If these constructs are learned well, programming tends to become much easier—it is easier because of the handful of techniques (constructs) that allow a flowchart to be created with a great deal of efficiency. The constructs are all converted into assembly language in the same manner that makes coding a program into assembly language much easier. The basic constructs of structured programming include sequence, if-then, if-then-else, repeat-until, do-while, and programmed-loop (a special case of repeat-until).

The Sequence Construct

The sequence construct, illustrated in Fig. 8–3, is one of the most basic of all structures. With this structure, control is transferred to it, a process is performed, and control exits it.

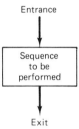

Figure 8–3 The flowchart sequence for the sequence construct.

A simple sequence structure that will compute the average and standard deviation of a test and print the results is illustrated in Fig. 8–4(a). Here four steps are required to solve for the average and standard deviation and print the results: two are predefined processes and two are output functions. Figure 8–4(b) illustrates the assembly language source equivalent of the flowcharted structured sequence of Fig. 8–4(a). In the assembly version of this program, subroutines are utilized because these basic operations are common and are probably used in other programs.

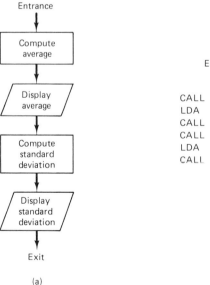

```
Entrance

CALL   AVERAGE
LDA    AVER
CALL   DISPLAY
CALL   STANDARD
LDA    STAND
CALL   DISPLAY

Exit

(b)
```

Figure 8–4 (a) The flowchart used to compute and print the average and standard deviation using the sequence construct; (b) the assembly language version of the sequence construct.

The If-Then Construct

The if-then construct is used to test a condition and then perform the sequence if the result of the test is true or false. The two basic forms of this construct are: if the condition is true, then perform a sequence, and if the condition is false, then perform a sequence. The if-true-then construct is illustrated in Fig. 8–5(a), and the if-false-then construct is illustrated in Fig. 8–5(b). Notice that both structures of the if-then construct have one entrance and one exit point, as do all constructs.

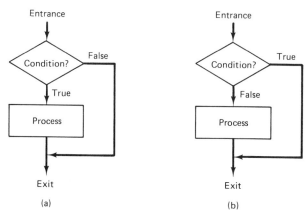

Figure 8–5   (a) The flowchart sequence for the if-true-then construct; (b) the flowchart sequence for the if-false-then construct.

Figure 8–6(a) shows how both constructs are used in an example flowchart for controlling a heating system, and Fig. 8–6(b) shows the listing of the assembly language source version of the program. Notice that the more complicated tasks are written as subroutines that are referenced by the assembly language source version of the program. Also notice that in the assembly language source version, the jump occurs if the condition is met, as when the temperature is tested and found that it is too cool to affect the heater. In many cases of the if-then construct, the compare instruction is used to test for a condition.

The If-Then-Else Construct

From the flowchart of Fig. 8–6 it is easy to see that a new construct can be created that handles the case where both true and false conditions cause a different event to occur. This new construct is the if-then-else construct, which takes the form of if-true do one sequence, else (false) do another sequence. The if-then-else construct is depicted in Fig. 8–7. As you can see, this structure allows both sequences to occur with only one test, which makes the flowchart and assembly language program easier to understand.

Suppose that the example in Fig. 8–6 is modified so that it uses the if-then-else construct. Notice from Fig. 8–8(a) that the length of the flowchart is shorter and easier to understand and the software of Fig. 8–8(b) is slightly shorter. The software is shorter because only one test is made instead of the two tests in Fig. 8–6.

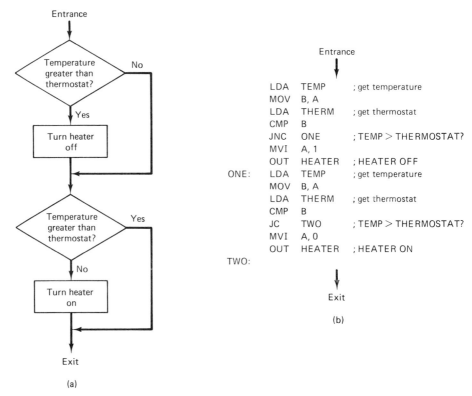

Figure 8-6 (a) The flowchart used to control a heater illustrating both the if-true-then and if-false-then constructs; (b) the assembly language version of the heater control sequence.

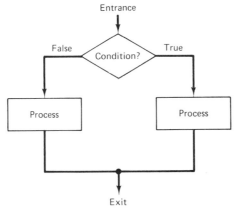

Figure 8-7 The flowchart sequence for the if-then-else construct.

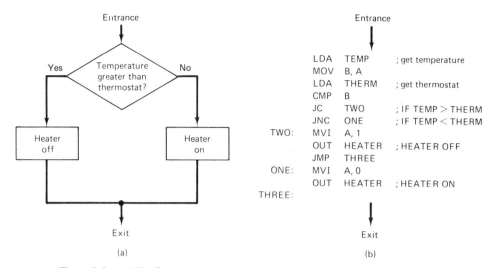

Figure 8-8 (a) The flowchart used to control a heater illustrating the if-then-else construct; (b) the assembly language version of the heater control sequence using the if-then-else construct.

The Repeat-Until Construct

The repeat-until construct allows a process to be executed or repeated until an event occurs. Whenever this construct is used, the process is first executed and then a condition is tested for a true or a false. It is important to remember that with this construct the process is executed even if the loop is not repeated. Figure 8-9(a) illustrates the repeat-until-true and Fig. 8-9(b) illustrates the repeat-until-false constructs.

An example of the repeat-until construct is depicted in the flowchart of Fig. 8-10(a) and the assembly language source listing of Fig. 8-10(b). Suppose that software is required to read a keyboard and store the keyboard data in a memory array until the CR (carriage return) character is detected by the program. Figure 8-10(a)

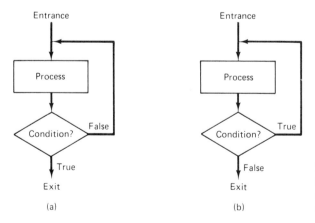

Figure 8-9 (a) The flowchart sequence for the repeat-until-true construct; (b) the flowchart sequence for the repeat-until-false construct.

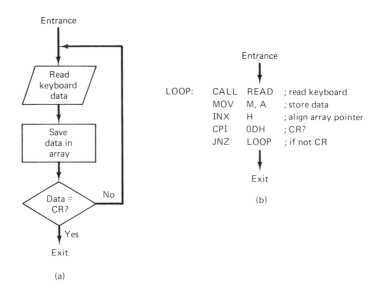

Figure 8-10   (a) The flowchart used to read a key from a keyboard, save the keycodes in a memory array and repeat-until a CR (carriage return) is detected; (b) the assembly language source version of the flowchart.

shows how the repeat—reading the keyboard until a CR is detected—flowchart is constructed. Notice that the software of Fig. 8–10(b) is as simple to develop as the flowchart.

The Do-While Construct

The do-while construct is comparable to the repeat-until construct except for one basic difference. The repeat-until construct performs the process before checking a condition, and the do-while construct checks the condition and then, if required, performs the process and repeats the check. There are two forms (see Fig. 8–11) of the do-while construct: (1) do-while-false and (2) do-while-true.

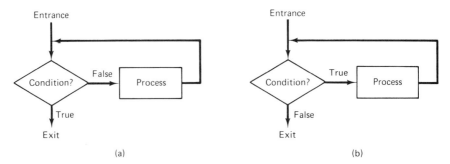

Figure 8-11   (a) The flowchart sequence of the do-while-false construct; (b) the flowchart sequence of the do-while-true construct.

Again let us use the keyboard as an example for this construct. Figure 8–12 illustrates both the flowchart and assembly language software for the keyboard. If Fig. 8–12 is compared with Fig. 8–10, the only difference is that in Fig. 8–10 the CR is stored in memory together with the other characters entered into the keyboard, and in Fig. 8–12 only the characters entered before the CR are stored in the memory. Notice that the read keyboard data process block seems to be misplaced in Fig. 8–12. It is not misplaced—it is really a part of the testing of the condition to determine if the keyboard data comprise a carriage return.

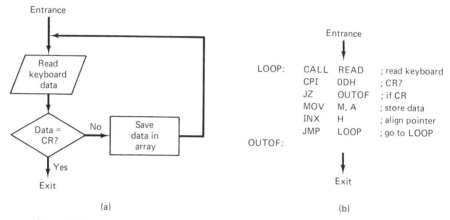

(a)   (b)

Figure 8–12   (a) The flowchart used to read a key from a keyboard, save the keycodes in a memory array using the do-while-false construct; (b) the assembly language source version of the flowchart.

The Programmed-Loop Construct (A Special Case of Repeat-Until)

Although this structure is not normally considered a structure, it is included here because of its common use in assembly language programming. Some textbooks call this a for-next construct, but the name does not really fit its function in assembly language programming. It may be argued that this construct is a form of the repeat-until construct, and it is, but again it is presented separately because of its common application.

Figure 8–13 shows how the flowchart of this construct appears. The first step loads a counter with the number of iterations required for the process block that follows. After the process is executed, the next flowchart block decrements the counter, and finally a test is made to determine if the counter has reached zero. If the counter has not reached zero the loop is repeated—repeat-until the counter equals zero. The significance of this construct is that a process is repeated the number of times originally loaded into the counter.

Suppose that exactly 12 characters are to be read from a keyboard and stored in a memory array. About the only way that this task can be easily accomplished is with the programmed-loop construct presented in Fig. 8–13. Here the counter is

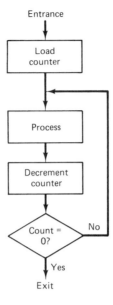

Figure 8-13 The flowchart sequence of the programmed-loop construct which loops through the process counter number of times.

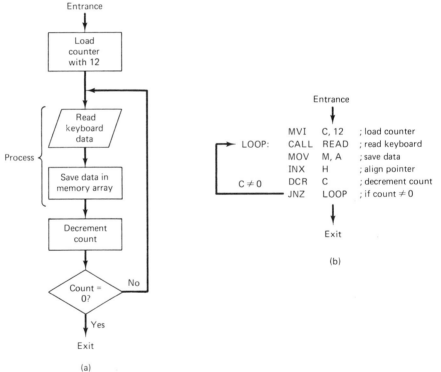

Figure 8-14 The flowchart used to read 12 keys from a keyboard and save the key-codes in a memory array; (b) the assembly language source version of the flowchart.

loaded with a 12 so that the process—read the keyboard and store the character read in a memory array—is repeated exactly 12 times. Figure 8–14 illustrates the flowchart and assembly language program for this programmed loop.

In the 8085A microprocessor, the value of the number loaded into the counter determines whether the counter is a single 8-bit register or a 16-bit register pair. The software used with the single register counter and the register pair counter differs somewhat, as illustrated in Fig. 8–15. In Fig. 8–15(a) a DCR instruction is used to decrement the count stored in a register, and in Fig. 8–15(b) the DCX is used to decrement the count stored in a register pair. Notice that a few instructions follow the DCX instruction. These are required because the 8085A does not change the flag bits for a DCX instruction. Remember that the flags are tested by the conditional jump instructions, so the software must modify the flags when the counter is decremented to determine if the counter has reached a value of zero. The MOV and ORA instructions that follow DCX allow the zero flag bit to reflect the condition of the BC register pair—the counter. The only time that the zero flag indicates a zero condition is when both B and C contain zeros. Remember that 0 OR 0 equals 0 and 1 OR anything equals 1.

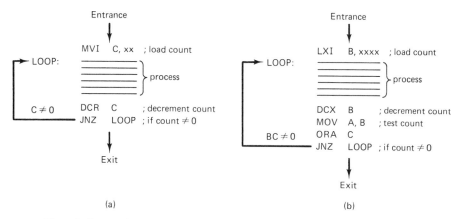

Figure 8-15   (a) The program used to go through a process up to 256 times (XX = 00) using a single register counter; (b) the program used to go through a process up to 65,536 times (XXXX = 0000) using a register pair counter.

8-4 EXAMPLE PROGRAM STRUCTURES

To become proficient with structured flowcharting using the constructs presented in Section 8-2, some example flowcharts are needed. In this section we present three structured flowcharting examples using the basic constructs.

Program Example 1

This example illustrates how a flowchart is developed for reading a series of grades from a keyboard, finding the average of the series of grades, and listing the average on a CRT screen. Before this flowchart can be developed, more detail is required. The number of grades to be entered is probably variable in size. It is therefore necessary that some code be entered following valid grades so that the program can count the number of grades entered into the program. For this example the number 101 (larger than 100 percent, or perfect) is typed to indicate that all grades are entered. This is enough detail to begin developing the flowchart.

Reading and counting the grades.   The first portion of the program must read grades until the 101 is encountered, count the number of grades entered, and store them in the memory for later use (see Fig. 8-16). The do-while construct or the repeat-until construct can be used to read and store the grades. Remember the example that stored the carriage return (repeat-until) and the other example (do-while) that didn't? In this program we do not need to store the 101, so the do-while construct is selected. The process for this first structure reads a grade or the number 101 and stores it in memory and also counts how many grades are entered.

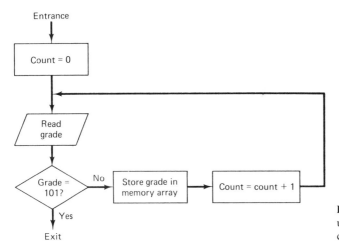

Figure 8-16 The flowchart sequence using the do-while structure to read and count grades for example one.

Computing and displaying the average.   The second part of this example, illustrated in Fig. 8-17, is required to find the average of the test grades and display that average. To generate the average, the grades are added together and then the sum is divided by the total number of grades. Because the grades are counted in the first part of this problem, it is easy to use the programmed-loop construct to add them all together. Once they are added to form the sum, the sequence construct is used to generate the average and display the result.

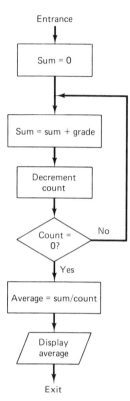

Figure 8-17 The flowchart used to determine and display the average for example one.

A simplified flowchart of example 1. If the prior flowcharts are examined closely, it will be seen that some of the functions can be combined to generate a new and much improved form. First, if the average is all that interests us, the grades do not need to be stored in the memory. If this is the case then only one loop is required to form the sum of all of the grades. Refer to Fig. 8-18 for a shortened version of the combination of Figs. 8-16 and 8-17.

Program Example 2

Suppose that software for a dollar-bill changer is required for your company's new bill changer and you are assigned the task of developing the software for the changer. The changer mechanism contains a sensor that detects paper in the bill slot, a motor to run the bill into and out of the changer, another sensor to detect a valid $1 bill, and a solenoid that returns a mechanically loaded dollar's worth of change to the customer. No provision other than an idiot light is provided to indicate that the machine is out of change. Customers lose their dollars if they do not see the out-of-change light. (Most changers seem to work this way.)

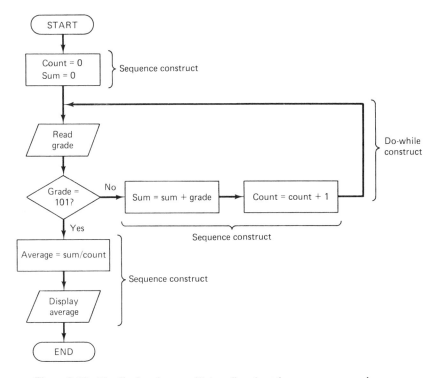

Figure 8-18   The final and most efficient flowchart for program example one.

The flowchart for this program is illustrated in Fig. 8-19. Notice that the repeat-until, if-then, and sequence constructs are used in this flowchart. Also notice that this program never ends. The first portion of this program uses the repeat-until structure to test the paper sensor—repeat-until a bill or other piece of paper is in the coin changer's slot. Once a bill is detected in the slot, the motor is run, pulling it into position to be tested for a valid $1 bill. Here the if-then structure is used to determine if the bill is a valid dollar. If it is not a valid bill, the piece of paper is run back out of the slot by the motor and the entire sequence is repeated. If it is a valid dollar, the bill is run into a collection bin within the machine and change is dispensed.

Program Example 3

Suppose that 100 student test scores are stored in a memory array and a program is needed to determine how many students received A, B, C, D, or F test scores. The first construct that comes to mind is the programmed-loop construct, which allows a number of processes to be executed a fixed number of times. In this case 100 test

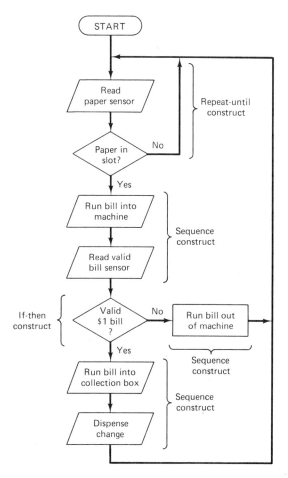

Figure 8-19   The flowchart of the program for a dollar bill changer.

scores must be examined to determine how many of them are various letter grades. To count each grade category, if-then constructs are used. This program example is illustrated in Fig. 8–20.

Here the programmed loop is extremely applicable because 100 test scores are to be checked for a particular range of values. The scores are tested by a series of if-then statements that are used to determine if the score lies within a grade range. If the score is within the range, the program increments a counter so that it can be counted. Then this process is repeated 100 times, so that each and every test score can be tested and counted.

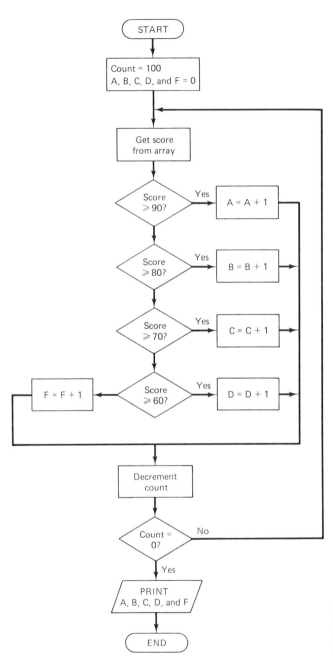

Figure 8-20 The flowchart of the program for determining how many students received A, B, C, D or F grades.

8-5 SUMMARY

1. Structured programming is a programming methodology that aids in the development of complex programs by using a series of standard constructs.

2. A flowchart is used to illustrate the flow of a program for the programmer and also for the lay person. The flowchart is an important portion of the program's documentation that allows later modifications to be made with ease.

3. Flowcharts are normally constructed with six standard flowcharting symbols: process, predefined process, input/output, decision, connector, and terminal.

4. The process flowcharting symbol is used to indicate a process, and the predefined process symbol is used to indicate a subroutine which is a predefined process.

5. The input/output flowcharting symbol is used to indicate any I/O operation, such as read keyboard, write printer, and so on.

6. The decision flowcharting symbol allows the program to ask a simple question, usually with two outcomes, such as true–false, yes–no, and positive–negative.

7. The connector flowcharting symbol indicates a break in the flow of the program that is continued at another connector. Connectors normally appear in pairs and contain either a number or a letter for identification.

8. The terminal flowcharting symbol is used to indicate the start or end of a program or predefined process.

9. Structured programming is accomplished via uniform flowcharting groupings called constructs. A construct is a sequence of steps that has one entrance and one exit point.

10. There are five constructs that are used to create a flowchart to solve any problem—sequence, if-then, if-then-else, repeat-until, and do-while. In addition to these five constructs, another, the programmed-loop construct, appears so often in programming that it is also included.

11. The sequence construct is the most basic of all constructs, usually containing a series of process, predefined process, and input/output flowchart symbols.

12. The if-then construct allows the programmer the ability to ask a question in a program. The if-true-then or if-false-then constructs are the two forms of this structure.

13. On occasion both true and false are possible process-oriented answers to a question. In this case the if-then-else construct applies.

14. The repeat-until construct allows a process to be repeated until a particular condition occurs. An example is starting your automobile. You repeat, keeping pressure applied to the turned ignition key until the roar of the engine is heard.

15. The do-while construct is very similar to the repeat-until construct. In fact, the only difference is that the repeat-until construct does the process before the test and the do-while construct executes the process only after the condition is tested.

16. The programmed-loop construct is a combination of the repeat-until and the if-then constructs. It allows a process to be executed *X* number of times.

8-6 GLOSSARY

Construct   A grouping of flowchart symbols that performs one of the following tasks: sequence, if-then, if-then-else, repeat-until, and do-while.

Flowchart   A grouping of symbols that are used to show the flow of a program. The flowchart is used to write a program and also to document it.

For-next   A statement found in the BASIC and Pascal languages which allows a process to be repeated a set number of times.

Process   A single or a group of steps in the flowchart of a program.

Programmed loop   A programmed loop is a construct that allows a process to be repeated a fixed number of times.

Structured programming.   A programming technique that uses a small set of constructs to form the flowchart for a program.

QUESTIONS AND PROBLEMS

8-1. What is a flowchart?

8-2. Draw and label the six flowcharting symbols most often used with assembly language programming.

8-3. What is normally found inside the process flowcharting symbol?

8-4. What predefined process symbol is used most often to envoke what type of predefined process?

8-5. What normally appears inside the input/output flowcharting symbol?

8-6. Is there any limit to the type of questions that may appear inside the decision flowcharting symbol?

8-7. What is a construct?

8-8. List the constructs that are used in structured assembly language programming.

8-9. Develop an example sequence construct that can be used to show someone how to open a door.

8-10. Using the if-then construct, develop a flowchart that can be used to show someone how to check to see if a door is locked and then lock it if it is not.

8-11. Repeat Question 8-10 using the opposite if-then construct (i.e., if you used the if-true-then construct, use the if-false-then construct).

8-12. Using the if-then-else construct, show how someone can decide whether to exit a bedroom through the door or through a window. (Assume that the house is on fire and the door is closed.)

8-13. Your house is being robbed and you tell your spouse (friend) to call the police. Develop a flowchart that shows how to do this using the repeat-until construct.

8-14. Is it possible to draw a flowchart for Question 8-13 using the do-while construct? (You are not allowed to precede the do-while construct with a sequence construct.)

8-15. What is the main difference between the repeat-until construct and the do-while construct?

8-16. Develop a flowchart that will search through 100 grades to determine if any of them are a zero. If there is a zero, indicate it by setting a flag (placing a logic 1 in the flag).

8-17. Why does the DCX instruction in a programmed loop need to be followed by a MOV and ORA?

8-18. Show another way to test a register pair for a zero condition after a DCX instruction.

_____ chapter nine _____

DATA MANIPULATION

As mentioned in earlier chapters, data manipulation is one of the more common tasks performed by the microprocessor in most microprocessor-based systems. In those early chapters, data were transferred a byte or word at a time. In this chapter we concentrate on block data transfers and exchanges which are used to transfer large groups of bytes or words. We also introduce character string transfers and exchanges, which are important software techniques that are used in larger microprocessor-based systems. A character string is a grouping of bytes that contains ASCII-coded characters which often form a name or other phrase in a computer system's memory.

9-1 OBJECTIVES

Upon completion of this chapter, you will be able to:

1. Develop software to transfer blocks of data (bytes or words) from one section of memory to another
2. Develop software that exchanges data (bytes or words) in one part of the memory with another
3. Represent any alphanumeric data in character string form
4. Develop software to transfer variable-length character strings from one section of the memory to another
5. Develop software to exchange character strings of different lengths

136

9-2 BLOCK DATA TRANSFERS

As stated in the introduction to this chapter, a block of data is a grouping of bytes or words of data in the microprocessor's memory. In many systems it is often required that blocks of information be transferred from one place to another in the microprocessor's memory.

Transferring Blocks of Bytes

Suppose that a block of 10 bytes of data, beginning at memory location 2080H, is to be transferred to a block of memory beginning at location 2090H. Many methods can be used to accomplish this transfer. One, the simplest, is to use the LDA and STA instruction to transfer each byte. The main problem with this technique is the length of the program. It takes 10 LDA and 10 STA instructions, each three bytes in length, to accomplish the transfer.

A more efficient way to transfer a block of data is to use the programmed-loop construct presented in Chapter 8. Remember that any time anything is to be accomplished a fixed number of times, it is important to use the programmed-loop construct for developing the program. Figure 9-1 illustrates the flowchart using this construct to transfer a block of 10 bytes of data from 2080H to 2090H.

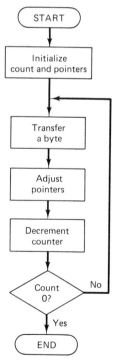

Figure 9-1 Flowchart required to transfer a block of bytes from one area of memory to another.

   A small-byte block transfer.   The program written from the flowchart, as
illustrated in Example 9-1, uses the HL register pair to indirectly address the source
block of data beginning at memory location 2090H and the DE register pair is used
to indirectly address the destination block beginning at memory location 2080H.
Transfers are made using a MOV, A,M instruction to load the accumulator from
the source block and the STAX D instruction to store the accumulator data from
the source block into the destination block. The B register is used as a counter in
this example.

(EXAMPLE 9-1)

```
                              ORG   2000H
                          ;
                          ;program to transfer COUNT number
                          ;of bytes from block SOUR to block
                          ;DEST
                          ;
                          ;COUNT <= 256
                          ;
2000 06-0A       START: MVI   B,COUNT ;load counter
2002 11-90-20           LXI   D,DEST  ;point to DEST
2005 21-80-20           LXI   H,SOUR  ;point to SOUR
2008 7E          LOOP:  MOV   A,M     ;transfer byte
2009 12                 STAX  D
200A 23                 INX   H       ;adjust pointers
200B 13                 INX   D
200C 05                 DCR   B       ;decrement counter
200D C2-08-20           JNZ   LOOP    ;if counter not zero
2010 C3-10-20    ENDP:  JMP   ENDP    ;end program
2013 0A-00       COUNT: EQU   10      ;define COUNT
2013 80-20       DEST:  EQU   2080H   ;define DEST
2013 90-20       SOUR:  EQU   2090H   ;define SOUR
2013                    END           ;end listing
```

   Earlier in the text it is stated that subroutines are very useful in the programming environment because they reduce the amount of time required to code a program. (Once a subroutine is written it never has to be rewritten if properly debugged.)
This program can be converted to a subroutine by replacing the JMP ENDP instruction with a RET instruction. Also notice that the only thing required to change the
length of the block and source and destination locations is changing the EQU statements that apply to each.

   A large-byte block transfer.   The flowchart presented in Fig. 9-1 is used to
transfer any size block of data. Suppose that a block of bytes beginning at location
0100H is transferred to a block of bytes beginning at location 2800H. The length
of this block is 300 (12CH) bytes. Because the number of bytes transferred is larger
than 256, this program requires that a register pair be used as the counter. Example
9-2 shows how the program of Example 9-1 is modified to effect this new transfer.
Notice that there is only a minor change in the program. The change is required because the DCX instruction does not affect the flag bits. To test for a count of zero,

(EXAMPLE 9-2)

```
                          ORG    2000H
                     ;
                     ;program to transfer COUNT number
                     ;of bytes from block SOUR to block
                     ;DEST
                     ;
                     ;COUNT <= 65,536
                     ;
2000 01-2C-01  START: LXI    B,COUNT ;load counter
2003 11-00-28         LXI    D,DEST  ;point to DEST
2006 21-00-01         LXI    H,SOUR  ;point to SOUR
2009 7E        LOOP:  MOV    A,M     ;transfer byte
200A 12               STAX   D
200B 23               INX    H       ;adjust pointers
200C 13               INX    D
200D 0B               DCX    B       ;decrement counter
200E 78               MOV    A,B     ;test counter
200F B1               ORA    C
2010 C2-09-20         JNZ    LOOP    ;if counter not zero
2013 C3-13-20  ENDP:  JMP    ENDP    ;end program
2016 2C-01     COUNT: EQU    300     ;define COUNT
2016 00-28     DEST:  EQU    2800H   ;define DEST
2016 00-01     SOUR:  EQU    0100H   ;define SOUR
2016                  END            ;end listing
```

the B register is ORed with the C register. If both registers contain zero, the outcome of the test is zero and the next sequential instruction (JNZ) does not jump to loop.

Transferring Blocks of Words

In certain applications, 16-bit words of data must be transferred. The only difference in the flowchart of Fig. 9–1 is a change in the block labeled "transfer a byte," which is changed to "transfer a word." Figure 9–2 shows the flowchart for the word block transfer as a subroutine move word (MWORD). To make this subroutine as flexible as possible, the task of loading the pointers and counter is left to the calling sequence. Example 9–3 shows a typical calling sequence for this subroutine, which

(EXAMPLE 9-3)

```
                          ORG    2000H    ;define start
                     ;
                     ;equates for calling sequence MWORD
                     ;
2000 00-28     DEST:  EQU    2800H    ;define DEST
2000 00-00     SOUR:  EQU    0000H    ;define SOUR
2000 00-02     COUNT: EQU    0200H    ;define COUNT
                     ;
                     ;calling sequence for subroutine MWORD
                     ;
2000 11-00-28         LXI    D,DEST   ;point to DEST
2003 21-00-00         LXI    H,SOUR   ;point to SOUR
2006 11-00-02         LXI    B,COUNT  ;load COUNT
2009 CD-50-20         CALL   MWORD    ;move words
```

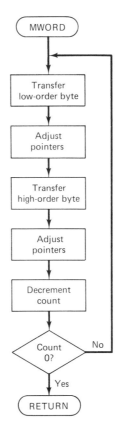

Figure 9-2 The flowchart of a subroutine that moves a block of words from one area of memory to another.

(EXAMPLE 9-4)

```
                    ORG 2050H    ;start at 2050H
              ;
              ;subroutine to transfer words from the
              ;memory location addressed by HL into
              ;the memory location addressed by DE.
              ;
              ;the number of bytes transferred is
              ;held in the BC pair.
              ;
2050 7E       MWORD: MOV  A,M     ;move low-order byte
2051 12              STAX D
2052 13              INX  D       ;adjust pointers
2053 23              INX  H
2054 7E              MOV  A,M     ;move high-order byte
2055 12              STAX D
2056 13              INX  D       ;adjust pointers
2057 23              INX  H
2058 0B              DCX  B       ;decrement counter
2059 78              MOV  A,B     ;test counter
205A B1              ORA  C
205B C2-50-20        JNZ  MWORD   ;if counter not zero
205E C9              RET          ;end subroutine
```

uses HL to address the source block, DE to address the destination block, and BC as a counter. Here, changing the EQU statements in the main program causes the location of both the source and destination block to change and also the count or number of words to be transferred.

The subroutine for transferring words is slightly different from the program that transferred bytes. Compare Examples 9–2 and 9–4 and notice the difference required for word transfers.

9–3 BLOCK EXCHANGES

Block exchanges are extremely similiar to block transfers except that the data are taken from one block of memory and exchanged with the data in a second block of memory. Although exchanges are not as common as transfers, they do have some application in microprocessor-based systems.

Byte Block Exchanges

Suppose that it is required to exchange the 80H bytes of a block of memory beginning at location 2800H with the 80H bytes of a block of memory beginning at location 2880H. Again the programmed-loop construct is very useful in writing this program and, in fact, the flowchart of Fig. 9–3 looks very similar to the flowchart

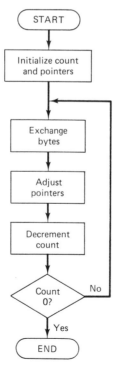

Figure 9-3 Flowchart required to exchange a block of bytes in one area of memory with another.

of Fig. 9–1. Please compare these two flowcharts and note their minor differences.

The program, which is written from the flowchart, appears in Example 9–5. Notice that to accomplish the exchange, data are held temporarily in the C register. This is required in order to exchange the data in these two blocks of memory. Also notice that this program uses the B register to hold the number of bytes to be exchanged, and the register pairs, HL and DE, are used to index the data.

(EXAMPLE 9–5)

```
                        ORG   2000H     ;originate program
                   ;
                   ;program to exchange byte data in block
                   ;SOUR with block DEST.  The count is
                   ;held in the B register.
                   ;
2000 06-80  START: MVI   B,COUNT   ;load counter
2002 11-80-28      LXI   D,DEST    ;point to DEST
2005 21-00-28      LXI   H,SOUR    ;point to SOUR
2008 4E     LOOP:  MOV   C,M       ;exchange bytes
2009 1A            LDAX  D
200A 77            MOV   M,A
200B 79            MOV   A,C
200C 12            STAX  D
200D 23            INX   H         ;adjust pointers
200E 13            INX   D
200F 05            DCR   B         ;decrement counter
2010 C2-08-20      JNZ   LOOP      ;if counter not zero
2013 C3-13-20 ENDP: JMP  ENDP      ;end program
2016 80-00  COUNT: EQU   80H       ;define COUNT
2016 80-28  DEST:  EQU   2880H     ;define DEST
2016 00-28  SOUR:  EQU   2800H     ;define SOUR
2016               END             ;end listing
```

Word Block Exchanges

Like word transfers, word exchanges are accomplished in a very similar manner. The only difference between their flowcharts is the exchange word instead of exchange byte. This example exchange word software is written as a subroutine and is listed in Example 9–7 with the calling sequence listed in Example 9–6.

(EXAMPLE 9–6)

```
                        ORG   2000H     ;define start
                   ;
                   ;equates for calling sequence EWORD
                   ;
2000 00-28  DEST:  EQU   2800H     ;define DEST
2000 00-00  SOUR:  EQU   0000H     ;define SOUR
2000 00-02  COUNT: EQU   0200H     ;define COUNT
                   ;
                   ;calling sequence for subroutine EWORD
                   ;
2000 11-00-28      LXI   D,DEST    ;point to DEST
2003 21-00-00      LXI   H,SOUR    ;point to SOUR
2006 11-00-02      LXI   B,COUNT   ;load COUNT
2009 CD-50-20      CALL  EWORD     ;move words
```

(EXAMPLE 9-7)

```
                      ORG 2050H  ;start at 2050H
             ;
             ;subroutine to exchange words from the
             ;memory location addressed by HL into
             ;the memory location addressed by DE.
             ;
             ;the number of words exchanged is
             ;held in the BC pair.
             ;
2050 C5      EWORD: PUSH B       ;save count
2051 4E             MOV  C,M     ;exchange low-order byte
2052 1A             LDAX D
2053 77             MOV  M,A
2054 79             MOV  A,C
2055 12             STAX D
2056 13             INX  D       ;adjust pointers
2057 23             INX  H
2058 4E             MOV  C,M     ;exchange high-order byte
2059 1A             LDAX D
205A 77             MOV  M,A
205B 79             MOV  A,C
205C 12             STAX D
205D 13             INX  D       ;adjust pointers
205E 23             INX  H
205F C1             POP  B       ;restore counter
2060 0B             DCX  B       ;decrement counter
2061 78             MOV  A,B     ;test counter
2062 B1             ORA  C
2063 C2-50-20       JNZ  EWORD   ;if counter not zero
2066 C9             RET          ;end subroutine
```

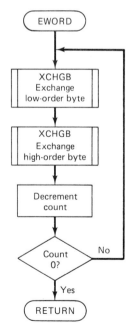

Figure 9-4 The flowchart of a subroutine that exchanges a block of words in one area of memory with another.

(EXAMPLE 9-8)

```
                    ORG  2050H   ;start at 2050H
                    ;
                    ;subroutine to exchange words
                    ;addressed by DE and HL.
                    ;
                    ;BC indicates the number of
                    ;words exchanged
                    ;
2050 CD-5D-20 EWORD: CALL XCHGB ;exchange low-order bytes
2053 CD-5D-20        CALL XCHGB ;exchange high-order bytes
2056 0B              DCX  B     ;decrement counter
2057 78              MOV  A,B   ;test counter
2058 B1              ORA  C
2059 C2-50-20        JNZ  EWORD ;if counter not zero
205C C9              RET        ;end subroutine
                    ;
                    ;subroutine to exchange one byte
                    ;addressed by DE with one byte
                    ;addressed by HL.
                    ;
205D C5       XCHGB: PUSH B     ;save counter
205E 4E              MOV  C,M   ;exchange bytes
205F 1A              LDAX D
2060 77              MOV  M,A
2061 79              MOV  A,C
2062 12              STAX D
2063 13              INX  D     ;adjust pointers
2064 23              INX  H
2065 C1              POP  B     ;restore counter
2066 C9              RET        ;end subroutine
```

Notice that the subroutine EWORD contains two identical sequences of instructions, one to exchange the low-order bytes and one to exchange the high-order bytes. This sequence can be written as a subroutine, improving the readability of the subroutine. In this example the length of the subroutine is equal, saving nothing, but this does not mean that the effort is a waste of time. Readability is much more important than length. Also notice that the counter is moved to the stack to allow the C register to be used for the exchange. This improved version of EWORD is listed in Example 9-8 and the flowchart is depicted in Fig. 9-4.

9-4 STRING TRANSFERS

What is a character string? A character string is a grouping of ASCII-coded characters (see Appendix C for a detailed list) that are most often terminated by an ASCII carriage return (0DH) and a line feed (0AH). (Table 9-1 illustrates many different-length character strings.) Character strings are usually variable in length and normally contain from no characters, a null string, to up to hundreds of characters. At times they also include a count of the number of characters stored in the string. Character strings are used in systems that deal with ASCII-coded data, which today include many systems.

TABLE 9-1 REPRESENTATIVE ASCII-CODED
CHARACTER STRINGS

String	ASCII-coded string
WHAT	57–49–41–54–0D–0A
ABC	41–42–43–0D–0A
12	31–32–0D–0A
	0D–0A (null string)
to be	74–6F–20–62–65–0D–0A
4.9	34–2E–39–0D–0A

Character String Transfers

A program, or more appropriately a subroutine, that transfers a variable-length sub-routine from one part of the memory to another is illustrated in the flowchart of Fig. 9–5. Notice that the programmed-loop construct is not used to develop the flow-chart as with block data transfers. Instead, the repeat-until construct is used to transfer data as long as the data are not a line feed. This means that the character string length is normally limited to the width of the CRT screen or the printer page. (A carriage return moves the print head or cursor to the left-hand margin of the CRT screen or the printed page. The line feed moves the print head or cursor to a new line on the CRT screen or printed page.) This subroutine transfers the character string from the block of memory indexed by the HL register pair into the block of memory in-dexed by the DE register pair. The calling sequence is illustrated in Example 9–9 and the subroutine itself is illustrated in Example 9–10.

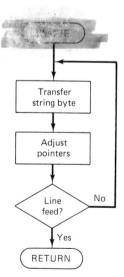

Figure 9-5 The flowchart of a subroutine used to transfer a character string from one area of memory to another.

(EXAMPLE 9-9)

```
                              ORG   2000H   ;define start
                       ;
                       ;data for this example
                       ;
2000 41-42-0D-0A             DB    'AB',0DH,0AH
                       ;
                       ;equates for this example
                       ;
2004 00-28             DEST:  EQU   2800H    ;define DEST
2004 00-20             SOUR:  EQU   2000H    ;define SOUR
                       ;
                       ;program to transfer the
                       ;character string.
                       ;
2004 11-00-28          START: LXI   D,DEST   ;point to DEST
2007 21-00-00                 LXI   H,SOUR   ;point to SOUR
200A CD-50-20                 CALL  SMOVE    ;move string
200D C3-0D-20          ENDP:  JMP   ENDP     ;end program
2010                          END            ;end listing
```

(EXAMPLE 9-10)

```
                              ORG   2050H   ;originate subroutine
                       ;
                       ;subroutine to transfer the
                       ;character string addressed by HL into
                       ;the location addressed by DE.
                       ;
2050 7E                SMOVE: MOV   A,M      ;transfer string byte
2051 12                       STAX  D
2052 23                       INX   H        ;adjust pointers
2053 13                       INX   D
2054 FE-0A                    CPI   LF       ;test for line feed
2056 C2-50-20                 JNZ   SMOVE    ;repeat-until line feed
2059 C9                       RET
                       ;
                       ;equates for SMOVE
                       ;
205A 0A-00             LF:    EQU   0AH      ;define line feed
```

9-5 STRING EXCHANGES

The software for string exchanges is not quite as easy to write as for string transfers because the strings to be exchanged can be of different lengths. If each area of memory contains only one character string, the exchange is rather simple, but if each area of memory contains many strings, as they often do, the program for exchanging strings becomes fairly difficult.

Character Strings as Stored in a Memory Array

Table 9-2 illustrates the method employed when character strings are stored in the memory as an array. Notice that each string ends with a carriage return and a line

TABLE 9-2 CHARACTER STRINGS AS STORED IN A MEMORY ARRAY

			Hex-coded strings					*ASCII-coded strings*
2800 41	42	43	0D	0A	43	41	52	ABC..CAR
2808 0D	0A	57	41	54	45	52	0D	..WATER.
2810 0A	57	45	4C	4C	0D	0A	1A	.WELL...

Notes: The ASCII characters that do not normally print a character appear as periods in the listing of ASCII-coded characters. Also note that the end of the string array is depicted by a control Z (1AH).

feed and the end of the string area is depicted with the control Z character (1AH). A control Z is often used to indicate the end of a grouping of character strings or a file in some operating systems.

Exchanging Character Strings

The main difficulty in exchanging character strings is that different-length strings require that other strings in the memory be moved about. If the strings are of the same length, no problem exists.

Figure 9-6 illustrates the flowchart that is used to exchange two character strings in the memory. The HL register pair is used to point to the string in the lowest-numbered memory location and the DE register pair is used to point to the string in the highest-numbered memory location. When these two pointers are loaded with the addresses of the two strings to be exchanged and the subroutine (SWAP) is called, the strings are exchanged until a line feed is detected in either string. At this a return

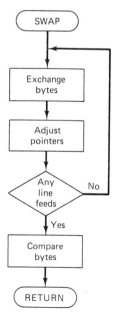

Figure 9-6 The flowchart of the SWAP subroutine which exchanges the contents of two character strings until a line feed is found in either string.

is made from the subroutine, with the zero flag indicating whether the strings are of equal (Z = 1) or unequal length (Z = 0). (Refer to Example 9-11 for the listing of this subroutine.)

```
(EXAMPLE 9-11)
                           ORG    2050H    ;origin
                     ;
                     ;subroutine to swap the character
                     ;strings addressed by HL and DE.
                     ;
    2050 46          SWAP:  MOV  B,M       ;swap string bytes
    2051 1A                 LDAX D
    2052 77                 MOV  M,A
    2053 4F                 MOV  C,A
    2054 FE-0A              CPI  LF         ;test for line feed
    2056 78                 MOV  A,B
    2057 12                 STAX D
    2058 23                 INX  H          ;adjust pointers
    2059 13                 INX  D
    205A CA-62-20           JZ   SWAP1      ;if line feed
    205D FE-0A              CPI  LF         ;test for line feed
    205F C2-50-20           JNZ  SWAP       ;if not line feed
    2062 B9          SWAP1: CMP  C          ;adjust zero flag
    2063 C9                 RET
                     ;
                     ;equates
                     ;
    2064 0A-00       LF:    EQU  10         ;define line feed
```

Example 9-12 shows how this subroutine is called from a program so that string 1 (ABC) and string 3 (WATER) from Table 9-2 are exchanged. Because these two strings are of unequal length, subroutine ADJ is called in this program. If, instead, strings 1 and 2 were exchanged, the program would not call ADJ because these two strings are of equal length.

```
(EXAMPLE 9-12)
                           ORG    2000H    ;origin
                     ;
                     ;calling sequence for subroutine
                     ;SWAP
                     ;
    2000 31-60-28    START: LXI SP,2860H   ;point to stack
    2003 21-00-28           LXI H,STR1     ;point to string 1
    2006 11-0A-28           LXI D,STR3     ;point to string 3
    2009 CD-50-20           CALL SWAP      ;exchange strings
    200C CA-12-20           JZ   ENDP      ;if strings equal
    200F CD-70-20           CALL ADJ       ;swap unequal strings
    2012 C3-12-20    ENDP:  JMP  ENDP      ;end program
                     ;
                     ;equates
                     ;
    2015 00-28       STR1:  EQU  2800H     ;define string 1
    2015 0A-28       STR3:  EQU  280AH     ;define string 3
```

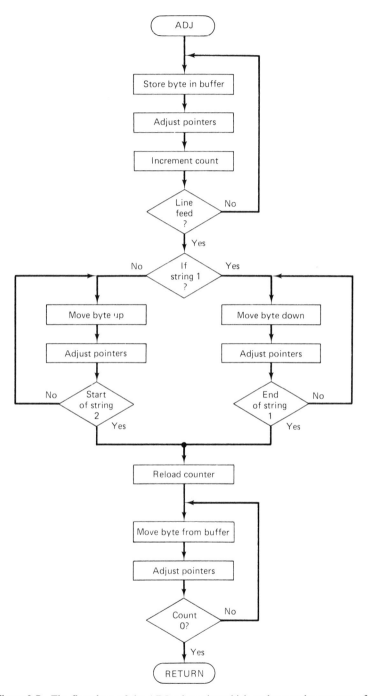

Figure 9-7   The flowchart of the ADJ subroutine which exchanges the contents of two character strings of unequal length.

Exchanging Strings of Unequal Length

Exchanging strings of unequal lengths is a very difficult task, as witnessed by the large flowchart in Fig. 9–7. There are actually three parts to this flowchart. The first portion takes the remaining unexchanged characters in the larger string and moves them into a buffer memory. The next portion of the subroutine determines whether the strings between the two that are exchanged needs to be moved up or down in the memory. Once this is decided, the correct direction of the move takes effect. Finally, the last portion of the subroutine takes the data from the buffer and appends them to the position of the longest string. The completed subroutine is listed in Example 9–13. If you have an SDK-85 or other programming aide it is suggested that this subroutine, the prior subroutine, and the program be placed in the memory and executed.

```
(EXAMPLE 9-13 page 1 of 2)

                        ORG   2070H  ;origin
                    ;
                    ;subroutine ADJ exchanges the remainder of
                    ;unequal strings.
                    ;
2070 FE-0A     ADJ:   CPI  LF      ;test for line feed
2072 C2-76-20         JNZ  ADJ1    ;if string 2
2075 EB               XCHG
2076 E5        ADJ1:  PUSH H       ;save registers
2077 D5               PUSH D
2078 0E-00            MVI  C,0     ;load counter
207A 11-80-28         LXI  D,BUF   ;point to buffer
207D 7E        ADJ2:  MOV  A,M     ;save string in buffer
207E 12               STAX D
207F 23               INX  H       ;adjust pointers
2080 13               INX  D
2081 0C               INR  C       ;increment counter
2082 FE-0A            CPI  LF      ;test for line feed
2084 C2-7D-20         JNZ  ADJ2    ;if not line feed
2087 79               MOV  A,C
2088 32-C4-20         STA  COUNT   ;save count
208B D1               POP  D       ;restore register
208C 78               MOV  A,B
208D C1               POP  B       ;restore register
208E FE-0A            CPI  LF
2090 C2-B1-20         JNZ  ADJ6    ;if string 2
2093 0B        ADJ3:  DCX  B       ;adjust pointers
2094 2B               DCX  H
2095 0A               LDAX B       ;transfer byte
2096 77               MOV  M,A
2097 79               MOV  A,C
2098 BB               CMP  E
2099 C2-93-20         JNZ  ADJ3    ;if DE <> BC
209C 78               MOV  A,B
209D BA               CMP  D
209E C2-93-20         JNZ  ADJ3    ;if DE <> BC
20A1 21-80-28 ADJ4:   LXI  H,BUF   ;point to buffer
20A4 3A-C4-20         LDA  COUNT   ;get count
20A7 4F               MOV  C,A
```

(EXAMPLE 9-13 page 2 of 2)

```
20A8 7E       ADJ5:   MOV  A,M    ;transfer a byte
20A9 12               STAX D
20AA 23               INX  H      ;adjust pointers
20AB 13               INX  D
20AC 0D               DCR  C      ;decrement counter
20AD C2-A8-20         JNZ  ADJ5   ;if count not zero
20B0 C9               RET
20B1 7E       ADJ6:   MOV  A,M    ;transfer a byte
20B2 02               STAX B
20B3 23               INX  H      ;adjust pointers
20B4 03               INX  B
20B5 7B               MOV  A,E
20B6 BD               CMP  L
20B7 C2-B1-20         JNZ  ADJ6   ;if DE <> HL
20BA 7A               MOV  A,D
20BB BC               CMP  H
20BC C2-B1-20         JNZ  ADJ6   ;if DE <> HL
20BF 50               MOV  D,B
20C0 59               MOV  E,C
20C1 C3-A1-20         JMP  ADJ4   ;finish subroutine
20C4 00       COUNT:  DB   0      ;define counter
                      ;
                      ;equate buffer area
                      ;
20C5 80-28    BUF:    EQU  2880H  ;define buffer
```

9-6 SUMMARY

1. Block data transfers are used to transfer a group of bytes or words from one area of memory to another area of memory.

2. Block data exchanges are used to exchange the byte-wide or word-wide contents of two blocks of memory.

3. The programmed-loop and repeat-until constructs proved useful in this chapter for both data and string manipulations.

4. This chapter showed the importance of subroutines in many programming techniques.

5. A character string is a group of ASCII characters that is terminated with a carriage return (an ASCII 0DH) and a line feed (an ASCII 0AH).

6. Character strings may be of any length, although they are usually at most one printed line in length. If a character string contains no characters, except for the carriage return and line feed, it is called a null string.

7. If character strings are stored in a memory array, the group of strings is usually terminated with the control Z character (an ASCII 1AH).

8. Character string transfers are used to move an ASCII-coded word, phrase, or sentence from one area of memory to another.

9. The character string exchange is useful for sorting alphanumeric data, as discussed in Chapter 14.

9-7 GLOSSARY

Array *See* Memory array.

Block data exchange A technique that is used to exchange the contents of bytes or words in one section of the memory with another section.

Block data transfer A technique that is used to transfer a section of bytes or words from one part of the memory to another.

Calling sequence The group of instructions in a program preceding and including the CALL to a subroutine.

Carriage return The ASCII-coded character (0DH) that is used to return the print head on a printer or the cursor on a CRT terminal to the left-hand margin of the paper or screen.

Character string Character strings are groupings of ASCII-coded characters that are terminated with a carriage return (an ASCII 0DH) and a line feed (an ASCII 0AH) in most systems.

Control Z Control Z (an ASCII 1AH) is used to indicate the end of an ASCII character string memory array.

Line feed The ASCII-coded character (0AH) that is used to advance the cursor in a CRT terminal or print head on a printer to the next line on the screen or paper.

Memory array A section of the memory that contains a grouping of bytes, words, or character strings is often called a memory array.

Null character string Null character strings contain only a carriage return and a line feed.

QUESTIONS AND PROBLEMS

9-1. Using the LDA and the STA instructions, write a program that will transfer five bytes of memory from locations 2800H through 2804H to locations 2820H through 2824H.

9-2. Redo the program written in Question 9-1 using the programmed-loop construct illustrated in Section 9-1.

9-3. The program listed in Example 9-1 transfers data from memory locations _____ through _____ to memory locations _____ through _____ .

9-4. If the count is initialized to 00H in programming Example 9-1, how many bytes of data will be transferred?

9-5. List one important feature of any subroutine.

9-6. What are the differences between the program in Examples 9-1 and 9-2?

9-7. Why must the value of the BC register pair be tested to determine if it's zero in programming Example 9-2?

9-8. Is the program listed in Example 9-3 complete? Explain your answer.

9-9. What advantages are evident in the subroutine MWORD listed in Example 9-4?

9-10. Compare the main difference in the software of a block data transfer and a block data exchange.

9-11. If 100 (64H) words are to be transferred from one area of memory to another, could a byte transfer program be used that transfers 200 (C8H) bytes? Which program is more efficient, and why?

9-12. When writing software, is readability an important consideration? Explain your answer.

9-13. Develop a flowchart and the program that will transfer 100 bytes of data from memory area 0000H through 0063H into areas 2800H through 2863H and also 2000H through 2063H. (*Hint:* Because you will need three register pairs to point to these memory locations, you may need to store the counter in the memory or on the stack.)

9-14. Write the hexadecimal versions of the following ASCII character strings in a form suitable for use in a computer system.
   (a) What are you doing?
   (b) I don't know.
   (c) Explain that!
   (d) Well, so I can.
   (e) Whom do you trust?

9-15. Is there any limit to the size of a number stored in a character string?

9-16. Explain what the carriage return and line feed codes accomplish on a printer.

9-17. What programming construct is used when a single character string is transferred from one area of memory to another?

9-18. Modify the subroutine in Example 9-10 so that five character strings are moved from the locations indirectly addressed by the HL register pair into the locations indexed by the DE register pair.

9-19. What is the significance of the control Z (1AH) ASCII code in a character string array?

9-20. Why is it much more difficult to exchange character strings than it is to transfer them?

9-21. Why does subroutine SWAP (Example 9-11) test for a line feed in both character strings? What happens if both character strings are unequal in length?

9-22. What three main events occur in the subroutine listed in Example 9-13?

9-23. The program listed in Example 9-12 calls two subroutine (SWAP and ADJ). Rewrite this sequence of calls so that a new subroutine called EXCHG is formed and show the calling sequence.

_____ chapter ten _____

FIXED-POINT ARITHMETIC

Chapter 9 presented data and string manipulation, which is an important portion of many programs. In this chapter we present fixed-point arithmetic, which is also a fairly important portion of many programs. Included are: 8-bit binary addition, subtraction, multiplication and division; multiple byte binary addition, subtraction, multiplication, and division; and BCD addition and subtraction. These operations will allow a programmer to accomplish most tasks required in machine or assembly language for most 8085A software-based systems.

10-1 OBJECTIVES

Upon completion of this chapter, you will be able to:

1. Use binary addition to form the sum of lists of data
2. Use binary subtraction to find the difference of two lists of data
3. Multiply and divide both 8- and 16-bit numbers
4. Add and subtract multiple-byte binary numbers
5. Add and subtract BCD numbers

10-2 EIGHT-BIT BINARY ADDITION AND SUBTRACTION

The programmer has a complete set of instructions for accomplishing single 8-bit additions or subtractions in the 8085A microprocessor. These instructions include:

two immediate, many register addressed, and two register pair indirect addressed forms. (Refer to Tables 5-1, 5-2, 5-5, and 5-6 for a complete listing of these instructions.)

Eight-Bit Binary Addition

Suppose that the ten 8-bit numbers stored at memory locations 2800H through 2809H are to be added together. To accomplish this, one of the 8-bit addition instructions is selected, but which one and what structured programming construct? Whenever a set of numbers are added together from the memory an ADD M instruction is used, and since 10 numbers are added in this example, the programmed-loop construct is applicable. A flowchart for this program is illustrated in Fig. 10-1 and the program is listed in Example 10-1.

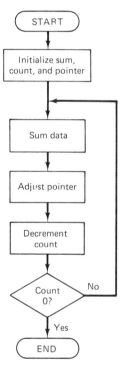

Figure 10-1 The flowchart of a program that sums a set of memory data.

What is wrong with the program listed in Example 10-1? The main problem with this program is that the largest sum can only be FFH. This is fine if the 10 numbers are small, but programs are supposed to work with any set of data. In this case a provision must be included to handle overflows after each addition. A simple modification to this program can easily correct this omission. The C register is used to store any overflows that occur, so that the 16-bit result is stored in the C and A registers after executing the program listed in Example 10-2.

(EXAMPLE 10-1)

```
                         ORG   2000H    ;origin
                 ;
                 ;example program that adds 10
                 ;bytes of data together and leaves
                 ;the 8-bit sum in the accumulator.
                 ;
2000 21-00-28 START:  LXI   H,2800H ;address data
2003 06-0A            MVI   B,10    ;load counter
2005 AF               XRA   A       ;clear sum
2006 86       LOOP:   ADD   M       ;sum data
2007 23               INX   H       ;adjust pointer
2008 05               DCR   B       ;decrement counter
2009 C2-03-20         JNZ   LOOP    ;if count <> 0
200C C3-0C-20 ENDP:   JMP   ENDP    ;end program
200F                  END           ;end listing
```

(EXAMPLE 10-2)

```
                         ORG   2000H    ;origin
                 ;
                 ;example program that adds 10
                 ;bytes of data together and leaves
                 ;the 16-bit sum in the C register
                 ;and the accumulator.
                 ;
2000 21-00-28 START:  LXI   H,2800H ;address data
2003 06-0A            MVI   B,10    ;load counter
2005 AF               XRA   A       ;clear sum
2006 4F               MOV   C,A     ;clear MSB sum
2007 86       LOOP:   ADD   M       ;sum data
2008 D2-0C-20         JNC   DOWN    ;if no carry
200B 0C               INR   C       ;add carry to MSB sum
200C 23       DOWN:   INX   H       ;adjust pointer
200D 05               DCR   B       ;decrement counter
200E C2-07-20         JNZ   LOOP    ;if count <> 0
2011 C3-11-20 ENDP:   JMP   ENDP    ;end program
2014                  END           ;end listing
```

Eight-Bit Binary Subtraction

Subtraction is a little different from addition because a list of numbers are not normally subtracted from each other. Suppose that two lists of numbers, each 10H bytes long, appear in the memory: list 1 is stored at location 2800H through 280FH and list 2 is stored at location 2810H through 281FH.

The program is to take the number stored at list 2 and subtract it from the number stored at list 1 and then store the difference at a location in list 2. This same operation is repeated 10H times until all 16 sets of numbers are subtracted. Again the programmed-loop construct is used to develop the flowchart (Fig. 10-2) and program (Example 10-3) for this task.

The main difference between the addition problem illustrated in Fig. 10-1 and this problem is that two sets of numbers are addressed by the microprocessor in this example. The DE register pair is used to indirectly address list 1 and the HL register

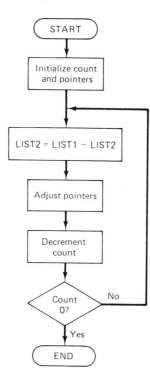

Figure 10-2 The flowchart of a program that forms the differences for two sets of numbers stored in the memory.

(EXAMPLE 10-3)

```
                    ORG   2000H    ;origin
              ;
              ;program to subtract LIST2 data
              ;from LIST1 data and store the
              ;difference in LIST2
              ;
2000 21-10-28 START:  LXI   H,LIST2  ;address LIST2
2003 11-00-28         LXI   D,LIST1  ;address LIST1
2006 06-10            MVI   B,10H    ;load counter
2008 12       LOOP:   LDAX  D        ;get LIST1
2009 96               SUB   M        ;subtract LIST2
200A 77               MOV   M,A      ;difference to LIST2
200B 23               INX   H        ;adjust pointers
200C 13               INX   D
200D 05               DCR   B        ;decrement counter
200E C2-08-20         JNZ   LOOP     ;if count <> 0
2011 C3-11-20 ENDP:   JMP   ENDP     ;end program
              ;
              ;equates
              ;
2014 00-28    LIST1:  EQU   2800H    ;define LIST1
2014 10-28    LIST2:  EQU   2810H    ;define LIST2
2014                  END            ;end listing
```

pair indirectly addresses list 2. This order cannot be reversed because memory data can be subtracted only by using the HL pair to indirectly address the memory.

10-3 BINARY MULTIPLICATION

Unfortunately, the 8085A microprocessor cannot multiply without a program. This section develops the algorithms required to perform binary multiplication so that programs can be written using this operation. Three techniques (repeated addition and two techniques of shift and add) are presented for binary multiplication. In addition to these different methods of multiplication, both signed and unsigned multiplication techniques are developed.

Unsigned Multiplication by Repeated Addition

Repeated addition is the simplest method of multiplication to understand and for small numbers a very useful method. The principle behind this technique is the structured programming construct, the programmed loop construct. If two 8-bit numbers are multiplied, one of the numbers can be used as the loop counter and the other number can be added to itself the loop counter number of times. Example 10-4 illustrates how the number 7 can be multiplied by 3 using repeated addition. Notice from this example that the product of 7×3 is generated by adding 7 three times. If the product of 6×4 is required, 6 could be added four times.

(Example 10-4)

$$7 \times 3 = 21$$

or

$$7 + 7 + 7 = 21$$

A subroutine that uses this technique is illustrated in the flowchart of Fig. 10-3 and the subroutine itself is listed in Example 10-6 with the subroutine calling sequence listed in Example 10-5. Notice that the product, which is formed by multiplying the accumulator times the B register, is a double-length product found in the HL register pair after returning from the subroutine. The reason that a double-length product is used is so that the two numbers that are multiplied together by the subroutine can result in a product that is larger than 256.

Unsigned Constant Multiplication

In many cases the number 10 or another fixed or constant number is used as a multiplier. Rather than use the repeated addition technique presented earlier, another technique is often used that results in a much faster multiplication.

Suppose that a program requires the number in the HL register pair to be multiplied by a 4. The easiest way to accomplish this is by using the DAD H instruction. Remember that DAD H doubles the contents of the HL register pair. If HL

(EXAMPLE 10-5)

```
                         ORG    2000H    ;origin
                    ;
                    ;The calling sequence for MULT
                    ;
2000 06-03    START: MVI   B,XX      ;load multiplier
2002 3E-06           MVI   A,YY      ;load multiplicand
2004 CD-50-20        CALL  MULT      ;HL = YY x XX
2007 C3-07-20 ENDP:  JMP   ENDP      ;end program
                    ;
                    ;equates
                    ;
200A 03-00    XX:    EQU   3         ;define multiplier
200A 06-00    YY:    EQU   6         ;define multiplicand
200A                 END             ;end listing
```

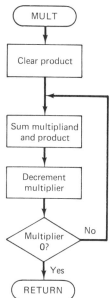

Figure 10-3 The flowchart used to multiply 2 numbers via the repeated addition technique.

(EXAMPLE 10-6)

```
                         ORG    2050H    ;origin
                    ;
                    ;subroutine that multiplies the
                    ;accumulator times the B register
                    ;and leaves the 16-bit product in
                    ;the HL register pair.
                    ;
2050 21-00-00 MULT:  LXI   H,0       ;clear product
2053 5F              MOV   E,A       ;form 16-bit multiplicand
2054 16-00           MVI   D,0
2056 19       LOOP:  DAD   D         ;form partial product
2057 05              DCR   B         ;decrement multiplier
2058 C2-56-20        JNZ   LOOP      ;if multiplier <> 0
205B C9              RET             ;return
```

is doubled twice, it is multiplied by 4. (See the subroutine listed in Example 10–7.) This example is almost too simple to write as a subroutine.

```
(EXAMPLE 10-7)

                          ORG  2060H    ;origin
         2060 29   MULT4: DAD  H        ;times 2
         2061 29          DAD  H        ;times 4
         2062 C9          RET           ;return
```

Suppose now that it is desired to multiply the number by a 10. How can this be accomplished? The first step is to convert the number to binary (see Example 10–8) and then use the one positions to form the product by adding their binary power of two values together. In this example, multiplication by 10 is formed by adding a 2 and an 8 times the original multiplicand. If 2 times and 8 times the multiplicand are added together, the result is 10 times the multiplicand. If the multiplicand is a 6, the product is 60. Example 10–9 shows the subroutine that is written to multiply the HL register pair by 10.

(Example 10-8)

$$8\ 4\ 2\ 1\quad \text{(weights)}$$

$$10 = 1\ 0\ 1\ 0$$

$$\begin{array}{rl}
12 & \text{(2 times 6)} \\
+\ 48 & \text{(8 times 6)} \\
\hline
60 & \text{the product}
\end{array}$$

```
(EXAMPLE 10-9)

                       ORG   2080H   ;origin
                     ;
                     ;subroutine that multiplies the
                     ;HL register pair by 10.
                     ;
        2080 29   MUL10: DAD  H       ;2 times HL
        2081 55          MOV  D,H     ;save 2 times HL
        2082 5D          MOV  E,L
        2083 29          DAD  H       ;4 times HL
        2084 29          DAD  H       ;8 times HL
        2085 19          DAD  D       ;sum 8 and 2 times HL
        2086 C9          RET
```

The Unsigned Multiplication Algorithm

The most flexible version of multiplication is the unsigned multiplication shift-and-add algorithm. This algorithm is developed by observing the steps required to multiply two binary numbers with a piece of paper and a pencil. If the multiplier bit is a 1, the multiplicand is added to the product, and if the multiplier bit is a 0, no addition takes place. Besides addition, the multiplication process requires that the multiplicand be shifted each time it is added to the product. Look at the example binary multiplication illustrated in Example 10-10 so that you understand how the partial products are shifted to the left and also notice that the product is double width.

(Example 10-10)

$$
\begin{array}{rl}
1001 & (9) \\
\times\ 1111 & (15) \\
\hline
1001 & (9) \\
10010 & (18) \\
100100 & (36) \\
1001000 & (72) \\
\hline
10000111 & (135)
\end{array}
$$

In addition to shifting the multiplicand left to form each partial product, the multiplier must be interrogated to determine whether or not a partial product is added to the product. On paper your finger is used to keep track of each bit, but in the computer no finger is available, so another technique must be developed. If the multiplier is shifted right, each bit is moved into the carry flag one at a time so that it can be checked for a 1 or 0 to determine if a partial product is added. If the multiplier becomes a zero, this process is complete. The flowchart for this algorithm is illustrated in Fig. 10-4 and the subroutine that multiplies the accumulator by the E register is listed in Example 10-11. This subroutine leaves the result in the HL register pair upon returning to the main program. The result, after a 9 is multiplied by a 5, is illustrated in the register trace of this subroutine (Table 10-1).

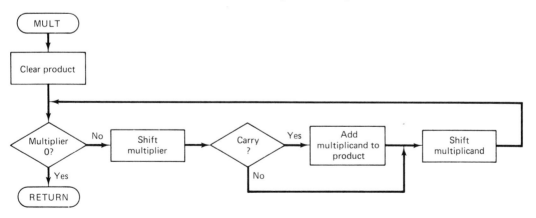

Figure 10-4   An algorithm illustrating binary multiplication using the shift and add technique.

(EXAMPLE 10-11)

```
                        ORG   2040H    ;origin
                   ;
                   ;subroutine that multiplies A X E
                   ;and leaves the 16-bit product in
                   ;the HL register pair.
                   ;
2040 21-00-00 MULT:    LXI   H,0      ;clear product
2043 55                MOV   D,H      ;clear MSB of multiplicand
2044 B7       LOOP:    ORA   A        ;test multiplier
2045 CA-53-20          JZ    ENDS     ;if zero
2048 1F                RAR            ;shift multiplier right
2049 D2-4D-20          JNC   LOOP1    ;if no carry
204C 19                DAD   D        ;add multiplicand
204D EB       LOOP1:   XCHG           ;shift multiplicand
204E 29                DAD   H
204F EB                XCHG
2050 C3-44-20          JMP   LOOP     ;repeat
2053 C9       ENDS:    RET            ;return
```

(EXAMPLE 10-12)

```
                        ORG   2060H    ;origin
                   ;
                   ;subroutine that multiplies the
                   ;signed number A X E and leaves the
                   ;16-bit signed product in the HL
                   ;register pair.
                   ;
2060 F5       SMULT:   PUSH  PSW      ;save multiplier
2061 AB                XRA   E        ;generate sign
2062 47                MOV   B,A      ;save sign
2063 7B                MOV   A,E      ;get multiplicand
2064 B7                ORA   A        ;test multiplicand
2065 F2-6B-20          JP    S1       ;if positive
2068 2F                CMA            ;negate multiplicand
2069 3C                INR   A
206A 6F                MOV   E,A
206B F1       S1:      POP   PSW      ;restore multiplier
206C B7                ORA   A        ;test multiplier
206D F2-72-20          JP    S2       ;if positive
2070 2F                CMA            ;negate multiplier
2071 3C                INR   A
2072 CD-40-20 S2:      CALL  MULT     ;multiply
2075 78                MOV   A,B      ;get sign
2076 B7                ORA   A        ;test sign
2077 F2-81-20          JP    S3       ;if product positive
207A 7C                MOV   A,H      ;negate product
207B 2F                CMA
207C 67                MOV   H,A
207D 7D                MOV   A,L
207E 2F                CMA
207F 6F                MOV   L,A
2080 23                INX   H
2081 C9       S3:      RET            ;return
```

TABLE 10-1 REGISTER TRACE OF THE MULTIPLICATION SUBROUTINE DEPICTED IN EXAMPLE 10–11 FOR THE NUMBERS 5 TIMES 9

PC	Cy	A	DE	HL	Instruction
2040	X	05	XX09	0000	LXI H,0
2043	x	05	0009	0000	MOV D,H
2044	0	05	0009	0000	ORA A
2045	0	05	0009	0000	JZ 2053
2048	1	02	0009	0000	RAR
2049	1	02	0009	0000	JNC 204D
204C	0	02	0009	0009	DAD D
204D	0	02	0009	0009	XCHG
204E	0	02	0009	0012	DAD H
204F	0	02	0012	0009	XCHG
2050	0	02	0012	0009	JMP 2044
2044	0	02	0012	0009	ORA A
2045	0	02	0012	0009	JZ 2053
2048	0	01	0012	0009	RAR
2049	0	01	0012	0009	JNC 204D
204D	0	01	0009	0012	XCHG
204E	0	01	0009	0024	DAD H
204F	0	01	0024	0009	XCHG
2050	0	01	0024	0009	JMP 2044
2044	0	01	0024	0009	ORA A
2045	0	01	0024	0009	JZ 2053
2048	1	00	0024	0009	RAR
2049	1	00	0024	0009	JNC 204D
204C	0	00	0024	002D	DAD D
204D	0	00	002D	0024	XCHG
204E	0	00	002D	0048	DAD H
204F	0	00	0048	002D	XCHG
2050	0	00	0048	002D	JMP 2044
2044	0	00	0048	002D	ORA A
2045	0	00	0048	002D	JZ 2053
2053	0	00	0048	002D	RET

Note: The HL register pair contains the product of 5 times 9, as 45 decimal (002DH) at the RET instruction.

Signed Multiplication

In certain applications signed arithmetic is used and the multiplication techniques presented thus far will not correctly generate signed results. Remember that if the signs of the multiplicand and multiplier are alike, the product is positive and if the signs are not alike, the product is negative. Using this mathematical rule, the subroutine presented in Example 10–11 can be modified to correctly multiply signed numbers. Example 10–12 illustrates the SMULT subroutine (see Fig. 10–5 for the flowchart) which multiplies signed numbers using the MULT subroutine of Example 10–11. To accomplish this, the multiplicand and multiplier are exclusive-ORed together and the result, which indicates the sign of the product, is saved in the B register. Both numbers are then adjusted so that they are positive before calling the MULT subroutine. Upon returning from the MULT subroutine, the sign of the B register is examined. If it is negative, the product in the HL register pair is negated.

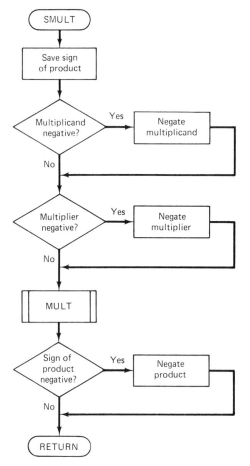

Figure 10-5 Signed multiplication using the MULT subroutine of Fig. 10-4.

10–4 BINARY DIVISION

Binary division, as binary multiplication, is used in some advanced applications software for the microprocessor. In this section we present two techniques (shift and add, and shift and subtract) for performing unsigned binary division. After these processes have been clarified, signed binary division is presented.

Division by a Constant

If data are shifted to the left, they are multiplied by 2 for each bit position of the shift as described in Section 10-3. If data are shifted to the right, they are divided by 2 for each bit position of the shift. Knowing this and the technique used to multiply by a constant, a technique can be developed so that any number can be divided by any power of 2. For example (see Example 10-13), if a number is to be divided by 4, it can be shifted right two places. Each shift divides by 2, so two shifts divide by 2 twice, or they divide by 4. Notice in this example that the wrong answer resulted. If the carry is added to the answer, it is rounded up to the correct result. The carry is always added to the result to obtain a rounded answer, and if carry is not added, the answer is truncated. A subroutine that divides the accumulator register by 4 and rounds the answer is illustrated in Example 10-14.

(Example 10-13)

Number	CY	
1100110	0 =	102
110011	0 =	51 (shifted once)
11001	1 =	25 (shifted twice)

(EXAMPLE 10-14)

```
                    ORG    2060H   ;set origin
                ;
                ;subroutine to divide the accumulator
                ;by 4 and round the result.
                ;
2060 B7         DIV4:  ORA    A       ;shift right
2061 1F                RAR
2062 B7                ORA    A       ;shift right
2063 1F                RAR
2064 CE-00             ACI    0       ;round result
2066 C9                RET            ;return
```

Signed division by a constant.   The subroutine listed in Example 10-14 can be modified so that it divides the signed number in the accumulator by 4 by using an arithmetic right shift. The arithmetic right shift copies the sign bit through the number when it is shifted right. In Example 10-14 a 0 is shifted in the left end of the accumulator by using the ORA A instruction to clear the carry before the shift.

Example 10-15 shows how the signed contents of the accumulator are divided by 4 with the result rounded. Notice that a shift left is used to copy the sign bit into the carry flag before shifting right twice. Each time that this is done the signed number is correctly divided by a 2.

The Unsigned Division Algorithm

To divide a number by any integer value, the division algorithm is normally used

(EXAMPLE 10-15)

```
                          ORG   2070H   ;origin
                      ;
                      ;subroutine to divide the signed
                      ;number in the accumulator by 4 and
                      ;round the result.
                      ;
2070 07      SDIV3:    RLC             ;sign to carry
2071 1F                RAR             ;original number, Cy = sign
2072 1F                RAR             ;arithmetic shift
2073 07                RLC             ;second arithmetic shift
2074 1F                RAR
2075 1F                RAR
2076 CE-00             ACI   0         ;round result
2078 C9                RET             ;return
```

to develop a subroutine. The division algorithm uses a combination of shifting left, comparing, subtracting, and setting bits to perform binary division. Before it can be understood, a review of binary division on paper is in order, as illustrated in Example 10–16.

In this example a 27 (11011) is divided by a 3 (11) and the result is a 9 (1001). To accomplish this division, the divisor is compared with a portion of the dividend. The first comparison is 11 with 1. Because 11 is larger than 1, a 0 is placed quotient. Next, the 11 is compared with 11 because the first 2 bits of the dividend are now

(Example 10-16)

$$
\begin{array}{r}
01001 \\
11\overline{)11011} \\
11 \\
\hline
11 \\
11 \\
\hline
\end{array}
$$

(EXAMPLE 10-17)

```
                          ORG   2040H   ;origin
                      ;
                      ;subroutine that divides L by C
                      ;leaving the quotient in L and the
                      ;remainder in H.
                      ;
2040 06-08   DIV:     MVI   B,8       ;load counter
2042 26-00            MVI   H,0       ;clear qoutient
2044 29      DIV1:    DAD   H         ;shift left
2045 7C               MOV   A,H       ;compare
2046 B9               SUB   C
2047 DA-4C-20         JC    DIV2      ;if dividend < divisor
204A 67               MOV   H,A
204B 2C               INR   L
204C 05      DIV2:    DCR   B         ;decrement counter
204D C2-44-20         JNZ   DIV1      ;if counter <> 0
2050 C9               RET             ;return
```

compared with the divisor. This time they are equal. If the divisor and the portion of the dividend it is compared with are equal or the portion of the dividend is larger, a subtraction occurs and a 1 is placed in the quotient. This comparison is continued until all the bits of the dividend are compared with the divisor. The flowchart illustrating this algorithm is shown in Fig. 10-6.

Using this flowchart as a guide, the subroutine listed in Example 10-17 divides the L register by the C register. The quotient is placed in the L register and the remainder is placed in the H register upon return from this subroutine. The dividend may not exceed 127 for this subroutine to function properly.

To assure correct operation of this subroutine, the register trace is illustrated in Table 10-2 for a 72 (1001000) divided by an 11 (1011).

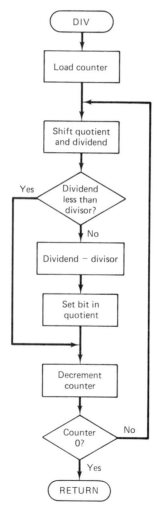

Figure 10-6 The flowchart of the divide algorithm.

(EXAMPLE 10-18)

```
                          ORG   2060H   ;origin
                   ;
                   ;subroutine to divide L by C and
                   ;leave the signed quotient in L
                   ;and the signed remainder in H.
                   ;
2060 7D            SDIV:   MOV   A,L     ;check sign
2061 A9                    XRA   C
2062 57                    MOV   D,A     ;save result sign
2063 7D                    MOV   A,L     ;test dividend
2064 B7                    ORA   A
2065 F2-6B-20              JP    SD1     ;if positive
2068 2F                    CMA           ;negate dividend
2069 3C                    INR   A
206A 6F                    MOV   L,A     ;save dividend
206B 79            SD1:    MOV   A,C     ;test divisor
206C B7                    ORA   A
206D F2-73-20              JP    SD2     ;if divisor positive
2070 2F                    CMA           ;negate divisor
2071 3C                    INR   A
2072 4F                    MOV   C,A     ;save divisor
2073 CD-40-20      SD2:    CALL  DIV     ;divide
2076 7A                    MOV   A,D     ;get sign
2077 B7                    ORA   A       ;test sign
2078 F2-83-20              JP    SD3     ;if positive
207B 7C                    MOV   A,H     ;negate remainder
207C 2F                    CMA
207D 3C                    INR   A
207E 67                    MOV   H,A
207F 7D                    MOV   A,L     ;negate quotient
2080 2F                    CMA
2081 3C                    INR   A
2082 6F                    MOV   L,A
2083 C9            SD3:    RET           ;return
```

TABLE 10-2 REGISTER TRACE OF SUBROUTINE DIV (EXAMPLE 10–17) USING A 72 DIVIDED BY AN 11

PC	A	Cy	B	C	H	L	Instruction
2040	XX	X	8	0B	XX	48	MVI B,8
2042	XX	X	8	0B	00	48	MVI H,0
2044	XX	0	8	0B	00	90	DAD H
2045	00	0	8	0B	00	90	MOV A,H
2046	F5	1	8	0B	00	90	SUB C
2047	F5	1	8	0B	00	90	JC 204C
204C	F5	1	7	0B	00	90	DCR B
204D	F5	1	7	0B	00	90	JNZ 2044
2044	F5	0	7	0B	01	20	DAD H
2045	01	0	7	0B	01	20	MOV A,H
2046	F6	1	7	0B	01	20	SUB C
2047	F6	1	7	0B	01	20	JC 204C
204C	F6	1	6	0B	01	20	DCR B

TABLE 10–2 (Cont'd.)

PC	A	Cy	B	C	H	L	Instruction
204D	F6	1	6	OB	01	20	JNZ 2044
2044	F6	O	6	OB	02	40	DAD H
2045	02	O	6	OB	02	40	MOV A,H
2046	F7	1	6	OB	02	40	SUB C
2047	F7	1	6	OB	02	40	JC 204C
204C	F7	1	5	OB	02	40	DCR B
204D	F7	1	5	OB	02	40	JNZ 2044
2044	F7	O	5	OB	04	80	DAD H
2045	04	O	5	OB	04	80	MOV A,H
2046	F9	1	5	OB	04	80	SUB C
2047	F9	1	5	OB	04	80	JC 204C
204C	F9	1	4	OB	04	80	DCR B
204D	F9	1	4	OB	04	80	JNZ 2044
2044	F9	O	4	OB	09	00	DAD H
2045	09	O	4	OB	09	00	MOV A,H
2046	FE	1	4	OB	09	00	SUB C
2047	FE	1	4	OB	09	00	JC 204C
204C	FE	1	3	OB	09	00	DCR B
204D	FE	1	3	OB	09	00	JNZ 2044
2044	FE	O	3	OB	12	00	DAD H
2045	12	O	3	OB	12	00	MOV A,H
2046	07	O	3	OB	12	00	SUB C
2047	07	O	3	OB	12	00	JC 204C
204A	07	O	3	OB	07	00	MOV H,A
204B	07	O	3	OB	07	01	INR L
204C	07	O	2	OB	07	01	DCR B
204D	07	O	2	OB	07	01	JNZ 2044
2044	07	O	2	OB	OE	02	DAD H
2045	OE	O	2	OB	OE	02	MOV A,H
2046	03	O	2	OB	OE	02	SUB C
2047	03	O	2	OB	OE	02	JC 204C
204A	03	O	2	OB	03	02	MOV H,A
204B	03	O	2	OB	03	03	INR L
204C	03	O	1	OB	03	03	DCR B
204D	03	O	1	OB	03	03	JNZ 2044
2044	03	O	1	OB	06	06	DAD H
2045	06	O	1	OB	06	06	MOV A,H
2046	FB	1	1	OB	06	06	SUB C
2047	FB	1	1	OB	06	06	JC 204C
204C	FB	1	O	OB	06	06	DCR B
204D	FB	1	O	OB	06	06	JNZ 2044
2050		(return)					

Note: The quotient (L) is a 6 and the remainder (H) is a 6. (72/11 = 6, remainder 6.)

Signed Binary Division

Signed binary division is treated in the same manner as signed multiplication. In fact, the flowchart of Fig. 10–5 is used for signed division as well as signed multiplication. The only differences are that the DIV subroutine is called rather than the MULT subroutine and the terms are exchanged so that the multiplier and multiplicand are changed to divisor and dividend and the product is changed to the quotient and remainder. (Both the quotient and remainder are negative if the result is negative.) A program that uses this flowchart and the DIV subroutine to perform signed division appears in Example 10–18.

10–5 MULTIPLE-BYTE ADDITION AND SUBTRACTION ━━━━━━━━

In Section 10–2 addition and subtraction were discussed. In this section, a continuation of that early discussion, we expand it to include multiple-byte addition and subtraction. Here 16-bit and larger numbers are added and subtracted so that a method can be developed for handling numbers that are larger than the register store provides for internally.

Multiple-Byte Addition

Of course, the DAD instruction performs 16-bit addition, but in this section we show how wider numbers can be added together. Suppose that two 32-bit numbers are to be added together using a subroutine. One 32-bit number is stored at the memory locations indirectly addressed by the HL register pair and the second 32-bit number is stored at the memory locations indirectly addressed by the DE register pair. The result is to be stored on top of the second number stored at the locations indirectly addressed by the DE register pair. (Remember that multiple-byte numbers are stored with the least significant portion in the lowest-numbered memory location.) When each 8-bit segment of the number is added, a carry may be generated, which must be transferred into the next-higher-order byte. The ADC M instruction is used to add the carry to the next-higher-order byte in this subroutine. A flowchart of this subroutine is illustrated in Fig. 10–7 and a listing of the software appears in Example 10–19.

Multiple-Byte Subtraction

Multiple-byte subtraction is very similar to multiple-byte addition in that the carry must be transferred from the low-order byte toward the high-order byte, except that in subtraction the carry flag bit is used to hold the borrow, not the carry. The subroutine to subtract two 32-bit numbers is almost identical to the subroutine to add two 32-bit numbers. Here, too, HL points to one number and DE points to the other. Example 10–20 illustrates a subroutine that subtracts two 32-bit numbers.

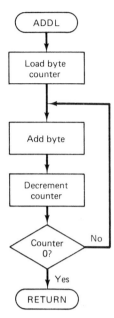

Figure 10-7 The flowchart of a subroutine that adds multiple byte numbers together.

(EXAMPLE 10-19)

```
                    ORG   2040H    ;origin
              ;
              ;subroutine to add multiple byte numbers
              ;
              ;HL addresses first number.
              ;DE addresses second number and sum.
              ;B can be adjusted to add any length
              ;number.
              ;
2040 06-04    ADDL:   MVI   B,4      ;load byte counter
2042 B7               ORA   A        ;clear carry
2043 12       ADDL1:  LDAX  D        ;sum byte
2044 8E               ADC   M
2045 77               MOV   M,A
2046 23               INX   H        ;adjust pointers
2047 13               INX   D
2048 05               DCR   B        ;decrement counter
2049 C2-43-20         JNZ   ADDL1    ;if counter <> 0
204C C9               RET            ;return
```

If the subroutines for addition and subtraction are compared, the only instruction that is different is the ADC M instruction, which is changed to SBB M for subtraction. If larger numbers are added or subtracted, the only change to either subroutine is a change in the count. A count of 4 causes 32-bit (four-byte) numbers to be added or subtracted. If 64-bit (eight-byte) numbers are added or subtracted, the count is changed to 8.

(EXAMPLE 10-20)

```
                        ORG   2060H    ;origin
                   ;
                   ;subroutine to subtract multiple
                   ;byte numbers
                   ;
                   ;the number addres by HL is subtracted
                   ;from the number addres by DE.  The
                   ;result is stored in the location
                   ;addressed HL.
                   ;
                   ;B can be adjusted to subtract any
                   ;size number
                   ;
2060 06-04         SUBL:  MVI   B,4      ;load byte counter
2062 B7                   ORA   A        ;clear borrow
2063 12            SUBL1: LDAX  D        ;subtract byte
2064 9E                   SBB   M
2065 77                   MOV   M,A
2066 23                   INX   H        ;adjust pointers
2067 13                   INX   D
2068 05                   DCR   B        ;decrement counter
2069 C2-63-20             JNZ   SUBL1    ;if counter <> 0
206C C9                   RET            ;return
```

10-6 BINARY-CODED-DECIMAL ADDITION AND SUBTRACTION ━━━━━━

Why is binary-coded-decimal (BCD) arithmetic important? In many microprocessor-based systems data are entered from a keyboard in BCD and then processed for displaying in BCD. If the system requires simple arithmetic, it is pointless to convert the data from BCD to binary for arithmetic and then back again to BCD for display. There are two basic forms of BCD numbers used in computer systems: packed BCD and unpacked BCD. Packed BCD numbers are stored with two digits per byte and unpacked BCD numbers are stored with one digit per byte. Data from keyboards and for displays are normally in unpacked form, and data for arithmetic and memory storage are in packed form.

Packing and Unpacking BCD Data

Before discussing BCD addition and subtraction, which require packed BCD numbers, it is wise to study packing and unpacking the BCD data from a keyboard and for a display. Both tasks are relatively simple and require some form of shifting to accomplish.

Packing BCD data.   By packing BCD data, the amount of memory required to store a number is reduced by a factor of 2. This results in a significant savings in the amount of memory required to store this type of data.

Suppose that an area of memory, indirectly addressed by the HL register pair, contains a string of unpacked BCD data and a subroutine is required to convert them into packed BCD data beginning at the location indirectly addressed by the DE register pair. Also, the unpacked string ends with a FFH code, so that its length is variable. This same code is used at the end of the packed data to indicate their ending. (Remember that all 8085A memory data, except for character strings, are stored with the least significant part in the lowest-numbered memory location.) A flowchart describing this subroutine appears in Fig. 10-8 and Example 10-21 contains a listing of the subroutine. The data from memory are checked for an FFH. If an FFH is encountered, the subroutine ends by storing any unpacked data in the memory and the FFH. If an FFH is not encountered, unpacked data are combined to form packed BCD data.

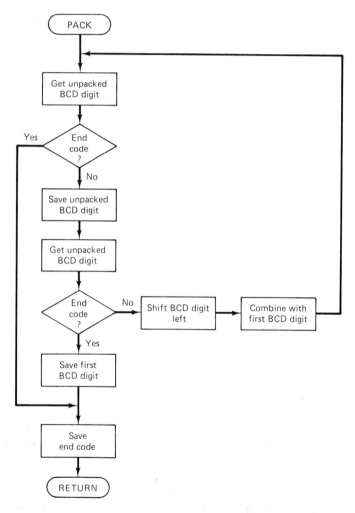

Figure 10-8   A flowchart for the PACK subroutine which combines unpacked BCD digits into packed, 2 per byte, BCD numbers.

(EXAMPLE 10-21)

```
                          ORG   2040H    ;origin
                    ;
                    ;subroutine to pack 2 BCD characters
                    ;per byte.
                    ;
2040 7E             PACK:  MOV   A,M      ;get unpacked data
2041 B7                    ORA   A        ;test it
2042 FA-5C-20             JM    PACK2    ;if end
2045 47                    MOV   B,A      ;save LSBCD digit
2046 23                    INX   H
2047 7E                    MOV   A,M      ;get upacked data
2048 B7                    ORA   A        ;test it
2049 FA-57-20             JM    PACK1    ;if end
204C 23                    INX   H
204D 07                    RLC            ;shift left 4
204E 07                    RLC
204F 07                    RLC
2050 07                    RLC
2051 80                    ADD   B        ;combine two digits
2052 12                    STAX  D        ;save packed BCD
2053 13                    INX   D
2054 C3-40-20             JMP   PACK     ;repeat packing
2057 78             PACK1: MOV   A,B      ;save digit
2058 12                    STAX  D
2059 13                    INX   D
205A 3E-FF                MVI   A,OFFH
205C 12             PACK2: STAX  D        ;save end
205D C9                    RET            ;return
```

Unpacking BCD data.   Unpacking BCD data is the reverse of packing except that a leading 0, which may occur, must be removed. Again HL points to the start of the unpacked BCD data and DE points to the start of the packed BCD data. A flowchart of this subroutine appears in Fig. 10-9 and a complete listing of the software appears in Example 10-22. Here the packed data are first checked for an FFH (end code) to determine if the packed BCD number is a 0, and if it is, the subroutine is excited by storing an FFH in the unpacked string. If the first BCD digit is not a 0, all the packed digits are unpacked and stored in the memory location indirectly addressed by the HL register pair. After unpacking, any leading 0's are suppressed and the end code is stored in the memory.

BCD Addition

BCD addition is basically the same as binary addition except that the binary ADD command is followed by a special instruction called decimal accumulator adjust (DAA). The DAA instruction adds 00H, 06H, 60H, or 66H to reconvert the result of adding two BCD numbers together back into BCD. Example 10-23 illustrates some BCD additions and the effect of the DAA instruction on the result. In Example 10-23(a) a 06 is added to correct the result, and in Example 10-23(b) a 66 is added. In Example 10-25(b) the result generates a carry, which is considered the one hundred's position of the BCD result.

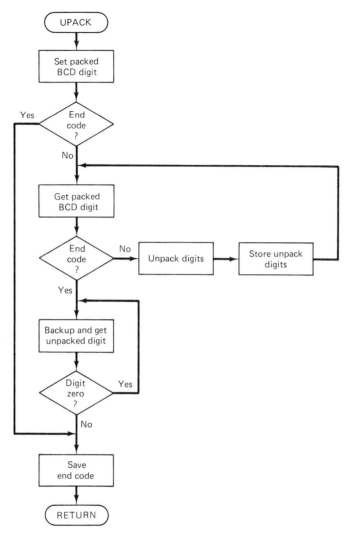

Figure 10-9   A flowchart for the UPACK subroutine which unpacks BCD digits into unpacked, 1 per byte, BCD numbers.

Suppose that two four-byte BCD packed numbers are stored in memory locations 2800H through 2803H and 2804H through 2807H. The result is stored in memory locations 2808H through 280CH (it takes an extra byte to store an overflow into the ninth digit if it occurs). To write a program for this problem, three pointers are required to address these three areas of the memory. A counter is also required so that the four bytes can be added. Figure 10-10 depicts the flowchart required to add these two numbers together; the program is listed in Example 10-24. The biggest problem in this program is using the registers to hold three addresses and a counter. The solu-

(EXAMPLE 10-22)

```
                          ;
                          ;subroutine to unpack BCD data
                          ;and suppress leading zeros.
                          ;
2060 1A          UPACK:   LDAX D          ;get packed data
2061 FE-FF                CPI  ENDC       ;check for zero
2063 FA-86-20             JM   UPK3       ;if zero
2066 1A          UPK1:    LDAX D          ;get packed data
2067 FE-FF                CPI  ENDC       ;check for end
2069 FA-7D-20             JM   UPK2       ;if end
206C E6-0F                ANI  ENDC       ;mask off MSBCD digit
206E 77                   MOV  M,A        ;save unpacked digit
206F 23                   INX  H
2070 F1                   LDAX D          ;get packed BCD
2071 13                   INX  D
2072 0F                   RRC             ;position MSBCD digit
2073 0F                   RRC
2074 0F                   RRC
2075 0F                   RRC
2076 E6-0F                ANI  0FH        ;mask off MSBCD digit
2078 77                   MOV  M,A        ;save unpacked digit
2079 23                   INX  H
207A C3-66-20             JMP  UPK1       ;repeat
207D 2B          UPK2:    DCX  H          ;backup
207E 7E                   MOV  A,M        ;check for zero
207F B7                   ORA  A
2080 C2-7D-20             JNZ  UPK2       ;if zero
2083 23                   INX  H
2084 3E-FF                MVI  A,ENDC     ;save end code
2086 77          UPK3:    MOV  M,A
2087 C9                   RET             ;return
2088 FF-00       ENDC:    EQU  0FFH       ;define end code
```

(Example 10-23)

(a)   0001 1000   (18 BCD)
     +   001 0010   + (12 BCD)
     ─────────────   ──────────
         0010 1010   (XX BCD)
     +   0000 0110   + (06)   DAA instruction
     ─────────────   ──────────
         0011 0000   (30 BCD)

(b)   1001 0111   (97 BCD)
     +   0100 1001   + (49 BCD)
     ─────────────   ──────────
         1110 0000   (XX BCD)
     +   0110 0110   + (66)   DAA instruction
     ─────────────   ──────────
         0100 0110   (46 BCD)   (carry = 1 for 146 BCD)

tion chosen is to store one of the pointers on the stack and use the XTHL instruction to access it. The XTHL instruction exchanges the number in the HL pair with the number on the stack, effectively allowing a program to use four register pairs.

(EXAMPLE 10-24)

```
                          ORG    2000H    ;origin
                 ;
                 ;program to add two BCD numbers.
                 ;
2000 11-00-28 START: LXI   D,NUMB1  ;point to first number
2003 21-08-28        LXI   H,ANS    ;point to answer
2006 E5              PUSH  H        ;stack answer pointer
2007 21-04-28        LXI   H,NUMB2  ;point to second number
200A 06-04           MVI   B,4      ;load counter
200C B7              ORA   A        ;clear carry
200D 12       LOOP:  LDAX  D        ;get first number
200E 8E              ADC   M        ;add second number
200F 27              DAA            ;correct answer
2010 E3              XTHL
2011 77              MOV   M,A      ;save answer
2012 23              INX   H        ;increment pointers
2013 E3              XTHL
2014 23              INX   H
2014 13              INX   D
2015 05              DCR   B        ;decrement counter
2016 C2-0D-20        JNZ   LOOP     ;if counter <> 0
2019 E1              POP   H        ;clear stack
201A C3-19-20 ENDP:  JMP   ENDP     ;end program
                 ;
                 ;equates
                 ;
201D 00-28    NUMB1: EQU   2800H    ;define NUMB1
201D 04-28    NUMB2: EQU   2804H    ;define NUMB2
281D 08-28    ANS:   EQU   2808H    ;define answer
```

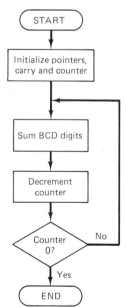

Figure 10-10 The flowchart for adding two 4-byte BCD numbers.

(Example 10-25)

Problem: 83 BCD
              – 14 BCD
                 ─────
                 69 BCD

Solution: 1001 1010 (9AH)
              – 0001 0100 (14 BCD)
                 ─────────
                 1000 0110 (86—ten's complement)
              + 1000 0011 (83 BCD)
                 ─────────
                 0000 1001
              + 0110 0000 DAA instruction
                 ─────────
                 0110 1001 (69 BCD)

(EXAMPLE 10-26)

```
                         ORG    2000H    ;origin
                      ;
                      ;program to subtract two BCD numbers.
                      ;
2000 11-00-28 START: LXI    D,NUMB1  ;point to first number
2003 21-08-28        LXI    H,ANS    ;point to answer
2006 E5              PUSH   H        ;stack answer pointer
2007 21-04-28        LXI    H,NUMB2  ;point to second number
200A 06-04           MVI    B,4      ;load counter
200C 37              STC             ;set carry
200D F5       LOOP:  PUSH   PSW      ;save carry
200E 3E-99           MVI    99H      ;generate 10's complement
200F 96              SUB    M
2010 4F              MOV    C,A      ;save 10's complement
2011 F1              POP    PSW      ;restore carry
2012 1A              LDAX   D        ;get first number
2013 89              ADC    C        ;form difference
2014 27              DAA             ;correct answer
2015 E3              XTHL
2016 77              MOV    M,A      ;save answer
2017 23              INX    H        ;increment pointers
2018 E3              XTHL
2019 23              INX    H
201A 13              INX    D
201B 05              DCR    B        ;decrement counter
201C C2-0D-20        JNZ    LOOP     ;if counter <> 0
201F E1              POP    H        ;clear stack
2020 C3-20-20 ENDP:  JMP    ENDP     ;end program
                     ;
                     ;equates
                     ;
2821 00-28    NUMB1: EQU    2800H    ;define NUMB1
2821 04-28    NUMB2: EQU    2804H    ;define NUMB2
2821 08-28    ANS:   EQU    2808H    ;define answer
```

BCD Subtraction

Unfortunately, the DAA instruction does not correct the result of a BCD subtraction in the 8085A microprocessor. This is easily overcome if the ten's complement of the subtrahend is added to the minuend. To form the ten's complement of a BCD number, the number is subtracted from a 9AH or a 99H plus 1. Example 10–25 illustrates this operation and also the BCD subtraction via ten's-complement addition.

The program listed in Example 10–24 is modified by including a series of instructions that generate the difference between the two BCD numbers as listed in Example 10–26. Here the carry is initially set and the number is ten's-complemented by subtracting it from 99H. The initial carry adds the 1 to the 99H, so that it becomes a 9AH.

10-7 SUMMARY

1. Eight-bit binary addition and subtraction is accomplished via immediate, register, and register indirect addressing, and 16-bit binary addition is accomplished via the double-addition instruction (DAD).
2. Whenever 8-bit numbers are summed, it is important to leave enough room for the result. In most cases 16 bits are required to hold the sum of even just a few 8-bit numbers.
3. Binary multiplication is carried out using any of three techniques: repeated addition and two methods of shifting and adding.
4. When numbers are multiplied together, the product is always a double-width product.
5. Signed multiplication requires that the signs of the multiplicand and multiplier be tested to see if they are the same or different. If they are different, the product is two's-complemented after multiplying, to change its sign to minus.
6. Binary multiplication is accomplished by one of two techniques: shifting and adding or shifting, comparing, subtracting, and setting bits in the quotient.
7. The quotient and the remainder are often binary integers that are equal in width to the divisor.
8. For signed division, the same rules that applied to signed multiplication apply except that the remainder and the quotient are both two's-complemented if negative.
9. Multiple-byte addition and subtraction require that the carry or borrow be rippled through the result from the least to the most significant byte. This carry or borrow ripple is accomplished by using either an add-with-carry instruction or a subtract-with-borrow instruction.
10. BCD numbers appear in a computer system's memory in two different forms: packed and unpacked. Packed BCD numbers are stored two digits per byte and unpacked BCD numbers are stored one digit per byte.

11. When BCD numbers are added, they are added as if they are binary numbers. The only difference between adding BCD numbers and binary numbers is that a BCD addition is followed by the execution of the DAA instruction, which adjusts the result.

12. The DAA instruction adjust the result of a BCD addition by adding a 00H, 06H, 60H, or 66H.

13. Because the DAA instruction will not adjust the result of a BCD subtraction, subtraction must be accomplished using the ten's-complement addition technique. The ten's complement is formed by subtracting the BCD number from a 99H and then adding 1 to it.

10-8 GLOSSARY

Borrow ripple   During multiple-byte subtraction a carry may occur in the least significant digit that must be rippled through to another more significant digit. If this occurs, it is often called a borrow ripple. (The borrow ripples through the carry flag in the 8085A microprocessor.)

Carry ripple   Whenever multiple-byte numbers are added, the carry that occurs and is transferred into a higher-order byte is called a carry ripple or sometimes a ripple carry.

Decimal accumulator adjust (DAA)   An instruction in the 8085A microprocessor instruction set that allows the sum of a BCD addition to be corrected into a BCD result.

Double-length product   Double-length products occur whenever numbers are multiplied together, and are always twice the width of the multiplier.

Multiple-byte number   Any number that is wider than B bits is considered a multiple-byte number.

Packed BCD number   A packed BCD number is constructed by placing two BCD digits in a byte.

Unpacked BCD number   Unpacked BCD numbers are stored a digit per byte.

QUESTIONS AND PROBLEMS

10-1. Write a sequence of instructions that will add the contents of the B register to the C register.

10-2. Write a sequence of instructions that will add the contents of the BC register pair to the DE register pair.

10-3. Modify the program listed in Example 10-2 so that it is capable of adding 300 numbers together.

10-4. Modify the program listed in Example 10-3 so that the answer after each subtraction is stored beginning at memory location 2820H. (*Hint:* This new program requires three pointers.)

10-5. Using the repeated-addition method of multiplication, write a subroutine that will multiply the HL register pair by the accumulator and leave the 32-bit most significant portion of the result in the DE register pair and the least significant part in the HL register pair.

10-6. Using the unsigned constant method of multiplication, develop a subroutine that will multiply the contents of the HL register pair times 13 decimal. The result should be left in the HL register pair.

10-7. Modify the unsigned multiplication subroutine of Example 10-11 so that it multiplies the accumulator times the 16-bit number in the HL register pair. The product is a 16-bit number in the HL register pair for this modification.

10-8. Continue the modification started in Question 10-7 so that the product is a 24-bit product stored in the BHL registers.

10-9. Can the accumulator be multiplied by $\frac{3}{8}$ using a modified unsigned constant-multiplication subroutine? If so, write the new subroutine.

10-10. Develop a signed binary division subroutine that will divide the number in the HL register pair by 8.

10-11. Convert the subroutine in Example 10-17 so that it divides the number in the HL register pair by the number in the C register.

10-12. What modification is required to allow the subroutine listed in Example 10-19 to add together two 64-bit numbers?

10-13. Why is the carry cleared in the subroutine listed in Example 10-20 before the actual subtraction occurs?

10-14. Would the PACK subroutine listed in Example 10-21 be shorter if it always packed eight BCD digits? If yes, write this new subroutine.

10-15. The DAA instruction can only be used to adjust the result of a BCD _____ .

10-16. Why is a POP H instruction included at the end of the subroutine listed in Example 10-24?

10-17. Why are XTHL instructions used in the subroutine listed in Example 10-24?

10-18. BCD subtraction is accomplished by adding the _____ complement of the subtrahend to the minuend.

10-19. Write a program that will subtract the number in the BC register pair from the number in the DE register pair and store the difference in the HL register pair. (You may not use the subtract-with-borrow instruction.)

10-20. Repeat Question 10-19 using the subtract with borrow instruction.

_____ chapter eleven _____

FLOATING-POINT ARITHMETIC

Floating-point arithmetic, or as it is sometimes called, real arithmetic, is found on occasion in microprocessor-based systems as user-written software. (Remember that a floating-point number is scientific notation in binary; refer to Section 3–4 if a brief review of floating-point numbers is necessary.) On most occasions the floating-point software is located within an interpreter or compiler program such as BASIC or Pascal. We present this chapter so that, if required, floating-point numbers, as generated by BASIC or Pascal, can be dealt with or, on the rare occasion requiring the user to write floating-point arithmetic subroutines, as a guide.

11–1 OBJECTIVES

Upon completion of this chapter, you will be able to:

1. Describe the makeup of an ANSI and an IEEE floating-point number
2. Convert between fixed-point and floating-point numbers
3. Add and subtract floating-point numbers
4. Multiply and divide floating-point numbers
5. Incorporate floating-point subroutines into software that you develop

11–2 FORMS OF FLOATING-POINT NUMBERS

There are two main forms of floating-point numbers in use today from the following organizations that determine standards: ANSI (American National Standards Institute)

182

and IEEE (Institute of Electrical and Electronic Engineers). Both forms find wide application, with the proposed IEEE standard used by many integrated arithmetic processing circuits such as the Intel 8087 Floating Point Processor. In this text we use the 32-bit or standard-length floating-point number. Due to increased accuracy requirements, some systems use a 64-bit version called a long real number.

ANSI Floating-Point Numbers

Figure 11–1 illustrates the ANSI four-byte floating point number and some examples. The first byte of a floating-point number is called its exponent or as it is sometimes called a characteristic or power. In addition to holding the 6-bit exponent of the floating-point number, byte 1 also contains the sign bit of the mantissa or as it is sometimes called, a coefficient, significand, or fraction and the sign bit of the exponent. The exponent is in true form if positive and in two's-complement form if negative. The next three bytes of the floating-point number contain a fractional binary mantissa which is normalized. A normalized mantissa is a fractional number that is less than 1 but greater or equal to 0.1. (A zero is a special case where all 32 bits of the floating-point number are 0.) This type of floating-point number is capable of storing a decimal number with about seven decimal digits of accuracy. The exponent allows a decimal exponent of about 10^{-19} to 10^{+19}.

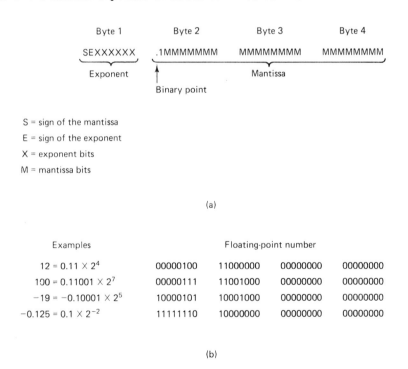

(a)

Examples	Floating-point number			
$12 = 0.11 \times 2^4$	00000100	11000000	00000000	00000000
$100 = 0.11001 \times 2^7$	00000111	11001000	00000000	00000000
$-19 = -0.10001 \times 2^5$	10000101	10001000	00000000	00000000
$-0.125 = 0.1 \times 2^{-2}$	11111110	10000000	00000000	00000000

(b)

Figure 11-1   ANSI 32-bit floating point numbers. (a) Byte format; (b) example ANSI floating point numbers.

IEEE Floating-Point Numbers

Figure 11–2 illustrates the standard form of a four byte IEEE floating-point number (IEEE-754, version 10.0), and some examples as used by many popular arithmetic floating-point processors. Byte 1 contains the sign of the mantissa and also 7 bits of the 7-bit biased exponent. (The eighth bit of the exponent is stored in the leftmost bit position of byte 2). The bias (modulo) used for an 8-bit exponent is 127 (7FH). If the number 12 converted to binary and normalized, it equals 1.1×2^3. The exponent (3) is added to the bias (7FH) and this is the number (82H) stored as the biased exponent. The remaining bits of the last three bytes contain a 23-bit mantissa with an implied 1. The left-hand bit of a normalized floating-point mantissa is always a 1. Since a 1 always appears in the left-hand bit, it is not stored in this form of a floating mantissa; instead, it is implicit or understood to be present. For the number 12 (1.1×2^3) the mantissa is a 0.1 instead of a 1.1 because of the implied 1-bit. This type of floating-point number is capable of storing a decimal number with about seven decimal digits of accuracy. The exponent allows a decimal exponent of about 10^{-38} to 10^{38}. A long IEEE floating-point number, which has a bias of 1023 and a 51-bit mantissa, is capable of storing a decimal number with about 18 decimal digits of accuracy. The exponent for the long floating-point number allows a decimal exponent of about 10^{-307} to 10^{308}—a very large number.

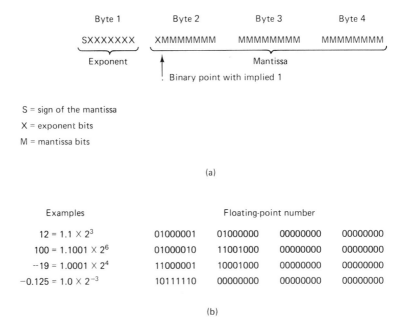

Figure 11-2   The proposed IEEE 32-bit floating point numbers, (a) Byte format; (b) example IEEE floating point numbers.

11-3 NUMERIC CONVERSION

In this section we describe how binary integers are converted to floating-point numbers. We also show how floating-point numbers are converted back to fixed-point numbers containing both integers and fractions.

Normalizing Binary Integers

Before a binary number can be used with floating-point arithmetic, it must be converted to a normalized floating-point number. (As stated in Section 11–2, in this text we use the proposed IEEE-754 version 10.0 floating-point number. To allow relatively short subroutines, for educational purposes, a modified 24-bit IEEE floating-point number is used that has a mantissa of 15 bits plus an implied 1-bit instead of the standard 23 bits plus an implied 1-bit, as illustrated in Fig. 11–3.) The subroutine will convert the signed 16-bit integer located in the HL register pair to a floating-point number located in the EHL registers, where E holds the sign of the mantissa and the exponent and HL contain a bit of the exponent and the 15-bit mantissa.

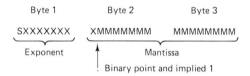

	Byte 1	Byte 2	Byte 3
	SXXXXXXX	XMMMMMMM	MMMMMMMM

Exponent   Mantissa

Binary point and implied 1

S = sign of the mantissa
X = exponent bits
M = mantissa bits

(a)

Examples   Floating-point numbers

$12 = 1.1 \times 2^3$	01000001	01000000	00000000
$100 = 1.1001 \times 2^6$	01000010	11001000	00000000
$-19 = 1.0001 \times 2^4$	11000001	10001000	00000000
$-0.125 = -1.0 \times 2^{-3}$	10111110	00000000	00000000
$4.5 = 1.001 \times 2^2$	01000000	10010000	00000000

(b)

Figure 11-3 The modified IEEE 24-bit floating point numbers used for the examples throughout this chapter. (a) Byte format; (b) example IEEE floating point numbers.

Figure 11–4 shows the flowchart for this subroutine, which is called NORM for normalize and Example 11–1 lists the subroutine itself. The NORM subroutine first checks to see if the integer is 0. If it is a 0, a 0 is placed in all three bytes of the result and the subroutine is ended. Next, the subroutine checks the sign of the

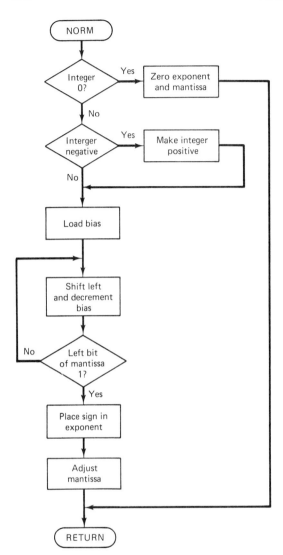

Figure 11-4 The flowchart of a subroutine that converts a 16-bit integer into a 24-bit floating point number.

integer to determine if it is negative. If it is negative, the integer is made positive and noted for later inclusion in the sign bit of the result in the E register. (The COMP subroutine is used to perform this negation, and it is used here and in the next portion of this section of the text.) Finally, an 8EH is loaded into the E register and HL are shifted left until the left position of H becomes a logic 1. For each shift the number in the E register is decremented. For example, if HL contains an 1000_2 the subroutine shifts it left 0CH places and a 0CH is subtracted from E. This leaves an 82H as the exponent (7FH + 3 = 82H). Once the number is normalized and the exponent is computed, it is shifted right and the carry is stored on top of the left

(Example 11-1.)

```
                         ORG   2020H      ;origin
2020 7C         NORM:    MOV   A,H        ;test for zero
2021 B5                  ORA   L
2022 5F                  MOV   E,A
2023 CA-40-20            JZ    ENDS       ;if zero
2026 7C                  MOV   A,H        ;test sign
2027 87                  ADD   A
2028 F5                  PUSH  PSW        ;save sign for later
2029 D2-2F-20            JNC   NORM1      ;if positive
202C CD-41-20            CALL  COMP       ;make positive
202F 1E-8F      NORM1:   MVI   E,8FH      ;load bias
2031 29         NORM2:   DAD   H          ;shift number
2032 1D                  DCR   E          ;decrement bias
2033 7C                  MOV   A,H        ;test for end
2034 B7                  ORA   A
2035 F2-31-20            JP    NORM2
2038 F1                  POP   PSW        ;get sign
2039 7B                  MOV   A,E        ;combine with exponent
203A 1F                  RAR
203B 5F                  MOV   E,A
203C 7C                  MOV   A,H        ;bit of exponent to H
203D 17                  RAL
203E 0F                  RRC
203F 67                  MOV   H,A
2040 C9         ENDS:    RET              ;return
                ;
                ;complement HL
                ;
2041 7C         COMP:    MOV   A,H        ;make negative
2042 2F                  CMA
2043 67                  MOV   H,A
2044 7D                  MOV   A,L
2045 2F                  CMA
2046 6F                  MOV   L,A
2047 23                  INX   H
2048 C9                  RET              ;return
```

bit of the H register. Next, the sign is added to the exponent to form byte 1 of the normalized floating-point number.

Converting a Floating-Point Number to a Fixed-Point Number

When a number is converted from floating-point form back into fixed-point form, there are generally two parts: an integer and a fraction. A subroutine that converts the floating-point number from the EHL registers into a 16-bit integer in BC and a 16-bit fraction in AD is listed in Example 11-2. The flowchart for this subroutine and the form of the results are illustrated in Fig. 11-5.

The floating-point number is first tested for a zero condition, and if it is zero, the integer and fraction are cleared and a return occurs. If the number is not zero, it is next checked to see if it is within the bounds of a 16-bit integer and fraction.

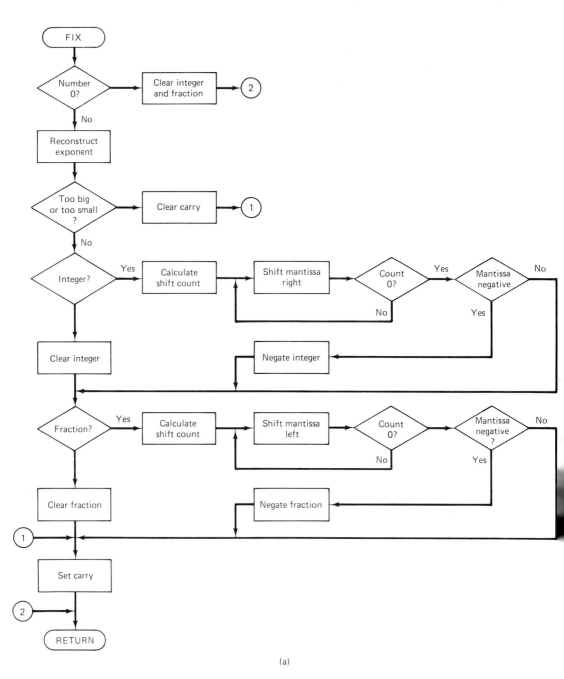

(a)

Figure 11-5   (a) A flowchart for converting a floating point number into an integer and fraction;
(b) the format of the 16-bit integer and 16-bit fraction.

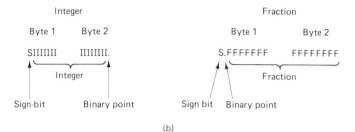

Figure 11-5 *(Continued)*

```
(Example 11-2 page 1 of 2)

                          ORG   2049H      ;origin
2049 7B          FIX:     MOV   A,E        ;test for zero
204A B4                   ORA   H
204B B5                   ORA   L
204C 47                   MOV   B,A
204D 4F                   MOV   C,A
204E 57                   MOV   D,A
204F CA-A5-20             JZ    ENDF       ;if zero
2052 7C                   MOV   A,H        ;reform exponent
2053 17                   RAL
2054 7B                   MOV   A,E
2055 17                   RAL
2056 47                   MOV   B,A        ;save it for fraction
2057 FE-8F                CPI   8FH        ;check exponent bounds
2059 D2-A6-20             JNC   ENDX       ;if too large
205C FE-71                CPI   71H
205E 3F                   CMC
205F D2-A6-20             JNC   ENDX       ;if too small
2062 E5                   PUSH  H          ;save mantissa
2063 3E-8F                MVI   A,8FH      ;form shift count
2065 90                   SUB   B
2066 57                   MOV   D,A
2067 FE-01                CPI   1          ;check for integer
2069 D2-72-20             JNC   FIX1       ;if integer
206C 21-00-00             LXI   H,0
206F C3-80-20             JMP   FIX3       ;go convert fraction
2072 7C          FIX1:    MOV   A,H        ;set implied one
2073 F6-80                ORI   80H
2075 67                   MOV   H,A
2076 CD-B0-20 FIX2:       CALL  SRI        ;shift HL right
2079 15                   DCR   D          ;decrement shift count
207A C2-76-20             JNZ   FIX2       ;if count <> 0
207D CD-A7-20             CALL  NEG        ;check for negative
2080 E3          FIX3:    XTHL             ;integer to stack
2081 E5                   PUSH  H          ;save mantissa
2082 7C                   MOV   A,H        ;set implied one
2083 F6-80                ORI   80H
2085 67                   MOV   H,A
2086 78                   MOV   A,B        ;form shift count
2087 D6-7F                SUI   7FH
2089 57                   MOV   D,A
208A CA-9B-20             JZ    FIX5
```

(Example 11-2 page 2 of 2)

```
208D  D2-96-20           JNC   FIX4      ;if fraction
2090  21-00-00           LXI   H,0
2093  C3-A1-20           JMP   FIX6
2096  29          FIX4:  DAD   H         ;adjust fraction
2097  15                 DCR   D
2098  C2-96-20           JNZ   FIX4      ;shift count <> 0
209B  CD-B0-20  FIX5:    CALL  SRI       ;adjust result
209E  CD-A7-20           CALL  NEG       ;check for negative
20A1  7C          FIX6:  MOV   A,H       ;place fraction in AD
20A2  55                 MOV   D,L
20A3  E1                 POP   H         ;restore mantissa
20A4  C1                 POP   B         ;place integer in BC
20A5  37          ENDF:  STC             ;set carry if valid
20A6  C9          ENDX:  RET             ;end subroutine
                  ;
                  ;subroutine to test for a negative mantissa
                  ;and negate HL.
                  ;
20A7  7B          NEG:   MOV   A,E       ;test for negative
20A8  B7                 ORA   A
20A9  F2-AF-20           JP    NEG1      ;if positive
20AC  CD-41-20           CALL  COMP      ;make positive
20AF  C9          NEG1:  RET             ;return
                  ;
                  ;subroutine to shift HL right
                  ;
20B0  B7          SRI:   ORA   A         ;clear carry
20B1  7C                 MOV   A,H       ;shift mantissa right
20B2  1F                 RAR
20B3  67                 MOV   H,A
20B4  7D                 MOV   A,L
20B5  1F                 RAR
20B6  6F                 MOV   L,A
20B7  C9                 RET             ;return
```

If it is out of bounds, a return occurs. Next, the integer portion is extracted by using some shifts. Similarly, the fractional portion is also generated by using shifts, leaving a 16-bit fraction in the AD registers. If the floating-point number is negative, both the integer and fractional portions are two's-complemented to make them negative. When the return occurs, the carry is set to indicate that AD and BC contain a valid fixed-point number. If the carry is cleared upon return, the original floating-point number was either too large or too small to convert to a fixed-point number.

11-4 FLOATING-POINT ADDITION AND SUBTRACTION

When adding or subtracting floating-point numbers, the binary points must be aligned just as with any other form (decimal) of addition or subtraction. If the exponents of the two numbers are equal, their binary points are aligned and addition or subtraction may be accomplished by adding or subtracting the mantissas. If the exponents are not equal, the smaller floating-point number's mantissa is shifted right. For each bit of shift, the exponent is incremented until it is equal to the exponent of the other number; then the addition or subtraction occurs.

Subroutine for Floating-Point Addition

A complete flowchart for floating-point addition is listed in Fig. 11–6. In the subroutine, depicted by this flowchart and Example 11–3, the floating-point number in the DBC registers is added to the floating-point number in the EHL registers and the sum is placed in the EHL registers. (Note that this subroutine destroys the original contents of the DBC registers.)

Notice that a series of tests are made on the two numbers before the actual addition occurs. The first test checks the signs of the mantissas to see if they differ. If the signs are different, a subtraction is indicated and the sign of DBC is complemented, followed by a jump to the floating-point subtraction subroutine (SUBF).

```
(Example 11-3 page 1 of 2.)

                        ORG   2800H    ;origin
                  ;
                  ;floating point addition EHL = EHL + DBC
                  ;return carry = overflow
                  ;
2800 7A      ADDF:  MOV   A,D      ;check sign bits
2801 AB             XRA   E
2802 F2-0C-28       JP    ADDF1    ;if signs are same
2805 7A             MOV   A,D      ;change sign
2806 EE-80          XRI   80H
2808 57             MOV   D,A
2809 C3-84-28       JMP   SUBF     ;go subtract
280C 7A      ADDF1: MOV   A,D      ;check for zero
280D B0             ORA   B
280E B1             ORA   C
280F CA-71-28       JZ    ADDF8    ;if zero
2812 7B             MOV   A,E      ;check for zero
2813 B4             ORA   H
2814 B5             ORA   L
2815 C2-1E-28       JNZ   ADDF2    ;if not zero
2818 CD-73-28       CALL  XCH      ;exchange numbers
281B C3-71-28       JMP   ADDF8
281E 7A      ADDF2: MOV   A,D
281F 32-72-28       STA   SIGN     ;save sign
2822 CD-7A-28       CALL  REC      ;reconstruct exponent
2825 CD-73-28       CALL  XCH      ;exchange numbers
2828 CD-7A-28       CALL  REC      ;reconstruct exponent
282B 7B             MOV   A,E      ;compare exponents
282C 92             SUB   D
282D D2-35-28       JNC   ADDF3    ;if positive
2830 CD-73-28       CALL  XCH      ;exchange numbers
2833 7B             MOV   A,E      ;compare numbers
2834 92             SUB   D
2835 CA-54-28 ADDF3: JZ   ADDF6    ;if exponents equal
2838 FE-10          CPI   16       ;check bounds
```

(Example 11-3 page 2 of 2)

```
283A DA-48-28          JC    ADDF4    ;if shift count < 16
283D 7B                MOV   A,E
283E 92                SUB   D
283F D2-5F-28          JNC   ADDF7    ;if positive
2842 CD-73-28          CALL  XCH
2845 C3-5F-28          JMP   ADDF7
2848 5F        ADDF4:  MOV   E,A
2849 CD-73-28          CALL  XCH
284C CD-B0-20 ADDF5:   CALL  SRI      ;shift right
284F 1C                INR   E
2850 15                DCR   D        ;decrement shift count
2851 C2-4C-28          JNZ   ADDF5    ;if shift count <> 0
2854 09        ADDF6:  DAD   B        ;add mantissas
2855 D2-5F-28          JNC   ADDF7    ;if no carry
2858 1C                INR   E
2859 CA-71-28          JZ    ADDF8    ;on error
285C CD-B0-20          CALL  SRI      ;shift right
285F 3A-72-28 ADDF7:   LDA   SIGN     ;get sign
2862 87                ADD   A        ;sign to carry
2863 7B                MOV   A,E      ;fix exponent
2864 57                MOV   D,A      ;save exponent
2865 1F                RAR
2866 5F                MOV   E,A
2867 7C                MOV   A,H
2868 E6-7F             ANI   7FH
286A 67                MOV   H,A      ;fix mantissa
286B 7A                MOV   A,D
286C 0F                RRC
286D E6-80             ANI   80H
286F B4                ORA   H
2870 67                MOV   H,A
2871 C9        ADDF8:  RET
               ;
2872           SIGN:   DS    1        ;reserve sign
               ;
               ;exchange DBC and EHL
               ;
2873 C5        XCH:    PUSH  B        ;exchange numbers
2874 E3                XTHL
2875 C1                POP   B
2876 7A                MOV   A,D
2877 53                MOV   D,E
2878 5F                MOV   E,A
2879 C9                RET            ;return
               ;
               ;reconstruct exponent and mantissa
               ;
287A 7C        REC:    MOV   A,H      ;reconstruct exponents
287B 87                ADD   A        ;to carry
287C 7B                MOV   A,E
287D 17                RAL
287E 5F                MOV   E,A
287F 7C                MOV   A,H      ;set implied one
2880 F6-80             ORI   80H
2882 67                MOV   H,A
2883 C9                RET            ;return
```

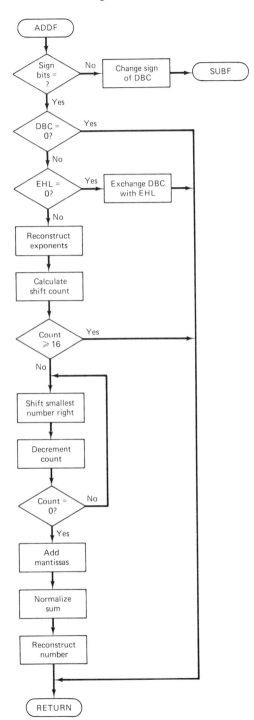

Figure 11-6   Flowchart for the floating point addition subroutine (ADDF) which adds the floating point number in DBC to EHL and leaves the sum in EHL.

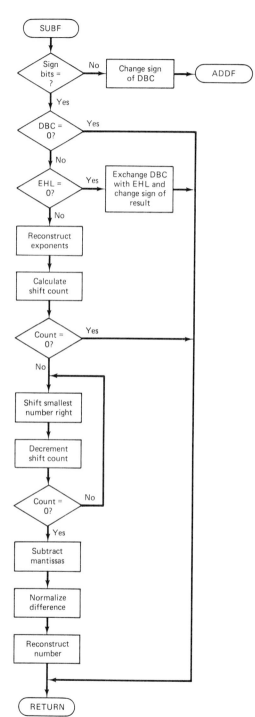

Figure 11-7 Flowchart for the floating point subtraction subroutine (SUBF) which subtracts DBC from EHL and leaves the result in EHL.

The next test determines if either of the floating-point numbers is zero. If either is zero, the result is the nonzero floating-point number, which is moved into EHL followed by a return. The exponents are now compared to see if they are equal. If equal, the mantissas are added and the sum is adjusted so that it is returned as a normalized floating-point number. If the exponents are not equal, the smallest mantissa is shifted right until they are equal or until it becomes a zero. If it becomes zero, the opposite number is returned from the subroutine as the sum, and if it is not zero, the two mantissas are added and the normalized sum is returned in the EHL registers. An error condition, indicated by a carry on return, is detected if the result exceeds the capacity of the floating-point number—an exponent overflow condition.

Subroutine for Floating-Point Subtraction

Floating-point subtraction is similar to addition except that the magnitudes of the numbers must be checked so that the smaller number is subtracted from the larger. This, and a few other checks, are depicted in the flowchart of Fig. 11–7 and the subroutine listing of Example 11–4. Notice that this flowchart is not all that different from the addition flowchart in Fig. 11–6.

```
(Example 11-4 page 1 of 3.)

                        ;
                        ;floating point subtraction EHL = EHL - DBC
                        ;return carry = underflow
                        ;
        2884 7A         SUBF:   MOV   A,D       ;check sign bits
        2885 AB                 XRA   E
        2886 F2-90-28           JP    SUBF1     ;if signs are same
        2889 7A                 MOV   A,D       ;change sign
        288A EE-80              XRI   80H
        288C 57                 MOV   D,A
        288D C3-00-28           JMP   ADDF      ;go add
        2890 7A         SUBF1:  MOV   A,D       ;check for zero
        2891 B0                 ORA   B
        2892 B1                 ORA   C
        2893 CA-33-29           JZ    SUBFB     ;if subtrahend is zero
        2896 7B                 MOV   A,E       ;check for zero
        2897 B4                 ORA   H
        2898 B5                 ORA   L
        2899 C2-A6-28           JNZ   SUBF2     ;if minuend <> 0
        289C CD-73-28           CALL  XCH       ;exchange numbers
        289F 7B                 MOV   A,E
        28A0 EE-80              XRI   80H       ;change sign
        28A2 5F                 MOV   E,A
        28A3 C3-33-29           JMP   SUBFB
        28A6 7B         SUBF2:  MOV   A,E       ;save sign
        28A7 32-72-28          STA   SIGN
        28AA CD-7A-28          CALL  REC       ;reconstruct exponent
        28AD CD-73-28          CALL  XCH       ;exchange numbers
        28B0 CD-7A-28          CALL  REC       ;reconstruct exponent
        28B3 92                 SUB   D         ;compare exponents
        28B4 C2-CF-28           JNZ   SUBF4
        28B7 78                 MOV   A,B       ;compare mantissas
```

(Example 11-4 page 2 of 3)

```
28B8 BC                    CMP  H
28B9 C2-BE-28              JNZ  SUBF3
28BC 79                    MOV  A,C
28BD BD                    CMP  L
28BE D2-0D-29 SUBF3:  JNC  SUBF8     ;go subtract
28C1 CD-73-28              CALL XCH       ;exchange numbers
28C4 3A-72-28              LDA  SIGN      ;change sign
28C7 EE-80                 XRI  80H
28C9 32-72-28              STA  SIGN
28CC C3-0D-29              JMP  SUBF8     ;go subtract
28CF 3A-72-28 SUBF4:  LDA  SIGN
28D2 EE-80                 XRI  80H
28D4 32-72-28              STA  SIGN
28D7 7B                    MOV  A,E       ;compare exponents
28D8 92                    SUB  D
28D9 D2-E9-28              JNC  SUBF5     ;if positive
28DC 3A-72-28              LDA  SIGN
28DF EE-80                 XRI  80H
28E1 32-72-28              STA  SIGN
28E4 CD-73-28              CALL XCH       ;exchange numbers
28E7 7B                    MOV  A,E       ;compare numbers
28E8 92                    SUB  D
28E9 FE-10    SUBF5:   CPI  16        ;check bounds
28EB DA-01-29              JC   SUBF6     ;if shift count < 16
28EE 7B                    MOV  A,E
28EF 92                    SUB  D
28F0 D2-21-29              JNC  SUBFA     ;if positive
28F3 3A-72-28              LDA  SIGN
28F6 EE-80                 XRI  80H
28F8 32-72-28              STA  SIGN
28FB CD-73-28              CALL XCH
28FE C3-21-29              JMP  SUBFA
2901 5F       SUBF6:   MOV  E,A
2902 CD-73-28              CALL XCH
2905 CD-B0-20 SUBF7:  CALL SRI       ;shift right
2908 1C                    INR  E
2909 15                    DCR  D         ;decrement shift count
290A C2-05-29              JNZ  SUBF7     ;if shift count <> 0
290D 79       SUBF8:   MOV  A,C       ;subtract
290E 95                    SUB  L
290F 6F                    MOV  L,A
2910 78                    MOV  A,B
2911 9C                    SBB  H
2912 67                    MOV  H,A
2913 7C       SUBF9:   MOV  A,H       ;normalize?
2914 B7                    ORA  A
2915 FA-21-29              JM   SUBFA     ;normalized
2918 1D                    DCR  E
2919 37                    STC
291A CA-33-29              JZ   SUBFB     ;on underflow
291D 29                    DAD  H
291E C3-13-29              JMP  SUBF9
2921 3A-72-28 SUBFA:  LDA  SIGN      ;get sign
2924 87                    ADD  A         ;sign to carry
2925 7B                    MOV  A,E       ;fix exponent
2926 57                    MOV  D,A       ;save exponent
2927 1F                    RAR
```

(Example 11-4 page 3 of 3)

```
2928 5F                  MOV   E,A
2929 7C                  MOV   A,H
292A E6-7F               ANI   7FH
292C 67                  MOV   H,A        ;fix mantissa
292D 7A                  MOV   A,D
292E 0F                  RRC
292F E6-80               ANI   80H
2931 B4                  ORA   H
2932 67                  MOV   H,A
2933 C9        SUBFB:    RET              ;return
```

Again, as with addition, the EHL registers holds the result and, for subtraction, the floating-point number in DBC (subtrahend) is subtracted from the contents of EHL (minuend). The first thing tested by the subtraction subroutine is a comparison of the signs of the floating-point numbers. If the signs differ, the number in the DBC registers is negated and the subroutine continues with the addition subroutine (ADDF). This conforms to standard practices for signed numbers. If the signs are the same, a check is made to determine if either number is zero. If one of the numbers is zero, the subroutine ends with the nonzero number in the EHL registers and the sign adjusted as required. Finally, the numbers' binary points are adjusted so that they are equal and the subtraction occurs, with the difference placed in the EHL registers. In certain cases this result must be normalized or shifted left and the sign may also require adjustment. During the normalization process an underflow may occur, resulting in an error. If an underflow occurs, a return is made with the carry flag set.

11–5 FLOATING-POINT MULTIPLICATION AND DIVISION

Floating-point multiplication and division are somewhat different from floating-point addition and subtraction because the mantissas do not need to be aligned before multiplying or dividing. Instead, the exponents are added together for multiplication or subtracted for division before the mantissas are multiplied or divided. Errors that occur during these operations are overflow for multiplication or division and a divide-by-zero error.

Subroutine for Floating-Point Multiplication

The subroutine illustrated in the flowchart of Figure 11–8 and the listing of Example 11–5 multiplies the floating-point number in the DBC registers times the floating-point number in the EHL register and leaves the product in the EHL registers. If an overflow condition (sum of exponents too large) is encountered, the carry flag is set and a return occurs. If the product is valid, a return occurs with carry cleared and the product is found in the EHL registers.

As you can see from the flowchart, the first thing checked is whether either number is zero. If either number is zero, the subroutine returns the zero as the result of the multiplication.

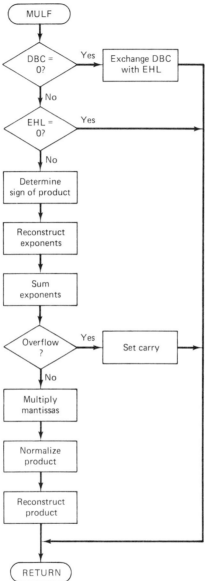

Figure 11-8 Flowchart for the floating point multiplication subroutine (MULF) which multiplies EHL by DBC and leaves the product in EHL.

Next, the signs are compared to determine the sign of the product (like signs produce a positive product and unlike signs produce a negative product). The exponents are now added together and their sum is checked for an overflow condition, which results in an overflow error. If no overflow occurs, the mantissas are now multiplied together, producing the product. After multiplying the mantissas together, the product is normalized, if required, and the sign is adjusted as indicated by the earlier comparison before a return from the sutroutine occurs with the product in the EHL registers.

(Example 11-5 page 1 of 2)

```
                      ;
                      ;subroutine to multiply where EHL = DBC x EHL
                      ;return carry = overflow
                      ;
2934 7B         MULF:  MOV   A,E      ;test multiplicand for O
2935 B4                ORA   H
2936 B5                ORA   L
2937 CA-99-29          JZ    MULF7    ;if zero
293A 7A                MOV   A,D      ;test multiplier for O
293B BO                ORA   B
293C B1                ORA   C
293D C2-46-29          JNZ   MULF1    ;if not zero
2940 CD-73-28          CALL  XCH      ;exchange numbers
2943 C3-99-29          JMP   MULF7    ;if zero
2946 7A        MULF1:  MOV   A,D      ;compare signs
2947 AB                XRA   E
2948 32-72-28          STA   SIGN     ;save sign of product
294B CD-7A-28          CALL  REC      ;reconstruct exponent
294E CD-73-28          CALL  XCH      ;exchange
2951 CD-7A-28          CALL  REC      ;reconstruct exponent
2954 7A                MOV   A,D      ;add exponents
2955 D6-7F             SUI   7FH
2957 57                MOV   D,A
2958 7B                MOV   A,E
2959 D6-7F             SUI   7FH
295B 82                ADD   D
295C DA-99-29          JC    MULF7    ;on overflow
295F C6-7F             ADI   7FH
2961 4F                MOV   C,A      ;save exponent
2962 58                MOV   E,B      ;truncate multiplicand
2963 16-00             MVI   D,O
2965 7C                MOV   A,H      ;truncate multiplier
2966 21-00-00          LXI   H,O      ;clear product
2969 B7        MULF2:  ORA   A        ;clear carry
296A CA-78-29          JZ    MULF4    ;if done
296D 1F                RAR            ;bit to carry
296E D2-72-29          JNC   MULF3    ;if no carry
2971 19                DAD   D
2972 EB        MULF3:  XCHG           ;adjust multiplicand
2973 29                DAD   H
2974 EB                XCHG
2975 C3-69-29          JMP   MULF2
2978 59        MULF4:  MOV   E,C      ;reload exponent
2979 7C        MULF5:  MOV   A,H      ;normalize product
297A B7                ORA   A
297B FA-87-29          JM    MULF6    ;if normalized
297E 29                DAD   H
297F 1D                DCR   E
2980 37                STC
2981 CA-99-29          JZ    MULF7    ;on overflow
2984 C3-79-29          JMP   MULF5
2987 7C        MULF6:  MOV   A,H      ;reconstruct mantissa
2988 E6-7F             ANI   7FH
298A 67                MOV   H,A
298B 7B                MOV   A,E
298C OF                RRC
298D E6-80             ANI   80H
```

(Example 11-5 page 2 of 2)

```
298F B4                ORA  H
2990 67                MOV  H,A
2991 3A-72-28          LDA  SIGN    ;reconstruct exponent
2994 87                ADD  A       ;sign to carry
2995 7B                MOV  A,E
2996 1F                RAR
2997 5F                MOV  E,A
2998 B7                ORA  A       ;clear carry
2999 C9         MULF7: RET          ;return
```

Subroutine for Floating-Point Division

The main differences between floating-point multiplication and floating-point division are that the exponents are subtracted instead of added and the mantissas are divided instead of multiplied. The subroutine for division divides the number in the DBC registers into the number in the EHL registers and leaves the quotient in the EHL registers. See Fig. 11-9 for the flowchart of this subroutine and Example 11-6 for the subroutine listing. When the flowcharts for multiplication and division are compared, there are only a few differences. One difference is that the result is zero only if the dividend is initially zero and an error occurs if the divisor is initially zero. The only other differences are that the exponents are subtracted instead of added and the mantissas are divided instead of multiplied. Again an error condition—divide overflow or divide by zero—is indicated by a return with the carry set.

(Example 11-6 page 1 of 2)

```
                       ;
                       ;subroutine to divide where EHL = EHL / DBC
                       ;return carry = overflow
                       ;
299A 7B         DIVF:  MOV  A,E     ;test dividend for zero
299B B4                ORA  H
299C B5                ORA  L
299D CA-13-2A          JZ   DIVF6   ;if zero
29A0 7A                MOV  A,D     ;test multiplier for zero
29A1 B0                ORA  B
29A2 B1                ORA  C
29A3 37                STC
29A4 CA-13-2A          JZ   DIVF6   ;if zero error
29A7 7A                MOV  A,D     ;compare signs
29A8 AB                XRA  E
29A9 32-72-28          STA  SIGN    ;save sign of quotient
29AC CD-7A-28          CALL REC     ;reconstruct exponent
29AF CD-73-28          CALL XCH     ;exchange
29B2 CD-7A-28          CALL REC     ;reconstruct exponent
29B5 CD-73-28          CALL XCH     ;reposition numbers
29B8 7B                MOV  A,E     ;calculate exponent
29B9 92                SUB  D
29BA C6-80             ADI  80H     ;add bias
29BC 32-14-2A          STA  EXP     ;save exponent
```

(Example 11-6 page 2 of 2)

```
29BF CD-B0-20            CALL SRI
29C2 CD-73-28            CALL XCH
29C5 CD-B0-20            CALL SRI
29C8 CD-73-28            CALL XCH
29CB EB                  XCHG
29CC 21-00-00            LXI  H,0        ;clear quotient
29CF 3E-10               MVI  A,16       ;load count
29D1 F5                  PUSH PSW
29D2 C3-DA-29            JMP  DIVF2
29D5 F5         DIVF1:   PUSH PSW        ;save count
29D6 29                  DAD  H          ;shift left
29D7 EB                  XCHG
29D8 29                  DAD  H
29D9 EB                  XCHG
29DA D5         DIVF2:   PUSH D
29DB 7B                  MOV  A,E        ;compare
29DC 91                  SUB  C
29DD 5F                  MOV  E,A
29DE 7A                  MOV  A,D
29DF 98                  SBB  B
29E0 57                  MOV  D,A
29E1 DA-E7-29            JC   DIVF3      ;if dividend smaller
29E4 F1                  POP  PSW
29E5 2C                  INR  L
29E6 D5                  PUSH D
29E7 D1         DIVF3:   POP  D
29E8 F1                  POP  PSW        ;get count
29E9 3D                  DCR  A          ;decrement count
29EA C2-D5-29            JNZ  DIVF1
29ED 3A-14-2A            LDA  EXP
29F0 5F                  MOV  E,A
29F1 7C         DIVF4:   MOV  A,H        ;normalize quotient
29F2 B7                  ORA  A
29F3 FA-FF-29            JM   DIVF5
29F6 29                  DAD  H
29F7 1D                  DCR  E
29F8 37                  STC
29F9 CA-13-2A            JZ   DIVF6
29FC C3-F1-29            JMP  DIVF4
29FF 7C         DIVF5:   MOV  A,H        ;adjust mantissa
2A00 E6-7F               ANI  7FH
2A02 67                  MOV  H,A
2A03 7B                  MOV  A,E        ;get exponent
2A04 1F                  RAR
2A05 5F                  MOV  E,A        ;save exponent
2A06 1F                  RAR
2A07 E6-80               ANI  80H
2A09 B4                  ORA  H
2A0A 67                  MOV  H,A        ;combine with mantissa
2A0B 3A-72-28            LDA  SIGN
2A0E E6-80               ANI  80H        ;get sign bit
2A10 B3                  ORA  E
2A11 5F                  MOV  E,A        ;place sign in exponent
2A12 B7                  ORA  A
2A13 C9         DIVF6:   RET             ;return
                ;
2A14            EXP:     DS   1          ;reserve for exponent
```

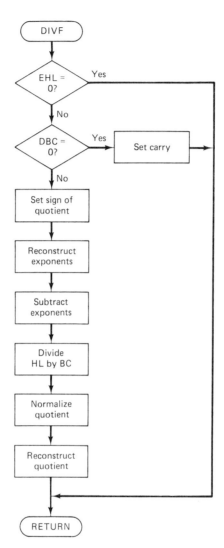

Figure 11-9 Flowchart for the floating point division subroutine (DIVF) which divides EHL by DBC and leaves the result in EHL.

11-6 SUMMARY

1. Floating-point arithmetic (binary scientific notation) is often called real arithmetic and it is used because of its ability to represent integers, fractions, and mixed numbers.

2. Two main forms of floating-point numbers are found in widespread use today: ANSI (American Standards Institute) and IEEE-754 version 10.0 (a standard proposed by the Institute of Electrical and Electronic Engineers).

3. A floating-point number is composed of two parts: the exponent, which is used to indicate the placement of the binary point in the mantissa, and the mantissa,

which holds a fraction between 0.1_2 and less than 1.0_2 for ANSI and between 1.0 and less than 2.0 for IEEE.

4. The exponent of a floating-point number is often called a characteristic or power and the mantissa of a floating-point number is often called a coefficient, significand, or fraction.

5. The ANSI form of the floating-point number is four bytes in length, with the first byte containing the signs of both the exponent and mantissa and also the exponent. The remaining three bytes contain a binary fraction that is equal or greater than 0.1_2 and less than 1.0_2.

6. The IEEE (IEEE-754 version 10.0) form of the floating-point number is four bytes in length, with the first byte containing the sign of the mantissa and part (7 bits) of the biased 8-bit exponent. The remaining three bytes hold the remaining bit of the exponent and an implied one-bit mantissa.

7. When a number is normalized, it is shifted to the left until the left bit of the result is a 1. As it is shifted, the exponent is increased in value by one for each bit of the shift.

8. If a floating-point number is converted to a fixed-point number, there are generally two parts: an integer and a fraction.

9. To add or subtract floating-point numbers, the binary points must be aligned. This is accomplished by shifting the smaller of the numbers to the right until the points are aligned. Once aligned, the numbers are added or subtracted and normalized to produce the floating-point sum or difference.

10. Floating-point multiplication and division are similar because for multiplication the exponents are added and then the mantissas are multiplied, and for division the exponents are subtracted and then the mantissas are divided. Multiplication and division can result in an overflow, and division can result in a divide-by-zero error.

11-7 GLOSSARY

ANSI The American National Standards Institute.

ANSI floating-point format A form of floating-point number that contains a 6-bit exponent, a 24-bit mantissa, and 2 sign bits, one for the mantissa and one for the exponent.

Bias The value added to the binary power of 2 to form the exponent in the IEEE format floating-point number.

Characteristic *See* Exponent.

Coefficient *See* Mantissa.

Exponent The portion of a floating-point number that is used to locate the binary point. If the exponent is $+2$, the binary point of the mantissa is moved to the right two places to convert it back into a mixed binary number.

Floating-point number The binary counterpart to scientific notation where the fraction is a binary number ranging in value from 0.1_2 to less than 1.0_2 and the exponent is a binary power.

Fraction   See Mantissa.

IEEE   The Institute of Electrical and Electronic Engineers.

IEEE floating-point number   A form of floating-point number that contains an 8-bit biased exponent, a 23-bit mantissa, plus an implied 1-bit and a sign bit for the mantissa. This form is proposed in the standard—IEEE-754 version 10.0.

Implied 1   In a floating-point number this is the logic 1 bit in the leftmost bit position that is not present but implied to be present. The implied 1 saves one bit of storage in the floating-point mantissa, allowing greater accuracy in a given number of bits.

Mantissa   The fractional portion of a floating-point number whose value is greater than or equal to 0.1_2 and less than 1.0_2. The only exception to this is for a number equal to zero; here the mantissa is zero. In certain standards, if the number overflows, the mantissa and exponent are all ones.

Normalized   A normalized floating-point number is one in which the left-hand bit of the mantissa is a logic 1.

Power   See Exponent.

Real number   See Floating-point number.

Significand   See Mantissa.

QUESTIONS AND PROBLEMS

11-1. Floating-point numbers are often called _____ numbers.

11-2. Floating-point numbers are often found used with what type of software?

11-3. What two types of floating-point numbers are found in widespread application?

11-4. List another name for the exponent of a floating-point number.

11-5. List another name for the mantissa of a floating-point number.

11-6. Describe the ANSI format of a floating-point number.

11-7. Describe the IEEE format of a floating-point number.

11-8. Convert the following decimal numbers to ANSI format floating-point numbers.
   (a) 1.0
   (b) 2.5
   (c) 1023.75
   (d) − 16.0625
   (e) − 212.125

11-9. Repeat Question 11–8 converting to the IEEE format floating-point number.

11-10. Convert the following binary representations of ANSI floating-point numbers to decimal.
   (a) 00000010 11000000 00000000 00000000
   (b) 10001111 10110000 10000000 00000000
   (c) 01111110 10001000 00000000 00000000
   (d) 00000000 00000000 00000000 00000000
   (e) 11111011 11111000 00000000 00000000

11-11. Convert the following binary representations of IEEE floating-point numbers to
decimal.
   (a) 01000000 00000000 00000000 00000000
   (b) 01000010 11100100 00000000 00000000
   (c) 10111111 00100000 00000000 00000000
   (d) 00000000 00000000 00000000 00000000
   (e) 01000011 11001000 00000000 00000000

11-12. Rewrite the binary floating-point numbers of Question 11–11 in the three-byte IEEE
format used in most of this chapter.

11-13. What does the NORM subroutine (Example 11–1) generate if the HL register pair equals
0000H when it is called?

11-14. Explain how the COMP subroutine (Example 11–1) two's-complements the number
in the HL register pair.

11-15. Why does the FIX subroutine (Example 11–2) check the range of the integer and
fraction?

11-16. Write a program that uses the floating-point addition subroutine (ADDF) to add decimal
number 100 to decimal number 52.

11-17. Write a program that uses the floating-point subtraction subroutine (SUBF) to subtract a 200 decimal from a 300 decimal.

11-18. Describe the differences between the floating-point multiplication subroutine and the
floating-point division subroutine.

11-19. Using the floating-point subroutines presented in this chapter, write a program that
will solve the following equation. (Assume that number A is stored at memory location 3000H through 3002H, B is stored at 3003H through 3005H, C is at 3006H through
3008H, and D is at 3009H through 300BH.)

$$A = B + (C*D)/2$$

chapter twelve

DATA CONVERSION ALGORITHMS

In many systems, much of the microprocessor's time is spent converting data from one form to another. An example is a keyboard. Whenever data are entered through a keyboard, they are entered one decimal character at a time. A 109 is entered as a 1, followed by a 0, followed by a 9. Unfortunately, many systems require numbers in binary form, so these three decimal digits are converted into binary by a data conversion subroutine.

This chapter covers a wide variety of data conversion algorithms that are sure to be found in routine programming for most microprocessor-based systems. Some of the conversions explained are: ASCII to BCD, BCD to ASCII, BCD to binary, binary to BCD, and string extraction and scanning.

12-1 OBJECTIVES

Upon completion of this chapter, you will be able to:

1. Convert ASCII data into hexadecimal or BCD and convert BCD or hexadecimal into ASCII
2. Convert BCD data as entered from a keyboard into binary as used by many systems
3. Convert binary data into BCD data for use on printers and displays
4. Extract an ASCII character string from an array of character strings
5. Remove an ASCII-coded number from any character string

12-2 ASCII CODE CONVERSION

At first glance ASCII code conversion seems trivial because it is rather easy to convert from an ASCII-coded number into a BCD number, or vice versa. The ASCII-coded numbers range from 30H through 39H (see Appendix D) for the decimal numbers 0 through 9. To convert from BCD to ASCII, a 30H is added to the ASCII number, and to convert from ASCII to BCD, a 30H is subtracted from the ASCII number. It is more difficult to convert between hexadecimal and ASCII code.

ASCII-to-Hexadecimal Code Conversion

Again refer to the ASCII codes listed in Appendix D and notice that the letters A through F are coded with 41H through 46H. It would be much easier for code conversion if these letters would be coded 3AH through 3FH. A 30H could be subtracted from any ASCII-coded hexadecimal number 0 through F. Because the numbers and letters are separated by a bias of 7, the ASCII-coded characters must be examined to determine if they are numbers (0 through 9) or letters (A through F). If they are numbers, a 30H is subtracted, and if they are letters, a 37H is subtracted. This process is illustrated in the flowchart of Fig. 12-1 and subroutine listing in Example 12-1.

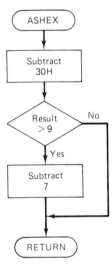

Figure 12-1 Flowchart for converting ASCII hexadecimal data to hexadecimal data.

(EXAMPLE 12-1)

```
                        ;
                        ;subroutine to convert ASCII to hexadecimal
                        ;
2800 D6-30     ASHEX:  SUI   30H     ;reduce by 30H
2802 FE-0A             CPI   0AH     ;test for letter
2804 DA-09-28          JC    ASHX1   ;if number
2807 D6-07             SUI   7       ;reduce by 7 more
2809 C9        ASHX1:  RET           ;return
```

Hexadecimal-to-ASCII Code Conversion

Converting from hexadecimal to ASCII code is almost the same as converting from ASCII code to hexadecimal except that instead of subtracting 30H (numbers) or 37H (letters), they are added to the hexadecimal number to generate the ASCII code. This is illustrated in the flowchart of Fig. 12–2 and the subroutine listing of Example 12–2.

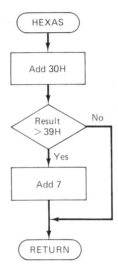

Figure 12-2 Standard flowchart for converting hexadecimal data to ASCII hexadecimal data.

(EXAMPLE 12–2)

```
                    ;
                    ;subroutine to convert hexadecimal to ASCII
                    ;10 bytes in length
                    ;
280A C6-30    HEXAS:  ADI   30H   ;increase by 30H
280C FE-3A            CPI   3AH   ;test for letter
280E DA-13-28         JC    HXAS1 ;if number
2811 C6-07            ADI   7     ;increase by 7 more
2813 C9       HXAS1:  RET         ;return
```

A secondary hexadecimal-to-ASCII conversion algorithm.   A shorter technique for this conversion is available on the 8085A microprocessor if the DAA instruction is a part of the conversion to ASCII (see Example 12–3). In this subroutine, which is very short, the number is adjusted with the DAA instruction so that its most significant half-byte (MSHB) is 0 or 1. (A number 0 through 9 results in a MSHB of 0 and a letter A through F results in a MSHB of 1.)

Next, an F0H is added so that the carry is set for a letter and cleared for a number. (A number results in an F in the MSHB with no carry and a letter results in a 0 for the MSHB with a carry.) Finally, a 40H is added with the carry generated, resulting in the ASCII codes 30H through 39H for numbers and the ASCII codes 41H through 46H for letters.

(EXAMPLE 12-3)

```
                      ;
                      ;short subroutine to convert hexadecimal to ASCII
                      ;7 bytes in length
                      ;
2814 B7      SHXA:   ORA  A       ;clear carrys
2815 27              DAA          ;adjust accumulator
2816 C6-F0           ADI  0F0H    ;add bias
2818 CE-40           ACI  40H     ;convert to ASCII
281A C9              RET          ;return
```

12-3 BCD-TO-BINARY CONVERSION

Converting BCD numbers into binary numbers is easy if the number is between 0 and 9 because there is no conversion. It is more difficult when the number exceeds 9. The most common method for BCD-to-binary conversion is to take the BCD number and multiply the ten's digit by 10 and add it to the unit digit. This works fine as long as the number is a two-digit BCD number. A three-digit number has its hundred's position multiplied by 100, its ten's digit multiplied by 10, and then the hundred's, ten's, and unit's digits are added together.

The BCD-to-Binary Conversion Algorithm (Integers)

From the prior description of BCD-to-binary conversion, it is easy to generate the conversion algorithm. Starting with the most significant digit of a variable-length BCD number and a 0 value for the binary result, multiply the result by 10 and add the digit. This is repeated until all the BCD digits of the number are added to the result. Example 12-4 shows how a few BCD numbers are converted to binary using this algorithm. (Of course, in the computer the result, multiplication by 10, and the addition are accomplished in binary.)

(Example 12-4)

(a) Convert 109 BCD to binary:

$$0 \times 10 + 1 = 1$$
$$1 \times 10 + 0 = 10$$
$$10 \times 10 + 9 = 109$$

(b) Convert 2001 BCD to binary:

$$0 \times 10 + 2 = 2$$
$$2 \times 10 + 0 = 20$$
$$20 \times 10 + 0 = 200$$
$$200 \times 10 + 1 = 2001$$

The flowchart for this algorithm is illustrated in Fig. 12–3 and the subroutine is listed in Example 12–5. In this example software the BCD number is assumed to be stored beginning at the memory location indirectly addressed by the DE register pair and the result is returned in the HL register pair. The number can be anything from 0 through 65,535 in value and it is assumed to end with an ASCII carriage return code (ODH). The number could also be in ASCII code if a SUI 30H (ASCII-to-BCD conversion) is placed in the subroutine as the first instruction.

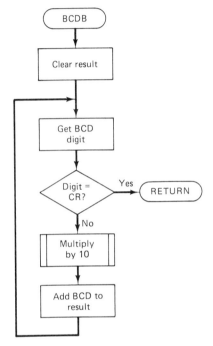

Figure 12-3 Flowchart for converting BCD integers into binary integers. The flowchart for multiply by 10 is not shown.

(EXAMPLE 12-5)

```
              ;
              ;subroutine to convert BCD to binary (integer)
              ;result = HL register pair
              ;DE indirectly address BCD number
              ;BCD number must end with a CR
              ;range 0 -- 65,536
              ;
2800 21-00-00 BCDB:  LXI  H,O    ;clear result
2803 1A       BCDB1: LDAX D      ;get BCD digit
2804 FE-OD           CPI  ODH    ;check for end
2806 CA-16-28        JZ   BCDB2  ;if CR end subroutine
2809 CD-17-28        CALL MUL10  ;multiply result times 10
280C 85              ADD  L      ;add BCD digit to result
280D 6F              MOV  L,A
280E 7C              MOV  A,H
280F CE-00           ACI  O
2811 67              MOV  H,A
2812 13              INX  D      ;address next digit
```

```
2813 C3-03-28            JMP   BCDB1  ;convert next digit
2816 C9          BCDB2: RET          ;return
                       ;
                       ;multiply HL times 10
                       ;
2817 29          MUL10: DAD   H      ;2 X HL
2818 44                 MOV   B,H    ;save 2 X HL
2819 4D                 MOV   C,L
281A 29                 DAD   H      ;4 X HL
281B 29                 DAD   H      ;8 X HL
281C 09                 DAD   B      ;10 X HL
281D C9                 RET          ;return
```

Example 12-5 *(Continued)*

The BCD-to-Binary Conversion Algorithm (Fractions)

The conversion algorithm for converting a BCD fraction to a binary fraction is similar to the integer conversion algorithm except that the numbers are divided by 10. Example 12-6 illustrates a few BCD fractions being converted to binary. Notice that the first digit is divided by 10, the second by 100, and so on. The results of these divisions are added together to produce a binary fraction.

(Example 12-6)

(a) Convert 0.25 BCD to binary:

$$2/10 = 0.2$$
$$5/100 = \underline{0.05}$$
$$0.25$$

(b) Convert 0.013 BCD to binary:

$$0/10 = 0.0$$
$$1/100 = 0.01$$
$$3/1000 = \underline{0.003}$$
$$0.013$$

This conversion algorithm is illustrated in Fig. 12–4 and the subroutine is listed in Example 12-7. Notice that the subroutine uses the MUL10 subroutine from Example 12-5 to change the number used for division by a factor of 10 each time the

```
(EXAMPLE 12-7 page 1 of 2)

                       ;
                       ;subroutine to convert BCD to binary (fraction)
                       ;result = HL register pair
                       ;DE indirectly address BCD number
                       ;BCD number must end with a CR
                       ;range 0 -- 1/65,535
                       ;
281E 21-00-00 BCDF:    LXI   H,0    ;clear result
2821 01-0A-00          LXI   B,10   ;start divisor at 10
```

(EXAMPLE 12-7 page 2 of 2)

```
2824 1A        BCDF1: LDAX D      ;get BCD digit
2825 FE-0D            CPI  0DH    ;test for end
2827 CA-3B-28         JZ   BCDF2  ;if CR detected
282A D5               PUSH D
282B CD-3C-28         CALL DIV    ;divide A by BC, result DE
282E 19               DAD  D      ;add to result in HL
282F D1               POP  D
2830 C5               PUSH B      ;position divisor
2831 E3               XTHL
2832 CD-17-28         CALL MUL10  ;multiply by 10
2835 E3               XTHL        ;reposition divisor
2836 C1               POP  B
2837 13               INX  D      ;index next BCD digit
2838 C3-24-28         JMP  BCDF1  ;convert next digit
283B C9        BCDF2: RET         ;return
                      ;
                      ;divide A by BC and place result in DE
                      ;
283C E5        DIV:   PUSH H      ;save HL
283D C5               PUSH B      ;save BC
283E 21-00-00         LXI  H,0    ;clear quotient
2841 B7               ORA  A      ;check for zero
2842 CA-73-28         JZ   DIV4   ;if 0
2845 5F               MOV  E,A    ;place dividend in DE
2846 16-00            MVI  D,0
2848 3E-11            MVI  A,17   ;load counter
284A F5               PUSH PSW    ;save counter
284B C3-53-28         JMP  DIV2   ;go divide
284E F5        DIV1:  PUSH PSW    ;save counter
284F 29               DAD  H      ;shift left
2850 EB               XCHG
2851 29               DAD  H
2852 EB               XCHG
2853 D5        DIV2:  PUSH D
2854 7B               MOV  A,E    ;compare
2855 91               SUB  C
2856 5F               MOV  E,A
2857 7A               MOV  A,D
2858 98               SBB  B
2859 57               MOV  D,A
285A DA-60-28         JC   DIV3   ;if dividend smaller
285D F1               POP  PSW
285E 2C               INR  L
285F D5               PUSH D
2860 D1        DIV3:  POP  D
2861 F1               POP  PSW    ;get count
2862 3D               DCR  A      ;decrement count
2863 C2-4E-28         JNZ  DIV1   ;if count not zero
2866 78               MOV  A,B    ;divide BC by 2
2867 1F               RAR
2868 47               MOV  B,A
2869 79               MOV  A,C
286A 1F               RAR
286B 4F               MOV  C,A
286C 93               SUB  E      ;round up quotient
286D 78               MOV  A,B
286E 9A               SBB  D
```

```
286F DA-73-28          JC   DIV4   ;if not rounded
2872 23                INX  H      ;round up quotient
2873 EB        DIV4:   XCHG        ;place quotient in DE
2874 C1                POP  B      ;restore BC
2875 E1                POP  H      ;restore HL
2876 C9                RET         ;return
```

Example 12-7 *(Continued)*

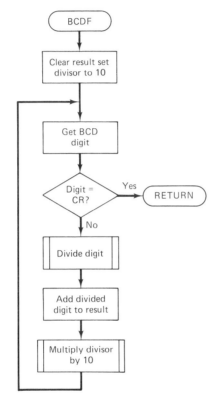

Figure 12-4 Flowchart for converting BCD fractions into binary fractions. The flowcharts for dividing and multiplying by 10 are not shown.

subroutine converts another BCD digit. Like Example 12–5 this subroutine converts a BCD fractional number stored in the memory location indexed by the DE register pair into a binary fraction in the HL register pair. The range of the fraction must be within 0.0 to 1/65,535, and the result may contain a slight rounding error due to the repeated divisions.

12-4 BINARY-TO-BCD CONVERSION

Binary-to-BCD conversions are required to output decimal data in any computer system. This type of conversion is as simple as BCD-to-binary conversion except that the process is a little different. To convert from binary to BCD, the binary number is divided by 10 and the remainders become the BCD digits of the decimal equivalent.

Binary-to-BCD Conversion Algorithm (Integers)

From the prior description of binary-to-BCD conversion it is rather simple to write an algorithm for binary-to-BCD conversion. Starting with the binary number to be converted, divide by 10. The remainder becomes the least significant digit of the BCD number and the quotient is again divided by 10. The division process continues until the quotient becomes a zero. Example 12-8 shows how a few binary numbers are converted to BCD using this algorithm.

(Example 12-8)

(a) Convert 100101_2 to BCD:

$$100101_2/1010_2 \;=\; q.\; 11_2 \quad r.\; 111_2 \qquad (7)$$
$$11_2/1010_2 \;=\; q.\; 0 \quad r.\; 11_2 \qquad (3)$$

(b) Convert 1100110_2 to BCD:

$$1100110_2/1010_2 \;=\; q.\; 1010_2 \quad r.\; 10_2 \qquad (2)$$
$$1010_2/1010_2 \;=\; q.\; 1_2 \quad r.\; 0 \qquad (0)$$
$$1_2/1010_2 \;=\; q.\; 0 \quad r.\; 1_2 \qquad (1)$$

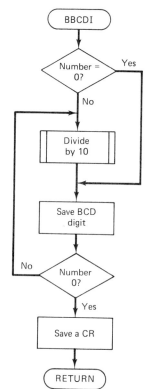

Figure 12-5 Flowchart for converting binary integers into BCD integers. The flowchart for dividing by 10 is not shown.

Figure 12-5 illustrates the flowchart written from the algorithm and Example 12-9 lists the subroutine developed from this flowchart. Notice that the subroutine converts the binary number stored in the HL register pair into a string of BCD digits stored beginning at the memory location indirectly addressed by the BC register pair. In addition to storing the BCD equivalent of HL, this subroutine also stores a carriage return at the end of the string of BCD digits.

```
(EXAMPLE 12-9)

                        ;
                        ;subroutine to convert the binary integer in HL
                        ;into a BCD string of numbers stored at the
                        ;location indexed by the BC pair.
                        ;
2020 7C         BBCDI:  MOV   A,H     ;test for zero
2021 B5                 ORA   L
2022 CA-28-20           JZ    BBDI2   ;if zero
2025 CD-33-20   BBDI1:  CALL  DIV10   ;divide HL by 10
2028 02         BBDI2:  STAX  B       ;save BCD digit
2029 03                 INX   B       ;index next location
202A 7C                 MOV   A,H     ;test for zero
202B B5                 ORA   L
202C C2-25-20           JNZ   BBDI1   ;continue dividing
202F 3E-0D              MVI   A,0DH   ;get CR
2031 02                 STAX  B       ;save CR
2032 C9                 RET           ;return
                        ;
                        ;subroutine to divide HL by 10 and place
                        ;quotient in HL and remainder in A.
                        ;
2033 C5         DIV10:  PUSH  B       ;save BC
2034 06-10              MVI   B,16    ;load counter
2036 11-00-00           LXI   D,0     ;clear quotient
2039 EB         DIV11:  XCHG          ;shift quotient left
203A 29                 DAD   H
203B EB                 XCHG
203C 29                 DAD   H       ;shift dividend left
203D D2-41-20           JNC   DIV12   ;if no carry
2040 1C                 INR   E
2041 D5         DIV12:  PUSH  D
2042 7B                 MOV   A,E     ;compare with 10
2043 D6-0A              SUI   10
2045 5F                 MOV   E,A
2046 7A                 MOV   A,D
2047 DE-00              SBI   0
2049 57                 MOV   D,A
204A DA-50-20           JC    DIV13   ;if dividend smaller
204D F1                 POP   PSW
204E 2C                 INR   L
204F D5                 PUSH  D
2050 D1         DIV13:  POP   D
2051 05                 DCR   B       ;decrement count
2052 C2-39-20           JNZ   DIV11
2055 7B                 MOV   A,E     ;position remainder
2056 C1                 POP   B       ;restore BC
2057 C9                 RET           ;return
```

Binary-to-BCD Conversion Algorithm (Fractions)

Converting a binary fraction to a BCD fraction is accomplished by multiplying the fraction by 10. After each multiplication the integer portion of the result is kept as a BCD digit. This process is repeated until the original fraction becomes a 0, as illustrated by the example conversions of Example 12-10. The result appears as a BCD digit, one at a time, after each multiplication.

(Example 12-10)

(a) Convert 0.1101_2 to BCD:

$$0.1101_2 \times 1010_2 = \quad 1000_2 \quad \text{r. } 0.001_2$$
$$0.001_2 \times 1010_2 = \quad \quad 1_2 \quad \text{r. } 0.01_2$$
$$0.01_2 \times 1010_2 = \quad \quad 10_2 \quad \text{r. } 0.1_2$$
$$0.1_2 \times 1010_2 = \quad \quad 101_2 \quad \text{r. } 0.0$$
$$\text{answer} \quad = \quad 0.8125_{10}$$

(b) Convert 0.10001_2 to BCD:

$$0.10001_2 \times 1010_2 = \quad 101_2 \quad \text{r. } 0.0101_2$$
$$0.0101_2 \times 1010_2 = \quad \quad 11_2 \quad \text{r. } 0.001_2$$
$$0.001_2 \times 1010_2 = \quad \quad 1_2 \quad \text{r. } 0.01_2$$
$$0.01_2 \times 1010_2 = \quad \quad 10_2 \quad \text{r. } 0.1_2$$
$$0.1_2 \times 1010_2 = \quad \quad 101_2 \quad \text{r. } 0.0$$
$$\text{answer} \quad = \quad 0.53125_{10}$$

Figure 12-6 illustrates this algorithm in flowchart form and Example 12-11 lists the subroutine written from this flowchart. This subroutine stores an ASCII period followed by the BCD digits of the result in the memory location indirectly addressed by the BC pair. (If the original number is 0, this subroutine stores only a carriage return.) The original fraction is placed in the HL register pair prior to calling the subroutine. Once the entire binary fraction is converted to BCD, the subroutine stores a carriage return following the last digit and returns to the program. Note that the BCD result may contain an error for certain fractions because some fractions cannot be completely represented in 16 bits. An example is 0.1_{10}. This error can be corrected by rounding if necessary.

(EXAMPLE 12-11 page 1 of 2)

```
                   ;
                   ;subroutine to convert the binary fraction in HL
                   ;into a BCD string of numbers stored at the
                   ;location indexed by the BC pair.
                   ;
2080 7C            BBCDF: MOV  A,H   ;test for zero
```

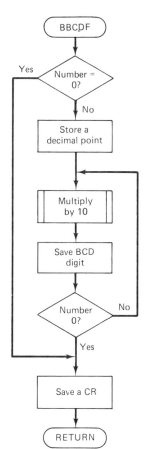

Figure 12-6 Flowchart for converting binary fractions into BCD fractions. The flowchart for multiplying by 10 is not shown.

(EXAMPLE 12-11 page 2 of 2)

```
2081 B5                 ORA   L
2082 CA-93-20           JZ    BBDF2 ;if zero
2085 3E-2E              MVI   A,'.' ;store a decimal point
2087 02                 STAX  B
2088 03                 INX   B
2089 CD-97-20 BBDF1:    CALL  MU10  ;multiply HL by 10
208C 02                 STAX  B     ;save BCD digit
208D 03                 INX   B     ;index next location
208E 7C                 MOV   A,H   ;test for zero
208F B5                 ORA   L
2090 C2-89-20           JNZ   BBDF1 ;continue dividing
2093 3E-0D    BBDF2:    MVI   A,0DH ;get CR
2095 02                 STAX  B     ;save CR
2096 C9                 RET         ;return
              ;
              ;subroutine to multiply HL by 10 and place
              ;remaining fractional part of the product in HL
              ;and the integer product in A.
              ;
2097 C5       MU10:     PUSH B      ;save BC
```

```
2098 1E-00                MVI   E,0    ;clear part of product
209A CD-AF-20             CALL  SLEHL  ;EHL X 2
209D 53                   MOV   D,E    ;save EHL X 2
209E 4D                   MOV   C,L
209F 44                   MOV   B,H
20A0 CD-AF-20             CALL  SLEHL  ;EHL X 4
20A3 CD-AF-20             CALL  SLEHL  ;EHL X 8
20A6 09                   DAD   B      ;form EHL X 10
20A7 D2-AB-20             JNC   MU11   ;if no carry
20AA 14                   INR   D
20AB 7A        MU11:      MOV   A,D
20AC 83                   ADD   E
20AD C1                   POP   B
20AE C9                   RET          ;return
               ;
               ;shift EHL left one bit
               ;
20AF 7B        SLEHL:     MOV   A,E
20B0 87                   ADD   A
20B1 5F                   MOV   E,A
20B2 29                   DAD   H
20B3 D2-B7-20             JNC   SLHL1  ;if no carry
20B6 1C                   INR   E
20B7 C9        SLHL1:     RET          ;return
```

Example 12-11 *(Continued)*

12-5 STRING SCANNING AND EXTRACTION

Although string scanning and extraction is not a data conversion technique, it does use some of the software developed in this chapter. This section shows how to find numbers in ASCII-coded character strings(string scanning) and convert them into binary numbers (extraction) stored in an area of memory.

String Scanning Software

Before a number can be extracted from an ASCII character string, it must be found in the string. A subroutine is developed to search through the string for a number (or a plus and minus sign in the case of signed numbers) and return with the starting address of the first digit of the number. This is a simple task as illustrated by the flowchart of Fig. 12-7 and the subroutine of Example 12-12. When this subroutine (SCAN) is called, the HL register pair points to the beginning of the ASCII character string and a return occurs whenever a number is found. If the carry is set upon returning, an ASCII-coded number is found, and if carry is cleared on the return, the string did not contain any numbers.

```
(EXAMPLE  12-12)

                 ORG   2800H
            ;
            ;subroutine to scan through a character string and
            ;locate the first numeric character.
```

```
                       ;
                       ;HL is used to point to the first character of the
                       ;string.
                       ;
                       ;on the return, HL points to the first numeric
                       ;character in the string or to a carriage return
                       ;if no number exists.
                       ;
                       ;return carry = 0 means carriage return
                       ;return carry = 1 means valid number
                       ;
2800 7E         SCAN:   MOV   A,M     ;get string character
2801 FE-0D              CPI   0DH     ;test for carriage return
2803 CA-14-28           JZ    SCAN2   ;if carriage return
2806 FE-30              CPI   30H     ;test for less than 0
2808 DA-10-28           JC    SCAN1   ;if less than 0
280B FE-3A              CPI   3AH     ;test for greater than 9
280D DA-14-28           JC    SCAN2   ;if not greater than 9
2810 23         SCAN1:  INX   H       ;point to next character
2811 C3-00-28           JMP   SCAN    ;check next character
2814 C9         SCAN2:  RET           ;return
```

Example 12-12 *(Continued)*

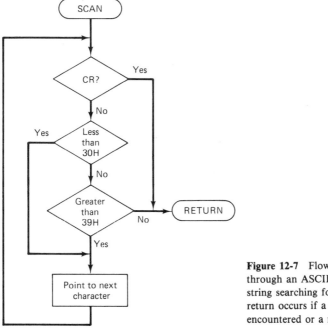

Figure 12-7 Flowchart for scanning through an ASCII coded character string searching for any number. A return occurs if a carriage return is encountered or a number.

Extracting the ASCII-Coded Number and Converting It to BCD

Once the number is found using SCAN, it must be extracted from the ASCII string and converted into BCD so that it can ultimately be converted to binary. A subroutine is written to remove ASCII numbers from the character string addressed by the HL register pair and place them in a table for later conversion into binary. Figure 12-8 illustrates a flowchart for extracting the ASCII number and Example 12-13 lists the subroutine (EXT).

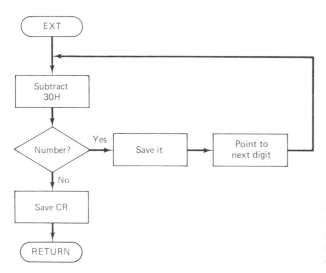

Figure 12-8 Flowchart for extracting and converting an ASCII coded BCD number from a character string. A return occurs if a non-number is encountered in the character string.

(EXAMPLE 12-13)

```
                    ;
                    ;subroutine to extract the ASCII coded number from
                    ;the string addressed by HL, convert it to BCD and
                    ;store it in the table addressed by the BC pair.
                    ;
                    ;the table entry is followed by a carrage return.
                    ;
2815 7E       EXT:    MOV  A,M    ;get string character
2816 D6-30            SUI  30H    ;convert to BCD
2818 DA-26-28         JC   EXT1   ;if not number
281B FE-0A            CPI  10     ;number?
281D D2-26-28         JNC  EXT1   ;if not number
2820 02               STAX B      ;save digit
2821 03               INX  B      ;index next table location
2822 23               INX  H      ;point to next ASCII code
2823 C3-15-28         JMP  EXT    ;check next character
2826 3E-0D    EXT1:   MVI  A,0DH  ;save carriage return
2828 02               STAX B
2829 03               INX  B
282A C9               RET         ;return
```

In subroutine EXT, HL points to the first digit of the number and BC points to the starting address of a list of numbers in the memory. The subroutine itself extracts the number digit by digit, subtracts a 30H from each digit converting to BCD, and stores the digits in the table addressed by BC. The subroutine ends when a non-numeric ASCII code is encountered and stores a carriage return following the entry into the table addressed by the BC register pair.

Forming a Master Subroutine to Scan and Extract Many Numbers from One ASCII-Coded String

The next logical step is to write a universal subroutine that scans a string, removes all the numbers present, and stores the numbers in a table. This is an easy task because most of the work is done by SCAN and EXT. The only additional software required is a counter to determine how many numbers are extracted from the ASCII character string. The flowchart for this subroutine (MSEXT) appears in Fig. 12-9 and the listing appears in Example 12-14.

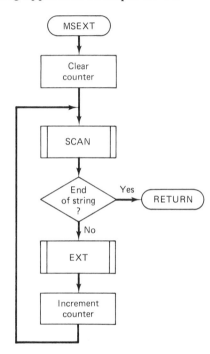

Figure 12-9 Flowchart for finding, extracting and converting ASCII coded BCD numbers from a character string. This subroutine removes all ASCII coded numbers from the string and stores them in a separate table.

(EXAMPLE 12-14)

```
              ;
              ;subroutine that converts all of the numbers present
              ;in the character string addressed by the HL pair
              ;into a series of BCD numbers stored in a table
              ;addressed by the BC pair.
              ;
              ;on return the D register indicates how many numbers
              ;are found in the character string
              ;
282B 16-00    MSEXT: MVI  D,0    ;load counter with zero
282D CD-00-28 MEXT1: CALL SCAN   ;find number
2830 D2-3A-28        JNC  MEXT2  ;if end of string
2833 CD-15-28        CALL EXT    ;extract a number
2836 14              INR  D      ;count the number
2837 C3-2D-28        JMP  MEXT1  ;do another
283A C9       MEXT2: RET         ;return
```

With MSEXT the calling program provides the starting address of the character string and the location of the table for storing the BCD numbers. On a return from this subroutine the D register indicates the number of BCD numbers stored in the table so that they can be processed. This processing in most cases involves converting the numbers into binary and storing them in another table for later program use. This conversion can be accomplished with the BCD-to-binary conversion algorithm discussed earlier in this chapter.

12-6 SUMMARY

1. Data conversion is important because the form of the data never seem to fit the application. For example, keyboards often generate different data than those that displays require.
2. Binary-coded decimal-to-ASCII code conversion is accomplished by adding a 30H to the BCD number. ASCII-to-BCD conversion is accomplished by subtracting 30H from the ASCII-coded character.
3. ASCII-to-hexadecimal conversion is effected by subtracting a 30H if the original ASCII character is a number or 37H if it is a letter. Hexadecimal-to-ASCII conversion is accomplished by adding a 30H to a number and a 37H to a letter.
4. The DAA instruction is used to speed up and shorten the length of hexadecimal-to-ASCII conversion software.
5. Converting BCD integers to binary integers is accomplished by starting with a binary value of 0. After starting at 0, as each BCD digit is encountered, the binary number is divided by 10 and the BCD digit is added to it to generate the final binary equivalent.
6. When BCD fractions are converted to binary, the first BCD digit is divided by 10, the second by 100, and so on. The results of all the divisions are then summed to generate the equivalent binary fraction. (Note that errors may occur because not all fractions convert directly.)
7. Binary integers are converted to BCD integers by dividing the binary number by 10 and saving each remainder as a significant BCD digit. Division continues until the quotient becomes a 0.
8. Whenever binary fractions are converted to BCD, the original binary fraction is multiplied by 10 until it becomes a 0. After each multiplication a BCD digit (0 through 9) is generated and stored in the memory.
9. Although string scanning and extraction is not a data conversion technique, it fits well with the conversion techniques described in this chapter. This technique is used to scan through an ASCII-coded character string, remove all of the ASCII-coded numbers, and convert them to BCD. Once the numbers are removed by this technique, they can be converted to binary by one of the conversion algorithms.

12-7 GLOSSARY

BCD fraction   BCD fractions are normal BCD numbers that are assumed to be fractions. Their ASCII representation is often started with a period (2EH).

Binary fraction   A number that has its binary point located just outside the leftmost bit position of the binary number so that the leftmost bit is weighted as a 2^{-1}.

Conversion error   When used with algorithms to convert from or to binary or BCD fractions, it refers to the inherent error built into the conversion process. An example is a 0.1_{10}, which cannot be converted exactly to binary or from binary to BCD.

String extraction   A technique used to remove (copy) ASCII-coded numbers or other data from a character string into a separate table in the memory.

String scanning   A term that refers to a technique used to locate a particular ASCII-coded character string. Generally used to remove numeric data from ASCII-coded character strings.

QUESTIONS AND PROBLEMS

12-1. Why is there a need for data conversion software?

12-2. ASCII numbers are converted to BCD numbers by subtracting what hexadecimal number?

12-3. BCD numbers are converted to ASCII by adding what hexadecimal number?

12-4. When converting from hexadecimal to ASCII, what problem is encountered if one number is added to the BCD value to accomplish the conversion?

12-5. Explain the operation of the hexadecimal-to-ASCII conversion algorithm of Example 12–3.

12-6. Using the subroutine illustrated in Example 12–3, write an additional subroutine that converts the hexadecimal contents of the accumulator into two ASCII-coded characters stored in the BC register pair. (B should hold the leftmost hexadecimal ASCII-coded character and C should hold the rightmost hexadecimal ASCII-coded character.)

12-7. Whenever a BCD integer is converted to binary, it is added to a binary quantity that is multiplied by a _____ before the addition for each BCD digit.

12-8. Modify the BCD-to-binary conversion subroutine of Example 12–5 so that if memory location SIGN contains an 0FFH, the binary result is returned in negative two's-complement form.

12-9. Briefly describe how BCD fractions are converted to binary fractions.

12-10. Binary integers are converted to BCD integers by dividing by _____ _____ and saving the _____ after each successive division.

12-11. Modify Example 12–9 so that it generates an ASCII-coded number instead of a BCD-coded number.

12-12. Binary fractions are converted to BCD fractions by multiplying by _____ until the original fraction becomes a 0.

12-13. Modify the subroutine in Example 12-11 so that it generates an ASCII fraction instead of a BCD fraction.

12-14. Modify the string scanning subroutine of Example 12-12 so that it stops scanning for a number, plus sign, minus sign, or a carriage return. [The carry (0) must still indicate that a carriage return is encountered.]

12-15. Modify the extraction subroutine listed in Example 12-13 so that it can use the output generated in Question 12-14. It should only store the BCD number for any positive number and a 0FH prior to storing a negative number.

12-16. Using the subroutines generated in Questions 12-14 and 12-15, modify Example 12-14 so that it scans an ASCII string and stores the signed results in a table.

12-17. Using the table of BCD numbers stored by Example 12-14, develop the software (in subroutine form) that will convert each number to binary and store the numbers at another table in memory.

chapter thirteen

TABLE LOOKUP AND TIME DELAYS

Table-lookup techniques are used in data conversion problems that have no simple mathematical solution as did BCD-to-ASCII conversion in Chapter 12. Examples of cases where table-lookup conversions are the only solution are: binary-to-seven-segment display code and conversion from many other codes. Besides their usefulness in converting from one code to another, lookup tables are also useful for filing data—you might call them the computer's version of a table of contents or an index.

Another important programming technique is the time delay. Although it does not fit too well with table-lookup techniques, it is an extremely important technique that is very common with I/O control software. Tables, in particular the seven-segment table, are also used with I/O, so it fits in this chapter better than any other.

13-1 OBJECTIVES

Upon completion of this chapter, you will be able to:

1. Use tables and the table-lookup technique to convert from any code to any other code
2. Construct menu-driven software by using the jump table
3. Use a binary search to find data in a table
4. Construct an ASCII data table to hold any form of information
5. Reference data through the use of a data pointer table
6. Create software time delays with delays of from a few microseconds to many hours

13–2 DIRECT TABLE LOOKUP FOR DATA CONVERSION ▬▬▬▬▬▬

As mentioned in the introduction to this chapter, one of the important functions of the table-lookup technique is for data conversion. One fairly common data conversion that uses this technique is BCD or hexadecimal-to-seven-segment code for LED, fluorescent, or LCD display devices.

Hexadecimal-to-Seven-Segment Code Conversion

Figure 13–1 illustrates a seven-segment LED display device and the bit positions that apply to its lettered segments. Here the most significant bit is undefined and can be used to control the decimal point on the display if desired. There are two basic types of seven-segment LED displays available: the common-anode display and the common-cathode display. Common-anode displays are connected so that 5 V is applied to all the internal anodes of the LED diodes. Common-anode displays require a logic 0 to illuminate a segment. Common-cathode displays are connected so that ground is connected to all the internal cathodes of the LED diodes. Common-cathode displays require a logic 1 to illuminate a segment.

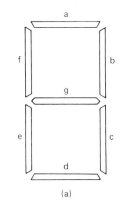

(a)

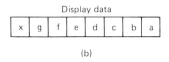

Display data

(b)

Figure 13-1 (a) The segment pattern of a 7-segment LED or LCD display device; (b) the binary bit pattern of the data used to control each segment of the 7-segment display device.

Seven-segment lookup table. Suppose that common-cathode displays are used and a table is required for coding each of the numbers 0 through 9 and the hexadecimal letters A through F. A table for each character is formed as illustrated in Example 13–1. This table will be used with a subroutine for converting hexadecimal code into seven-segment code for display.

Lookup conversion subroutine. Software that uses the table formed in Example 13–1 refers to the table by using the hexadecimal data as a portion of the

(EXAMPLE 13-1)

```
                            ORG    2800H
                       ;
                       ;MSB = 0
                       ;hexadecimal to 7-segment conversion table
                       ;common cathode or common anode with
                       ;inverters.
                       ;
     2800 3F           TABLE: DB     3FH    ;0
     2801 06                  DB     06H    ;1
     2802 5B                  DB     5BH    ;2
     2803 4F                  DB     4FH    ;3
     2804 66                  DB     66H    ;4
     2805 6D                  DB     6DH    ;5
     2806 7D                  DB     7DH    ;6
     2807 27                  DB     27H    ;7
     2808 7F                  DB     7FH    ;8
     2809 6F                  DB     6FH    ;9
     280A 77                  DB     77H    ;A
     280B 7C                  DB     7CH    ;b
     280C 39                  DB     39H    ;C
     280D 5E                  DB     5EH    ;d
     280E 79                  DB     79H    ;E
     280F 71                  DB     71H    ;F
```

memory address. Notice that the first location of the table contains the seven-segment code for a 0, the second contains the code for a 1, and so on. If the HL register pair is loaded with the starting address of the table (2800H) and the hexadecimal data are moved into L, then HL will point to the correct seven-segment data for the hexadecimal number. A short subroutine that references the table is listed in Example 13-2. This subroutine is very useful if the table begins at a location that ends with 00H. If the table begins at any other location, a bias must be added to the hexadecimal number before it is moved into the L register. Suppose that the table begins at location 2832H. The bias is 32H and it must be added to the hexadecimal number as illustrated in Example 13-3. If the table crosses a page boundary (100H), the bias must be added to the HL register pair after the hexadecimal data are moved into L. Because of this problem, it is more efficient to begin all the lookup tables at the beginning of a page boundary.

(EXAMPLE 13-2)

```
                       ;
                       ;table lookup subroutine that refers to TABLE
                       ;for the 7-segment code.
                       ;this subroutine converts the contents of the
                       ;accumulator (0 -- F) to 7-segment code.
                       ;
     2810 26-28        LOOK:   MVI   H,28H ;address table
     2812 6F                   MOV   L,A
     2813 7E                   MOV   A,M    ;replace with 7-seg code
     2814 C9                   RET          ;return
```

(EXAMPLE 13-3)

```
                          ;
                          ;table lookup subroutine that refers to TABLE
                          ;for the 7-segment code.
                          ;this subroutine converts the contents of the
                          ;accumulator (0 -- F) to 7-segment code.
                          ;
2810 26-28    LOOK:   MVI  H,28H ;address table
2812 C6-32            ADI  32H   ;add bias
2814 6F               MOV  L,A
2815 7E               MOV  A,M   ;replace with 7-seg code
2816 C9               RET        ;return
```

Direct table lookup is a very efficient way of converting from one code to another and finds an application for converting ASCII code to EBCDIC (a code used in some large mainframe computer systems) and various other codes found in many different systems.

Using Table Lookup for Jump Tables

Today, many programs are menu driven. A menu-driven program is one in which a menu of options are presented to the operator, who chooses the option required to perform a given task. Figure 13-2 illustrates a menu that might be encountered for a program that corrects the spelling of a text file stored on a disk. The user enters the numerical choice and the computer executes the function described by the choice.

CORRECT, the spelling program
written by Barry B. Brey, copyright 1984

0 — Correct the spelling in a text file.
1 — Erase a word from the dictionary.
2 — Add a word to the dictionary.
3 — Print the dictionary.
4 — Set up the printer.
5 — Create a new dictionary.
6 — Delete a dictionary.

Enter your choice:

Figure 13-2 Display presented by a menu-driven spelling program. All the user does is enter the numerical choice from the menu and the function will execute.

The software that handles the menu is a jump table-lookup subroutine. After the numeric choice is entered, it appears in the accumulator and subroutine JUMP is called. JUMP, as listed in Example 13-4, refers to a jump table, which contains the addresses of each program for CORRECT. Once the 16-bit address is located, the HL register pair is loaded with it and a PCHL instruction is executed. PCHL is the instruction that copies the HL register pair into the program counter so that the next instruction executed is at the location indexed by the HL register pair. A few programming concepts are important in this example, such as the ADD A instruction, which is used to double the contents of the accumulator. Doubling the accumulator is required because each table entry is 16 bits (two bytes) in length. Also important is the addition of the doubled lookup number to the beginning address

(EXAMPLE 13-4)

```
                         ORG      2800H
                         ;
                         ;subroutine to reference the jump table
                         ;for the address of the program that
                         ;corresponds to the number in the
                         ;accumulator.
                         ;
                         ;accumulator must equal 0 -- 6
                         ;
     2800 21-0E-28 JUMP:  LXI   H,JTAB ;address jump table
     2803 87             ADD   A       ;double number
     2804 5F             MOV   E,A     ;place number in DE
     2805 16-00          MVI   D,0
     2807 19             DAD   D       ;adjust address
     2808 5E             MOV   E,M     ;get jump address
     2809 23             INX   H
     280A 56             MOV   D,M
     280B E1             POP   H       ;clear return address
     280C EB             XCHG          ;place address in HL
     280D E9             PCHL          ;go execute program
                         ;
                         ;jump table for program CORRECT
                         ;
     280E 00-29 JTAB:    DW    CORR    ;correct spelling
     2810 2A-2A          DW    ERA     ;erase word
     2812 63-2A          DW    ADDW    ;add word
     2814 8F-2A          DW    PRI     ;print
     2816 02-2B          DW    SETU    ;setup
     2818 33-2B          DW    CRE     ;create
     281A 03-2C          DW    DLE     ;delete
```

of the jump table. This is required because no origin is specified for the table. This allows the table to be placed anywhere in the memory by the assembler. Because assemblers are used for software development, this step is very important if no origin is specified.

13-3 BINARY SEARCHING

On many occasions tables are used to store data that change from time to time. Examples include data for game programs, samples taken in a data aquisition system, and tax tables in electronic point-of-sales terminals (POS). In this section we present the techniques required to search a table for a particular key or code and return with either a count or a yes–no answer.

The Yes-No Binary Search

This type of binary table search is very important to games and artificial intelligence programs. An example is the table used with a tic-tac-toe game. The lookup table for this game is initialized with nine entries, each containing a zero indicating that the box is not selected. Part of the software required to create this game must check the table after each player chooses a box for an X or an 0. (The X's and 0's can be stored in ASCII code.) Whenever a box is selected, it is addressed with an X- and Y-coordinate. For example, the upper right-hand box is address 0,2.

The subroutine to check the table for an entry is listed in Example 13-5. Upon calling this subroutine, the X-coordinate is in the C register and the Y-coordinate is in the B register. When a return occurs, the zero flag is a 1 for no (no X or 0 in the table entry) and a 0 for a yes (an X or 0 present in the table entry). The subroutine first multiplies the X-coordinate by 3 and adds the Y-coordinate to the result. This yields a number between 0 and 8 for each of the boxes in the game. The number (0 through 8) is then added to the address of the table and a test of the contents of this address is made to determine if an X or 0 exists.

```
(EXAMPLE 13-5)

                    ORG     2800H
                    ;
                    ;subroutine to reference a tic-tac-toe
                    ;table.
                    ;register B = Y-coordinate (0 - 2)
                    ;register C = X-coordinate (0 - 2)
                    ;return zero = if square not occupied
                    ;
2800 16-03  CHEX:   MVI     D,3      ;load 3
2802 3E-FD          MVI     A,-3     ;load -3
2804 82     CHEX1:  ADD     D        ;multiply C * 3
2805 0D             DCR     C
2806 F2-04-28       JP      CHEX1
2809 80             ADD     B        ;add B
280A 4F             MOV     C,A      ;form 16-bit bias
280B 06-00          MVI     B,0
280D 21-14-28       LXI     H,TTAB   ;address table
2810 19             DAD     D
2811 7E             MOV     A,M      ;test entry
2812 B7             ORA     A
2813 C9             RET              ;return
                    ;
2814        TTAB:   DS      9        ;reserve 9 for table
```

Sales Tax Lookup Table

Another fairly common use of a table is to store data that must be searched by a program. A very common application is sales tax tables in electronic point-of-sales terminals (POS).

Suppose that a sales tax table is required for a particular POS. The sales tax is to be determined for a 6% tax rate at up to $2. In many states the tax breaks on the first few dollars are weighted so that a straight percentage calculation cannot be used to determine the tax. A table illustrating some hypothetical breaks is presented in Example 13-6.

The subroutine that references this table appears in flowchart form in Fig. 13-3 and the software is listed in Example 13-7. Notice that the numbers in the table are

(EXAMPLE 13-6)

```
                 ORG    2800H
                 ;
                 ;a hypothetical sales tax table for 6%.
                 ;each entry represents the break point
                 ;for the next higher cent of tax.
                 ;
2800 0B     TAX:     DB     11      ;0.00 - 0.10 = $0.01
2801 11              DB     17      ;0.11 - 0.16 = $0.02
2802 1E              DB     30      ;0.17 - 0.29 = $0.03
2803 30              DB     48      ;0.30 - 0.47 = $0.04
2804 4A              DB     74      ;0.48 - 0.73 = $0.05
2805 65              DB     101     ;0.74 - 1.00 = $0.06
2806 78              DB     120     ;1.01 - 1.19 = $0.07
2807 87              DB     135     ;1.20 - 1.34 = $0.08
2808 99              DB     153     ;1.35 - 1.52 = $0.09
2809 B0              DB     176     ;1.53 - 1.75 = $0.10
280A C2              DB     194     ;1.76 - 1.93 = $0.11
```

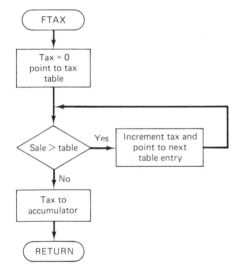

Figure 13-3 Flowchart of a subroutine that looks up the sales tax (6%) and return with that tax in the accumulator.

(EXAMPLE 13-7)

```
                 ;
                 ;subroutine that converts the unsigned
                 ;binary integer in the accumulator to
                 ;a tax from the TAX table.
                 ;
                 ;integer is assumed to be no greater than $2.
                 ;
280B 0600   FTAX:    MVI    B,0      ;start tax at $0.00
280D 21-00-28        LXI    H,TAX    ;reference TAX table
2810 BE     FTAX1:   CMP    M        ;compare tax table
2811 23              INX    H        ;point to next entry
2812 04              INR    B        ;increment rate
2813 D2-10-28        JNC    FTAX1    ;if not found
2816 78              MOV    A,B      ;move tax to A
2817 C9              RET             ;return
```

compared with the sales amount in the accumulator. After each comparison, the location in the table and the tax counter are incremented. This continues until the comparison results in a carry, after which the tax is moved from the tax counter to the accumulator before the return. On the return the correct sales tax is found in the accumulator. If more than $2 in sales is to be handled by the software, a POS usually takes any amount over $2 and multiplies it by the sales tax percentage. This does not require a lookup table.

13-4 VARIABLE-LENGTH SEARCHING

In certain applications, tabled data may be of different binary lengths. An application of a table that contains data of different lengths is a list of names in ASCII code. This list could be a dictionary of words, a directory of actual names, or an index of items. If a name is to be found in such a list, a variable-length search must be accomplished.

Entabling Variable-Length ASCII Data

In most cases, variable-length ASCII data are entabled so that the last ASCII-coded character of each entry is negative (bit 7 set) and any other ASCII character in the entry is positive (bit 7 cleared). This is done so that a special character need not be used to indicate the end of an entry, which saves memory space. A special character (00H) is used, though, to indicate the end of the table. This form of data storage is used because of its efficiency.

Example 13-8 shows how some ASCII-coded words are stored in the memory to form a table containing variable-length ASCII data.

```
(EXAMPLE 13-8)

                          ORG 2800H
                   ;ASCII variable length table.
                   ;
                   ;each entry ends with a negative ASCII
                   ;code.
                   ;
                   ;the table ends with a 00H.
                   ;
2800 44-4F-C7      TABA:  DB   'DO','G'+80H   ;DOG
2803 41-D3                DB   'A','S'+80H    ;AS
2805 49-D3                DB   'I','S'+80H    ;IS
2807 46-49-4E-C4          DB   'FIN','D'+80H  ;FIND
280B 57-48-D9             DB   'WH','Y'+80H   ;WHY
280E C1                   DB   'A'+80H        ;A
280F 00                   DB   O              ;end of table
```

Subroutine to Search a Variable-Length Table

The subroutine used to search a table, such as the one illustrated in Example 13–8, must point to the start of the table and also to an ASCII character string stored elsewhere in the memory. (The string being searched for must also end with its last character negative.) The table is searched to determine if a match exists between the stored character string and any entry in the table. Figure 13–4 illustrates the flowchart for this subroutine and Example 13–9 lists the software.

Notice that this subroutine uses the HL register pair to address the ASCII-coded character string being searched for, and the DE register pair is used to address the table. The subroutine searches through the table until either the ASCII string is found or until the end of the table is encountered. If no match occurs, the return occurs with the carry set, and if a match occurs, the carry is cleared with the starting address of the table entry in the DE register pair.

```
        (EXAMPLE 13-9)
                             ;
                             ;subroutine to search the table addressed
                             ;by the DE register pair for the ASCII
                             ;coded character string addressed by the
                             ;HL register pair.
                             ;
                             ;upon return DE addresses the starting
                             ;address of the character string in the
                             ;table if it is found.  If not found the
                             ;carry flag is set upon returning.
                             ;
        2810 E5      SEAR:   PUSH H      ;save address of string
        2811 D5              PUSH D      ;save address of entry
        2812 1A      SEAR1:  LDAX D      ;get table data
        2813 B7              ORA  A      ;test it
        2814 CA-34-28        JZ   SEAR5  ;if end of table
        2817 FA-23-28        JM   SEAR2  ;if end of entry
        281A BE              CMP  M      ;compare entry
        281B C2-27-28        JNZ  SEAR3  ;if different
        281E 23              INX  H      ;address next
        281F 13              INX  D
        2820 C3-12-28        JMP  SEAR1  ;check next
        2823 BE      SEAR2:  CMP  M      ;compare entry
        2824 CA-35-28        JZ   SEAR6  ;if found
        2827 E1      SEAR3:  POP  H      ;scan to next entry
        2828 3E-80           MVI  A,80H  ;set A negative
        282A BE      SEAR4:  CMP  M
        282B 23              INX  H
        282C D2-2A-28        JNC  SEAR4  ;if last not found
        282F EB              XCHG
        2830 E1              POP  H
        2831 C3-10-28        JMP  SEAR   ;repeat search
        2834 37      SEAR5:  STC         ;set carry
        2835 D1      SEAR6:  POP  D      ;restore addresses
        2836 E1              POP  H
        2837 C9              RET         ;return
```

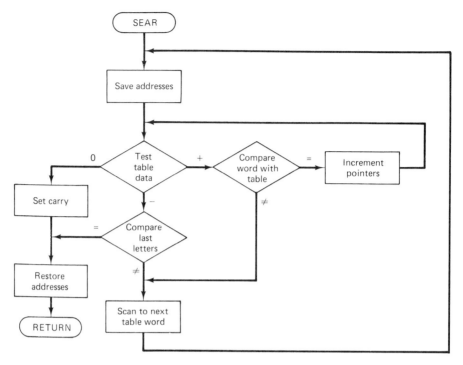

Figure 13-4   Flowchart of a subroutine that searches a table for an ASCII character string. If a match occurs return is made with carry cleared and if no match is made carry is set before returning.

13-5 REFERENCING A TABLE THROUGH POINTERS

The searching technique presented in Section 13-4 works efficiently as long as the table being searched is not too long. To circumvent the problem associated with a long table, another table can be used to point to segments of the main table. Suppose that the table is organized in alphabetical order or that it is organized in sections with words of equal length. If the starting address of each section is known, a section of the main table can be located quickly so that a short search of the section can be accomplished in a relatively short period of time. A second table is often used to store pointers for reference to the longer main table.

The Reference Table

Suppose that a table of words (LETA) is organized in alphabetical order as illustrated in Example 13-10. (Only a portion of the actual table appears because of its length.) Notice that each segment of the table ends with a 00H code. Actually, LETA is con-

(EXAMPLE 13-10)

```
                            ;
                            ;ASCII variable length table.
                            ;
                            ;each entry ends with a negative ASCII code.
                            ;
                            ;each segment of the table ends with a OOH.
                            ;
                            ;begin A segment
                            ;
2838 C1             LETA:   DB   'A'+80H          ;A
2839 41-4C-CC               DB   'AL','L'+80H     ;ALL
283C 41-4E-C4               DB   'AN','D'+80H     ;AND
283F 00                     DB   O               ;end segment
                            ;
                            ;begin B segment
                            ;
2840 42-C5          LETB:   DB   'B','E'+80H      ;BE
2842 42-45-4C-CC            DB   'BEL','L'+80H    ;BELL
2846 42-4F-41-D4            DB   'BOA','T'+80H    ;BOAT
284A 42-55-D9               DB   'BU','Y'+80H     ;BUY
284D 00                     DB   O               ;end segment
                            ;
                            ;begin C segment
                            ;
284E 43-41-CE       LETC:   DB   'CA','N'+80H     ;CAN
  .    .   .  .             .    .    .            .
  .    .   .  .             .    .    .            .
  .    .   .  .             .    .    .            .
                            ;
                            ;begin Z segment
                            ;
297D 5A-4F-CF       LETZ:   DB   'ZO','O'+80H     ;ZOO
2980 00                     DB   O               ;end segment
                            ;                     end table
```

structed from many smaller tables—one for each letter of the alphabet (LETA, LETB, etc.).

A second table (TABL) that contains a pointer to this first table appears, in part, in Example 13–11. Notice that each entry is two bytes in length and contains the beginning address of a letter segment of the main table. TABL is used to locate a letter segment in the main table before the search subroutine (SEAR; see Section 13–4) is called. This reduces considerably the amount of time needed to search the table.

Subroutine to Search via the Reference Table

Now that an efficient method of addressing a large ASCII table is understood, a subroutine is written that uses the reference table (TABL) to search through the larger main table. To accomplish this, the first character of the ASCII-coded word, to be

(EXAMPLE 13-11)

```
                        ;
                        ;
                        ;table that refers to each segment
                        ;of the ASCII coded table LETA.
                        ;
2981  38-28     TABL:   DW     LETA   ;refer to letter A
2983  40-28             DW     LETB   ;refer to letter B
2985  4E-28             DW     LETC   ;refer to letter C
  .     .  .      .      .      .      .
  .     .  .      .      .      .      .
  .     .  .      .      .      .      .
  .     .  .      .      .      .      .
29B3  7D-29             DW     LETZ   ;refer to letter Z
                        ;               end of reference table
```

searched for in the main table, must be interrogated so that the proper reference address may be found. A subroutine that uses SEAR and some additional commands appears in the flowchart of Fig. 13-5, and a listing of the software appears in Example 13-12.

This subroutine (MSEAR), as did SEAR, assumes that the HL register pair addresses the ASCII-coded word to be located. The DE register pair must contain the

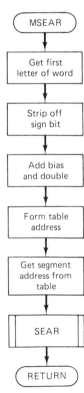

Figure 13-5 Flowchart of a subroutine that searches a table for an ASCII character string. This is accomplished by using the first letter of the string to locate the address of a lettered segment of the main table.

(EXAMPLE 13-12)

```
                        ;
                        ;subroutine to reference TABL so that
                        ;SEAR can be used to search a lettered
                        ;segment.
                        ;
                        ;HL points to ASCII word
                        ;
                        ;if found, DE addresses table entry
                        ;
                        ;if not found, carry = 1
                        ;
29B5 7E         MSEAR:  MOV  A,M       ;get first letter
29B6 E6-7F              ANI  7FH       ;strip sign bit
29B8 D6-41              SUI  41H       ;subtract bias
29BA 87                 ADD  A         ;double number
29BB E5                 PUSH H         ;save HL
29BC 21-81-29           LXI  H,TABL    ;address reference table
29BF 4F                 MOV  C,A       ;A to BC
29C0 06-00              MVI  B,0
29C2 09                 DAD  B         ;add to table address
29C3 5E                 MOV  E,M       ;get segment address
29C4 23                 INX  H
29C5 56                 MOV  D,M
29C6 E1                 POP  H         ;restore HL
29C7 CD-10-28           CALL SEAR      ;search segment
29CA C9                 RET            ;return
```

address of the reference table instead of the ASCII-coded data table as with SEAR. The subroutine moves the first character of the word to be searched for into the accumulator and subtracts a 41H from it. This leaves a number whose value ranges from 0 (letter A) through 25_{10} (letter Z).

Next, the number is doubled so that the 16-bit address of the correct letter segment can be referenced in the table. The address is loaded into the DE register pair and subroutine SEAR is called so that a segment of the table can be searched. As with SEAR, a return carry indicates that the ASCII-coded word is not found, and if it is found, the DE register pair points to its location in the main table.

13-6 TIME-DELAY SOFTWARE

Time-delay software is required for a wide variety of I/O interfacing and also for some forms of programs. Examples of some time delays that are required with I/O include: keyboard contact debouncing, controlled pulse-width generation (monostable multivibrator similation), and the generation of periodic waveforms (symmetrical or asymmetrical). Examples of time delays for programs include: delays required for the operator to read a message, and allowing the operator a certain amount of time to respond to a question.

Using Appendix A to Determine Instruction Execution Time

Appendix A lists the instructions available for use with the 8085A microprocessor and the number of system clock cycles required to execute them. A clock cycle is normally equal to the period of one-half the crystal clock frequency. If the 8085A uses a 6.0-MHz crystal, the cycle time is equal to $\frac{1}{3}$ μs. Many systems use either a 6.144-MHz or 6.0-MHz crystal. This text will assume that the 8085A uses a 6.0-MHz crystal in all the timing calculations.

Most of the instructions listed contain a single number of clocks for execution, but a few contain two numbers (9/18). The CALL instruction requires 18 clocks to execute and the CC (call on carry) instruction requires 9/18 clocks to execute. This means that if the call occurs (carry = 1), it takes 18 clocks to execute, and if the call does not occur (carry = 0), it takes nine clocks to execute. This same logic is applied to the conditional return and conditional jump instructions listed in Appendix A.

Short Time Delays

Short time delays are easy to implement because a single loop and an 8-bit counter can be used for the software. Example 13-13 illustrates a simple technique for obtaining short time delays. In this listing, the comments indicate how many clocks and the amount of time required for the execution of each of the instructions. Here the accumulator is loaded with count XX and the program passes through the loop XX number of times before returning from the subroutine. The amount of time required is equal to the time it takes to execute the CALL to the subroutine, to return from the subroutine, and to load the accumulator with the count (XX) plus XX times the time required to execute the DCR A and the JNZ SDEL1 instructions. Example 13-14 shows equations that are used to calculate the value of XX for a particular delay time in microseconds or the time in microseconds for a given count. (The largest value for XX is 256 when XX = 00.) If 256 is used for a count, the longest delay is slightly over 1.0 milliseconds (ms).

```
(EXAMPLE 13-13)

                        ORG   2800H
                   ;
                   ;subroutine for a short time delay using
                   ;a single 8-bit counter.
                   ;
                   ;c = clocks
                   ;us = microseconds
                   ;
2800 3E-XX    SDEL:  MVI   A,XX    ;7 c, 2 1/3 us
2802 3D       SDEL1: DCR   A       ;4 c, 1 1/3 us
2803 C2-02-28        JNZ   SDEL1   ;7/10 c, 2 1/3 or 3 1/3 us
2806 C9              RET           ;10 c, 3 1/3 us
```

(Example 13-14)

If XX is known:

$$\text{time} = 15\tfrac{1}{3}\ \mu s + (XX - 1)\ (4\tfrac{2}{3}\ \mu s)$$

If time is known:

$$XX = \frac{\text{time} - 15\tfrac{1}{3}\ \mu s}{4\tfrac{2}{3}\ \mu s} + 1$$

Long Time Delays

In many instances more than a 1.0-ms time delay is required. This is attainable by using a register pair as a counter instead of a single register. Example 13-15 illustrates a time-delay subroutine that is able to generate delays of slightly more than $\tfrac{1}{2}$ second. Example 13-16 depicts equations that are used with this subroutine to calculate either the time in microseconds, if the count is known, or the count, if the time in microseconds is known. Note that the maximum count is 65,536 when XXXX = 0.

```
(EXAMPLE 13-15)

                    ORG          2810H
                ;
                ;subroutine for a long time delay using
                ;the BC pair as a counter.
                ;
                ;c = clocks
                ;us = microseconds
                ;
2810 01-XX-XX LDEL:   LXI   B,XXXX  ;10 c, 3 1/3 us
2813 0B       LDEL1:  DCX   B       ;6 c, 2 us
2814 78               MOV   A,B     ;4 c, 1 1/3 us
2815 B1               ORA   C       ;4 c, 1 1/3 us
2816 C2-13-28         JNZ   LDEL1   ;7/10, 2 1/3 or 3 1/3 us
2819 C9               RET           ;10 c, 3 1/3 us
```

(Example 13-16)

If XXXX is known:

$$\text{time} = 19\tfrac{2}{3}\ \mu s + (XXXX - 1)\ (8.0\ \mu s)$$

If time is known:

$$XXXX = \frac{\text{time} - 19\tfrac{2}{3}\ \mu s}{8.0\ \mu s} + 1$$

Extremely Long Time Delays

Extremely long time delays are created by using the long time-delay subroutine LDEL in nested loops. If LDEL is set to delay for $\tfrac{1}{2}$ second, time delays in multiples of

$\frac{1}{2}$ second are easily created. Example 13–17 shows how a time delay of 1 hour is generated using LDEL and another register pair for timing.

```
(EXAMPLE 13-17)

                          ORG    2800H
                       ;1 hour time delay
                       ;
     2800 11-20-1C HOUR:  LXI    D,7200   ;load counter
     2803 CD-10-28 HOUR1: CALL   LDEL     ;wait 1/2 second
     2806 1B              DCX    D        ;loop 7200 times
     2807 7A              MOV    A,D
     2808 B3              ORA    E
     2809 C2-03-28        JNZ    HOUR1
     280C C9              RET             ;return after 1 hour
                       ;
                       ;subroutine for a 1/2 second time delay
                       ;
                          ORG    2810H
     2810 01-66-F7 LDEL:  LXI    B,63334  ;load count
     2813 0B       LDEL1: DCX    B        ;loop 63334 times
     2814 78              MOV    A,B
     2815 B1              ORA    C
     2816 C2-13-28        JNZ    LDEL1
     2819 C9              RET             ;return after 1/2 second
```

13-7 SUMMARY

1. Table-lookup techniques are excellent for converting codes, referencing programs through jump tables, and looking up data in either binary or ASCII form.

2. The only efficient, and possibly the only method of converting from BCD or hexadecimal data to seven-segment code for use with LED or LCD displays is via direct table lookup.

3. A very efficient method for handling menu-driven software incorporates a jump table to pass program control to a subprogram that corresponds to an item in the menu.

4. Binary searching allows tables to be used for conversion such as tax information and hold information for games such as tic-tac-toe.

5. Many types of data are stored in tables that have entries that are of variable length. The variable-length search allows this type of data to be located with a minimum amount of software.

6. ASCII string data stored in a table normally end with the last character negative in order to reduce the length of the table.

7. Pointers are very useful when trying to locate data in a large table. A pointer table holds addresses of various data segments in a larger table so that the data can be located more efficiently.

8. Time-delay software is used in many programs and also for I/O device control. In the 8085A, time delays can range from a few microseconds to years in length.

13-8 GLOSSARY

Clock cycle time   The time required for one complete cycle of the system clock. This is often either 333 nanoseconds (ns) or 320 ns in the 8085A microprocessor.

Jump table   Jump tables contain memory addresses of subprograms or subroutines stored elsewhere in the memory. Reference to these subprograms or subroutines is made through the jump table.

Menu   A selection of functions that are presented to the computer user through a numbered or lettered list of options displayed on the CRT screen.

Menu driven   Software that is selected and executed through a menu is considered to be menu-driven software. An entire system can be menu driven if all the available software options are presented to the operator through a menu.

Page   A page of computer memory is equal to 256 bytes.

Pointer   A memory address that points to or indexes data located in a table.

Point-of-sales terminal   Often abbreviated POS, the point-of-sales terminal is another name for an electronic cash register.

Reference table   Sometimes refers to a table of pointers or memory addresses which refer to sections of data or beginning addresses of subprograms or subroutines.

Table lookup   A programming technique that uses a table to store data and a key that references the data in the table. Often used to convert codes and store and reference any data that are tabular in nature.

Time-delay software   Software that is written to execute in an accurate and predictable amount of time. This is possible because instruction execution times are known.

QUESTIONS AND PROBLEMS

13-1. Modify the lookup table presented in Example 13-1 so that it contains entries for codes 10H through 13H, which contain the following characters: 10H = n, 11H = U, 12H = H, and 13H = r.

13-2. Write a subroutine that uses Example 13-2 to convert the contents of the accumulator into two seven-segment characters returned in the BC register pair. (B = leftmost half-byte; C = rightmost half-byte.)

13-3. If the POP H instruction is removed from Example 13-4, can each subprogram be followed by a return, converting them into subroutines so that control is returned to the main program?

13-4. Modify the subroutine of Example 13-5 so that it checks to see if an X− , Y − coordinate contains an X.

13-5. Write a subroutine that uses Example 13-7 to calculate the sales tax on any value. (*Hint:* If the sale is larger than $2, compute the sales tax by multiplication.)

13-6. Is it possible to store ASCII-coded sentences in the table of Example 13-8?

13-7. If the answer to Question 13-6 is yes, explain which character is a negative number.

13-8. What applications do you foresee for the reference table concept presented in Section 13-5?

13-9. In Example 13–12, a bias a 41H is subtracted from the accumulator. If the data contained both upper- and lowercase letters, would the same bias be subtracted?

13-10. How much time is required to execute an XTHL instruction if the 8085A clock frequency is 6 MHz?

13-11. What count (XX) is used in Example 13–13 so that the time delay is 500 μs ± 2 percent?

13-12. How much time delay is generated in Example 13–13 if a count of 12H is used for XX?

13-13. What count (XXXX) is used in Example 13–15 so that a 100 ms ± 2 percent time delay is developed?

13-14. Using the technique presented in Example 13–17, develop a 1 minute ± 5 percent time delay.

13-15. If all three register pairs are used for a time delay and each count is 65,565, what is the time delay within ± 1 hour?

SORTING NUMERIC AND ALPHANUMERIC DATA

Many applications of the microprocessor require that various forms of data be sorted. Data may appear in the form of numeric information of all types (integer and floating point) and in the form of ASCII-coded character strings.

In this chapter we approach sorting by first discussing some of the more common techniques used for sorting numeric data. Some of the techniques included are the bubble sort and the Shell sort. In addition to these techniques, alphanumeric data are inserted into a list of ordered alphanumeric data.

14-1 OBJECTIVES

Upon completion of this chapter, you will be able to:

1. Sort both 8- and 16-bit numeric data by using the bubble sort or Shell sort
2. Insert new 8-bit or 16-bit data into an ordered list using the bubble sort
3. Sort data alphabetically using the insertion technique

14-2 BUBBLE SORTS

Bubble sorting is one of the easiest sorting methods to understand and, unfortunately, most often used sorting algorithm. It is unfortunate because the bubble sort is at times the least efficient sorting technique. It takes a bubble sort longer than any other sorting technique to sort a random list of data. It does have its moment, though, when used with an ordered list of data. If a number is to be inserted into a list of data that have been sorted previously, the bubble sort is the most efficient sorting (insertion) technique available.

Bubble-Sort Algorithm

Table 14-1 illustrates a list of five random numbers that are sorted by a bubble sort. With the bubble sort, adjacent data are compared for magnitude. If the result of the comparison indicates that an exchange is required, the exchange takes place. In the first iteration notice that all data pairs are compared starting with numbers 11 and 14. (Comparisons begin at the bottom of the list.) Because 11 is less than 14, an exchange occurs on the first comparison, as indicated in the second column of numbers. This is repeated until each pair of the original set of data are compared. Notice at the end of the first iteration (rightmost column) that the smallest number is at the top of the list. You could say that the smaller numbers are bubbling up to the top of the list. (This is where the term *bubble sort* originated.)

TABLE 14-1 SAMPLE BUBBLE SORT WITH RANDOMLY ORDERED DATA

Initial		*Iteration 1*	
10	10	10	10
19	19	19	11
12	12	11	19
14	11	12	12
11	14	14	14

Initial	*Iteration 2*
10	10
11	11
19	12
12	19
14	14

Initial	*Iteration 3*
10	10
11	11
12	12
19	14
14	19

If the remaining iterations are examined, notice that each iteration compares one fewer pair of numbers from the list. The second iteration ignores the very first number because it is the smallest number, the third iteration ignores the first two numbers, and so on. It may take up to $n - 1$ iterations to sort a list of numbers using the bubble-sorting technique. Sorting is complete when no additional exchanges take place in an iteration or when the last iteration occurs.

If the data have already been sorted, and one new datum is to be inserted, the bubble sort requires only one iteration. Table 14–2 illustrates an ordered list with a new number placed at the bottom of the list for insertion. As mentioned earlier, this second usage of the bubble sort is the most efficient technique for inserting numbers into an ordered list.

TABLE 14-2 SAMPLE BUBBLE SORT WITH AN
ORDERED LIST OF DATA ILLUSTRATING INSERTION

Initial	Iteration	
10	10	10
12	12	12
14	14	13
16	13	14
13	16	16

Subroutine Implementing a Numeric Bubble Sort

Suppose that a subroutine is required to sort twenty 8-bit numbers using the bubble sort. This is accomplished by using two programmed loops. The outer loop ensures that the data are iterated up to 19 times ($n - 1$ times). The inner loop assures that each iteration compares 19 pairs during the first iteration, 18 pairs during the second iteration, and so on. A flowchart of this subroutine is listed in Fig. 14–1 and a software listing appears in Example 14–1. Notice that a flag is set for each iteration if numbers are exchanged. The flag is then tested at the end of each iteration to determine if any numbers were exchanged. Remember that when numbers are no longer exchanged, or the last iteration occurs, the data are sorted. A more powerful version

```
(EXAMPLE 14-1)

                        ORG   2800H
                   ;
                   ;subroutine to bubble-sort X numbers.
                   ;
                   ;X is stored at the location LIST.
                   ;
                   ;the data is stored following X.
                   ;
2800 21-2B-28  BUB:    LXI   H,LIST  ;address count & data
2803 4E                MOV   C,M     ;get count
2804 06-00             MVI   B,0
2806 09                DAD   B       ;address list bottom
2807 0D                DCR   C       ;adjust count
2808 CA-2A-28          JZ    BUB4    ;if only 1 number
280B E5        BUB1:   PUSH  H       ;save address
280C 16-00             MVI   D,0     ;clear swap flag
280E 41                MOV   B,C     ;load inside count
280F 7E        BUB2:   MOV   A,M     ;compare pair
2810 2B                DCX   H
2811 BE                CMP   M
```

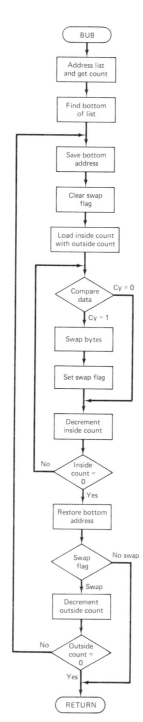

Figure 14-1 The flowchart of a subroutine that bubble-sorts the data at location LIST.

```
2812 D2-1D-28          JNC    BUB3      ;if no swap
2815 16-01             MVI    D,1       ;set swap flag
2817 5F                MOV    E,A       ;swap bytes
2818 7E                MOV    A,M
2819 73                MOV    M,E
281A 23                INX    H
281B 77                MOV    M,A
281C 2B                DCX    H
281D 05         BUB3:  DCR    B         ;decrement inside count
281E C2-0F-28          JNZ    BUB2      ;if inside count <> 0
2821 E1                POP    H         ;address list bottom
2822 15                DCR    D         ;check swap flag
2823 C2-2A-28          JNZ    BUB4      ;if no swap
2826 0D                DCR    C         ;decrement outside count
2827 C2-0B-28          JNZ    BUB1      ;if not done
282A C9         BUB4:  RET              ;return
                       ;
                       ;example data
                       ;
282B 14         LIST:  DB     20            ;count
282C 0A-11-63-16       DB     10,17,99,22   ;data
2830 05-02-0C-42       DB     5,2,12,66
2834 64-03-0B-62       DB     100,3,11,98
2838 37-17-12-01       DB     55,23,18,1
283C 05-14-82-6E       DB     5,20,130,110
```

Example 14-1 *(Continued)*

of Example 14–1 appears in Example 14–2. This modified version of the subroutine is capable of sorting up to 32K words of 16-bit data. As with Example 14–1, no data are passed to the subroutine through the registers. It might be useful to modify both subroutines so that the starting address of the data is passed to the subroutine through the HL register pair. This makes the subroutines more flexible in its application.

```
(EXAMPLE 14-2 page 1 of 2)

                     ORG       2800H
                     ;
                     ;Subroutine to bubble-sort 16-bit X
                     ;numbers.  X is stored at the location
                     ;LIST.  The data is stored following X.
                     ;
2800 21-4B-28  BUBW:  LXI    H,LIST    ;address count & data
2803 5E               MOV    E,M       ;get count
2804 23               INX    H
2805 56               MOV    D,M
2806 2B               DCX    H
2807 D5               PUSH   D
2808 EB               XCHG             ;double count
2809 29               DAD    H
280A EB               XCHG
280B 19               DAD    D         ;address list bottom
280C D1               POP    D
280D 1B               DCX    D         ;adjust count
```

(EXAMPLE 14-2 page 2 of 2)

```
280E 7A                         MOV  A,D
280F B3                         ORA  E
2810 CA-4A-28                   JZ   BUBW5     ;if only 1 number
2813 D5            BUBW1: PUSH  D              ;save count
2814 E5                         PUSH H         ;save address
2815 06-00                      MVI  B,0       ;clear swap flag
2817 4E            BUBW2: MOV   C,M            ;compare numbers
2818 23                         INX  H
2819 7E                         MOV  A,M
281A 2B                         DCX  H
281B 2B                         DCX  H
281C BE                         CMP  M
281D 2B                         DCX  H
281E DA-29-28                   JC   BUBW3     ;if exchange needed
2821 C2-38-28                   JNZ  BUBW4     ;if no exchange needed
2824 79                         MOV  A,C
2825 BE                         CMP  M
2826 D2-38-28                   JNC  BUBW4     ;if no exchange
2829 06-01         BUBW3: MVI   B,1            ;set swap flag
282B 7E                         MOV  A,M       ;swap words
282C 71                         MOV  M,C
282D 23                         INX  H
282E 4E                         MOV  C,M
282F 23                         INX  H
2830 77                         MOV  M,A
2831 23                         INX  H
2832 7E                         MOV  A,M
2833 71                         MOV  M,C
2834 2B                         DCX  H
2835 2B                         DCX  H
2836 77                         MOV  M,A
2837 2B                         DCX  H
2838 1B            BUBW4: DCX   D              ;decrement inside count
2839 7A                         MOV  A,D       ;test count for zero
283A B3                         ORA  E
283B C2-17-28                   JNZ  BUBW2     ;if inside count <> 0
283E E1                         POP  H         ;address list bottom
283F D1                         POP  D         ;get outside count
2840 05                         DCR  B         ;check swap flag
2841 C2-4A-28                   JNZ  BUBW5     ;if no swap
2844 1B                         DCX  D         ;decrement outside count
2845 7A                         MOV  A,D       ;test outside count
2846 B3                         ORA  E
2847 C2-13-28                   JNZ  BUBW1     ;if not done
284A C9            BUBW5: RET                  ;return
                          ;
                          ;example data
                          ;
284B 0A-00         LIST:  DW    10            ;count
284D 64-00-C8-00          DW    100,200 ;data
2851 02-00-1A-01          DW    2,282
2855 B6-00-E8-03          DW    182,1000
2859 2C-01-04-00          DW    300,4
285D F4-01-2C-00          DW    500,44
```

14-3 SHELL SORTS

An important increase in sorting efficiency (a factor of several times for the aver-age-size list) can be obtained by using another sorting technique, called a Shell sort. The Shell sort is actually a modified bubble sort first proposed by D. L. Shell in 1959. The Shell sort is efficient only when used to sort a randomly ordered list of numbers; the bubble sort is more efficient for inserting one number into an ordered list of numbers.

The Shell-Sort Algorithm

In a Shell sort, adjacent data are not compared as in a bubble sort. Instead, numbers that are a half the distance of the total number of data in the list apart are compared. For example, if eight numbers are to be sorted, numbers that are 4 apart are first compared, followed by numbers that are 3 apart, followed by numbers that are 2 apart, and followed by numbers that are adjacent. It takes four passes to accomplish a Shell sort of eight numbers, compared to seven passes to sort the same eight numbers using a bubble sort. As one can imagine, as the size of the group of numbers is in-creased, the time saved becomes even more dramatic.

   The starting interval is computed by dividing the total number of items in the list by 2. The result is a truncated integer. In $n = 8$, the 8 divided by 2 = 4. Four is the distance between the first two numbers that are compared in the sort. If $n = 9$, then 9 divided by 2 = 4 because the result is not rounded up. Table 14–3 shows a series of nine random numbers that are sorted with four iterations using the Shell sort. Notice that the first pass compares numbers that are 4 apart, the second pass numbers that are 3 apart, and so on. After the last comparison (under $i = 1$) the numbers are sorted in numeric order. It takes far less time to pass through the numbers four times (Shell sort) then seven times (bubble sort).

TABLE 14-3 SERIES OF NINE NUMBERS THAT ARE SORTED USING THE SHELL-SORT ALGORITHM

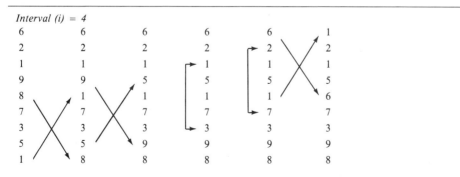

TABLE 14-3 *(Cont.)*

Interval (i) = 3

1	1	1	1	1	1	1
2	2	2	2	2	2	2
1	1	1	1	1	1	1
5	5	5	3	3	3	3
6	6	6	6	6	6	6
7	7	7	7	7	7	7
3	3	3	5	5	5	5
9	9	9	9	9	9	9
8	8	8	8	8	8	8

Interval (i) = 2

1	1	1	1	1	1	1	1
2	2	2	2	2	2	2	2
1	1	1	1	1	1	1	1
3	3	3	3	3	3	3	3
6	6	6	5	5	5	5	5
7	7	7	7	7	7	7	7
5	5	5	6	6	6	6	6
9	9	9	9	9	9	9	9
8	8	8	8	8	8	8	8

Interval (i) = 1

1	1	1	1	1	1	1	1
2	2	2	2	2	2	2	1
1	1	1	1	1	1	1	2
3	3	3	3	3	3	3	3
5	5	5	5	5	5	5	5
7	7	7	6	6	6	6	6
6	6	6	7	7	7	7	7
9	8	8	8	8	8	8	8
8	9	9	9	9	9	9	9

Shell-Sort Software

Figure 14–2 illustrates the flowchart of the Shell sort algorithm. Notice that it is very similar to the flowchart of the bubble sort as illustrated in Fig. 14–1. Example 14–3 lists the subroutine that is written for the Shell sort. Here a list of 8-bit numbers are sorted using this technique. The starting value for *i* is determined by dividing the number of items in the list by a factor of 2.

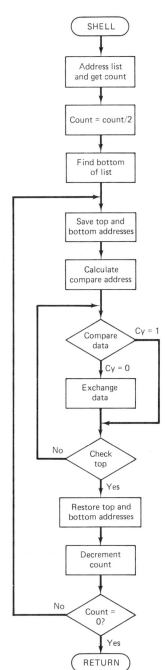

Figure 14-2 Flowchart of subroutine SHELL which performs a shell-sort of the data at location LIST.

(Example 14-3 page 1 of 2)

```
                              ORG    2800H
                    ;
                    ;subroutine to shell-sort X numbers.
                    ;X is stored at the location LIST.
                    ;the data is stored following X.
                    ;
                    ;(the count must be 2 or greater)
                    ;
2800 21-36-28       SHELL: LXI    H,LIST
2803 7E                    MOV    A,M      ;get count
2804 B7                    ORA    A        ;divide by 2
2805 1F                    RAR
2806 4F                    MOV    C,A
2807 5E                    MOV    E,M
2808 16-00                 MVI    D,0
280A 23                    INX    H
280B E5                    PUSH   H        ;save top address
280C 19                    DAD    D        ;find bottom address
280D 2B                    DCX    H
280E D1                    POP    D
280F E5             SHEL1: PUSH   H        ;save bottom address
2810 D5                    PUSH   D        ;save top address
2811 7D                    MOV    A,L      ;form comparison address
2812 91                    SUB    C
2813 5F                    MOV    E,A
2814 7C                    MOV    A,H
2815 DE-00                 SBI    O
2817 57                    MOV    D,A
2818 1A             SHEL2: LDAX   D        ;compare data
2819 BE                    CMP    M
281A DA-21-28             JC     SHEL3    ;if correct order
281D 46                    MOV    B,M      ;exchange data
281E 77                    MOV    M,A
281F 78                    MOV    A,B
2820 12                    STAX   D
2821 E3             SHEL3: XTHL            ;get top address
2822 7A                    MOV    A,D      ;compare addresses
2823 BC                    CMP    H
2824 C2-29-28             JNZ    SHEL4
2827 7B                    MOV    A,E
2828 BD                    CMP    L
2829 E3             SHEL4: XTHL
282A 2B                    DCX    H        ;adjust pointers
282B 1B                    DCX    D
282C C2-18-28             JNZ    SHEL2    ;continue pass
282F D1                    POP    D        ;get top address
2830 E1                    POP    H        ;get bottom address
2831 0D                    DCR    C        ;adjust (i)
2832 C2-0F-28             JNZ    SHEL1    ;if (i) <> 0
2835 C9                    RET
                    ;
                    ;example data
                    ;
2836 0A             LIST:  DB     10       ;count
2837 64-C8                 DB     100,200  ;data
2839 02-B6                 DB     2,182
283B B5-0A                 DB     181,10
283D 1E-04                 DB     30,4
283F 32-2C                 DB     50,44
```

14-4 ALPHANUMERIC SORTS

Alphanumeric sorting uses either the bubble sort discussed in Section 14–2 or the Shell sort discussed in Section 14–3. If the list of alphanumeric data is completely random, the Shell sort is best, and if it is ordered or even semiordered, the bubble sort is best. Alphanumeric data are stored in the memory as proposed in Chapter 13, so that each entry's last digit is a negative value.

The main difference between numeric sorting and alphanumeric sorting is the length of the data. When numbers are sorted, they are always the same width. When alphanumeric data are sorted, the width varies from one byte to almost any width. Alphanumeric sorting therefore requires special comparisons and exchanges that accommodate the variable nature of each character string. (See Table 14–4 for an example set of character strings.)

TABLE 14-4 EXAMPLE LIST OF CHARACTER STRINGS (DOG, DOGGY, EDWARD, GO, WATER, WELL, and ZOO) ILLUSTRATING THAT EACH ENTRY ENDS WITH A NEGATIVE VALUE AND THAT THE END OF THE LIST CONTAINS A CONTROL-Z CHARACTER (1A)

Address	Hexadecimal	ASCII
2000	44 4E C7 44 4E 47 47 D9	DO.DOGG.
2008	45 44 57 41 52 C4 47 CE	EDWAR.G.
2010	57 41 54 45 D2 57 45 4C	WATE.WEL
2018	CC 5A 4E CE 1A 00 00 00	.ZO . . . . .

This section is devoted to inserting a string in an ordered list, because this is the most common way that alphanumeric data are stored in a list in the memory. To accomplish this, two main subroutines are required: compare and insert. The compare subroutine is charged with determining if the string should be inserted, and the insert subroutine is used to store the new string in the ordered list.

Subroutine to Compare Two ASCII-Coded Alphanumeric Character Strings

Before insertion can be accomplished, a few subroutines must be developed. One of these is a subroutine that compares two variable-length ASCII-coded character strings. The outcome of the comparison must indicate which of the strings is nearer the beginning of the alphabet, so that a decision can be made for exchanging the two strings.

The subroutine to accomplish comparison is listed in flowchart form in Fig. 14–3 and the flowchart is translated into software in Example 14–4. Subroutine COMPS requires that the HL register pair address a string in the list of data being sorted, and the DE register pair addresses the string being compared with the list. Upon a return from this subroutine, the carry flag indicates whether the string in

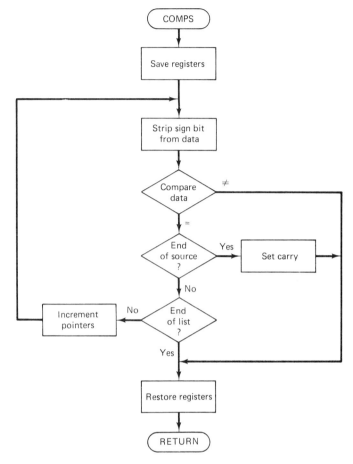

Figure 14-3 Subroutine COMPS compare the source string against the List string. If the end of the source string or a case where the source is nearer the end of the alphabet occurs a return with carry is made.

(EXAMPLE 14-4)

```
        ORG   2800H
;
;subroutine to compare the source
;string addressed by the DE register
;pair with the list string addressed
;by the HL register pair.
;
;upon return carry = 0 if source is
;equal or below list string and
;carry = 1 if source is above list
;string.
;
;both HL and DE remain unchanged by
;this subroutine.
```

```
                            ;
        2800 E5             COMPS:  PUSH  H          ;save registers
        2801 D5                     PUSH  D
        2802 C5                     PUSH  B
        2803 7E             COMPS1: MOV   A,M        ;compare data
        2804 E6-7F                  ANI   7FH
        2806 47                     MOV   B,A
        2807 1A                     LDAX  D
        2808 E6-7F                  ANI   7FH
        280A B8                     CMP   B
        280B C2-1E-28               JNZ   COMPS2     ;if not equal
        280E 1A                     LDAX  D          ;end source string?
        280F B7                     ORA   A
        2810 37                     STC
        2811 FA-1E-28               JM    COMPS2     ;if end source
        2814 7E                     MOV   A,M        ;end list string?
        2815 B7                     ORA   A
        2816 FA-1E-28               JM    COMPS2     ;if end list string
        2819 23                     INX   H          ;adjust pointers
        281A 13                     INX   D
        281B C3-03-28               JMP   COMPS1
        281E C1             COMPS2: POP   B          ;restore registers
        281F D1                     POP   D
        2820 E1                     POP   H
        2821 C9                     RET              ;return
```

Example 14-4 *(Continued)*

the list is above, equal, or below the string being compared to it in the alphabet. A carry of 0 indicates that the string being compared to the list is equal or below the string in the list alphabetically, and a carry of 1 indicates that the string being compared to the list is above the string in the list alphabetically.

Subroutine to Insert an ASCII-Coded Character String into an Ordered List

Once a comparison of the new string is made with the list and it is found that the new string should be inserted, the insert (INSR) subroutine is called. INSR, as illustrated in the flowchart of Fig. 14-4 and the software listing of Example 14-5, is used to insert the character string into the ordered list. As with COMPS, INSR uses HL to address the list and DE to address the new string to be inserted into the list.

```
        (EXAMPLE 14-5 page 1 of 2)

                            ;
                            ;subroutine to insert the string
                            ;addressed by the DE register
                            ;pair into the list at the
                            ;location addressed by the HL
                            ;register pair.
                            ;
                            ;DE and HL do not change.
                            ;
        2822 C5             INSR:   PUSH  B          ;save registers
        2823 D5                     PUSH  D
```

(EXAMPLE 14-5 page 2 of 2)

```
2824 E5                     PUSH  H
2825 01-00-00               LXI   B,0       ;count source string
2828 03          INSR1:     INX   B
2829 1A                     LDAX  D
282A 13                     INX   D
282B B7                     ORA   A
282C F2-28-28               JP    INSR1     ;if end not found
282F 3E-1A                  MVI   A,1AH     ;find control-Z
2831 BE          INSR2:     CMP   M
2832 23                     INX   H
2833 C2-31-28               JNZ   INSR2     ;if not found
2836 2B                     DCX   H
2837 54                     MOV   D,H       ;save address of end
2838 5D                     MOV   E,L
2839 09                     DAD   B         ;form new end address
283A C1                     POP   B         ;get insert address
283B C5                     PUSH  B
283C 1A          INSR3:     LDAX  D         ;move data
283D 77                     MOV   M,A
283E 2B                     DCX   H
283F 1B                     DCX   D
2840 79                     MOV   A,C       ;test for insert address
2841 BB                     CMP   E
2842 C2-3C-28               JNZ   INSR3     ;if not done
2845 78                     MOV   A,B
2846 BA                     CMP   D
2847 C2-3C-28               JNZ   INSR3     ;if not done
284A 1A                     LDAX  D         ;save last character
284B 77                     MOV   M,A
284C E1                     POP   H         ;get insert address
284D D1                     POP   D         ;get source address
284E D5                     PUSH  D         ;save addresses
284F E5                     PUSH  H
2850 1A          INSR4:     LDAX  D         ;insert string
2851 77                     MOV   M,A
2852 23                     INX   H
2853 13                     INX   D
2854 B7                     ORA   A         ;test for end of string
2855 F2-50-28               JP    INSR4     ;if not end
2858 E1                     POP   H         ;restore registers
2859 D1                     POP   D
285A C1                     POP   B
285B C9                     RET             ;return
```

INSR must first determine the length of string to be entered into the list and then make room for it in the list. Once room is made, the string is stored in the list at the location addressed by the HL register pair.

Subroutine to Locate the Correct Place and Insert a String into an Ordered List

The COMPS and INSR subroutines are now combined to form a master subroutine that will insert a character string into any ordered list. This new subroutine (PUT) uses the DE pair to address the new string and the HL register pair to address the

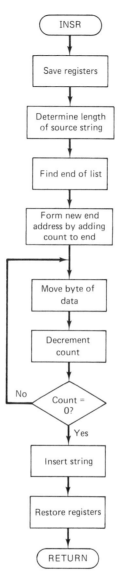

Figure 14-4 Flowchart of subroutine INSR. This flowchart is used to develop software to insert the character string addressed by DE into the LIST location addressed by HL.

top of the list where it is to be inserted. Refer to Fig. 14–5 for the flowchart of this subroutine and to Example 14–6 for the software listing.

Subroutine PUT first checks to see if the comparison point is at the bottom of the list. If the bottom of the list is encountered, the new character string is inserted at this point. If the bottom of the list is not encountered, the new string is compared with the first entry in the list. COMPS determines if the new string is to be entered at this point. If the new string is nearer the front of the alphabet, it is inserted (INSR) at this point. If the new string is nearer the end of the alphabet, PUT scans to the next entry and checks again with COMPS.

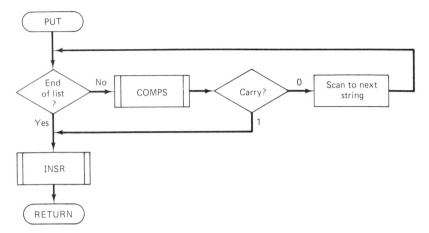

Figure 14-5   Flowchart of subroutine PUT. PUT inserts a new character string in the correct alphabetic position in an ASCII coded LIST.

(EXAMPLE 14-6)

```
                    ;
                    ;subroutine to scan through the
                    ;alphanumeric list addressed by
                    ;the HL register pair and put
                    ;the character string addressed
                    ;by the DE register pair into
                    ;the proper alphabetic position.
                    ;
                    ;all registers are destroyed by
                    ;this subroutine.
                    ;
285C 7E       PUT:    MOV   A,M     ;test for Control-Z
285D FE-1A            CPI   1AH
285F CA-71-28         JZ    PUT2    ;if end of list
2862 CD-00-28         CALL  COMPS   ;compare strings
2865 DA-71-28         JC    PUT2    ;if found
2868 7E       PUT1:   MOV   A,M     ;scan to next string
2869 B7               ORA   A
286A 23               INX   H
286B F2-68-28         JP    PUT1    ;if not end of string
286E C3-5C-28         JMP   PUT     ;check again
2871 CD-22-28 PUT2:   CALL  INSR    ;insert string
2874 C9               RET           ;return
```

14-5 SUMMARY

1. Data are often sorted using one of two common sorting algorithms: bubble sort and Shell sort.
2. Bubble sorts gain their name from the fact that the smaller numbers seem to bubble to the top of the list after each pass of the data in the list.

3. Shell sorts gain their name from the man who first proposed this sorting technique, D. L. Shell.

4. The most efficient sorting technique to use with a list of random data is the Shell sort.

5. The most efficient sorting technique to use with an ordered or semiordered list of data is the bubble sort.

6. Numeric sorting is far easier to accomplish than alphanumeric sorting because the data are of uniform width for numeric sorting.

7. When ASCII character strings are compared, they are compared from the first character to the last. If the two strings being compared are of unequal length and both are identical to the last character, the shorter string is nearer the beginning of the alphabet.

8. Inserting characters in an ordered list as discussed in Section 14–4 is the best method for sorting alphanumeric data. The reason is that only at most one pass of the data occurs for each new entry.

14-6 GLOSSARY

Alphanumeric insertion   A technique used to store new data in an ordered list of alphanumeric data. This technique is most often preferred, because data are usually stored in a list one at a time.

Alphanumeric sort   The ordering of ASCII-coded string data that contains both alphabetic and numeric data.

Bubble sort   A sorting technique where smaller numbers move to the top of the list—hence the name. This sorting technique compares adjacent data until all pairs of data have been compared up to $n - 1$ times.

Exchange flag   An indicator used in a bubble sort to improve the speed of the sort. The exchange flag indicates if an exchange occurred in a pass by the software. If no exchange occurred, the list of data is in sorted order.

Shell sort   A Shell sort is a modified bubble sort first proposed by D. L. Shell in 1959. This sorting technique compares pairs of numbers up to $(n - 1)/2$ times, making it much faster than the bubble sort.

QUESTIONS AND PROBLEMS

14-1. What two basic sorting techniques are presented in this chapter?

14-2. Which sorting technique takes longest to sort a random list of data?

14-3. What sorting technique is best suited to inserting data in an ordered list?

14-4. What sorting technique uses an exchange flag to indicate if an exchange has occurred during a pass?

14-5. If 200 numbers are sorted using the bubble sort, it takes _____ passes to sort the data.

14-6. If 200 numbers are sorted using a Shell sort, it takes _____ passes to sort the data.

14-7. What sorting technique always compares adjacent data?

14-8. Is it possible to modify the subroutine illustrated in Example 14-2 so that it sorts 24-bit numbers? Explain your answer.

14-9. Which sorting technique is best suited to sorting a random list of data?

14-10. If 81 numbers are sorted using a Shell sort, the first pass compares numbers that are _____ bytes apart.

14-11. Modify the subroutine of Example 14-3 so that it sorts 16-bit numbers.

14-12. Why do ASCII-coded string data always end with a negative character?

14-13. The insertion technique for sorting alphanumeric data is most efficient because _____.

14-14. Briefly explain the operation of the subroutine listed in Example 14-4.

14-15. A carry = 1 following the execution of the subroutine in Example 14-4 indicates what condition?

14-16. Briefly explain the operation of the insertion subroutine of Example 14-5.

14-17. Explain the operation of the subroutine illustrated in Example 14-6.

chapter fifteen

DIAGNOSTIC SOFTWARE

Diagnostic software is an extremely important feature of most modern micro-processor-based systems. Whenever most units are powered up, software checks the RAM, ROM, and sometimes the I/O equipment to determine if a fault exists. If a fault does exist, the operator is notified and the service technician is called to repair the defective unit.

In this chapter we detail the software required to check both the RAM and ROM memory of a system and develop diagnostics to test certain types of I/O equipment. This information is meant to be only an introduction to software testing, as there is no possible way that all tests for I/O devices can be covered in this text. Once each of these tests is discussed, the system test software is outlined so that a comprehensive software test can be developed for virtually any microprocessor-based system.

15-1 OBJECTIVES

Upon completion of this chapter, you will be able to:

1. Test any RAM memory for both static (hard) errors and dynamic (soft) errors
2. Test any ROM or EPROM using a checksum—either addition or exclusive-OR
3. Test I/O devices such as keyboards, printers, and RS-232C interfaces
4. Integrate diagnostic software into a diagnostic software package for system testing

15–2 RAM TESTING

The RAM (read/write) memory in a microprocessor-based system should be tested periodically by maintenance personnel or whenever a unit has power applied to it. There are two types of RAM tests that are commonly used: static and dynamic testing. This section details both tests and explains which is better for a particular system.

Static Error RAM Memory Testing

Static RAM testing is used to test any type of RAM to determine if it is functional. It will not find all possible RAM failures, but it does find most of them. A static failure is one where a bit or bits in a RAM are either always a logic 1 or always a logic 0. A static failure is also sometimes called a hard error.

Software to test for a static memory failure usually (1) stores a 00H in every memory location, (2) checks to see if every location is 00H, (3) stores an FFH in every memory location, and (4) tests to see if every memory location is an FFH. If the RAM responds favorably to this test, it has passed the static test and has no hard errors. Figure 15–1 illustrates a flowchart for this type of memory test and Example 15–1 lists a subroutine that follows this flowchart.

Subroutine HDER tests a 256-byte block of memory beginning at the memory location addressed by the HL register pair. Upon return from this subroutine, the HL register pair addresses the beginning location of the next 256-byte segment of

(EXAMPLE 15–1)

```
                              ORG      2000H
                         ;
                         ;subroutine to perform a test for
                         ;hard errors on a 256 byte block
                         ;of memory addressed by the HL
                         ;register pair.
                         ;
                         ;uses subroutine TST and CHK.
                         ;
2000 3E-00    HDER:      MVI   A,00H  ;load test pattern
2002 CD-14-20            CALL  TST    ;save test pattern
2005 CD-1A-20            CALL  CHK    ;check memory
2008 DA-12-20            JC    HDER1  ;if error
200B 2F                  CMA          ;change test pattern
200C CD-14-20            CALL  TST    ;save test pattern
200F CD-1A-20            CALL  CHK    ;check memory
2012 24       HDER1:     INR   H      ;address next block
2013 C9                  RET
                         ;
                         ;subroutine to store A in block
                         ;
2014 77       TST:       MOV   M,A    ;save test pattern
2015 2C                  INR   L      ;point to next
2016 C2-14-20            JNZ   TST    ;loop until L = 00
2019 C9                  RET          ;return
                         ;
                         ;subroutine to test memory for pattern
```

```
                        ;
201A BE            CHK:     CMP   M       ;test memory
201B C2-23-20              JNZ   CHK1    ;if error
201E 2C                    INR   L       ;point to next
201F C2-1A-20             JNZ   CHK     ;loop until L = 00
2022 C9                    RET           ;return no error
2023 37            CHK1:    STC           ;indicate error
2024 C9                    RET           ;return error
```

Example 15-1 *(Continued)*

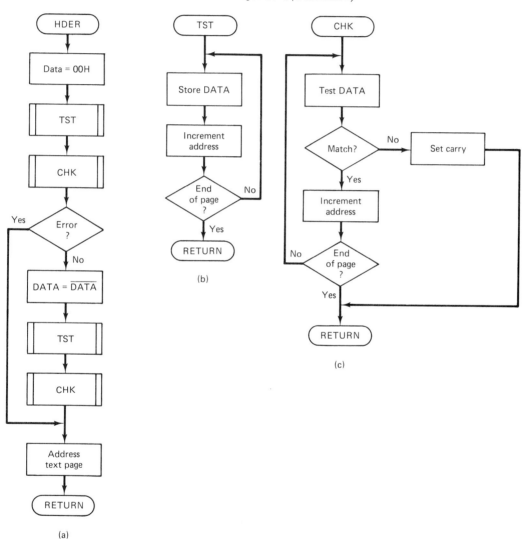

Figure 15-1   (a) Flowchart of the subroutine that tests a page of RAM, addressed by the HL register pair, for a hard error; (b) flowchart of the subroutine that stores data in a memory page; (c) flowchart of the subroutine that checks data in a memory page.

the memory. This allows the subroutine to be used to test any amount of memory by calling it repeatedly. If a hard error is detected, the return occurs with carry set, and if no error is detected, the return occurs with carry cleared.

Checkerboard test. A better method of testing the RAM for a hard error is the checkerboard test. This test is identical to the test performed in subroutine HDER except that instead of testing the RAM for a 00H and an FFH, it tests for a 55H and an AAH. Notice that the bits are alternately set and cleared—hence the name *checkerboard test*. Example 15–2 (subroutine HDCB) shows the modified version of HDER. This type of test can often detect a soft error in addition to a hard error. A soft error is an error in which an adjacent bit of memory can change. The checkerboard test will weed out some of these soft errors, but not all of them.

```
(EXAMPLE 15-2)

                          ORG     2000H
                    ;
                    ;subroutine to perform a checkerboard
                    ;test for hard errors on a 256 byte
                    ;block of memory addressed by the HL
                    ;register pair.
                    ;
                    ;uses subroutine TST and CHK.
                    ;
2000 3E-55    HDCB:   MVI   A,55H ;load test patern
2002 CD-14-20         CALL  TST   ;save test pattern
2005 CD-1A-20         CALL  CHK   ;check memory
2008 DA-12-20         JC    HDCB1 ;if error
200B 2F               CMA         ;change test pattern
200C CD-14-20         CALL  TST   ;save test pattern
200F CD-1A-20         CALL  CHK   ;check memory
2012 24       HDCB1:  INR   H     ;address next block
2013 C9               RET
```

Dynamic Error RAM Testing

Dynamic errors (soft errors) in RAMS are much harder to find because a bit changed in one memory location can change a bit in another memory location. For this reason the dynamic error test takes much more time to accomplish.

One of the more common tests for soft errors is the walking bit test. Table 15–1 shows the contents of the first 16 memory locations on the first and second passes of a walking bit test. After the first pass is completed, the data in each location are tested for correctness. The second pass stores the same data shifted by one location. To completely test a 256-byte block of memory requires 16 passes. This takes at least 16 times longer than the simple static error test described earlier.

The flowchart for a subroutine that performs a walking bit test appears in Figure 15–2, and the subroutine (WALK) is listed in Example 15–3. Subroutine WALK uses a sequence of four instructions to generate the walking bit pattern: RLC, RAR, CMC, and RAL. The RLC and RAR instructions copy the leftmost bit into the carry flag without modifying the contents of the accumulator. These two instructions are fol-

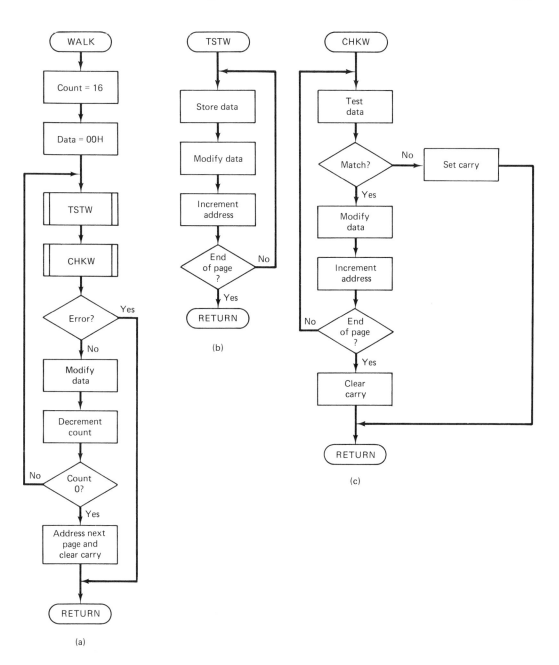

Figure 15-2   (a) Flowchart of the subroutine that tests RAM for soft errors by the walking bit method; (b) subroutine to store the walking bit pattern in a page of memory; (c) subroutine to check a page of memory for the walking bit pattern.

lowed by the CMC instruction, which complements the carry so that it can be moved into the least-significant-bit position of the accumulator with the RAL instruction.

TABLE 15-1 FIRST AND SECOND PASSES OF THE WALKING BIT TEST FOR SOFT ERRORS

Address	First pass	Second pass
XXX0	0000 0000	0000 0001
XXX1	0000 0001	0000 0011
XXX2	0000 0011	0000 0111
XXX3	0000 0111	0000 1111
XXX4	0000 1111	0001 1111
XXX5	0001 1111	0011 1111
XXX6	0011 1111	0111 1111
XXX7	0111 1111	1111 1111
XXX8	1111 1111	1111 1110
XXX9	1111 1110	1111 1100
XXXA	1111 1100	1111 1000
XXXB	1111 1000	1111 0000
XXXC	1111 0000	1110 0000
XXXD	1110 0000	1100 0000
XXXE	1100 0000	1000 0000
XXXF	1000 0000	0000 0000
XX10	0000 0000	0000 0001

Note: These patterns repeat every 16 memory locations.

(EXAMPLE 15-3 page 1 of 2)

```
                        ORG   2000H
              ;
              ;subroutine to perform a walking bit
              ;test for soft errors on a 256 byte
              ;block of memory addressed by the HL
              ;register pair.
              ;
              ;uses subroutine TSTW and CHKW.
              ;
2000 06-10    WALK:   MVI   B,16    ;set count
2002 3E-00            MVI   A,0     ;set start value
2004 CD-18-20 WALK1:  CALL  TSTW    ;store pattern
2007 CD-22-20         CALL  CHKW    ;test pattern
200A DA-17-20         JC    WALK2   ;on error
200D 07               RLC           ;modify pattern
200E 1F               RAR
200F 3F               CMC
2010 17               RAL
2011 05               DCR   B       ;decrement count
2012 C2-04-20         JNZ   WALK1   ;repeat 16 times
2015 24               INR   H       ;point to next block
```

(EXAMPLE 15-3 page 2 of 2)

```
2016 B7              ORA   A     ;clear carry
2017 C9      WALK2:  RET         ;return
             ;
             ;subroutine to store walking bit pattern
             ;in a block of memory.
             ;
2018 77      TSTW:   MOV   M,A   ;save byte
2019 07              RLC         ;modify pattern
201A 1F              RAR
201B 3F              CMC
201C 17              RAL
201D 2C              INR   L     ;point to next location
201E C2-18-20        JNZ   TSTW  ;repeat until L = 00
2021 C9              RET         ;return
             ;
             ;subroutine to test memory for the walking
             ;bit pattern.
             ;
2022 BE      CHKW:   CMP   M     ;check memory
2023 C2-30-20        JNZ   CHKW1 ;error
2026 07              RLC         ;modify pattern
2027 1F              RAR
2028 3F              CMC
2029 17              RAL
202A 2C              INR   L     ;point to next location
202B C2-22-20        JNZ   CHKW  ;repeat until L = 00
202E B7              ORA   A     ;indicate no error
202F C9              RET         ;return
2030 37      CHKW1:  STC         ;indicate error
2031 C9              RET         ;return
```

When WALK is called, the HL register pair must contain the address of the 256-byte block of memory to be tested. After testing this section of memory, the block address located in the HL register pair is automatically incremented before the return. A return carry = 0 indicates no error and a return with carry = 1 indicates a soft error in the section of memory tested by the subroutine.

15-3 ROM TESTING

ROM or EPROM testing is just as important as RAM testing in a microprocessor-based system. How do you test a ROM? Because the program and/or data on a ROM is known, it can be tested. Two methods are normally employed for testing a ROM, the addition checksum, and the exclusive-OR checksum. With the addition checksum all the data on the ROM are added together to form a sum. This sum is always equal to a particular value for a particular ROM. If the checksum is known, the ROM can be tested.

Exclusive-OR Checksum

The exclusive-OR checksum ROM testing technique is fairly common because it is very short. This test uses a subroutine that exclusive-ORs all the data on a ROM together to generate a unique checksum for the ROM. In practice, all but one of the bytes on a ROM contain data. The remaining byte contains a number that forces the checksum for the ROM to be a zero. This is done so that the software for checking the ROM can be simplified. Table 15-2 illustrates a tiny ROM (eight bytes) that contains seven bytes of data and an eighth byte to cause a checksum of 00H. Notice that the eighth byte is actually the exclusive-OR checksum of the first seven bytes.

TABLE 15-2 SMALL ROM CONTAINING SEVEN BYTES OF DATA AND AN EIGHTH BYTE THAT CAUSES THE EXCLUSIVE-OR CHECKSUM TO EQUAL 00H

Address	Data	
0	1010 0000	
1	1100 1111	
2	1001 1100	
3	1000 1000	
4	1111 1111	
5	0000 1010	
6	0000 0111	
7	1000 1001	Makes checksum 00H

Note: If all eight bytes are exclusive-ORed together, the result is a 00H.

Figure 15-3 illustrates a flowchart of a subroutine that performs an exclusive-OR checksum on ROM and Example 15-4 lists the software of the subroutine. Subroutine ROM1 tests the ROM addressed by the HL register pair, whose length is indicated by the number in the BC register pair. Upon return from ROM1, the zero flag indicates the status of the ROM—zero flag = 1, no error, and zero flag = 0, error. Also note that upon return the HL register pair points to the location in memory after the last address on the ROM.

(EXAMPLE 15-4)

```
                        ORG   2000H
                  ;
                  ;subroutine that uses the exclusive-OR
                  ;checksum to test a ROM.
                  ;
                  ;HL addresses starting location.
                  ;BC contains the length of the ROM.
                  ;
                  ;return zero = good ROM
                  ;retrun not zero = bad ROM
                  ;
2000 97           ROM1:   SUB  A      ;clear checksum
2001 AE           ROM1A:  XRA  M      ;exclusive-OR data
2002 23                   INX  H      ;point to next memory
```

```
2003 57           MOV   D,A    ;save checksum
2004 0B           DCX   B      ;decrement count
2005 78           MOV   A,B    ;test BC = 0
2006 B1           ORA   C
2007 7A           MOV   A,D    ;get checksum
2008 C2-01-20     JNZ   ROM1A  ;repeat BC times
200B B7           ORA   A      ;test checksum
200C C9           RET          ;return
```

Example 15-4 *(Continued)*

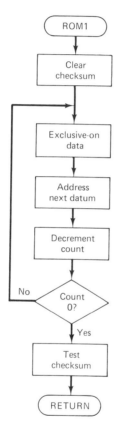

Figure 15-3 ROM1 uses the exclusive-OR technique of the checksum to test ROM.

Addition Checksum

The addition checksum requires a longer subroutine, but it is more accurate than the exclusive-OR checksum. With the addition checksum a 16-bit sum is formed by adding all the bytes of data on the ROM together except for the last two bytes. The last two bytes contain a 16-bit number that, when added to the addition checksum of all the other bytes, forms a sum of 0000H for the ROM.

Subroutine ROM2 is flowcharted in Fig. 15-4 and listed in Example 15-5. As with the exclusive-OR checksum, the addition checksum uses the HL register pair to address the starting location on the ROM and the BC pair to indicate the length of the ROM. Upon return from ROM2, a zero condition indicates no error and a nonzero condition indicates an error.

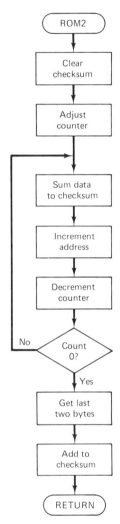

Figure 15-4 ROM2 uses the addition techniques of the checksum to test ROM.

(EXAMPLE 15-5)

```
        ORG   2000H
;
;subroutine that uses the addition
;checksum to test a ROM.
;
;HL addresses starting location.
;BC contains the length of the ROM.
;
```

```
                              ;return zero = good ROM
                              ;retrun not zero = bad ROM
                              ;
 2000  11-00-00   ROM2:    LXI   D,0      ;clear checksum
 2003  0B                  DCX   B        ;subtract 2 from count
 2004  0B                  DCX   B
 2005  7E        ROM2A:    MOV   A,M      ;get data
 2006  83                  ADD   E        ;add to checksum
 2007  5F                  MOV   E,A
 2008  D2-0C-20            JNC   ROM2B    ;if no carry
 200B  14                  INR   D
 200C  23        ROM2B:    INX   H        ;point to next byte
 200D  0B                  DCX   B        ;decrement count
 200E  78                  MOV   A,B      ;test BC = 0
 200F  B1                  ORA   C
 2010  C2-05-20            JNZ   ROM2A    ;if BC <> 0
 2013  4E                  MOV   C,M      ;get 16-bit number
 2014  23                  INX   H
 2015  46                  MOV   B,M
 2016  23                  INX   H
 2017  EB                  XCHG           ;add it to checksum
 2018  09                  DAD   B
 2019  EB                  XCHG
 201A  7A                  MOV   A,D      ;test checksum
 201B  B3                  ORA   E
 201C  C9                  RET            ;return
```

Example 15-5 *(Continued)*

15-4 I/O TESTING

I/O testing is much more varied than either RAM or ROM testing because of the wide variety of I/O devices interfaced to microprocessors. In this section we explain how a few common I/O devices are tested so that the testing methodology can be mastered. After studying this section you should be able to write your own software to test just about any I/O device that is connected to a microprocessor-based system.

Testing Methodology

Whenever an I/O device is tested, it must be tested completely. This means the minimum amount of testing possible to completely test the device. Always keep I/O or any other testing software as simple as possible.

For example, suppose that a microprocessor-based system contained some seven-segment LED displays. To test the displays, one is tempted to output various numbers to them. This is not necessary to completely test the displays. All the test needs to do is to display an 8 on each digit. This will indicate if each display is operating properly.

Another example is a keyboard. How can a keyboard be tested? About the only way that a keyboard can be tested is to type on each key and display the outcome on a CRT screen or LED display. The software for this type of test reads a key and displays the key data on the display device. The process is not completed until the last key on the keyboard is typed.

Printer Interface Testing

A very common I/O device connected to most microprocessor-based systems is some form of printer. To test a printer and its interface, a program is written that sends all the printable characters to the printer. Before the interface is tested, the printer is first tested. This is usually accomplished by turning the printer on while holding down either the line feed button or the form feed button. What you will see on the printer's paper is line after line of all the printable characters. If this functions correctly, the printer is working, but the interface may not be working. The interface is next exercised using a program that sends all the printable characters to the printer. The printer is turned on, placed in the on-line mode, and the program is executed. If the interface and printer are functioning, all the printable characters will appear on the printed page.

A subroutine to test the printer interface is listed in Example 15–6 and a flow-chart of this subroutine is illustrated in Fig. 15–5. Subroutine PRIT sends all the ASCII characters from 21H (!) through 7FH (■) to the printer. On some printers that are capable of graphics characters, the last character should be an FFH instead of a 7FH.

```
(EXAMPLE 15-6)
                              ORG   2000H
                         ;
                         ;subroutine to test the printer
                         ;and printer interface.
                         ;
                         ;prints all of the printable
                         ;characters on the printer.
                         ;
                         ;uses your print driver PRINT
                         ;
2000 3E-21      PRIT:    MVI  A,21H ;starting character
2002 CD-XX-XX   PRIT1:   CALL PRINT ;print character
2005 3C                  INR  A     ;get next character
2006 F2-02-20            JP   PRIT1 ;until 80H
2009 C9                  RET        ;return
```

RS-232C Serial Interface Testing

The RS-232C interface is commonly used to connect many microprocessor-based systems to modems or similar devices. To test this interface in many cases, but not always, the modem or other device is disconnected and pins 2 and 3 are connected together. This ties the transmit data to the receive data pin so that both sections of the interface can be tested. In some interfaces the $\overline{CTS}$ pin must also be activated. Because the receiver can now receive transmitted data, a subroutine can be written to completely test the interface.

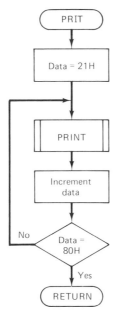

Figure 15-5 Flowchart that is used to develop software that test a printer interface.

A subroutine (RS232) is listed in Example 15-7 which sends and receives all the possible 8-bit characters that can be sent or received by many RS-232C interfaces. (Sometimes only 7 bits can be sent or received.) If an error is detected by the subroutine, it returns, indicating a nonzero condition.

(EXAMPLE 15-7)

```
                    ORG   2000H
                ;
                ;subroutine to test an RS-232C
                ;interface.
                ;
                ;this subroutine should be called
                ;more than one time to run a complete
                ;test on the interface.
                ;
                ;user must provide the SEND and RECV
                ;subroutines.
                ;
                ;return not zero = error
                ;
2000 06-00      RS232:  MVI  B,0     ;initialize first datum
2002 78         RS232A: MOV  A,B     ;send character
2003 CD-XX-XX           CALL SEND
2006 CD-XX-XX           CALL RECV    ;receive same character
2009 B8                 CMP  B       ;test it
200A C2-11-20           JNZ  RS232B  ;error
200D 04                 INR  B
200E C2-02-20           JNZ  RS232A  ;if B <> 0
2011 C9         RS232B: RET          ;return
```

15-5 SYSTEM TESTING

System testing is the integration of all the previously investigated tests into one program. Most systems start by testing at least the RAM and the ROM before the normal system software is entered. A method of developing the system test software is presented in this section.

System Testing Software

Before the system test software can be written, the memory map of the system must be known. Figure 15-6 illustrates a hypothetical memory map that is similar to what one would find in many microprocessor-based systems. Here the ROM memory begins at memory location 0000H and extends to 3FFFH, and the system RAM begins at location 4000H. The RAM is expandable, so that our software must take this into account.

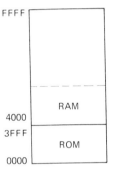

Figure 15-6 Memory map of the system memory used for the test software in Example 15-8.

Before any of the memory can be tested, the stack pointer (SP) must be loaded with a location in the RAM so that the testing subroutines can be called. This is accomplished by the first portion of the software listed in Example 15-8. Here each page of RAM memory is tested for the top of memory beginning at location 4100H. Once a location is found that cannot store a logic 0, the top of the memory is found. This address is loaded into the SP by the SPHL instruction so that the very top of the RAM becomes the stack.

```
(EXAMPLE 15-8 page 1 of 2)

                         ORG   0000H
                 ;
                 ;this system test software begins at
                 ;memory location 0000H because this
                 ;is where the 8085A begins executing
                 ;software when first turned on.
                 ;
0000 C3-80-00    RESET:  JMP   TEST      ;jump over RST vectors
                 ;
                 ;
                 ;find top of memory and load SP
                 ;
```

(EXAMPLE 15-8 page 2 of 2)

```
                        ORG   0080H
0080 21-00-40   TEST:   LXI   H,4000H ;address bottom RAM
0083 7D                 MOV   A,L     ;clear A
0084 24         FTOP:   INR   H       ;point to next page
0085 77                 MOV   M,A     ;store 00H
0086 BE                 CMP   M       ;memory?
0087 CA-84-00           JZ    FTOP    ;if memory
008A F9                 SPHL          ;load stack pointer
                        ;
                        ;test ROM
                        ;
                        ;error handler user provided
                        ;
008B E5                 PUSH  H        ;save top of memory
008C 21-00-00           LXI   H,0      ;load ROM start address
008F 01-00-40           LXI   B,4000H  ;load count
0092 CD-XX-XX           CALL  ROM1     ;call checksum subroutine
0095 C2-XX-XX           JNZ   ERROR    ;go to error handler
                        ;
                        ;test RAM
                        ;
                        ;error handler user provided
                        ;
0098 E1                 POP   H        ;get top of memory
0099 E5                 PUSH  H        ;save top of memory
009A 7C                 MOV   A,H      ;adjust for count
009B D6-41              SUI   41H      ;set count to memory
                                       ;minus one page
009D 47                 MOV   B,A      ;save count
009E CD-XX-XX   TEST1:  CALL  HDCB     ;test page
00A1 05                 DCR   B
00A2 DA-XX-XX           JC    ERROR    ;if bad RAM
00A5 C2-9E-00           JNZ   TEST1    ;if not done
                        ;
                        ;test last page of RAM
                        ;
00A8 C1                 POP   B        ;get top address
00A9 21-00-00           LXI   H,0      ;get SP
00AC 39                 DAD   SP
00AD 25                 DCR   H        ;drop SP down 1 page
00AE F9                 SPHL
00AF 69                 MOV   L,C      ;get top address
00B0 60                 MOV   H,B
00B1 25                 DCR   H        ;point at last page
00B2 CD-XX-XX           CALL  HDCB     ;test last page
00B5 DA-XX-XX           JC    ERROR
00B8 F9                 SPHL           ;reload SP with top
                        ;
                        ;system software begins here
                        ;
```

After the SP is loaded, the ROM is tested. This is accomplished by loading the HL register pair with the starting address of the ROM (0000H) and BC with the length of the ROM (4000H). Notice that this test software is located on the ROM that is being tested.

Once the ROM is tested, the RAM is next tested by getting the address of the top of the memory from the stack and forming a count that is equal to one less than the actual number of RAM pages of memory. This is done so that the stack area is not affected by the RAM test subroutine.

Once all but one page of the RAM is tested, the stack pointer is moved so that the top page of the RAM is tested. After testing the top page of the RAM, the SP is reloaded with the top of memory address and the system software is entered.

15–6 SUMMARY

1. Diagnostic software is an important part of the operating system of any modern microprocessor-based system because it frees the operator from determining whether a system is functioning.

2. Two types of errors commonly occur in RAM memory: static (hard) and dynamic (soft) error. A hard error occurs when a bit or bits inside the RAM stick high or low. A soft error occurs when a bit changes in a memory location due to a change at another memory location.

3. Static tests are performed in one or two ways. The first method (1) stores a 00H in each memory location, (2) checks each location for a 00H, (3) stores an FFH in each memory location, and (4) tests each location for an FFH. The second method is the same as the first except that 55H and AAH are used in place of 00H and FFH.

4. Dynamic tests are performed by using the walking bit test.

5. Checksums are used to test ROM or EPROM. Two types of checksums are commonly used for this test: addition and exclusive-OR.

6. The addition checksum adds all the data on the ROM together, except for the last two bytes, and forms a 16-bit sum. The last two bytes (a 16-bit number) are added to the 16-bit sum to (hopefully) generate a 0000H checksum.

7. The exclusive-OR checksum exclusive-ORs all of the data on the ROM together to generate a 00H checksum. One byte on the ROM is chosen so that the result is a 0.

8. I/O testing is dependent on the I/O device under test. For example, a seven-segment LED display is tested by displaying an 8.

9. System testing software normally includes both the ROM and RAM tests. When a system has power applied to it, the first portion of the program loads the stack pointer and then tests the ROM and RAM memories.

15–7 GLOSSARY

Checkerboard test   A special type of RAM memory test program that stores 55H and AAH alternately in the memory. This test finds all hard errors and some soft errors.

Checksum   A special testing technique that is used to check ROMs. A checksum is either the arithmetic sum of all the data on the ROM or the exclusive-OR of all the data on the ROM.

Diagnostic software   This is software used to test the microprocessor's memory and I/O.

Dynamic fault   A change in a bit or bits triggered by the change of another bit in a RAM memory device.

Hard error   See Static fault.

Modem   A *m*odulator/*dem*odulator is a communications device that allows a microprocessor-based system to communicate to other systems through telephone lines.

RS-232C   A serial interfacing standard that finds widespread application in microprocessor-based systems.

Soft error   See Dynamic fault.

Static fault   A permanent error resulting in a bit or bits remaining at a logic 1 or 0 level.

Walking bit test   A special test that detects soft errors in RAMs.

QUESTIONS AND PROBLEMS ███████████

15-1. What is a hard error?

15-2. What is a soft error?

15-3. Describe how a RAM can be tested for a hard error.

15-4. What is the difference between the subroutine of Examples 15-1 and 15-2?

15-5. In Example 15-2, why does the page address (HL register pair) point to the next page upon return from the subroutine?

15-6. Explain how the walking bit pattern is developed in Example 15-3.

15-7. What two techniques are often used to test a ROM?

15-8. Explain how the exclusive-OR checksum is used to test the ROM as outlined in Example 15-4.

15-9. Which type of checksum technique is more accurate, and why?

15-10. Explain how the zero flag is used to indicate an error in Example 15-5.

15-11. Explain how a seven-segment LED is tested.

15-12. How would you test the CRT screen in a video display terminal?

15-13. Explain how a printer interface is tested.

15-14. What two pins are connected when an RS-232C serial interface is tested?

15-15. Explain how the stack pointer is loaded in Example 15-8.

15-16. Why is the RAM tested in two parts in Example 15-8?

chapter sixteen

INTRODUCTION TO THE 8085A SYSTEM ARCHITECTURE

Before the 8085A microprocessor's hardware and interfacing can be studied, it is important to have a basic understanding of the 8085A microprocessor and the basic architecture of the system. In this chapter you are given the information that you will need to continue your studies of this microprocessor in another course. Why does this book spend so much time on software? Most systems are software based and consequently most of the design work is software. Without this type of basic exposure to software it is doubtful that much design or even understanding of the hardware is achievable.

16-1 OBJECTIVES

Upon completion of this chapter, you will be able to:

1. Understand the basic function of each pin on the 8085A microprocessor
2. Show how the 8085A address/data bus is demultiplexed for creating separate address and data buses
3. Explain how the system timing relates to the operation of basic system components such as memory and simple I/O
4. Describe the operation of the 8085A with its memory and I/O

16-2 THE 8085A PINOUT

The pinout of the 8085A is important because it illustrates which pin connections
are available for interfacing and also the function of each pin. This section details
the purpose of each pin, describes the characteristics of each pin, and discusses power
supply requirements and decoupling.

Pinout

Figure 16-1 illustrates the pinout of the 8085A microprocessor, which is packaged
in a 40-pin dual-in-line package (DIP). Pins 40 and 20 are used for the application
of $+5$ V and ground (0 V), respectively. This power supply arrangement is typical
of most 40-pin integrated circuits. In most circuitry it is a common practice to connect a capacitor (0.1 μF) across pins 20 and 40 to decouple the chip from the power
supply. Without the decoupling capacitor, transients might be generated that could
destroy data in the 8085A or other chips connected to the power supply.

The 8085A requires an average of approximately 170 mA of current (for the
8085A version) from the ± 10 percent $+5$-V power supply for proper operation. If

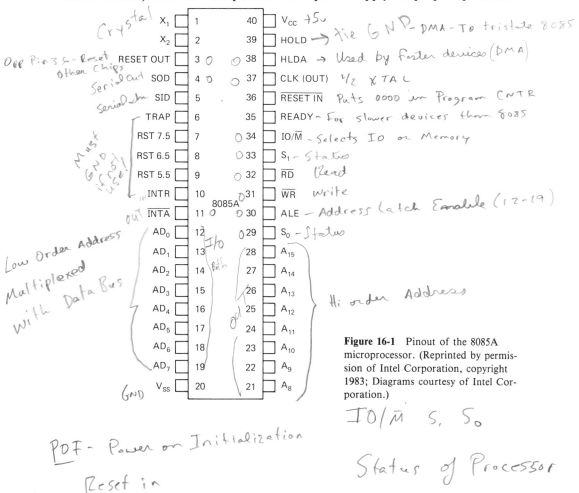

Figure 16-1   Pinout of the 8085A
microprocessor. (Reprinted by permission of Intel Corporation, copyright
1983; Diagrams courtesy of Intel Corporation.)

the supply voltage falls outside this range, the microprocessor will not function properly.

Pin characteristics in general. The 8085A can directly drive a wide variety of TTL and MOSFET digital integrated circuits. Table 16-1 illustrates the fanout (number of inputs that can be connected to one output) of the 8085A to various other logic circuits.

TABLE 16-1 FANOUT CAPABILITIES OF THE 8085A MICROPROCESSOR

Logic type	Part	Fanout
TTL	74XXX	1
TTL	74SXXX	1
TTL	74LSXXX	5
CMOS	CD4XXX	10[a]
HCMOS	74HCXXX	10[a]
MOS	Various	10[a]

[a]A fanout of 10 is limited by the maximum recommended bus capacitance of 150 pF. If the capacitive load is greater, all the timing is degraded.

The input pins represent a very light digital load of ± 10 μA at a very low capacitance of only about 10 pF. This means that the input connects are connected to other logic families (TTL and MOSFET) without any special interfacing circuitry.

Clock Pins

The 8085A has three pins that control or present the clock signal. X1 and X2 are used to determine the clock frequency, and clock output (CLK OUT) is a TTL square-wave clock output. Figure 16-2 illustrates a crystal connected across the X1 and X2 pins to generate the clock signal. X1 and X2 are connected to an internal oscillator which requires only an external timing component to generate the clock signal. Notice that CLK OUT is one-half the crystal frequency. The internal timing information and the clock presented in the timing diagrams of Section 16-2 are also at one-half

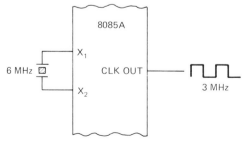

Figure 16-2 A 6MHz crystal connected across X1 and X2 to generate an internal operating frequency of 3 MHz and also a clock output frequency of 3MHz.

the crystal frequency. In many systems a 6.144-MHz or 6-MHz crystal is used to generate the system clock and CLK OUT signal of 3.072 MHz or 3.0 MHz.

Machine Status ` Bits

The machine status bits (S0, S1, and IO/$\overline{\text{M}}$) are used to indicate what type of operation the 8085A is currently executing. Table 16–2 illustrates a function table for these 3 bits. The main purpose of the IO/$\overline{\text{M}}$ signal is to indicate either a memory operation(IO/$\overline{\text{M}}$ = 0) or an I/O operation (IO/$\overline{\text{M}}$ = 1). IO/$\overline{\text{M}}$ is normally used to select the memory or I/O device in a system. In general, if S0 = 0, the operation is a read, and if S1 = 0, the operation is a write. S0 and S1 are normally used to detect an op-code fetch or a halt condition if required and may also be used to generate advanced read and write signals.

TABLE 16–2 MACHINE STATUS BITS S0, S1, AND IO/$\overline{\text{M}}$

S1	S0	IO/$\overline{\text{M}}$	Function
0	0	0	Halt
0	0	1	Halt
0	1	0	Memory write
0	1	1	I/O write
1	0	0	Memory read
1	0	1	I/O read
1	1	0	Op-code fetch
1	1	1	Op-code fetch or interrupt acknowledge

Note: During a hold or reset, all three pins are at their high-impedance state.

Read and Write Control

The $\overline{\text{RD}}$ and $\overline{\text{WR}}$ pins are used to time both memory and I/O for either a read or a write. If the $\overline{\text{RD}}$ = 0 at the same time that IO/$\overline{\text{M}}$ = 0, the operation being performed is a memory read. Similarly, if $\overline{\text{RD}}$ = 0 and IO/$\overline{\text{M}}$ = 1, the operation performed is an I/O read. Table 16–3 illustrates all the possible combinations of these important control signals.

Address and Address/Data Bus Connections

The 8085A has a 16-bit address bus and an 8-bit data bus. The 16-bit address bus allows the microprocessor to directly address 64K different memory locations and the 8-bit data bus allows 8 bits of data to be transferred to or from memory or I/O. In addition to addressing the memory, the address bus connections are also used to address I/O devices when IO/$\overline{\text{M}}$ is at a logic 1 level. The I/O address is an 8-bit number that appears simultaneously on both halves of the address bus.

TABLE 16-3 FUNCTIONS OF THE IO/$\overline{\text{M}}$, $\overline{\text{RD}}$, and $\overline{\text{WR}}$ READ AND WRITE
CONTROL SIGNALS

IO/$\overline{M}$	$\overline{RD}$	$\overline{WR}$	Function
0	0	0	Undefined
0	0	1	Memory read
0	1	0	Memory write
0	1	1	Undefined
1	0	0	Undefined
1	0	1	I/O read
1	1	0	I/O write
1	1	1	Undefined

Pins A15 through AB are used as the most significant half of the memory address and usually the address of the I/O device. The remaining 8 address bits are multiplexed with data on the address/data connections AD7 through AD0. (At times this bus contains memory addressing information, and at other times data that are sent to I/O or memory or received from I/O or memory. To extract the address information from the address/data bus, a special signal, ALE (address latch enable), is provided. Figure 16-3 illustrates the connection of a 74LS373 transparent gated latch which is normally used to demultiplex the address information from the address/data bus. The ALE signal is a clock pulse that causes the 74LS373 to grab the address information at ALE's 1-to-0 transition. The $\overline{\text{OE}}$ pin on the 74LS373 is connected to ground in some systems or to the HLDA output in others. More detail on HLDA is provided later in this section.

Figure 16-4 shows the system bus model of the 8085A microprocessor, illustrating the control, data, and address buses. The system model is used to interface both memory and most I/O devices to the 8085A. The address bus selects a memory location or I/O device, the data bus is used to convey the data to or from memory or I/O, and the control bus commands the memory or I/O to read or write data.

Resetting the 8085A

Two control pins ($\overline{\text{RESET IN}}$ and RESET OUT) are used for resetting the microprocessor and the system peripheral components. $\overline{\text{RESET IN}}$ is used to initialize the 8085A upon the application of dc power or at any time that the operator deems a reset necessary. Figure 16-5 illustrates the typical circuit that is connected to the $\overline{\text{RESET IN}}$ pin. If the 8085A is turned off for a long period, C discharges to 0 V. When dc power is applied, the $\overline{\text{RESET IN}}$ pin will initially see the 0 V on C. After a short period of time C charges to 5 V through R and the 8085A is allowed to continue normal operation. The typical values for R and C vary widely, but they usually have a time constant of 75–100 ms.

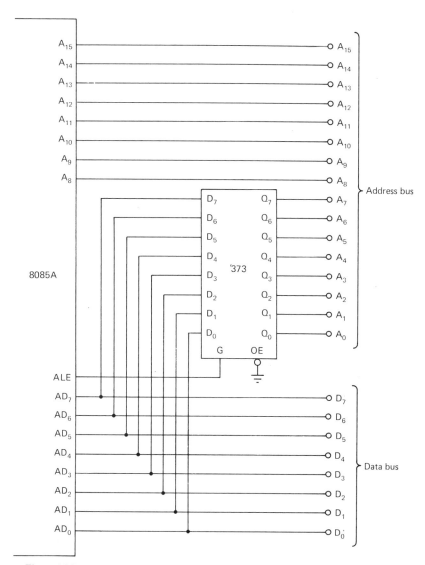

Figure 16-3   ALE used to demultiplex the address/data bus of the 8085A providing a separate address and data bus.

Whenever the 8085A is reset by applying dc power or pushing the pushbutton switch, it clears the program counter and some additional internal bits. If the program counter is cleared by a reset, the 8085A begins executing the program that is stored beginning at memory location 0000H. Table 16-4 illustrates the effect of the reset input. The RESET OUT pin becomes a logic 1 whenever the $\overline{\text{RESET IN}}$ pin is a logic 0. RESET OUT is normally used to reset peripheral equipment in an 8085A-based system.

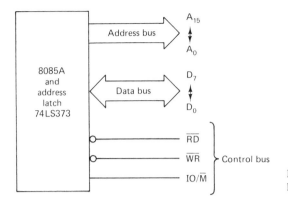

Figure 16-4 The 8085A and address latch which generate the system buses.

TABLE 16-4 EFFECT OF APPLYING 0 V TO THE RESET IN PIN

Internal device	State
Program counter	0000H (address of first instruction)
Instruction register	00H (NOP instruction)
INTE F-F	0 (interrupts off)
RST 7.5 F-F	0 (ignore RST 7.5 input)
TRAP F-F	0 (ignore TRAP input)
SOD F-F	0 (SOD pin = 0)
Machine state F-F	0 (start at first machine state)
Machine cycle F-F	0 (op-code fetch)
HOLD F-F	0 (prevent DMA)
INTR F-F	0 (prevent interrupt)
READY F-F	0 (indicate system ready)
RST 5.5 mask	1 (RST 5.5 pin off)
RST 6.5 mask	1 (RST 6.5 pin off)
RST 7.5 mask	1 (RST 7.5 pin off)

Note: F-F, flip-flop.

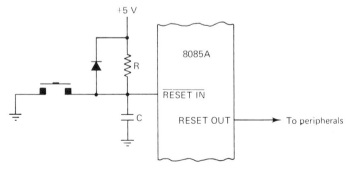

Figure 16-5 The circuit used to automatically reset the 8085A whenever DC power is applied. The pushbutton may also be used by the operator to reset the 8085A.

Interrupt Control Pins

There are five interrupt control inputs (TRAP, RST 7.5, RST 6.5, RST 5.5, and INTR) and one interrupt control output (INTA) available on the 8085A microprocessor. An interrupt is a hardware-initiated subroutine CALL. This means that if an interrupt pin is enabled and activated, a subroutine will be called, interrupting the program that is currently executing. Table 16–5 illustrates the locations of the subroutines called by each of the interrupt input pins. An interrupt is accepted by the 8085A at the end of each instruction if it is asserted (a logic 1 on an interrupt input).

TABLE 16-5 SUBROUTINE ADDRESSES
CALLED BY THE INTERRUPT INPUT PINS

Pin	Subroutine location
TRAP	0024H
RST 5.5	002CH
RST 6.5	0034H
RST 7.5	003CH
INTR	a

[a]The address of the subroutine called by this input is determined by the external hardware.

Figure 16–6 illustrates the usage of the INTR (interrupt request) input and the application of a RST instruction to the address/data bus in response to the INTA (interrupt acknowledge) pulse. If INTR is asserted, the 8085A responds with an INTA

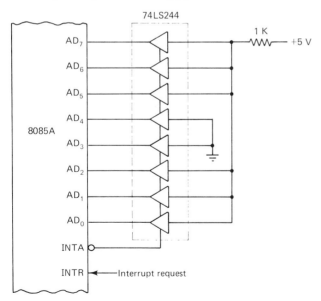

Figure 16-6 A circuit that causes an RST4 instruction (E7H) to be executed in response to an INTR.

pulse. During the $\overline{\text{INTA}}$ pulse, the 8085A expects to see an instruction applied to its data bus. The circuit of Fig. 16–6 applies a RST 4 instruction to the data bus in response to the INTR. The RST 4 instruction causes the subroutine stored beginning at 0020H to be executed. Any of the RST instructions can be applied during an $\overline{\text{INTA}}$ pulse.

Serial Data Pins

The 8085A has two pins that are used for inputting and outputting serial data: SID (serial data input) and SOD (serial data output) The SOD pin is controlled by the SIM instruction and the SID pin is read by the RIM instruction. These instructions are explained in Section 6–5.

Ready

The READY pin is an input that is used to indicate that the external memory and I/O are ready for the microprocessor to continue its operation. In most modern systems this pin is tied to a logic 1 level, indicating that the system is always ready. If a very slow (access time that is longer than 575 ns) memory or I/O device is attached to the 8085A, this pin is controlled. If a 0 is applied to READY, the 8085A enters into wait states. A wait state is a clocking period (at a 3-MHz clock rate, 1 wait = 333 ns). This allows the external memory to request as many wait states as are required to obtain the needed access time.

Another use of the READY pin is a run/stop function. If READY = 1, the microprocessor runs a program, and if READY = 0, the microprocessor waits for READY to become a logic 1. Figure 16–7 illustrates a simple toggle switch that is used to cause a run or a stop condition.

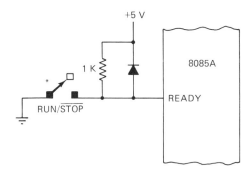

Figure 16-7 Implementing the RUN/STOP function by controlling the READY input to the 8085A microprocessor.

* Switch shown in the RUN position.

Direct Memory Access

The last two pins (HOLD and HLDA) are used for direct memory access (DMA). A DMA is an I/O technique where the external I/O device can request the use of the microprocessor buses. If HOLD = 1, the 8085A will place its address, data, and control pins at their high-impedance state and stop executing the program. This allows an external I/O device to gain access to the memory without the intervention of the 8085A. DMA action is signaled by the logic 1 condition on the HLDA (hold acknowl-edge pin) during a DMA. The DMA I/O technique allows external I/O devices to gain high-speed access to the memory. DMA transfers can proceed at rates of up to 2M bytes of data per second. Under programmed control, data transfer rates are normally limited to about 30,000 bytes per second. DMA data transfer is used for CRT terminals and sometimes disk memory systems because of the high rate of data transfer speed.

16-3 8085A READ AND WRITE TIMING

The timing of the microprocessor is important if the external memory and I/O opera-tion are to be understood with the execution of instructions. Timing also plays an important part in the selection of compatible memory and I/O devices.

This section details the operation of the basic read and write timing signals for the execution of instructions. It also explains how to determine the allowable mem-ory access time provided by the 8085A operating at any clock speed.

Basic Read Timing

Figure 16–8 depicts the basic timing signals required to read data from memory or I/O. At the top of this diagram the system clock signal is divided into T-states. A T-state is equal to one clock period beginning at the logic 1-to-0 transition and end-ing at the logic 1-to-0 transition.

Read timing is always composed of three T-states. (Some instructions may re-quire more states, but it takes exactly three to read data from memory or I/O.)

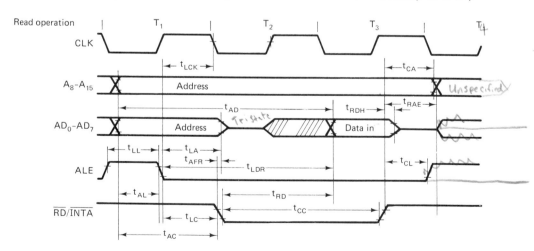

Figure 16-8   Basic 8085A read timing. (Reprinted by permission of Intel Corporation, copy-right 1983; Diagrams courtesy of Intel Corporation.)

State T1.   T1 is used by the 8085A to issue the address on the address bus (A15 through A8) and also the address/data bus (AD7 through AD0). In addition to sending the address to the memory or I/O, the following information is provided by the 8085A: the status bits (S1 and S0), IO/$\overline{\text{M}}$, and ALE. Remember that ALE is used to demultiplex the address/data bus, which contains only addressing information during T1.

State T2.   T2 is used by the 8085A to allow the memory enough time to access the data that are sampled during the next state, T3. It is also used to issue the $\overline{\text{RD}}$ signal to cause the memory or I/O to read data. The only other event that occurs during T2 is that the READY input is sampled. READY is sampled at the 0-to-1 transition of the clock during T2. If READY is a logic 1 at this time, the next state is T3, but if READY is a logic 0, the next state is Tw (wait state). If a wait state is caused, the READY input is also sampled in each Tw.

State T3.   T3 is used to read the data from the data bus into the microprocessor during this state. Assuming that the memory or I/O has applied the data to the data bus, data are sampled during T3 at the 0-to-1 transition of the clock.

Memory access time.   The 8085A allows the memory 575 ns of time to access data if operated at the maximum clock cycle time of 320 ns. If the clock time is longer, so is the access time. Memory access time is the time from where the memory address appears to where the data are read from the data bus by the microprocessor. In the timing diagram this is labeled TAD (time to access data). An access time of 575 ns is adequate to interface to almost any of today's standard memory and I/O components. It is difficult to find a device with an access time of longer than 450 ns.

Basic Write Timing

Figure 16–9 depicts the basic write timing for the 8085A microprocessor. Notice how similar this timing is to the read timing illustrated in Fig. 16–8. In fact, write timing

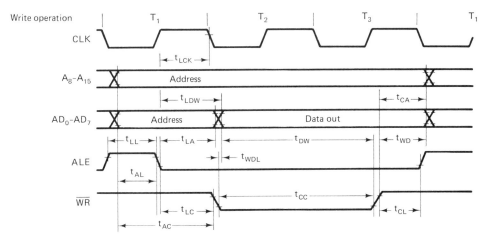

Figure 16-9 Basic 8085A write timing. (Reprinted by permission of Intel Corporation, copyright 1983; Diagrams courtesy of Intel Corporation.)

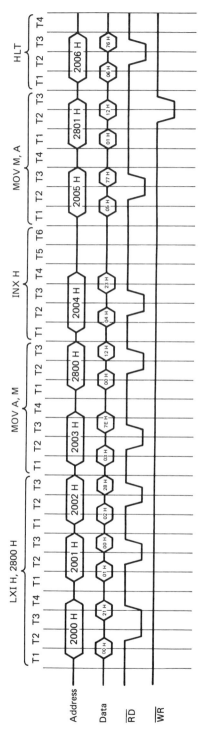

Figure 16-10 The timing sequence generated by program example (Example 16-11).

is different in only one respect from read timing—$\overline{WR}$ is asserted in place of $\overline{RD}$ during T2. Otherwise, the purpose of each machine state is identical to read timing. Instead of reading the data during T3, data are written to an external memory or I/O device from the data bus. Notice that the 0-to-1 transition of the $\overline{WR}$ signal is used to actually transfer the data from the data bus to the memory or I/O device.

Bus Reaction During the Execution of a Short Program

To gain a better understanding of the bus signals during the execution of software, Fig. 16-10 illustrates the timing realized from the execution of the short program listed in Example 16-1. Example 16-1 shows a short program that transfers the data stored at memory location 2800H into memory location 2801H. This program then ends in a HLT instruction, so that it could be ended in a reasonable amount of space. The timing diagrams point out exactly what information appears at each bus for each instruction as it is executed. This allows you to develop a better understanding of the bus signals as they appear to the memory.

```
(EXAMPLE 16-1)

                          ORG   2000H
                     ;
                     ;sample program used to illustrate
                     ;bus timing.
                     ;
     2000 21-00-28   START: LXI  H,2800H  ;address data
     2003 7E                MOV  A,M      ;get data
     2004 23                INX  H        ;address destination
     2005 77                MOV  M,A      ;save data
     2006 76                HLT           ;end program
```

16-4 MEMORY INTERFACE

This section introduces you to the basic memory interface and it is not intended to cover all possible memory devices or addressing techniques—that would require several chapters. Introduced are both the ROM and the static RAM, which are shown operating with the 8085A.

ROM Interface

Most microprocessor-based systems contain a ROM or EPROM for program storage. The purpose of the interface between the ROM and the microprocessor is to turn the ROM on for the appropriate range of memory addresses. This range of addresses varies from system to system, but in general the ROM normally functions beginning at memory location 0000H and upward.

Figure 16-11 illustrates a system that contains three 2732 EPROM (4K × 8) memory devices interfaced to the microprocessor through a 74LS138 3-line-to-8-line decoder.

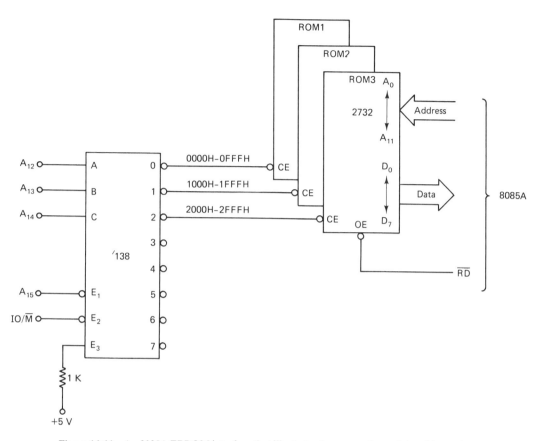

Figure 16-11   An 8085A EPROM interface that illustrates the connections of the address, data and control buses.

The 74LS138 decoder.   The purpose of the decoder is to decode the proper range of memory addresses for each EPROM. All the decoder's outputs are at a logic 1 unless the three enable (E) inputs are at their active levels. This means that $\overline{E1}$ and $\overline{E2}$ must be 0 and E3 must be 1 for any output to become a logic 0. Which output becomes a 0 when the decoder is enabled? The output that is selected by address inputs A, B, and C becomes a logic 0. Table 16-6 illustrates the operation of the decoder.

Explanation of Fig. 16-11.   In the circuit of Fig. 16-11, address pins A15 and IO/$\overline{M}$ are connected to decoder pins $\overline{E1}$ and $\overline{E2}$ and E3 is pulled up to a logic 1 through a pull-up resistor. This means that no output appears from the decoder until A15 = 0 and IO/$\overline{M}$ = 0. In other words, the only time that any EPROM connected to a decoder's output can be turned on is when the address begins with a binary 0 (locations 0000H through 7FFFH). In addition to A15, address bits A14, A13, and A12 are connected to decoder inputs C, B, and A. This means that these three ad-

TABLE 16-6 TRUTH TABLE OF A 74LS138 3-LINE-TO-8-LINE DECODER

Inputs						Outputs							
$\overline{E1}$	$\overline{E2}$	E3	C	B	A	$\overline{0}$	$\overline{1}$	$\overline{2}$	$\overline{3}$	$\overline{4}$	$\overline{5}$	$\overline{6}$	$\overline{7}$
1	×	×	×	×	×	1	1	1	1	1	1	1	1
×	1	×	×	×	×	1	1	1	1	1	1	1	1
×	×	0	×	×	×	1	1	1	1	1	1	1	1
0	0	1	0	0	0	0	1	1	1	1	1	1	1
0	0	1	0	0	1	1	0	1	1	1	1	1	1
0	0	1	0	1	0	1	1	0	1	1	1	1	1
0	0	1	0	1	1	1	1	1	0	1	1	1	1
0	0	1	1	0	0	1	1	1	1	0	1	1	1
0	0	1	1	0	1	1	1	1	1	1	0	1	1
0	0	1	1	1	0	1	1	1	1	1	1	0	1
0	0	1	1	1	1	1	1	1	1	1	1	1	0

Note: × = don't care (0 or 1).

dress bits select which output becomes active if A15 is 0. Table 16–7 lists the address ranges available at each output pin of this decoder.

Outputs $\overline{0}$, $\overline{1}$, and $\overline{2}$ are connected to $\overline{CE}$ pins on three different EPROMs. The $\overline{CE}$ input to an EPROM is used to enable (turn on) the EPROM. The EPROMS are enabled for the following addresses: EPROM0, 0000H through 0FFFH; EPROM1, 1000H through 1FFFH and EPROM2, 2000H through 2FFFH.

TABLE 16-7 ADDRESS RANGES OF THE OUTPUT PINS FOR THE DECODER OF FIG. 16–11

Address				Range	Output pin
A15	A14	A13	A12		
0	0	0	0	0000H–0FFFH	$\overline{0}$
0	0	0	1	1000H–1FFFH	$\overline{1}$
0	0	1	0	2000H–2FFFH	$\overline{2}$
0	0	1	1	3000H–3FFFH	$\overline{3}$
0	1	0	0	4000H–4FFFH	$\overline{4}$
0	1	0	1	5000H–5FFFH	$\overline{5}$
0	1	1	0	6000H–6FFFH	$\overline{6}$
0	1	1	1	7000H–7FFFH	$\overline{7}$

In addition to the $\overline{CE}$ input on each EPROM, there is also an $\overline{OE}$ connection. $\overline{OE}$ is used to enable the output buffers inside the EPROM. In this example $\overline{OE}$ is connected to the microprocessor's $\overline{RD}$ signal so that the EPROM's outputs are potentially enabled for a read. The outputs are enabled only if both $\overline{OE}$ and $\overline{CE}$ are 0, and that can only happen to one EPROM at a time because of the decoder circuit.

Finally, each EPROM has address bus connections A11 through A0 and data output pins D7 through D0. The address connections are connected to the 8085A address bus and the data output connections are connected to the data bus. Notice that each EPROM addresses 4K bytes of memory because of the 12 address inputs ($2^{12} = 4096$).

RAM Interface

The RAM interface illustrated in Fig. 16–12 is similar to the EPROM interface illustrated in Fig. 16–11. A few major differences exist: (1) the 2732 EPROMs are 4K × 8 and the 6116 RAMs are 2K × 8, and (2) the 6116s have an extra input ($\overline{WE}$) that is connected to the 8085A $\overline{WR}$ pin.

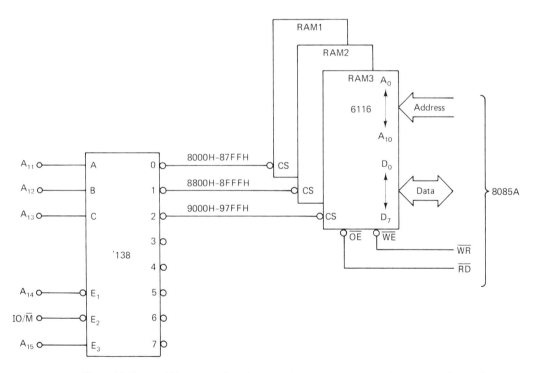

Figure 16-12   An 8085A RAM interface that illustrates the connections of the address, data and control buses.

RAM interface decoder.   The decoder in the RAM interface is connected so that A15 must be a logic 1 to enable any RAMs. Also, IO/$\overline{\text{M}}$ is connected to $\overline{\text{E1}}$, the address input A14 is attached to the $\overline{\text{E2}}$ input, and address inputs A13, A12, and A11 are connected to A, B, and C. This means that no decoder output can become active unless a memory operation occurs from memory address 8000H–BFFFH. Refer to Table 16–8 for a list of the addresses decoded by the 74LS138 in Fig. 16–12.

Explanation of Fig. 16–12.   If an address within the range 8000H through BFFFH appears on the 8085A address bus, the decoder is enabled. One of the eight output connections becomes a logic 0, which in turn selects one of the RAM memory devices. ($\overline{\text{CS}}$ is an input that selects or turns on the RAM.)

Once one of the RAMs is selected, the microprocessor issues either a $\overline{\text{RD}}$ or $\overline{\text{WR}}$ signal. If the $\overline{\text{RD}}$ signal is issued, the $\overline{\text{OE}}$ pin of the selected RAM is a 0, causing that RAM to output data to the microprocessor's data bus. If the $\overline{\text{WR}}$ signal is issued, the $\overline{\text{WE}}$ pin is at a logic 0, causing the selected RAM to write data from the data bus.

TABLE 16-8 ADDRESS RANGES OF THE OUTPUT PINS FOR THE DECODER OF FIG. 16-12

Address					Range	Output pin
A15	A14	A13	A12	A11		
1	0	0	0	0	8000H–87FFH	0
1	0	0	0	1	8800H–8FFFH	1
1	0	0	1	0	9000H–97FFH	2
1	0	0	1	1	9800H–9FFFH	3
1	0	1	0	0	A000H–A7FFH	4
1	0	1	0	1	A800H–AFFFH	5
1	0	1	1	0	B000H–B7FFH	6
1	0	1	1	1	B800H–BFFFH	7

16-5 I/O INTERFACE

I/O devices are available to accomplish any digital-to-human or digital-to-machine interface and also any human- or machine-to-digital interface. In this section we introduce the topic of I/O interfacing by looking at the basic input and output interface.

Basic Input Interface

To input data to the microprocessor, the 8085A executes an IN instruction. The IN instruction causes data from an external device to be input through the data bus connections into the accumulator. The form of the instruction is IN d8, where d8 is the address of the external I/O device. The device address appears on the address bus just as a memory address does except that it appears twice. IN 10H would address data at input device number 10H, which appears on the address bus as a 1010H.

Decoding the device address.   Because the device address appears on the address bus twice, either half can be decoded. In practice the most significant half is often decoded because it is available on the unmultiplexed address pins A15 through A8. Figure 16–13 illustrates an eight-input NAND gate that is used to decode address 10H from the most significant half of the address bus. The output of this decoded address is then combined with the IO/$\overline{M}$ signal and also $\overline{RD}$ to produce a unique signal for an IN 10H. The only time that the output of this circuit will ever go low is for an IN 10H. Because the output of this circuit goes low at $\overline{RD}$ time, it can be used to gate data directly onto the data bus for inputting into the 8085A. Figure 16–14 illustrates a series of eight toggle switches whose data are input to the data bus for the active-low $\overline{\text{IN 10H}}$ strobe generated by the decoder in Fig. 16–13. The switches are connected to the data bus through a series of eight three-state buffers. When the control input to the buffer becomes a logic 0, the data input is passed through to the output; otherwise, the buffer is an open circuit.

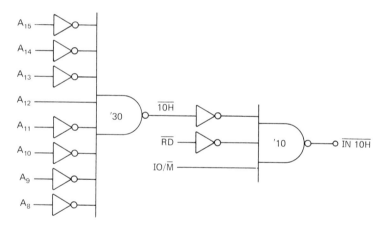

Figure 16-13   Circuit that decodes the IN10H instruction.

Basic Output Interface

To output data from the microprocessor, the 8085A executes an OUT instruction. The OUT instruction causes data from the accumulator to be output through the data bus connections to the external device. The form of the instruction is OUT d8, where d8 is the address of the external I/O device. The device address appears on the address bus just as it did for the IN instruction. OUT 1AH addresses data at output device number 1AH, which appears on the address bus as a 1A1AH.

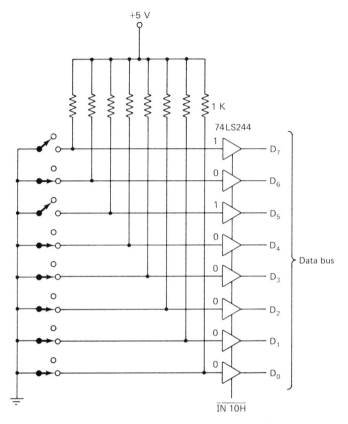

Figure 16-14   A set of 8 toggle switches that are input to the microprocessor for an IN10H instruction.

The basic output circuit.   The basic output circuit with a decoder used to decode the OUT 1AH instruction is illustrated in Fig. 16–15. Here the $\overline{\text{WR}}$ signal is combined with the output of the eight-input NAND gate and the IO/$\overline{\text{M}}$ signal in order to generate the $\overline{\text{OUT 1AH}}$ strobe. The active-low strobe is used as a clock pulse to a series of eight D-type flip-flops inside a 74LS374. (Notice that a positive edge-triggered latch is used here because the data are not stable on the data bus until the 0-to-1 transition of the $\overline{\text{WR}}$ signal.)

Whenever an OUT 1AH instruction is executed, the contents of the accumulator are placed onto the data bus. The data bus is connected to the D inputs of the flip-flops, which capture the information on the data bus at the trailing edge of the $\overline{\text{OUT 1AH}}$ strobe. The accumulator data are held in these eight flip-flops until the next time that an OUT 1AH instruction is executed.

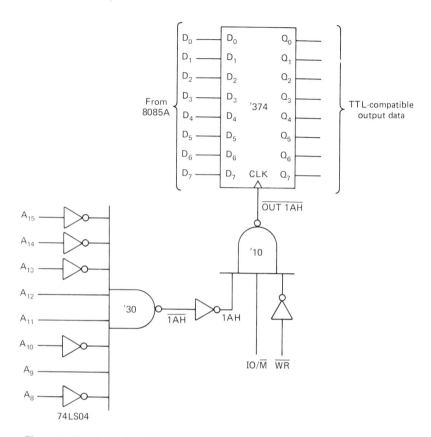

Figure 16-15   Circuit that holds data from the 8085A microprocessor's accumulator for an OUT 1AH.

16-6 SUMMARY

1. The 8085A microprocessor is an 8-bit machine that is packaged in a 40-pin DIP. Power supply requirements are + 5.0 V at approximately 170 mA of current.

2. The 8085A output pins are capable of driving one 74XXX, one 74SXXX, five 74LSXXX, approximately ten 74HCXXX, or approximately ten CD4XXX loads.

3. The 8085A normally functions with an external crystal of 6 MHz or 6.144 MHz which generates an internal operating frequency of either 3 MHz or 3.072 MHz.

4. The 8085A has a 16-bit address bus which allows it to directly address 64K different memory locations. The 8-bit data bus allows the microprocessor to address data in 8-bit widths.

5. The main control signals are IO/$\overline{\text{M}}$ (I/O or memory), $\overline{\text{RD}}$ (read), and $\overline{\text{WR}}$ (write).

6. The address/data bus is a multiplexed bus which at times contains address bit positions A7 through A0 and at other times contains data bus bit positions D7 through D0. The ALE (address latch enable) signal is used to separate the address information from the data bus.

7. Whenever the 8085A is reset, many things occur, but the most notable thing that happens is that the internal program counter is cleared to 0000H, so that the first instruction executed after a reset is at location 0000H.

8. Interrupts are available through a series of five interrupt inputs. Four of the interrupt inputs are internally decoded to automatically call subroutines. The fifth interrupt input requires that the user provide the subroutine call instruction via the $\overline{\text{INTA}}$ pin and the data bus.

9. SID (serial input data) and SOD (serial output data) are used to provide or receive serial data.

10. READY is used to cause the 8085A to enter wait states for slower memory components. It is also used to implement the run/stop function.

11. A special type of I/O technique that bypasses the microprocessor is available in the 8085A. This special I/O technique is called DMA (direct memory access).

12. Read and write timing is composed of three clocking periods (T-states). T1 is used to provide the memory with a memory address, T2 is used to issue the $\overline{\text{RD}}$ or $\overline{\text{WR}}$ command, and T3 is used to accomplish the read or write.

13. The 8085A microprocessor allows the memory 575 ns of time to access data.

14. The 74LS138 decoder is used to generate the $\overline{\text{CE}}$ (ROM) or $\overline{\text{CS}}$ (RAM) signal that is used to enable either the ROM or the RAM.

15. The IN and OUT instructions transfer data to and from the I/O device through the data bus. The I/O device address appears on the address bus.

16–7 GLOSSARY

Address bus   A set of connections used to address memory and I/O.

Address/data bus   A special bus available on many Intel microprocessors that contains both memory address information and data bus information.

ALE   Address latch enable is a special signal that is used to demultiplex the address/data bus in most Intel microprocessors.

Data Bus   A microprocessor bus that is used to transfer data to and from the memory and I/O in a computer system.

DMA   Direct memory access is an I/O technique where the I/O device turns the microprocessor off through the HOLD pin and directly accesses data in the memory.

Interrupt   A hardware-initiated subroutine call.

IO/$\overline{M}$ A special signal that indicates a memory operation (0) or an I/O operation (1).

Memory access time   This is the time allowed to the memory device to present the data to the data bus. It is measured from when the microprocessor outputs the address until the point where it samples the data.

Multiplexed bus   A bus that contains more than one piece of information. The term *multiplex* means to share.

$\overline{RD}$ The read signal is used to notify the memory or I/O that it is time to place the data on the data bus.

Strobe   A signal that indicates a unique event. For example, $\overline{RD}$ is a strobe because it indicates a unique event—read.

T-state   A T-state is one 8085A clocking period. T-states are used to explain the operation of the microprocessor timing.

Wait state   A special mode of operation where the microprocessor waits for slow memory or I/O. The only thing that changes during a wait state is the clock.

$\overline{WR}$ The write signal is used to notify the memory or I/O device that it is time to remove the data from the data bus.

QUESTIONS AND PROBLEMS

16-1. The 8085A is normally packaged in a _____ -pin DIP.

16-2. A _____ μF capacitor is normally used to decouple digital integrated circuits from the dc power supply.

16-3. How many 74LSXXX unit loads can be driven from an 8085A output pin?

16-4. What limits the number of MOS loads that can be connected to an 8085A output pin?

16-5. If the 8085A is operated at an internal clock frequency of 2 MHz, a _____ -MHz crystal must be connected across X1 and X2.

16-6. What does the $10/\overline{M}$ pin indicate?

16-7. A halt is indicated when S0 and S1 are both logic _____ levels.

16-8. Which two 8085A control pins are used to cause the memory or I/O to perform a read or a write operation?

16-9. Which 8085A bus is multiplexed?

16-10. A memory read operation is indicated when $IO/\overline{M}$ = _____ and $\overline{RD}$ = _____ .

16-11. An I/O write operation is indicated when $IO/\overline{M}$ = _____ and $\overline{WR}$ = _____ .

16-12. Explain the purpose of the ALE pin.

16-13. Explain how the reset circuit of Fig. 16-5 operates.

16-14. Whenever the 8085A is reset it begins executing the program located at memory location _____ .

16-15. If a logic 1 is placed on the TRAP pin, the interrupt service subroutine that begins at memory location _____ is called.

16-16. Develop a short sequence of instructions that will place a logic 1 on the SOD pin.

16-17. If a logic _____ is placed on the READY pin, the 8085A will enter into wait states.

16-18. What is DMA?

16-19. For a memory write, outline the purpose of 8085A clock states T1, T2, and T3.

16-20. How much time does the 8085A allow the memory to access data?

16-21. If a 74LS138 is connected so that $\overline{E1}$ and $\overline{E2}$ are logic 0's and E3 is a logic 1, which output pin becomes a logic 0 for the following bit pattern applied to C, B, and A: C = 1, B = 0, and A = 1?

16-22. What is the purpose of the $\overline{OE}$ pin on most ROMs?

16-23. What is the purpose of the $\overline{CE}$ pin on most ROMs?

16-24. What happens to the addresses decoded by the 74LS138 decoder in Fig. 17–11 if A15 is connected to E3 and $\overline{E1}$ is grounded?

16-25. Where is the $\overline{RD}$ pin connected on an EPROM? On a 6116 RAM?

16-26. Where is the $\overline{WR}$ pin connected on a 6116 RAM?

16-27. What are the main differences between the RAM and ROM selection logic?

16-28. A memory device that has 10 inputs (A9 through A0) has _____ memory locations.

16-29. What two signals are used to indicate an IN instruction?

16-30. What two signals are used to indicate an OUT instruction?

16-31. Describe how the IN 44H instruction functions to indicate the contents of the address bus, data bus, and the direction of the data flows.

16-32. Describe how the OUT 66H instruction functions to indicate the contents of the address bus, data bus, and the direction of the data flows.

8085A INSTRUCTION SUMMARY

Mnemonic	Op-code	bytes	clocks	Function	Flag Z	Cy	A	S	P
ACI d8	CE–d8	2	7	A = A + d8 + Cy	^	^	^	^	^
ADC B	88	1	4	A = A + B + Cy	^	^	^	^	^
ADC C	89	1	4	A = A + C + Cy	^	^	^	^	^
ADC D	8A	1	4	A = A + D + Cy	^	^	^	^	^
ADC E	8B	1	4	A = A + E + Cy	^	^	^	^	^
ADC H	8C	1	4	A = A + H + Cy	^	^	^	^	^
ADC L	8D	1	4	A = A + L + Cy	^	^	^	^	^
ADC M	8E	1	7	A = A + M + Cy	^	^	^	^	^
ADC A	8F	1	4	A = A + A + Cy	^	^	^	^	^
ADD B	80	1	4	A = A + B	^	^	^	^	^
ADD C	81	1	4	A = A + C	^	^	^	^	^
ADD D	82	1	4	A = A + D	^	^	^	^	^
ADD E	83	1	4	A = A + E	^	^	^	^	^
ADD H	84	1	4	A = A + H	^	^	^	^	^
ADD L	85	1	4	A = A + L	^	^	^	^	^
ADD M	86	1	7	A = A + M	^	^	^	^	^
ADD A	87	1	4	A = A + A	^	^	^	^	^
ADI d8	C6–d8	1	7	A = A + d8	^	^	^	^	^
ANA B	A0	1	4	A = A ∧ B	^	0	1	^	^
ANA C	A1	1	4	A = A ∧ C	^	0	1	^	^

Mnemonic	Op-code	bytes	clocks	Function	Z	Cy	A	S	P
ANA D	A2	1	4	A = A ∧ D	^	0	1	^	^
ANA E	A3	1	4	A = A ∧ E	^	0	1	^	^
ANA H	A4	1	4	A = A ∧ H	^	0	1	^	^
ANA L	A5	1	4	A = A ∧ L	^	0	1	^	^
ANA M	A6	1	7	A = A ∧ M	^	0	1	^	^
ANA A	A7	1	4	A = A ∧ A	^	0	1	^	^
ANI d8	E6–d8	2	7	A = A ∧ d8	^	0	1	^	^
CALL a16	CD–ll–hh	3	18	Call subr	*	*	*	*	*
CC a16	DC–ll–hh	3	9/18	Call subr if Cy = 1	*	*	*	*	*
CM a16	FC–ll–hh	3	9/18	Call subr if S = 1	*	*	*	*	*
CNC a16	D4–ll–hh	3	9/18	Call subr if Cy = 0	*	*	*	*	*
CNZ a16	C4–ll–hh	3	9/18	Call subr if Z = 0	*	*	*	*	*
CP a16	F4–ll–hh	3	9/18	Call subr if S = 0	*	*	*	*	*
CPE a16	EC–ll–hh	3	9/18	Call subr if P = 1	*	*	*	*	*
CPO a16	E4–ll–hh	3	9/18	Call subr if P = 0	*	*	*	*	*
CZ a16	CC–ll–hh	3	9/18	Call subr if Z = 1	*	*	*	*	*
CMA	2F	1	4	A = $\overline{A}$	*	*	*	*	*
CMC	3F	1	4	Cy = $\overline{Cy}$	^	*	*	*	*
CMP B	B8	1	4	Flags = A − B	^	^	^	^	^
CMP C	B9	1	4	Flags = A − C	^	^	^	^	^
CMP D	BA	1	4	Flags = A − D	^	^	^	^	^
CMP E	BB	1	4	Flags = A − E	^	^	^	^	^
CMP H	BC	1	4	Flags = A − H	^	^	^	^	^
CMP L	BD	1	4	Flags = A − L	^	^	^	^	^
CMP M	BE	1	7	Flags = A − M	^	^	^	^	^
CMP A	BF	1	4		1	0	0	0	1
CPI d8	FE–d8	2	7	Flags = A − d8	^	^	^	^	^
DAA	27	1	4	Decimal adjust A	^	^	^	^	^
DAD B	09	1	10	HL = BC + HL	*	^	*	*	*
DAD D	19	1	10	HL = DE + HL	*	^	*	*	*
DAD H	29	1	10	HL = HL + HL	*	^	*	*	*
DAD SP	39	1	10	HL = SP + HL	*	^	*	*	*
DCR B	05	1	4	B = B − 1	^	*	^	^	^
DCR C	0D	1	4	C = C − 1	^	*	^	^	^
DCR D	15	1	4	D = D − 1	^	*	^	^	^
DCR E	1D	1	4	E = E − 1	^	*	^	^	^
DCR H	25	1	4	H = H − 1	^	*	^	^	^
DCR L	2D	1	4	L = L − 1	^	*	^	^	^
DCR M	35	1	10	M = M − 1	^	*	^	^	^
DCR A	3D	1	4	A = A − 1	^	*	^	^	^
DCX B	0B	1	6	BC = BC − 1	*	*	*	*	*

					Flag				
Mnemonic	*Op-code*	*bytes*	*clocks*	*Function*	*Z*	*Cy*	*A*	*S*	*P*
DCX D	1B	1	6	DE = DE − 1	*	*	*	*	*
DCX H	2B	1	6	HL = HL − 1	*	*	*	*	*
DCX SP	3B	1	6	SP = SP − 1	*	*	*	*	*
DI	F3	1	4	Disable intr	*	*	*	*	*
EI	FB	1	4	Enable intr	*	*	*	*	*
HLT	76	1	4	Halt	*	*	*	*	*
IN d8	DB-d8	2	10	Input A	*	*	*	*	*
INR B	04	1	4	B = B + 1	^	*	^	^	^
INR C	0C	1	4	C = C + 1	^	*	^	^	^
INR D	14	1	4	D = D + 1	^	*	^	^	^
INR E	1C	1	4	E = E + 1	^	*	^	^	^
INR H	24	1	4	H = H + 1	^	*	^	^	^
INR L	2C	1	4	L = L + 1	^	*	^	^	^
INR M	34	1	10	M = M + 1	^	*	^	^	^
INR A	3C	1	4	A = A + 1	^	*	^	^	^
INX B	03	1	6	BC = BC + 1	*	*	*	*	*
INX D	13	1	6	DE = DE + 1	*	*	*	*	*
INX H	23	1	6	HL = HL + 1	*	*	*	*	*
INX SP	33	1	6	SP = SP + 1	*	*	*	*	*
JC a16	DA-ll-hh	3	7/10	Jump if Cy = 1	*	*	*	*	*
JM a16	FA-ll-hh	3	7/10	Jump if S = 1	*	*	*	*	*
JMP a16	C3-ll-hh	3	10	Jump	*	*	*	*	*
JNC a16	D2-ll-hh	3	7/10	Jump if Cy = 0	*	*	*	*	*
JNZ a16	C2-ll-hh	3	7/10	Jump if Z = 0	*	*	*	*	*
JP a16	F2-ll-hh	3	7/10	Jump if S = 0	*	*	*	*	*
JPE a16	EA-ll-hh	3	7/10	Jump if P = 1	*	*	*	*	*
JPO a16	E2-ll-hh	3	7/10	Jump if P = 0	*	*	*	*	*
JZ a16	CA-ll-hh	3	7/10	Jump if Z = 1	*	*	*	*	*
LDA a16	3A-ll-hh	3	13	A = ((a16))	*	*	*	*	*
LDAX B	0A	1	7	A = ((BC))	*	*	*	*	*
LDAX D	1A	1	7	A = ((DE))	*	*	*	*	*
LHLD a16	2A-ll-hh	3	16	HL = ((a16))	*	*	*	*	*
LXI B,d16	01-ll-hh	3	10	BC = d16	*	*	*	*	*
LXI D,d16	11-ll-hh	3	10	DE = d16	*	*	*	*	*
LXI H,d16	21-ll-hh	3	10	HL = d16	*	*	*	*	*
LXI SP,d16	31-ll-hh	3	10	SP = d16	*	*	*	*	*
MOV B,B	40	1	4	B = B	*	*	*	*	*
MOV B,C	41	1	4	B = C	*	*	*	*	*
MOV B,D	42	1	4	B = D	*	*	*	*	*
MOV B,E	43	1	4	B = E	*	*	*	*	*
MOV B,H	44	1	4	B = H	*	*	*	*	*

Mnemonic	Op-code	bytes	clocks	Function	Flag				
					Z	Cy	A	S	P
MOV B,L	45	1	4	B = L	*	*	*	*	*
MOV B,M	46	1	7	B = M	*	*	*	*	*
MOV B,A	47	1	4	B = A	*	*	*	*	*
MOV C,B	48	1	4	C = B	*	*	*	*	*
MOV C,C	49	1	4	C = C	*	*	*	*	*
MOV C,D	4A	1	4	C = D	*	*	*	*	*
MOV C,E	4B	1	4	C = E	*	*	*	*	*
MOV C,H	4C	1	4	C = H	*	*	*	*	*
MOV C,L	4D	1	4	C = L	*	*	*	*	*
MOV C,M	4E	1	7	C = M	*	*	*	*	*
MOV C,A	4F	1	4	C = A	*	*	*	*	*
MOV D,B	50	1	4	D = B	*	*	*	*	*
MOV D,C	51	1	4	D = C	*	*	*	*	*
MOV D,D	52	1	4	D = D	*	*	*	*	*
MOV D,E	53	1	4	D = E	*	*	*	*	*
MOV D,H	54	1	4	D = H	*	*	*	*	*
MOV D,L	55	1	4	D = L	*	*	*	*	*
MOV D,M	56	1	7	D = M	*	*	*	*	*
MOV D,A	57	1	4	D = A	*	*	*	*	*
MOV E,B	58	1	4	E = B	*	*	*	*	*
MOV E,C	59	1	4	E = C	*	*	*	*	*
MOV E,D	5A	1	4	E = D	*	*	*	*	*
MOV E,E	5B	1	4	E = E	*	*	*	*	*
MOV E,H	5C	1	4	E = H	*	*	*	*	*
MOV E,L	5D	1	4	E = L	*	*	*	*	*
MOV E,M	5E	1	7	E = M	*	*	*	*	*
MOV E,A	5F	1	4	E = A	*	*	*	*	*
MOV H,B	60	1	4	H = B	*	*	*	*	*
MOV H,C	61	1	4	H = C	*	*	*	*	*
MOV H,D	62	1	4	H = D	*	*	*	*	*
MOV H,E	63	1	4	H = E	*	*	*	*	*
MOV H,H	64	1	4	H = H	*	*	*	*	*
MOV H,L	65	1	4	H = L	*	*	*	*	*
MOV H,M	66	1	7	H = M	*	*	*	*	*
MOV H,A	67	1	4	H = A	*	*	*	*	*
MOV L,B	68	1	4	L = B	*	*	*	*	*
MOV L,C	69	1	4	L = C	*	*	*	*	*
MOV L,D	6A	1	4	L = D	*	*	*	*	*
MOV L,E	6B	1	4	L = E	*	*	*	*	*
MOV L,H	6C	1	4	L = H	*	*	*	*	*
MOV L,L	6D	1	4	L = L	*	*	*	*	*

Mnemonic	Op-code	bytes	clocks	Function	Z	Cy	A	S	P
MOV L,M	6E	1	7	L = M	*	*	*	*	*
MOV L,A	6F	1	4	L = A	*	*	*	*	*
MOV M,B	70	1	7	M = B	*	*	*	*	*
MOV M,C	71	1	7	M = C	*	*	*	*	*
MOV M,D	72	1	7	M = D	*	*	*	*	*
MOV M,E	73	1	7	M = E	*	*	*	*	*
MOV M,H	74	1	7	M = H	*	*	*	*	*
MOV M,L	75	1	7	M = L	*	*	*	*	*
MOV M,A	77	1	7	M = A	*	*	*	*	*
MOV A,B	78	1	4	A = B	*	*	*	*	*
MOV A,C	79	1	4	A = C	*	*	*	*	*
MOV A,D	7A	1	4	A = D	*	*	*	*	*
MOV A,E	7B	1	4	A = E	*	*	*	*	*
MOV A,H	7C	1	4	A = H	*	*	*	*	*
MOV A,L	7D	1	4	A = L	*	*	*	*	*
MOV A,M	7E	1	7	A = M	*	*	*	*	*
MOV A,A	7F	1	4	A = A	*	*	*	*	*
MVI B,d8	06–d8	2	7	B = d8	*	*	*	*	*
MVI C,d8	0E–d8	2	7	C = d8	*	*	*	*	*
MVI D,d8	16–d8	2	7	D = d8	*	*	*	*	*
MVI E,d8	1E–d8	2	7	E = d8	*	*	*	*	*
MVI H,d8	26–d8	2	7	H = d8	*	*	*	*	*
MVI L,d8	2E–d8	2	7	L = d8	*	*	*	*	*
MVI M,d8	36–d8	2	10	M = d8	*	*	*	*	*
MVI A,d8	3E–d8	2	7	A = d8	*	*	*	*	*
NOP	00	1	4	No operation	*	*	*	*	*
ORA B	B0	1	4	A = A V B	^	0	0	^	^
ORA C	B1	1	4	A = A V C	^	0	0	^	^
ORA D	B2	1	4	A = A V D	^	0	0	^	^
ORA E	B3	1	4	A = A V E	^	0	0	^	^
ORA H	B4	1	4	A = A V H	^	0	0	^	^
ORA L	B5	1	4	A = A V L	^	0	0	^	^
ORA M	B6	1	7	A = A V M	^	0	0	^	^
ORA A	B7	1	4	A = A V A	^	0	0	^	^
ORI d8	F6–d8	2	7	A = A V d8	^	0	0	^	^
OUT d8	D3–d8	2	10	Output A	*	*	*	*	*
PCHL	E9	1	6	PC = HL	*	*	*	*	*
POP B	C1	1	10	BC = STACK	*	*	*	*	*
POP D	D1	1	10	DE = STACK	*	*	*	*	*
POP H	E1	1	10	HL = STACK	*	*	*	*	*
POP PSW	F1	1	10	AF = STACK	^	^	^	^	^

Mnemonic	Op-code	bytes	clocks	Function	Z	Cy	A	S	P
PUSH B	C5	1	12	STACK = BC	*	*	*	*	*
PUSH D	D5	1	12	STACK = DE	*	*	*	*	*
PUSH H	E5	1	12	STACK = HL	*	*	*	*	*
PUSH PSW	F5	1	12	STACK = AF	*	*	*	*	*
RAL	17	1	4	Rotate A left through carry	*	^	*	*	*
RAR	1F	1	4	Rotate A right through carry	*	^	*	*	*
RC	D8	1	6/12	Return if Cy = 1	*	*	*	*	*
RET	C9	1	10	Return	*	*	*	*	*
RIM	20	1	4	Read interrupts	*	*	*	*	*
RLC	07	1	4	Rotate A left	*	^	*	*	*
RM	F8	1	6/12	Return if S = 1	*	*	*	*	*
RNC	D0	1	6/12	Return if Cy = 0	*	*	*	*	*
RNZ	C0	1	6/12	Return if Z = 0	*	*	*	*	*
RP	F0	1	6/12	Return if S = 0	*	*	*	*	*
RPE	E8	1	6/12	Return if P = 1	*	*	*	*	*
RPO	E0	1	6/12	Return if P = 0	*	*	*	*	*
RRC	0F	1	4	Rotate A right	*	^	*	*	*
RST 0	C7	1	12	CALL 0000H	*	*	*	*	*
RST 1	CF	1	12	CALL 0008H	*	*	*	*	*
RST 2	D7	1	12	CALL 0010H	*	*	*	*	*
RST 3	DF	1	12	CALL 0018H	*	*	*	*	*
RST 4	E7	1	12	CALL 0020H	*	*	*	*	*
RST 5	EF	1	12	CALL 0028H	*	*	*	*	*
RST 6	F7	1	12	CALL 0030H	*	*	*	*	*
RST 7	FF	1	12	CALL 0038H	*	*	*	*	*
RZ	C8	1	6/12	Return if Z = 1	*	*	*	*	*
SBB B	98	1	4	A = A − B − Cy	^	^	^	^	^
SBB C	99	1	4	A = A − C − Cy	^	^	^	^	^
SBB D	9A	1	4	A = A − D − Cy	^	^	^	^	^
SBB E	9B	1	4	A = A − E − Cy	^	^	^	^	^
SBB H	9C	1	4	A = A − H − Cy	^	^	^	^	^
SBB L	9D	1	4	A = A − L − Cy	^	^	^	^	^
SBB M	9E	1	7	A = A − M − Cy	^	Cy	^	A	^
SBB A	9F	1	4	A = A − A − Cy	^	^	^	^	^
SBI d8	DE−d8	2	7	A = A − d8 − Cy	^	^	^	^	^
SHLD a16	22−ll−hh	3	16	((a16)) = HL	*	*	*	*	*
SIM	30	1	4	Set interrupts	*	*	*	*	*
SPHL	F9	1	6	SP = HL	*	*	*	*	*
STA a16	32−ll−hh	3	13	((a16)) = A	*	*	*	*	*

Mnemonic	Op-code	bytes	clocks	Function	Z	Cy	A	S	P
STAX B	02	1	7	((BC)) = A	*	*	*	*	*
STAX D	12	1	7	((DE)) = A	*	*	*	*	*
STC	37	1	4	Cy = 1	*	1	*	*	*
SUB B	90	1	4	A = A − B	^	^	^	^	^
SUB C	91	1	4	A = A − C	^	^	^	^	^
SUB D	92	1	4	A = A − D	^	^	^	^	^
SUB E	93	1	4	A = A − E	^	^	^	^	^
SUB H	94	1	4	A = A − H	^	^	^	^	^
SUB L	95	1	4	A = A − L	^	^	^	^	^
SUB M	96	1	7	A = A − M	^	^	^	^	^
SUB A	97	1	4	A = A − A	1	0	0	0	1
SUI d8	D6−d8	2	7	A = A − d8	^	^	^	^	^
XCHG	EB	1	4	HL ↔ DE	*	*	*	*	*
XRA B	A8	1	4	A = A ∀ B	^	0	0	^	^
XRA C	A9	1	4	A = A ∀ C	^	0	0	^	^
XRA D	AA	1	4	A = A ∀ D	^	0	0	^	^
XRA E	AB	1	4	A = A ∀ E	^	0	0	^	^
XRA H	AC	1	4	A = A ∀ H	^	0	0	^	^
XRA L	AD	1	4	A = A ∀ L	^	0	0	^	^
XRA M	AE	1	7	A = A ∀ M	^	0	0	^	^
XRA A	AF	1	4	A = A ∀ A	1	0	0	0	1
XRI d8	EE−d8	1	7	A = A ∀ d8	^	0	0	^	^
XTHL	E3	1	16	HL ↔ STACK	*	*	*	*	*

Notes: *, no change; ^, changes; ↔, exchanged with; (()), contents of the location at a16, BC, or DE; a16, 16-bit address; d8, 8 bits of data; d16, 16 bits of data; M, memory location indirectly addressed by the HL register pair; ll = low-order byte of the address; hh = high-order byte of the address.

8085A DATA SHEETS

The following data sheets were reprinted
with permission from the
Intel Corporation.
Copyright, 1981.

8085AH/8085AH-2/8085AH-1
8-BIT HMOS MICROPROCESSORS

- **Single +5V Power Supply with 10% Voltage Margins**
- **3 MHz, 5 MHz and 6 MHz Selections Available**
- **20% Lower Power Consumption than 8085A for 3 MHz and 5 MHz**
- **1.3 μs Instruction Cycle (8085AH); 0.8 μs (8085AH-2); 0.67 μs (8085AH-1)**
- **100% Compatible with 8085A**
- **100% Software Compatible with 8080A**
- **On-Chip Clock Generator (with External Crystal, LC or RC Network)**

- **On-Chip System Controller; Advanced Cycle Status Information Available for Large System Control**
- **Four Vectored Interrupt Inputs (One is Non-Maskable) Plus an 8080A-Compatible Interrupt**
- **Serial In/Serial Out Port**
- **Decimal, Binary and Double Precision Arithmetic**
- **Direct Addressing Capability to 64K Bytes of Memory**
- **Available in EXPRESS**
  - **Standard Temperature Range**
  - **Extended Temperature Range**

The Intel® 8085AH is a complete 8 bit parallel Central Processing Unit (CPU) implemented in N-channel, depletion load, silicon gate technology (HMOS). Its instruction set is 100% software compatible with the 8080A microprocessor, and it is designed to improve the present 8080A's performance by higher system speed. Its high level of system integration allows a minimum system of three IC's [8085AH (CPU), 8156H (RAM/IO) and 8355/8755A (ROM/PROM/IO)] while maintaining total system expandability. The 8085AH-2 and 8085AH-1 are faster versions of the 8085AH.

The 8085AH incorporates all of the features that the 8224 (clock generator) and 8228 (system controller) provided for the 8080A, thereby offering a high level of system integration.

The 8085AH uses a multiplexed data bus. The address is split between the 8 bit address bus and the 8 bit data bus. The on-chip address latches of 8155H/8156H/8355/8755A memory products allow a direct interface with the 8085AH.

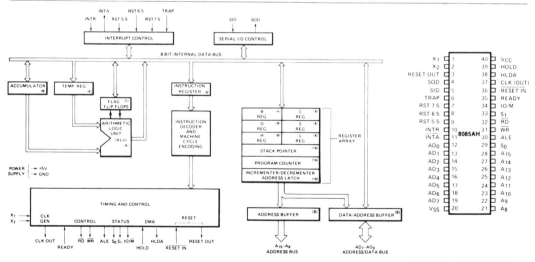

Figure 1. 8085AH CPU Functional Block Diagram

Figure 2. 8085AH Pin Configuration

Table 1. Pin Description

Symbol	Type	Name and Function
A_8–A_{15}	O	**Address Bus:** The most significant 8 bits of the memory address or the 8 bits of the I/O address, 3-stated during Hold and Halt modes and during RESET.
AD_0—$_7$	I/O	**Multiplexed Address/Data Bus:** Lower 8 bits of the memory address (or I/O address) appear on the bus during the first clock cycle (T state) of a machine cycle. It then becomes the data bus during the second and third clock cycles.
ALE	O	**Address Latch Enable:** It occurs during the first clock state of a machine cycle and enables the address to get latched into the on-chip latch of peripherals. The falling edge of ALE is set to guarantee setup and hold times for the address information. The falling edge of ALE can also be used to strobe the status information. ALE is never 3-stated.
S_0, S_1, and IO/$\overline{M}$	O	**Machine Cycle Status:**

IO/$\overline{M}$	S_1	S_0	Status
0	0	1	Memory write
0	1	0	Memory read
1	0	1	I/O write
1	1	0	I/O read
0	1	1	Opcode fetch
1	1	1	Opcode fetch
1	1	1	Interrupt Acknowledge
*	0	0	Halt
*	X	X	Hold
*	X	X	Reset

* = 3-state (high impedance)
X = unspecified

S_1 can be used as an advanced R/$\overline{W}$ status. IO/$\overline{M}$, S_0 and S_1 become valid at the beginning of a machine cycle and remain stable throughout the cycle. The falling edge of ALE may be used to latch the state of these lines.

Symbol	Type	Name and Function
$\overline{RD}$	O	**Read Control:** A low level on $\overline{RD}$ indicates the selected memory or I/O device is to be read and that the Data Bus is available for the data transfer, 3-stated during Hold and Halt modes and during RESET.
$\overline{WR}$	O	**Write Control:** A low level on $\overline{WR}$ indicates the data on the Data Bus is to be written into the selected memory or I/O location. Data is set up at the trailing edge of $\overline{WR}$. 3-stated during Hold and Halt modes and during RESET.

Symbol	Type	Name and Function
READY	I	**Ready:** If READY is high during a read or write cycle, it indicates that the memory or peripheral is ready to send or receive data. If READY is low, the cpu will wait an integral number of clock cycles for READY to go high before completing the read or write cycle. READY must conform to specified setup and hold times.
HOLD	I	**Hold:** Indicates that another master is requesting the use of the address and data buses. The cpu, upon receiving the hold request, will relinquish the use of the bus as soon as the completion of the current bus transfer. Internal processing can continue. The processor can regain the bus only after the HOLD is removed. When the HOLD is acknowledged, the Address, Data $\overline{RD}$, $\overline{WR}$, and IO/$\overline{M}$ lines are 3-stated.
HLDA	O	**Hold Acknowledge:** Indicates that the cpu has received the HOLD request and that it will relinquish the bus in the next clock cycle. HLDA goes low after the Hold request is removed. The cpu takes the bus one half clock cycle after HLDA goes low.
INTR	I	**Interrupt Request:** Is used as a general purpose interrupt. It is sampled only during the next to the last clock cycle of an instruction and during Hold and Halt states. If it is active, the Program Counter (PC) will be inhibited from incrementing and an $\overline{INTA}$ will be issued. During this cycle a RESTART or CALL instruction can be inserted to jump to the interrupt service routine. The INTR is enabled and disabled by software. It is disabled by Reset and immediately after an interrupt is accepted.
$\overline{INTA}$	O	**Interrupt Acknowledge:** Is used instead of (and has the same timing as) $\overline{RD}$ during the Instruction cycle after an INTR is accepted. It can be used to activate an 8259A Interrupt chip or some other interrupt port.
RST 5.5 RST 6.5 RST 7.5	I	**Restart Interrupts:** These three inputs have the same timing as INTR except they cause an internal RESTART to be automatically inserted. The priority of these interrupts is ordered as shown in Table 2. These interrupts have a higher priority than INTR. In addition, they may be individually masked out using the SIM instruction.

Table 1. Pin Description (Continued)

Symbol	Type	Name and Function
TRAP	I	**Trap:** Trap interrupt is a non-maskable RESTART interrupt. It is recognized at the same time as INTR or RST 5.5-7.5. It is unaffected by any mask or Interrupt Enable. It has the highest priority of any interrupt. (See Table 2.)
RESET IN	I	**Reset In:** Sets the Program Counter to zero and resets the Interrupt Enable and HLDA flip-flops. The data and address buses and the control lines are 3-stated during RESET and because of the asynchronous nature of RESET, the processor's internal registers and flags may be altered by RESET with unpredictable results. RESET IN is a Schmitt-triggered input, allowing connection to an R-C network for power-on RESET delay (see Figure 3). Upon power-up, RESET IN must remain low for at least 10 ms after minimum V_{CC} has been reached. For proper reset operation after the power-up duration, RESET IN should be kept low a minimum of three clock periods. The CPU is held in the reset condition as long as RESET IN is applied.

Symbol	Type	Name and Function
RESET OUT	O	**Reset Out:** Reset Out indicates cpu is being reset. Can be used as a system reset. The signal is synchronized to the processor clock and lasts an integral number of clock periods.
X_1, X_2	I	**X_1 and X_2:** Are connected to a crystal, LC, or RC network to drive the internal clock generator. X_1 can also be an external clock input from a logic gate. The input frequency is divided by 2 to give the processor's internal operating frequency.
CLK	O	**Clock:** Clock output for use as a system clock. The period of CLK is twice the X_1, X_2 input period.
SID	I	**Serial Input Data Line:** The data on this line is loaded into accumulator bit 7 whenever a RIM instruction is executed.
SOD	O	**Serial Output Data Line:** The output SOD is set or reset as specified by the SIM instruction.
V_{CC}		**Power:** +5 volt supply.
V_{SS}		**Ground:** Reference.

Table 2. Interrupt Priority, Restart Address, and Sensitivity

Name	Priority	Address Branched To (1) When Interrupt Occurs	Type Trigger
TRAP	1	24H	Rising edge AND high level until sampled.
RST 7.5	2	3CH	Rising edge (latched).
RST 6.5	3	34H	High level until sampled.
RST 5.5	4	2CH	High level until sampled.
INTR	5	See Note (2).	High level until sampled.

NOTES:
1. The processor pushes the PC on the stack before branching to the indicated address.
2. The address branched to depends on the instruction provided to the cpu when the interrupt is acknowledged.

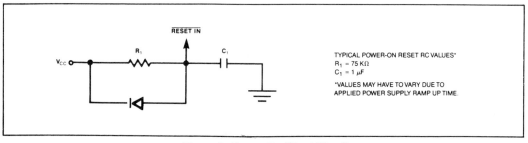

Figure 3. Power-On Reset Circuit

AFN-01835C

FUNCTIONAL DESCRIPTION

The 8085AH is a complete 8-bit parallel central processor. It is designed with N-channel, depletion load, silicon gate technology (HMOS), and requires a single +5 volt supply. Its basic clock speed is 3 MHz (8085AH), 5 MHz (8085AH-2), or 6 MHz (8085AH-1), thus improving on the present 8080A's performance with higher system speed. Also it is designed to fit into a minimum system of three IC's: The CPU (8085AH), a RAM/IO (8156H), and a ROM or EPROM/IO chip (8355 or 8755A).

The 8085AH has twelve addressable 8-bit registers. Four of them can function only as two 16-bit register pairs. Six others can be used interchangeably as 8-bit registers or as 16-bit register pairs. The 8085AH register set is as follows:

Mnemonic	Register	Contents
ACC or A	Accumulator	8 bits
PC	Program Counter	16-bit address
BC,DE,HL	General-Purpose Registers; data pointer (HL)	8 bits x 6 or 16 bits x 3
SP	Stack Pointer	16-bit address
Flags or F	Flag Register	5 flags (8-bit space)

The 8085AH uses a multiplexed Data Bus. The address is split between the higher 8-bit Address Bus and the lower 8-bit Address/Data Bus. During the first T state (clock cycle) of a machine cycle the low order address is sent out on the Address/Data bus. These lower 8 bits may be latched externally by the Address Latch Enable signal (ALE). During the rest of the machine cycle the data bus is used for memory or I/O data.

The 8085AH provides $\overline{RD}$, $\overline{WR}$, S_0, S_1, and IO/$\overline{M}$ signals for bus control. An Interrupt Acknowledge signal ($\overline{INTA}$) is also provided. HOLD and all Interrupts are synchronized with the processor's internal clock. The 8085AH also provides Serial Input Data (SID) and Serial Output Data (SOD) lines for simple serial interface.

In addition to these features, the 8085AH has three maskable, vector interrupt pins, one nonmaskable TRAP interrupt, and a bus vectored interrupt, INTR.

INTERRUPT AND SERIAL I/O

The 8085AH has 5 interrupt inputs: INTR, RST 5.5, RST 6.5, RST 7.5, and TRAP. INTR is identical in function to the 8080A INT. Each of the three RESTART inputs, 5.5, 6.5, and 7.5, has a programmable mask. TRAP is also a RESTART interrupt but it is nonmaskable.

The three maskable interrupts cause the internal execution of RESTART (saving the program counter in the stack and branching to the RESTART address) if the interrupts are enabled and if the interrupt mask is not set. The nonmaskable TRAP causes the internal execution of a RESTART vector independent of the state of the interrupt enable or masks. (See Table 2.)

There are two different types of inputs in the restart interrupts. RST 5.5 and RST 6.5 are *high level-sensitive* like INTR (and INT on the 8080) and are recognized with the same timing as INTR. RST 7.5 is *rising edge-sensitive*.

For RST 7.5, only a pulse is required to set an internal flip-flop which generates the internal interrupt request (a normally high level signal with a low going pulse is recommended for highest system noise immunity). The RST 7.5 request flip-flop remains set until the request is serviced. Then it is reset automatically. This flip-flop may also be reset by using the SIM instruction or by issuing a $\overline{RESET\ IN}$ to the 8085AH. The RST 7.5 internal flip-flop will be set by a pulse on the RST 7.5 pin even when the RST 7.5 interrupt is masked out.

The status of the three RST interrupt masks can only be affected by the SIM instruction and $\overline{RESET\ IN}$. (See SIM, Chapter 5 of the MCS-80/85 User's Manual.)

The interrupts are arranged in a fixed priority that determines which interrupt is to be recognized if more than one is pending as follows: TRAP—highest priority, RST 7.5, RST 6.5, RST 5.5, INTR—lowest priority. This priority scheme does not take into account the priority of a routine that was started by a higher priority interrupt. RST 5.5 can interrupt an RST 7.5 routine if the interrupts are re-enabled before the end of the RST 7.5 routine.

The TRAP interrupt is useful for catastrophic events such as power failure or bus error. The TRAP input is recognized just as any other interrupt but has the highest priority. It is not affected by any flag or mask. The TRAP input is both *edge and level sensitive*. The TRAP input must go high and remain high until it is acknowledged. It will not be recognized again until it goes low, then high again. This avoids any false triggering due to noise or logic glitches. Figure 4 illustrates the TRAP interrupt request circuitry within the 8085AH. Note that the servicing of any interrupt (TRAP, RST 7.5, RST 6.5, RST 5.5, INTR) disables all future interrupts (except TRAPs) until an EI instruction is executed.

AFN-01835C

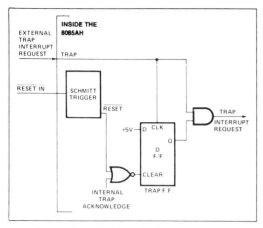

Figure 4. TRAP and RESET IN Circuit

The TRAP interrupt is special in that it disables interrupts, but preserves the previous interrupt enable status. Performing the first RIM instruction following a TRAP interrupt allows you to determine whether interrupts were enabled or disabled prior to the TRAP. All subsequent RIM instructions provide current interrupt enable status. Performing a RIM instruction following INTR, or RST 5.5–7.5 will provide current Interrupt Enable status, revealing that Interrupts are disabled. See the description of the RIM instruction in the MCS-80/85 Family User's Manual.

The serial I/O system is also controlled by the RIM and SIM instructions. SID is read by RIM, and SIM sets the SOD data.

DRIVING THE X_1 AND X_2 INPUTS

You may drive the clock inputs of the 8085AH, 8085AH-2, or 8085AH-1 with a crystal, an LC tuned circuit, an RC network, or an external clock source. The crystal frequency must be at least 1 MHz, and must be twice the desired internal clock frequency; hence, the 8085AH is operated with a 6 MHz crystal (for 3 MHz clock), the 8085AH-2 operated with a 10 MHz crystal (for 5 MHz clock), and the 8085AH-1 can be operated with a 12 MHz crystal (for 6 MHz clock). If a crystal is used, it must have the following characteristics:

Parallel resonance at twice the clock frequency desired
C_L (load capacitance) $\leq$ 30 pF
C_S (shunt capacitance) $\leq$ 7 pF
R_S (equivalent shunt resistance) $\leq$ 75 Ohms
Drive level: 10 mW
Frequency tolerance: $\pm$.005% (suggested)

Note the use of the 20 pF capacitor between X_2 and ground. This capacitor is required with crystal frequencies below 4 MHz to assure oscillator startup at the correct frequency. A parallel-resonant LC circuit may be used as the frequency-determining network for the 8085AH, providing that its frequency tolerance of approximately $\pm$10% is acceptable. The components are chosen from the formula:

$$f = \frac{1}{2\pi\sqrt{L(C_{ext} + C_{int})}}$$

To minimize variations in frequency, it is recommended that you choose a value for C_{ext} that is at least twice that of C_{int}, or 30 pF. The use of an LC circuit is not recommended for frequencies higher than approximately 5 MHz.

An RC circuit may be used as the frequency-determining network for the 8085AH if maintaining a precise clock frequency is of no importance. Variations in the on-chip timing generation can cause a wide variation in frequency when using the RC mode. Its advantage is its low component cost. The driving frequency generated by the circuit shown is approximately 3 MHz. It is not recommended that frequencies greatly higher or lower than this be attempted.

Figure 5 shows the recommended clock driver circuits. Note in D and E that pullup resistors are required to assure that the high level voltage of the input is at least 4V and maximum low level voltage of 0.8V.

For driving frequencies up to and including 6 MHz you may supply the driving signal to X_1 and leave X_2 open-circuited (Figure 5D). If the driving frequency is from 6 MHz to 12 MHz, stability of the clock generator will be improved by driving both X_1 and X_2 with a push-pull source (Figure 5E). To prevent self-oscillation of the 8085AH, be sure that X_2 is not coupled back to X_1 through the driving circuit.

AFN-01835C

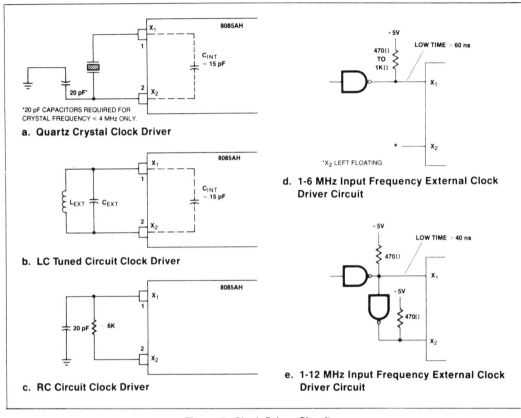

a. Quartz Crystal Clock Driver

*20 pF CAPACITORS REQUIRED FOR CRYSTAL FREQUENCY ≤ 4 MHz ONLY.

b. LC Tuned Circuit Clock Driver

c. RC Circuit Clock Driver

d. 1-6 MHz Input Frequency External Clock Driver Circuit

*X₂ LEFT FLOATING

e. 1-12 MHz Input Frequency External Clock Driver Circuit

Figure 5. Clock Driver Circuits

GENERATING AN 8085AH WAIT STATE

If your system requirements are such that slow memories or peripheral devices are being used, the circuit shown in Figure 6 may be used to insert one WAIT state in each 8085AH machine cycle.

The D flip-flops should be chosen so that
• CLK is rising edge-triggered
• CLEAR is low-level active.

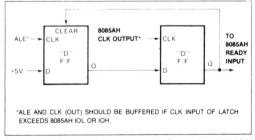

*ALE AND CLK (OUT) SHOULD BE BUFFERED IF CLK INPUT OF LATCH EXCEEDS 8085AH IOL OR IOH.

Figure 6. Generation of a Wait State for 8085AH CPU

AFN-01835C

314

As in the 8080, the READY line is used to extend the read and write pulse lengths so that the 8085AH can be used with slow memory. HOLD causes the CPU to relinquish the bus when it is through with it by floating the Address and Data Buses.

SYSTEM INTERFACE

The 8085AH family includes memory components, which are directly compatible to the 8085AH CPU. For example, a system consisting of the three chips, 8085AH, 8156H, and 8355 will have the following features:

- 2K Bytes ROM
- 256 Bytes RAM
- 1 Timer/Counter
- 4 8-bit I/O Ports
- 1 6-bit I/O Port
- 4 Interrupt Levels
- Serial In/Serial Out Ports

This minimum system, using the standard I/O technique is as shown in Figure 7.

In addition to standard I/O, the memory mapped I/O offers an efficient I/O addressing technique. With this technique, an area of memory address space is assigned for I/O address, thereby, using the memory address for I/O manipulation. Figure 8 shows the system configuration of Memory Mapped I/O using 8085AH.

The 8085AH CPU can also interface with the standard memory that does *not* have the multiplexed address/data bus. It will require a simple 8212 (8-bit latch) as shown in Figure 9.

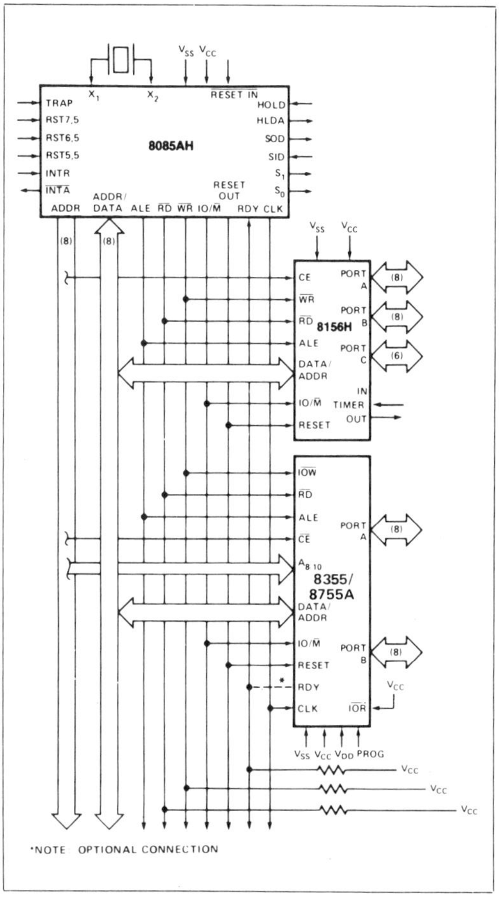

Figure 7. 8085AH Minimum System (Standard I/O Technique)

AFN-01835C

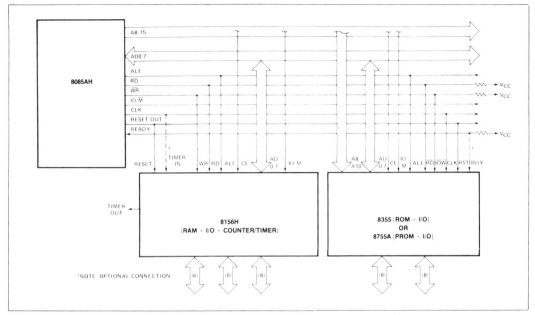

Figure 8. MCS-85® Minimum System (Memory Mapped I/O)

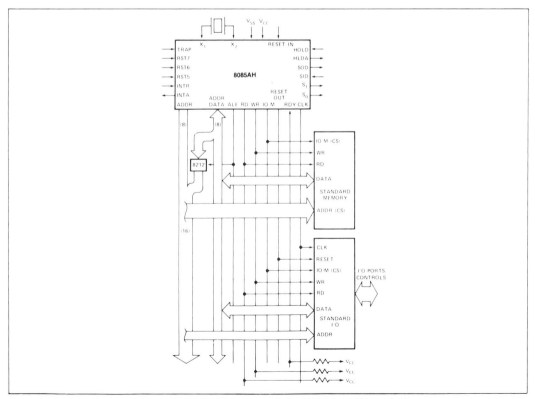

Figure 9. MCS-85® System (Using Standard Memories)

AFN-01835C

BASIC SYSTEM TIMING

The 8085AH has a multiplexed Data Bus. ALE is used as a strobe to sample the lower 8-bits of address on the Data Bus. Figure 10 shows an instruction fetch, memory read and I/O write cycle (as would occur during processing of the OUT instruction). Note that during the I/O write and read cycle that the I/O port address is copied on both the upper and lower half of the address.

There are seven possible types of machine cycles. Which of these seven takes place is defined by the status of the three status lines (IO/$\overline{\text{M}}$, S_1, S_0) and the three control signals ($\overline{\text{RD}}$, $\overline{\text{WR}}$, and $\overline{\text{INTA}}$). (See Table 3.) The status lines can be used as advanced controls (for device selection, for example), since they become active at the T_1 state, at the outset of each machine cycle. Control lines $\overline{\text{RD}}$ and $\overline{\text{WR}}$ become active later, at the time when the transfer of data is to take place, so are used as command lines.

A machine cycle normally consists of three T states, with the exception of OPCODE FETCH, which normally has either four or six T states (unless WAIT or HOLD states are forced by the receipt of READY or HOLD inputs). Any T state must be one of ten possible states, shown in Table 4.

Table 3. 8085AH Machine Cycle Chart

MACHINE CYCLE		STATUS			CONTROL		
		IO/$\overline{\text{M}}$	S1	S0	$\overline{\text{RD}}$	$\overline{\text{WR}}$	$\overline{\text{INTA}}$
OPCODE FETCH	(OF)	0	1	1	0	1	1
MEMORY READ	(MR)	0	1	0	0	1	1
MEMORY WRITE	(MW)	0	0	1	1	0	1
I/O READ	(IOR)	1	1	0	0	1	1
I/O WRITE	(IOW)	1	0	1	1	0	1
ACKNOWLEDGE OF INTR	(INA)	1	1	1	1	1	0
BUS IDLE	(BI): DAD	0	1	0	1	1	1
	ACK. OF RST.TRAP	1	1	1	1	1	1
	HALT	TS	0	0	TS	TS	1

Table 4. 8085AH Machine State Chart

Machine State	Status & Buses				Control		
	S1,S0	IO/$\overline{\text{M}}$	A_8-A_{15}	AD_0-AD_7	$\overline{\text{RD}}$,$\overline{\text{WR}}$	$\overline{\text{INTA}}$	ALE
T_1	X	X	X	X	1	1	1*
T_2	X	X	X	X	X	X	0
T_{WAIT}	X	X	X	X	X	X	0
T_3	X	X	X	X	X	X	0
T_4	1	0†	X	TS	1	1	0
T_5	1	0†	X	TS	1	1	0
T_6	1	0†	X	TS	1	1	0
T_{RESET}	X	TS	TS	TS	TS	1	0
T_{HALT}	0	TS	TS	TS	TS	1	0
T_{HOLD}	X	TS	TS	TS	TS	1	0

0 = Logic "0"   TS = High Impedance
1 = Logic "1"   X = Unspecified

* ALE not generated during 2nd and 3rd machine cycles of DAD instruction.
† IO/M = 1 during T_4-T_6 of INA machine cycle.

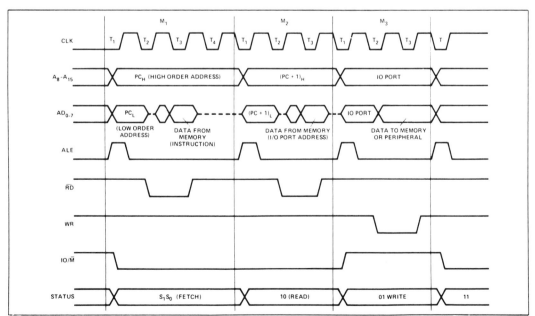

Figure 10. 8085AH Basic System Timing

AFN-01835C

8085AH/8085AH-2/8085AH-1

ABSOLUTE MAXIMUM RATINGS*

Ambient Temperature Under Bias .... 0°C to 70°C
Storage Temperature .... −65°C to +150°C
Voltage on Any Pin
  With Respect to Ground .... −0.5V to +7V
Power Dissipation .... 1.5 Watt

D.C. CHARACTERISTICS

8085AH, 8085AH-2: (T_A = 0°C to 70°C, V_{CC} = 5V ±10%, V_{SS} =0V; unless otherwise specified)*
8085AH-1: (T_A = 0°C to 70°C, V_{CC} = 5V ±5%, V_{SS} = 0V; unless otherwise specified)

Symbol	Parameter	Min.	Max.	Units	Test Conditions
V_{IL}	Input Low Voltage	−0.5	+0.8	V	
V_{IH}	Input High Voltage	2.0	V_{CC} +0.5	V	
V_{OL}	Output Low Voltage		0.45	V	I_{OL} = 2mA
V_{OH}	Output High Voltage	2.4		V	I_{OH} = −400μA
I_{CC}	Power Supply Current		135	mA	8085AH, 8085AH-2
			200	mA	8085AH-1 (Preliminary)
I_{IL}	Input Leakage		±10	μA	0 ≤ V_{IN} ≤ V_{CC}
I_{LO}	Output Leakage		±10	μA	0.45V ≤ V_{OUT} ≤ V_{CC}
V_{ILR}	Input Low Level, RESET	−0.5	+0.8	V	
V_{IHR}	Input High Level, RESET	2.4	V_{CC} +0.5	V	
V_{HY}	Hysteresis, RESET	0.25		V	

A.C. CHARACTERISTICS

8085AH, 8085AH-2: (T_A = 0°C to 70°C, V_{CC} = 5V ±10%, V_{SS} = OV)*
8085AH-1: (T_A = 0°C to 70°C, V_{CC} = 5V ±5%, V_{SS} = 0V)

Symbol	Parameter	8085AH[2] (Final) Min.	8085AH[2] (Final) Max.	8085AH-2[2] (Final) Min.	8085AH-2[2] (Final) Max.	8085AH-1 (Preliminary) Min.	8085AH-1 (Preliminary) Max.	Units
t_{CYC}	CLK Cycle Period	320	2000	200	2000	167	2000	ns
t_1	CLK Low Time (Standard CLK Loading)	80		40		20		ns
t_2	CLK High Time (Standard CLK Loading)	120		70		50		ns
t_r, t_f	CLK Rise and Fall Time		30		30		30	ns
t_{XKR}	X_1 Rising to CLK Rising	25	120	25	100	20	100	ns
t_{XKF}	X_1 Rising to CLK Falling	30	150	30	110	25	110	ns
t_{AC}	A_{8-15} Valid to Leading Edge of Control[1]	270		115		70		ns
t_{ACL}	A_{0-7} Valid to Leading Edge of Control	240		115		60		ns
t_{AD}	A_{0-15} Valid to Valid Data In		575		350		225	ns
t_{AFR}	Address Float After Leading Edge of READ (INTA)		0		0		0	ns
t_{AL}	A_{8-15} Valid Before Trailing Edge of ALE [1]	115		50		25		ns

*Note: For Extended Temperature EXPRESS use M8085AH Electricals Parameters.

AFN-01835C

A.C. CHARACTERISTICS (Continued)

Symbol	Parameter	8085AH[2] (Final)		8085AH-2[2] (Final)		8085AH-1 (Preliminary)		Units
		Min.	Max.	Min.	Max.	Min.	Max.	
t_{ALL}	A_{0-7} Valid Before Trailing Edge of ALE	90		50		25		ns
t_{ARY}	READY Valid from Address Valid		220		100		40	ns
t_{CA}	Address (A_{8-15}) Valid After Control	120		60		30		ns
t_{CC}	Width of Control Low ($\overline{RD}$, $\overline{WR}$, $\overline{INTA}$) Edge of ALE	400		230		150		ns
t_{CL}	Trailing Edge of Control to Leading Edge of ALE	50		25		0		ns
t_{DW}	Data Valid to Trailing Edge of $\overline{WRITE}$	420		230		140		ns
t_{HABE}	HLDA to Bus Enable		210		150		150	ns
t_{HABF}	Bus Float After HLDA		210		150		150	ns
t_{HACK}	HLDA Valid to Trailing Edge of CLK	110		40		0		ns
t_{HDH}	HOLD Hold Time	0		0		0		ns
t_{HDS}	HOLD Setup Time to Trailing Edge of CLK	170		120		120		ns
t_{INH}	INTR Hold Time	0		0		0		ns
t_{INS}	INTR, RST, and TRAP Setup Time to Falling Edge of CLK	160		150		150		ns
t_{LA}	Address Hold Time After ALE	100		50		20		ns
t_{LC}	Trailing Edge of ALE to Leading Edge of Control	130		60		25		ns
t_{LCK}	ALE Low During CLK High	100		50		15		ns
t_{LDR}	ALE to Valid Data During Read		460		270		175	ns
t_{LDW}	ALE to Valid Data During Write		200		120		110	ns
t_{LL}	ALE Width	140		80		50		ns
t_{LRY}	ALE to READY Stable		110		30		10	ns
t_{RAE}	Trailing Edge of $\overline{READ}$ to Re-Enabling of Address	150		90		50		ns
t_{RD}	$\overline{READ}$ (or $\overline{INTA}$) to Valid Data		300		150		75	ns
t_{RV}	Control Trailing Edge to Leading Edge of Next Control	400		220		160		ns
t_{RDH}	Data Hold Time After $\overline{READ}$ $\overline{INTA}$	0		0		0		ns
t_{RYH}	READY Hold Time	0		0		5		ns
t_{RYS}	READY Setup Time to Leading Edge of CLK	110		100		100		ns
t_{WD}	Data Valid After Trailing Edge of $\overline{WRITE}$	100		60		30		ns
t_{WDL}	LEADING Edge of $\overline{WRITE}$ to Data Valid		40		20		30	ns

8085AH/8085AH-2/8085AH-1

NOTES:
1. A_8–A_{15} address Specs apply IO/$\overline{M}$, S_0, and S_1 except A_8–A_{15} are undefined during T_4–T_6 of OF cycle whereas IO/$\overline{M}$, S_0, and S_1 are stable.
2. *Test Conditions:* t_{CYC} = 320 ns (8085AH)/200 ns (8085AH-2);/167 ns (8085AH-1); C_L = 150 pF.

3. For all output timing where $C_L \neq 150$ pF use the following correction factors:
   25 pF $\leq C_L <$ 150 pF: -0.10 ns/pF
   150 pF $< C_L \leq$ 300 pF: $+0.30$ ns/pF
4. Output timings are measured with purely capacitive load.
5. To calculate timing specifications at other values of t_{CYC} use Table 5.

A.C. TESTING INPUT, OUTPUT WAVEFORM

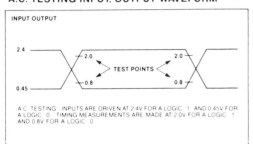

A.C. TESTING: INPUTS ARE DRIVEN AT 2.4V FOR A LOGIC 1 AND 0.45V FOR A LOGIC 0. TIMING MEASUREMENTS ARE MADE AT 2.0V FOR A LOGIC 1 AND 0.8V FOR A LOGIC 0.

A.C. TESTING LOAD CIRCUIT

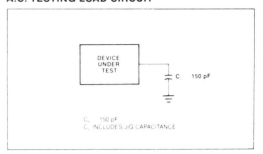

C_L = 150 pF
C_L INCLUDES JIG CAPACITANCE

Table 5. Bus Timing Specification as a T_{CYC} Dependent

Symbol	8085AH	8085AH-2	8085AH-1	
t_{AL}	(1/2) T − 45	(1/2) T − 50	(1/2) T − 58	Minimum
t_{LA}	(1/2) T − 60	(1/2) T − 50	(1/2) T − 63	Minimum
t_{LL}	(1/2) T − 20	(1/2) T − 20	(1/2) T − 33	Minimum
t_{LCK}	(1/2) T − 60	(1/2) T − 50	(1/2) T − 68	Minimum
t_{LC}	(1/2) T − 30	(1/2) T − 40	(1/2) T − 58	Minimum
t_{AD}	(5/2 + N) T − 225	(5/2 + N) T − 150	(5/2 + N) T − 192	Maximum
t_{RD}	(3/2 + N) T − 180	(3/2 + N) T − 150	(3/2 + N) T − 175	Maximum
t_{RAE}	(1/2) T − 10	(1/2) T − 10	(1/2) T − 33	Minimum
t_{CA}	(1/2) T − 40	(1/2) T − 40	(1/2) T − 53	Minimum
t_{DW}	(3/2 + N) T − 60	(3/2 + N) T − 70	(3/2 + N) T − 110	Minimum
t_{WD}	(1/2) T − 60	(1/2) T − 40	(1/2) T − 53	Minimum
t_{CC}	(3/2 + N) T − 80	(3/2 + N) T − 70	(3/2 + N) T − 100	Minimum
t_{CL}	(1/2) T − 110	(1/2) T − 75	(1/2) T − 83	Minimum
t_{ARY}	(3/2) T − 260	(3/2) T − 200	(3/2) T − 210	Maximum
t_{HACK}	(1/2) T − 50	(1/2) T − 60	(1/2) T − 83	Minimum
t_{HABF}	(1/2) T + 50	(1/2) T + 50	(1/2) T + 67	Maximum
t_{HABE}	(1/2) T + 50	(1/2) T + 50	(1/2) T + 67	Maximum
t_{AC}	(2/2) T − 50	(2/2) T − 85	(2/2) T − 97	Minimum
t_1	(1/2) T − 80	(1/2) T − 60	(1/2) T − 63	Minimum
t_2	(1/2) T − 40	(1/2) T − 30	(1/2) T − 33	Minimum
t_{RV}	(3/2) T − 80	(3/2) T − 80	(3/2) T − 90	Minimum
t_{LDR}	(4/2) T − 180	(4/2) T − 130	(4/2) T − 159	Maximum

NOTE: N is equal to the total WAIT states. T = t_{CYC}.

320

WAVEFORMS

CLOCK

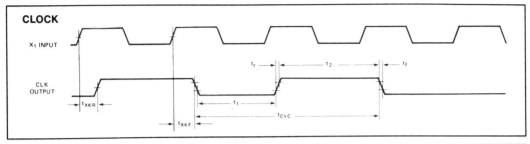

READ

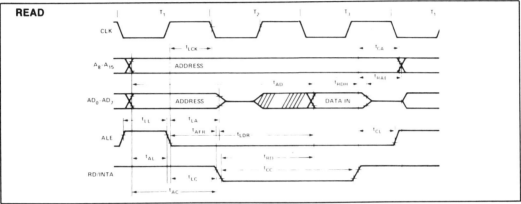

WRITE

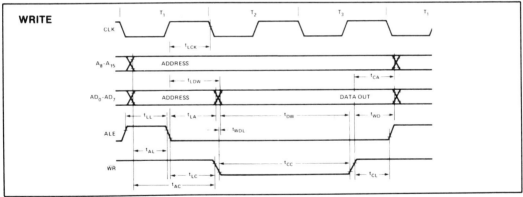

HOLD

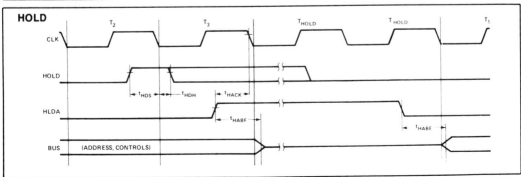

WAVEFORMS (Continued)

READ OPERATION WITH WAIT CYCLE (TYPICAL) — SAME READY TIMING APPLIES TO WRITE

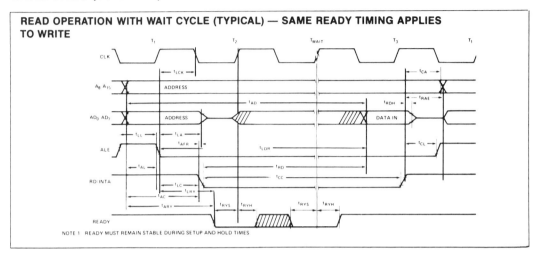

INTERRUPT AND HOLD

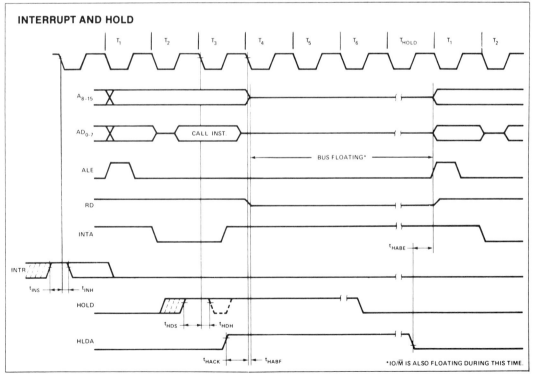

AFN-018350

appendix c

ASCII CODE

ASCII character	Binary code	Hexadecimal code	Decimal code
NUL	0000 0000	00	0
SOH	0000 0001	01	1
STX	0000 0010	02	2
ETX	0000 0011	03	3
EOT	0000 0100	04	4
ENQ	0000 0101	05	5
ACK	0000 0110	06	6
BEL	0000 0111	07	7
BS	0000 1000	08	8
HT	0000 1001	09	9
LF	0000 1010	0A	10
VT	0000 1011	0B	11
FF	0000 1100	0C	12
CR	0000 1101	0D	13
SO	0000 1110	0E	14
SI	0000 1111	0F	15
DLE	0001 0000	10	16
DC1	0001 0001	11	17
DC2	0001 0010	12	18
DC3	0001 0011	13	19
DC4	0001 0100	14	20

ASCII character	Binary code	Hexadecimal code	Decimal code
NAK	0001 0101	15	21
SYN	0001 0110	16	22
ETB	0001 0111	17	23
CAN	0001 1000	18	24
EM	0001 1001	19	25
SUB	0001 1010	1A	26
ESC	0001 1011	1B	27
FS	0001 1100	1C	28
GS	0001 1101	1D	29
RS	0001 1110	1E	30
US	0001 1111	1F	31
SP	0010 0000	20	32
!	0010 0001	21	33
''	0010 0010	22	34
#	0010 0011	23	35
$	0010 0100	24	36
%	0010 0101	25	37
&	0010 0110	26	38
'	0010 0111	27	39
(	0010 1000	28	40
)	0010 1001	29	41
*	0010 1010	2A	42
+	0010 1011	2B	43
,	0010 1100	2C	44
−	0010 1101	2D	45
.	0010 1110	2E	46
/	0010 1111	2F	47
0	0011 0000	30	48
1	0011 0001	31	49
2	0011 0010	32	50
3	0011 0011	33	51
4	0011 0100	34	52
5	0011 0101	35	53
6	0011 0110	36	54
7	0011 0111	37	55
8	0011 1000	38	56
9	0011 1001	39	57
:	0011 1010	3A	58
;	0011 1011	3B	59
<	0011 1100	3C	60
=	0011 1101	3D	61

ASCII character	Binary code	Hexadecimal code	Decimal code
>	0011 1110	3E	62
?	0011 1111	3F	63
@	0100 0000	40	64
A	0100 0001	41	65
B	0100 0010	42	66
C	0100 0011	43	67
D	0100 0100	44	68
E	0100 0101	45	69
F	0100 0110	46	70
G	0100 0111	47	71
H	0100 1000	48	72
I	0100 1001	49	73
J	0100 1010	4A	74
K	0100 1011	4B	75
L	0100 1100	4C	76
M	0100 1101	4D	77
N	0100 1110	4E	78
O	0100 1111	4F	79
P	0101 0000	50	80
Q	0101 0001	51	81
R	0101 0010	52	82
S	0101 0011	53	83
T	0101 0100	54	84
U	0101 0101	55	85
V	0101 0110	56	86
W	0101 0111	57	87
X	0101 1000	58	88
Y	0101 1001	59	89
Z	0101 1010	5A	90
[	0101 1011	5B	91
/	0101 1100	5C	92
]	0101 1101	5D	93
`	0101 1110	5E	94
__	0101 1111	5F	95
'	0110 0000	60	96
a	0110 0001	61	97
b	0110 0010	62	98
c	0110 0011	63	99
d	0110 0100	64	100
e	0110 0101	65	101
f	0110 0110	66	102

ASCII character	Binary code	Hexadecimal code	Decimal code
g	0110 0111	67	103
h	0110 1000	68	104
i	0110 1001	69	105
j	0110 1010	6A	106
k	0110 1011	6B	107
l	0110 1100	6C	108
m	0110 1101	6D	109
n	0110 1110	6E	110
o	0110 1111	6F	111
p	0111 0000	70	112
q	0111 0001	71	113
r	0111 0010	72	114
s	0111 0011	73	115
t	0111 0100	74	116
u	0111 0101	75	117
v	0111 0110	76	118
w	0111 0111	77	119
x	0111 1000	78	120
y	0111 1001	79	121
z	0111 1010	7A	122
{	0111 1011	7B	123
|	0111 1100	7C	124
}	0111 1101	7D	125
~	0111 1110	7E	126
□	0111 1111	7F	127

CONTROL CHARACTER DEFINITIONS

Character	Function
NUL	Null or blank
SOH	Start of heading
STX	Start of text
ETX	End of text
EOT	End of transmission
ENQ	Enquiry
ACK	Acknowledge
BEL	Bell
BS	Backspace
HT	Horizontal tab
LF	Line feed

Character	Function
VT	Vertical tab
FF	Form feed
CR	Carriage return (enter)
SO	Shift out
SI	Shift in
DLE	Data link escape
DC1	Direct control 1
DC2	Direct control 2
DC3	Direct control 3
DC4	Direct control 4
NAK	Negative acknowledge
SYN	Synchronous idle
ETB	End of transmission block
CAN	Cancel
EM	End of medium
SUB	Substitute
ESC	Escape
FS	Form separator
RS	Record separator
US	Unit separator
□	Delete or rubout

HIDDEN 8085A INSTRUCTIONS

The 8085A officially contains 246 different instructions. Because the op-code is an 8-bit number there are 256 different possible op-codes. What occurs when the remaining 10 op-codes are executed? Believe it or not, most versions of the 8085A have some powerful additional instructions that are not published by the manufacturer. This appendix details the operation of each of these additional instructions and two additional flag bits. Beware that not all versions of the 8085A will function with these instructions. (I have not found any, but there may be some out there somewhere.)

ADDITIONAL FLAG BITS

The flag register as presented earlier in the text contained three unused flag bit positions. Two of these are used as listed in Fig. D-1. The X flag bit is an overflow/underflow bit for the INX and DCX instructions. If the HL register pair

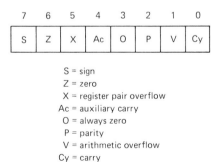

7	6	5	4	3	2	1	0
S	Z	X	Ac	O	P	V	Cy

S = sign
Z = zero
X = register pair overflow
Ac = auxiliary carry
O = always zero
P = parity
V = arithmetic overflow
Cy = carry

Figure D-1 The 8085A flag bits showing V and X.

contains an FFFFH and it is incremented by an INX H, the X flag bit will become a 1. This bit can be tested by two new instructions, as detailed later. Underflow is when a register pair changes from a 0000H to an FFFFH, as with a DCX instruction.

The V flag bit is an overflow bit that indicates an overflow after an addition or a subtraction. For example, if a signed 7FH (128) is added to a 01H, the result is 80H, but 80H is a −128. This is the wrong answer. Until this flag bit is used, it is very difficult to detect this type of overflow. Two instructions are available that test this flag bit in the 8085A.

HIDDEN INSTRUCTIONS

The 8085A contains 10 instructions (see Table D-1), that have not been announced by Intel.

TABLE D-1 HIDDEN 8085A INSTRUCTIONS

Symbolic	Machine	Comment
DSB	08	HL = HL − BC
JNX a16	DD–ll–hh	Jump on X = 0
JX a16	FD–ll–hh	Jump on X = 1
LDH d8	28–d8	DE = HL + d8
LDS d8	38–d8	DE = SP + d8
LHL	ED	Load HL from location addressed by DE
RHL	10	Arithmetic right shift of HL
RL	18	Rotate DE left through carry
RSTV	CB	Restart on overflow
SHL	D9	Store HL at location addressed by DE

Notes: a16, 16-bit memory address; d8, 8-bits of immediate data; ll, low-order address; hh, high-order address.

DSB subtracts the BC register pair from the HL register pair and the result is placed in the HL register pair. This instruction affects all the flags, including V and X.

JNX is used to test the X flag bit. If X = 0, a jump occurs, and if X = 1, the next sequential instruction is executed. No flags are affected by this instruction.

JX tests the X flag for a logic 1 condition. If X = 1, a jump occurs to the 16-bit memory address that is stored with the op-code.

LDH adds the immediate byte of data to the contents of the HL register pair and stores the sum in the DE register pair. This operation does not affect any of the flag bits.

LDS adds the immediate byte of data to the contents of the SP register and stores the sum in the DE register pair. No flags are affected by this addition.

LHL loads the HL register pair from the memory locations addressed by the DE register pair. L is loaded from address DE and H is loaded from address DE + 1.

RHL is used to shift the HL register pair to the right. This instruction performs an arithmetic right shift by copying the sign flag bit through the remaining portion of the HL register pair. Only the Cy flag is affected by this instruction.

RL rotates the DE register pair to the left through the carry flag bit.

RSTV calls the subroutine that begins at memory address 0040H if the overflow bit (V) is a logic 1.

SHL stores the contents of the HL register pair into memory beginning at the location addressed by the DE register pair. L is stored at the location addressed by DE and H is stored at the location addressed by DE + 1.

appendix e

ANSWERS TO THE EVEN-NUMBERED QUESTIONS

Chapter 1

1-2. Arcade games and calculators.

1-4. 8 bits.

1-6. NMOS technology.

1-8. 8086, Z8000, and the MC68000.

1-10. Microprocessor, memory, and I/O.

1-12. Data, control, and address.

1-14. Zero, sign, and parity.

1-16. RAM.

1-18. NMOS, CMOS, DRAM, and SRAM.

1-20. Motor, switch, DAC, and ADC.

1-22. Display memory and registers, store memory and registers, run a program, and single-step through a program.

Chapter 2

2-2. A VDT, an assembler, an editor, and a linker.

2-4. Move strings of characters, delete data, and move entire blocks of data.

2-6. A syntax error is an error of form.

2-8. Assembly language and library modules.

2-10. If teamwork is used properly, it reduces the amount of time required to develop software.

2-12. Top-down, modular, and structured.

2-14. Modular.

2-16. (1) Define the system, (2) design the system using top-down techniques, (3) determine which modules exist, (4) program the modules, (5) test the modules, (6) link the modules and test as a system, (7) determine whether the system must be redesigned or whether it can go into production.

2-18. Without good communications between members of a software design team it is doubtful that a system will ever be created.

2-20. A mnemonic code is an abbreviation for a standard operation such as addition or subtraction.

2-22. Symbolic code uses mnemonic codes, whereas binary machine code is coded in binary.

2-24. It detects errors the instant they occur.

Chapter 3

3-2. 64K.

3-4. Serial input and output data.

3-6. See Fig. E-1.

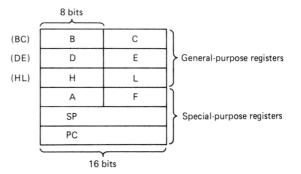

3-8. Register pair.

3-10. S: sign, P: parity, Ac: auxiliary carry between half-bytes, Z: zero, and Cy: carry out of the most significant bit of the result.

3-12. LIFO.

3-14. At the bottom of the memory beginning at location 0000H.

3-16. The microprocessor's connection to the outside world.

3-18. $156 = 1001\ \ 1100$, $522 = 10\ \ 0000\ \ 1010$, $1000 = 11\ \ 1110\ \ 1000$, $2009 = 111\ \ 1101\ \ 1001$, and $10000 = 10\ \ 0111\ \ 0001\ \ 0000$.

3-20. $12 = 0000\ \ 1100$, $-12 = 1111\ \ 0100$, $32 = 0010\ \ 0000$, $-63 = 1100\ \ 0001$, and $-100 = 1001\ \ 1100$.

3-22. A control H is typed.

3-24.
$$
\begin{array}{rllllllll}
12 = & 0100 & 0001 & 0100 & 0000 & 0000 & 0000 & 0000 & 0000\,, \\
-22 = & 1100 & 0001 & 1011 & 0000 & 0000 & 0000 & 0000 & 0000\,, \\
10.5 = & 0100 & 0001 & 1010 & 1000 & 0000 & 0000 & 0000 & 0000\,, \\
0.002 = & 0011 & 1011 & 0000 & 0011 & 0001 & 0010 & 0110 & 1110\,, \text{ and} \\
-4.25 = & 1100 & 0000 & 1000 & 1000 & 0000 & 0000 & 0000 & 0000\,.
\end{array}
$$

3-26. 246.

3-28. The data acted on by the opcode.

3-30. Byte 1 is the op-code and bytes 2 and 3 are the data or address. Byte 2 is the least significant part, and byte 3 is the most significant part.

3-32. Any instruction that is not an arithmetic or logic operation.

Chapter 4

4-2. 3.

4-4. 1000H = 00-10, 234AH = 4A-23, ABCDH = CD-AB, 5000H = 00-50, and 456FH = 6F-45.

4-6. Letter M refers to the memory location pointed to by the HL register pair.

4-8. LXI D,1200H = 11-00-12, MVI C,90H = 0E-90, LXI SP,1234H = 31-34-12, MVI M,10 = 36-0A, and MVI M,10H = 36-10.

4-10. See Example E-1.

(EXAMPLE E-1)

```
21-00-12   LXI H,1200H
36-16      MVI M,16H
2E-02      MVI L,02H
36-17      MVI M,17H
```

4-12. 1200H = 44H and 1201H = 22H.

4-14. 77H.

4-16. Because this instruction does not do anything!

4-18. See Example E-2.

(EXAMPLE E-2)

```
78      MOV A,B
42      MOV B,D
57      MOV D,A
79      MOV A,C
4B      MOV C,E
5F      MOV E,A
```

4-20. 2000H.

4-22. Processor status word: the accumulator and flags.

4-24. C.

4-26. LXI SP,d16, and SPHL.

Chapter 5

5-2.

	S	Cy	P	AC	Z
12H + 33H = 45H	0	0	0	0	0
F0H + 33H = 23H	0	1	0	0	0
0FH + 40H = 4FH	0	0	0	0	0
3FH + ABH = EAH	1	0	0	1	0

5-4. See Example E-3.

```
(EXAMPLE E-3)
7D      MOV A,H     ;get H
85      ADD L       ;A + L
6F      MOV L,A     ;answer to L
```

5-6. See Example E-4.

```
(EXAMPLE E-4)
7B      MOV A,E     ;get E
85      ADD L       ;A + L
6F      MOV L,A     ;answer to L
7A      MOV A,D     ;get D
8D      ADC H       ;A + H + Cy
67      MOV H,A     ;answer to H
```

5-8. Only the carry flag (Cy).

5-10. See Example E-5.

```
(EXAMPLE E-5)
47      MOV A,B     ;get B
85      ADD L       ;A + L
27      DAA         ;correct result
6F      MOV L,A     ;answer to L
```

5-12.

	S	Cy	P	AC	Z
12H − 33H = DFH	1	1	0	1	0
F0H − 33H = BDH	1	0	1	1	0
0FH − 40H = CFH	1	1	1	0	0
3FH − ABH = 94H	1	1	0	0	0

5-14. SUB M.

5-16. See Example E-6.

```
(EXAMPLE E-6)
7D      MOV A,L     ;get L
93      SUB E       ;A - E
6F      MOV L,A     ;answer to L
7C      MOV A,H     ;get H
9A      SBB D       ;A - D - Cy
67      MOV H,A     ;answer to H
```

5-18. Both instructions subtract except that the compare instruction only changes the flags, while the subtract changes the flags and stores the difference in the accumulator.

5-20. CMA.

5-22. Clear.

5-24. Invert.

5-26. It is used to test the accumulator.

5–28. Because the accumulator contains 8 bits, it does not matter whether the number is rotated four places to the right or to the left.

5–30. See Example E–7.

```
(EXAMPLE E-7)

79      MOV  A,C  ;get C
87      ADD  A    ;shift left
4F      MOV  C,A  ;answer to C
78      MOV  A,B  ;get B
8F      ADC  A    ;shift left + Cy
47      MOV  B,A  ;answer to B
```

Chapter 6

6–2. The JMP instruction jumps to the memory location stored in bytes 2 and 3 of the instruction, and the PCHL instruction jumps to the location stored in the HL register pair.

6–4. Z (zero), Cy (carry), S (sign), and P (parity).

6–6. The carry flag is used to indicate the relative magnitude of two numbers, and at times, this is important in software.

6–8. The parity flag is most often used in a data communications environment.

6–10. CALL.

6–12. The contents of the program counter always point to the next instruction to be executed; therefore, the CALL instruction, which places this number on the stack, is placing the address of the next instruction on the stack. This address is retrieved by the return instruction so that it can return to the program. For this reason, this number or address is called the return address.

6–14. The program counter.

6–16. See Example E–8.

```
(EXAMPLE E-8)

START: MVI  A,4    ;load A with test number
       CALL TRIP   ;triple A
       CALL TRIP   ;triple A
END:   JMP  END    ;end program
```

6–18. Nothing.

6–20. A reset or an interrupt.

6–22. An interrupt service subroutine is the subroutine called by the interrupt for the purpose of servicing the interrupt.

6–24. Off.

6–26. See Example E–9.

```
(EXAMPLE E-9)

TOGGLE: MVI  A,0COH  ;set SOD
        SIM
        MVI  A,40H   ;clear SOD
        SIM
        RET
```

Chapter 7

7-2. Source and object.

7-4. One-pass assemblers are rare because of the problem with forward addressing.

7-6. (a) Invalid because of the period before the 3. (b) Invalid because it's missing the colon (this may be allowed with some assemblers); (c) invalid because it starts with a number; (d) valid in most assemblers; (e) invalid because a space is not allowed.

7-8. 12 or 12D (decimal), 120 (octal), and 12H (hexadecimal).

7-10. The semicolon is used to indicate that any character(s) following it to the end of the line are considered comments.

7-12. DB 'WATERLOO'.

7-14. ORG 0800H.

7-16. False.

7-18. A linker is a program that is used to connect or link program modules together.

7-20. (a) V because the value of the operand is too great to be moved into A; (b) R because X is not a valid register; (c) S because a period is used to separate A and B instead of a comma; (d) E because the operand expression is invalid.

7-22. An assembler that can create new op-codes (macros).

7-24. A plus sign is used to set off a macro expansion.

Chapter 8

8-2. See Figure E-2.

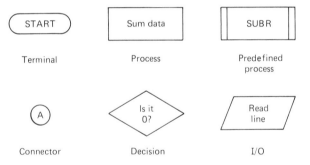

8-4. A subroutine.

8-6. Yes the question cannot have more than three direct answers.

8-8. Sequence, if-then, if-then-else, repeat-until, do-while, and often a programmed loop.

8-10. See Figure E-3.

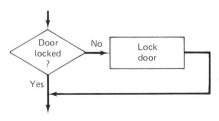

8-12. See Figure E-4.

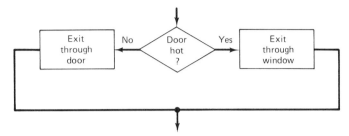

8-14. No, because you need to dial the police before you can determine if the telephone is busy.

8-16. See Figure E-5.

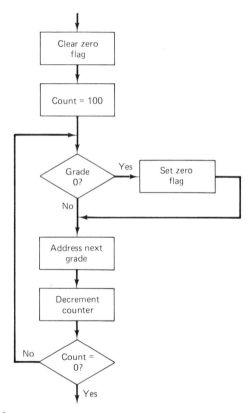

8-18. See Example E-10.

```
(EXAMPLE E-10)

(if BC is the counter)

        MVI   A,0
        CMP   B
        JNZ   LOOP
        CMP   C
        JNZ   LOOP
```

Chapter 9

9-2. See Example E-11.

```
(EXAMPLE E-11)

                        ORG   2000H
2000 06-05    START: MVI   B,5      ;load counter with 5
2002 21-00-28        LXI   H,2800H  ;point to 2800H
2005 11-20-28        LXI   D,2820H  ;point to 2820H
2008 7E       LOOP:  MOV   A,M      ;transfer a byte
2009 12              STAX  D
200A 23              INX   H        ;adjust pointers
200B 13              INX   D
200C 05              DCR   B        ;decrement counter
200D C2-08-20        JNZ   LOOP     ;if counter <> 0
2010 C3-10-20 ENDP:  JMP   ENDP     ;end program
```

9-4. 256.

9-6. The main difference is the counter is stored in the B register in Example 9-1 and in the BC register pair in Example 9-2.

9-8. No. It is not complete because when it returns from the CALL instruction there is no continuation of the program.

9-10. The only difference is the way that data are moved. In the transfer program the MOV A,M and STAX D instructions are used to transfer data, and in the exchange program additional instructions are required to exchange the data.

9-12. Readability is very important later when the software is modified.

9-14. (a) 57 68 61 74 20 61 72 65 20 79 6F 75 20 64 6F 69 67 3F; (b) 49 20 64 6F 6E 27 74 20 6B 6E 6F 77 2E; (c) 45 78 70 6C 61 69 6E 20 74 68 61 74 21; (d) 57 65 6C 6C 2C 20 73 6F 20 49 20 63 61 6E 2E; (e) 57 68 6F 70 20 64 6F 20 79 6F 75 20 74 72 75 73 74 3F.

9-16. The carriage return returns the print head or cursor to the left margin of the paper or CRT screen, and the line feed moves the cursor or print head down a line.

9-18. See Example E-12.

```
(EXAMPLE E-12)

                        ORG   2050H
2050 06-05    SMOVE: MVI   B,5      ;load counter
2052 7E       LOOP:  MOV   A,M      ;transfer byte
2053 12              STAX  D
2054 23              INX   H        ;adjust pointers
2055 13              INX   D
2056 FE-0A           CPI   LF       ;test for line feed
2058 C2-52-20        JNZ   LOOP     ;repeat-until LF
205B 05              DCR   B        ;decrement count
205C C2-52-20        JNZ   LOOP     ;if count <> 0
205F C9              RET
2060 0A-00    LF:    EQU   0AH      ;define line feed
```

9-20. It is much more difficult because when strings are of different lengths other strings must be moved around before the exchange can be completed.

9-22. (1) The remaining portion of the longest string is transferred to a buffer; (2) the strings in the array are moved to make room for the longer string; (3) the buffer is unloaded into the array in the place allocated by the move.

Chapter 10

10-2. See Example E-13.

```
(EXAMPLE E-13)

                        ORG   2000H    ;origin
2000 EB         START:  XCHG           ;DE to HL
2001 09                 DAD   B        ;DE + BC
2002 EB                 XCHG           ;answer to DE
2003 C3-03-20 ENDP:     JMP   ENDP     ;end program
```

10-4. See Example E-14.

```
(EXAMPLE E-14)

                        ORG   2000H    ;origin
2000 21-20-28 START: LXI  H,ANS    ;point to answer
2003 E5              PUSH H        ;save answer address
2004 21-10-28        LXI  H,LIST2  ;address LIST2
2007 11-00-28        LXI  D,LIST1  ;address LIST1
200A 06-0A           MVI  B,10     ;load counter
200C 12       LOOP:  LDAX D        ;get LIST1
200D 96              SUB  M        ;subtract LIST2
200E E3              XTHL
200F 77              MOV  M,A      ;difference to ANS
2010 23              INX  H        ;adjust pointers
2011 E3              XTHL
2012 23              INX  H
2013 13              INX  D
2014 05              DCR  B        ;decrement counter
2015 C2-0C-20        JNZ  LOOP     ;if count <> 0
2018 E1              POP  H        ;clear stack
2019 C3-19-20 ENDP:  JMP  ENDP     ;end program
201C 00-28    LIST1: EQU  2800H    ;define LIST1
201C 10-28    LIST2: EQU  2810H    ;define LIST2
201C 20-28    ANS:   EQU  2820H    ;define ANS
```

10-6. See Example E-15.

```
(EXAMPLE E-15)

                        ORG   2060H    ;origin
2060 E5        MUL13:  PUSH H         ;save 1X
2061 29                DAD  H         ;2X
2062 29                DAD  H         ;4X
2063 E5                PUSH H         ;save 4X
2064 29                DAD  H         ;8X
2065 D1                POP  D         ;get 4X
2066 19                DAD  D         ;generate 12X
2067 D1                POP  D         ;get 1X
2068 19                DAD  D         ;generate 13X
2069 C9                RET            ;return
```

10-8. See Example E-16.

```
(EXAMPLE E-16)

                          ORG    2040H    ;origin
        2040 06-00   MULT:  MVI    B,0      ;clear B
        2042 EB             XCHG
        2043 21-00-00       LXI    H,0
        2046 B7       LOOP:  ORA    A        ;test multiplier
        2047 CA-59-20       JZ     ENDS     ;if zero
        204A 1F             RAR             ;shift multiplier right
        204B D2-53-20       JNC    LOOP1    ;if no carry
        204E 19             DAD    D        ;add multiplicand
        204F D2-53-20       JNC    LOOP1
        2052 04             INR    B
        2053 EB       LOOP1: XCHG            ;shift multiplicand
        2054 29             DAD    H
        2055 EB             XCHG
        2056 C3-46-20       JMP    LOOP     ;repeat
        2059 C9       ENDS:  RET             ;return
```

10-10. See Example E-17.

```
(EXAMPLE E-17)

                          ORG    2070H    ;origin
        2070 07      SDIV8: RLC             ;sign to carry
        2071 1F             RAR             ;original number, C = sign
        2072 1F             RAR             ;arithmetic shift complete
        2073 07             RLC             ;second arithmetic shift
        2074 1F             RAR
        2075 1F             RAR
        2076 07             RLC             ;third arithmetic shift
        2077 1F             RAR
        2078 1F             RAR
        2079 CE-00          ACI    0        ;round result
        207B C9             RET             ;return
```

10-12. Change the count from 4 to 8.

10-14. Yes; see Example E-18.

```
(EXAMPLE E-18)

                          ORG    2040H    ;origin
        2040 06-04   PACK:  MVI    B,4      ;load counter
        2042 79      PCK1:  MOV    C,M      ;get byte
        2043 23             INX    H        ;adjust pointer
        2044 7E             MOV    A,M      ;get byte
        2045 23             INX    H        ;adjust pointer
        2046 07             RLC             ;shift left 4
        2047 07             RLC
        2048 07             RLC
        2049 07             RLC
        204A 81             ADD    C        ;combine bytes
        204B 12             STAX   D        ;store packed byte
        204C 13             INX    D        ;adjust pointer
        204D 05             DCR    B        ;decrement counter
        204E C2-42-20       JNZ    PCK1     ;if counter <> 0
        2051 C9             RET             ;return
```

10-16. It is used to clear the stack of the address of the answer.

10-18. Ten's complement.

10-20. See Example E-19.

```
(EXAMPLE E-19)

                             ORG   2000H    ;origin
       2000 7B       START:  MOV   A,E      ;form difference
       2001 91               SUB   C
       2002 6F               MOV   L,A
       2003 7A               MOV   A,D
       2004 98               SBB   B
       2005 67               MOV   H,A
       2006 C3-06-20 ENDP:   JMP   ENDP     ;end program
```

Chapter 11

11-2. BASIC and Pascal interpreters and compilers.

11-4. Power or characteristic.

11-6. The ANSI floating-point format consists of four bytes. Byte 1 contains the signs of both mantissa and exponent and the 6-bit exponent. The remaining three bytes contain the mantissa.

11-8. **(a)** 00000001 10000000 00000000 00000000
      (b) 00000010 10100000 00000000 00000000
      (c) 00001010 11111111 11110000 00000000
      (d) 10000101 10000000 10000000 00000000
      (e) 10001000 11010100 00100000 00000000

11-10. **(a)** 3.0
      (b) $-22,592$
      (c) 0.1328325
      (d) 0.0
      (e) -0.0302734375

11-12. **(a)** 01000000 00000000 00000000
      (b) 01000010 11100100 00000000
      (c) 10111111 00100000 00000000
      (d) 00000000 00000000 00000000
      (e) 01000011 11001000 00000000

11-14. This subroutine generates the two's complement by inverting each half of the HL register pair with the CMA instruction. The entire HL register pair is then incremented to generate the two's complement.

11-16. See Example E-20.

```
(EXAMPLE E-20)          ;
                        ;program that adds a 100
                        ;and 52 together.
                        ;
       2000 16-43    START: MVI   D,43H     ;load 100 into DBC
       2002 01-00-48        LXI   B,4800H
       2005 1E-42           MVI   E,42H     ;load 52 into EHL
       2007 21-00-D0        LXI   H,0D000H
       200A CD-00-28        CALL  ADDF      ;add number
       200D C3-0D-20 ENDP:  JMP   ENDP      ;end program
```

11-18. The differences are that the exponents are added for multiplication and subtracted for division and, of course, multiplication versus division for the mantissas.

Chapter 12

12-2. 30H.

12-4. The problem is that ASCII numbers and ASCII letters are separated by a bias of 7.

12-6. See Example E-21.

```
              (EXAMPLE E-21)
                            ;
                            ;subroutine to convert the accumulator
                            ;to two ASCII digits stored in BC.
                            ;
                                 ORG   2000H
              2000 F5        CONV:  PUSH PSW    ;save accumulator
              2001 E6-0F            ANI  0FH    ;mask left-most
              2003 CD-14-28         CALL SHXA   ;convert right-most
              2007 4F               MOV  C,A    ;save right-most
              2008 F1               POP  PSW    ;restore accumulator
              2009 0F               RRC         ;move right 4 bits
              200A 0F               RRC
              200B 0F               RRC
              200C 0F               RRC
              200D E6-0F            ANI  0FH    ;mask left-most
              2010 CD-14-28         CALL SHXA   ;convert left-most
              2013 47               MOV  B,A    ;save left-most
              2014 C9               RET
```

12-8. See Example E-22.

```
              (EXAMPLE E-22)
                            ;
                            ;subroutine to convert BCD to binary (integer)
                            ;result = HL register pair
                            ;DE indirectly addresses BCD number
                            ;BCD number must end with a CR
                            ;range 0 -- 65,536
                            ;
                            ;subroutine MUL10 is stored at 2017H
                            ;
              2800 21-00-00 BCDB:  LXI  H,0    ;clear result
              2803 1A       BCDB1: LDAX D      ;get BCD digit
              2804 FE-0D           CPI  0DH    ;check for end
              2806 CA-16-28        JZ   BCDB2  ;if CR end subroutine
              2809 CD-17-20        CALL MUL10  ;multiply result times 10
              280C 85              ADD  L      ;add BCD digit to result
              280D 6F              MOV  L,A
              280E 7C              MOV  A,H
              280F CE-00           ACI  0
              2811 67              MOV  H,A
              2812 13              INX  D      ;address next digit
              2813 C3-03-28        JMP  BCDB1  ;convert next digit
              2816 3A-25-28 BCDB2: LDA  SIGN   ;get sign
              2819 B7              ORA  A      ;test sign
```

```
281A F2-24-28          JP   BCDB3 ;if positive
281D 74                MOV  A,H   ;two complement HL
281E 2F                CMA
281F 67                MOV  H,A
2820 75                MOV  A,L
2821 2F                CMA
2822 6F                MOV  L,A
2823 23                INX  H
2824 C9      BCDB3:    RET        ;return
2825 ·       SIGN:     DS   1     ;reserve for sign
```

Example E-22 *(Continued)*

12-10. 10 and remainder.

12-12. 10.

12-14. See Example E-23.

(EXAMPLE E-23)

```
                    ORG   2800H
           ;
           ;subroutine to scan through a character string and
           ;locate the first numeric character.
           ;
           ;HL is used to point to the first character of the
           ;string.
           ;
           ;on the return, HL points to the first numeric
           ;character in the string or to a carriage return
           ;if no number exists.
           ;
           ;return carry = 0 means carriage return
           ;return carry = 1 means valid number
           ;
2800 7E    SCAN:   MOV  A,M    ;get string character
2801 FE-0D         CPI  0DH    ;test for carriage return
2803 CA-1F-28      JZ   SCAN3  ;if carriage return
2806 FE-2B         CPI  '+'    ;check for +
2808 CA-1E-28      JZ   SCAN2  ;if +
280B FE-2D         CPI  '-'    ;check for -
280D CA-1E-28      JZ   SCAN2  ;if -
2810 FE-30         CPI  30H    ;test for less than 0
2812 DA-1A-28      JC   SCAN1  ;if less than 0
2815 FE-3A         CPI  3AH    ;test for greater than 9
2817 DA-1F-28      JC   SCAN3  ;if not greater than 9
281A 23    SCAN1:  INX  H      ;point to next character
281B C3-00-28      JMP  SCAN   ;check next character
281E 37    SCAN2:  STC
281F C9    SCAN3:  RET         ;return
```

12-16. No modification is required.

12-18. See Example E-24.

(EXAMPLE E-24 page 1 of 2)

```
                    ORG   2830H
           ;subroutine to convert data in a table
```

(EXAMPLE E-24 page 2 of 2)

```
                        ;addressed by BC into a second table
                        ;addressed by HL.
                        ;count is in D register
                        ;
    2830 0A     BINB:    LDAX  B       ;get BCD data
    2831 FE-0F           CPI   0FH     ;check for minus
    2833 32-6F-28        STA   SIGN    ;save for later
    2836 C2-3A-28        JNZ   BINB1   ;if positive
    2839 03              INX   B
    283A D5     BINB1:   PUSH  D       ;save DE
    283B E5              PUSH  H       ;save HL
    283C 21-00-00        LXI   H,0     ;clear result
    283F 0A     BINB2:   LDAX  B       ;get digit
    2840 FE-0D           CPI   0DH     ;carriage return?
    2842 CA-52-28        JZ    BINB3   ;if carriage return
    2845 CD-70-28        CALL  MUL1    ;multply by 10
    2848 85              ADD   L       ;add BCD digit
    2849 6F              MOV   L,A
    284A 7C              MOV   A,H
    284B CE-00           ACI   0
    284D 67              MOV   H,A
    284E 03              INX   B       ;address next digit
    284F C3-3F-28        JMP   BINB2   ;convert next digit
    2852 3A-6F-28 BINB3: LDA   SIGN    ;test sign
    2855 FE-0F           CPI   0FH
    2857 C2-61-28        JNZ   BINB4   ;if positive
    285A 7D              MOV   A,L
    285B 2F              CMA
    285C 6F              MOV   L,A
    285D 7C              MOV   A,H
    285E 2F              CMA
    285F 67              MOV   H,A
    2860 23              INX   H
    2861 D1     BINB4:   POP   D       ;get address
    2862 7D              MOV   A,L     ;save binary number
    2863 12              STAX  D
    2864 13              INX   D
    2865 7C              MOV   A,H
    2866 12              STAX  D
    2867 13              INX   D
    2868 EB              XCHG          ;address back into HL
    2869 D1              POP   D       ;restore count
    286A 15              DCR   D       ;decrement count
    286B C2-30-28        JNZ   BINB    ;if another
    286E C9              RET           ;return
    286F        SIGN:    DS    1       ;reserve for sign
                        ;
                        ;
    2870 29     MUL1:    DAD   H       ;multiple HL by 10
    2871 54              MOV   D,H
    2872 5D              MOV   E,L
    2873 29              DAD   H
    2874 29              DAD   H
    2875 19              DAD   D
    2876 C9              RET           ;return
```

Chapter 13

13-2. See Example E-25.

(EXAMPLE E-25)

```
                        ORG   2000H
      2000 F5      DIP:  PUSH  PSW    ;save acc
      2001 E6-0F         ANI   0FH    ;mask of left-most
      2003 CD-10-28      CALL  LOOK   ;look up right-most
      2006 4F            MOV   C,A    ;store it
      2007 F1            POP   PSW    ;restore acc
      2008 0F            RRC          ;position left-most
      2009 0F            RRC
      200A 0F            RRC
      200B 0F            RRC
      200C E6-0F         ANI   0FH    ;mask left-most
      200E CD-10-28      CALL  LOOK   ;look up left-most
      2011 47            MOV   B,A    ;store it
      2012 C9            RET          ;return
```

13-4. See Example E-26.

(EXAMPLE E-26)

```
                  ORG     2800H
                  ;
                  ;subroutine to reference a tic-tac-toe
                  ;table.
                  ;register B = Y-coordinate (0 - 2)
                  ;register C = X-coordinate (0 - 2)
                  ;return zero = if square is an X
                  ;
   2800 16-03     CHEX:  MVI   D,3    ;load 3
   2802 3E-FD            MVI   A,-3   ;load -3
   2804 82        CHEX1: ADD   D      ;multiply C * 3
   2805 0D               DCR   C
   2806 F2-04-28         JP    CHEX1
   2809 80               ADD   B      ;add B
   280A 4F               MOV   C,A    ;form 16-bit bias
   280B 06-00            MVI   B,0
   280D 21-15-28         LXI   H,TTAB ;address table
   2810 19               DAD   D
   2811 7E               MOV   A,M    ;test entry
   2812 FE-58            CPI   'X'    ;check for X
   2814 C9               RET          ;return
                  ;
   2815           TTAB:  DS    9      ;reserve 9 for table
```

13-6. Yes.

13-8. Sorting data, referencing data as in data base management, and so on.

13-10. $5\frac{1}{3}\,\mu s$.

13-12. 94.7 μs.

13-14. Change the count in DE to 120_{10}.

Chapter 14

14-2. Bubble sort.

14-4. Bubble sort.

14-6. 100.

14-8. Yes, if the comparison is changed from a 16-bit to a 24-bit comparison and the exchange is changed to 24-bit.

14-10. 40.

14-12. This saves memory because nothing needs to be stored to indicate the end of a character string.

14-14. This subroutine compares data until either a mismatch occurs or the end of either string is reached. If a mismatch occurs, the return with carry set or cleared depends on the two characters compared. If the end of either string is reached, the carry is set for the end of the insertion string and cleared for the end of the list string.

14-16. This subroutine first determines how long the insertion string is, then makes room in the list addressed by the HL pair for the insertion string. Once room has been made, the subroutine stores the new string in the list.

Chapter 15

15-2. A soft error or, as it is sometimes called, a dynamic error is a condition where another bit or bits change if an adjacent bit is changed.

15-4. The only difference is that Example 15-1 starts with a data value of 00H and Example 15-2 starts with 55H.

15-6. The walking bit pattern is developed by moving the leftmost bit to the carry flag (RLC and RAR). Next, the carry bit is complemented before it is shifted into the rightmost bit of the accumulator (CMC and RAL).

15-8. After the checksum is initialized to 00H, the data on the ROM are exclusive-ORed together to generate a checksum.

15-10. If after a return, the zero flag indicates a zero condition, the ROM tested good. If it indicates a nonzero condition, the ROM tested bad.

15-12. Display a character at each screen location. This allows for a simple visual test and also for the alignment of the CRT.

15-14. 2 and 3.

15-16. It is tested in two parts so that the stack is not destroyed by the test software.

Chapter 16

16-2. 0.1.

16-4. The amount of capacitance that they add to the bus should not exceed 150 pF.

16-6. If 0, a memory operation, and if 1, an I/O operation.

16-8. $\overline{\text{RD}}$ and $\overline{\text{WR}}$.

16-10. IO/$\overline{\text{M}}$ = 0 and $\overline{\text{RD}}$ = 0.

16-12. The ALE pin is used to demultiplex (remove) the address information from the address/data bus.

16–14. 0000H.

16–16. See Example E–27.

(EXAMPLE E–27)

```
MVI   A,0C0H
SIM
```

16–18. Direct memory access is an I/O technique that allows the I/O device to suspend the microprocessor's operation through the HOLD pin and directly transfers data to or from the memory.

16–20. 575 ns.

16–22. Used to turn the output pins on if $\overline{\text{CE}}$ is also at a logic 0 level.

16–24. Address range = 8000H through FFFFH.

16–26. $\overline{\text{WE}}$.

16–28. 1024 (1K).

16–30. $\overline{\text{WR}}$ = 0 and IO/$\overline{\text{M}}$ = 1.

16–32. When an OUT 66H is executed, the microprocessor outputs a 6666H on the address bus and sends accumulator data to the I/O device through its data bus.

INDEX

A

Accumulator, 31
Addition:
  BCD, 68–69, 174–76
  with carry, 67–68
  8-bit, 65–67
  8-bit binary, 155–56
  floating-point, 191–95
  multiple-byte, 170
  16-bit, 68
Address/data bus, 28
Addressing modes, 48–50
ALE, 282
ALU (Arithmetic and logic unit), 5, 28
AND operation, 74–75
Architecture, 28–30, 278–97
Arithmetic instructions:
  ACI, 65–67
  ADC, 67–68
  ADD, 65–67
  ADI, 65–67
  CMP, CPI, 73
  DAA, 68–69
  DAD, 68
  DCR, DCX, 72
  INR/INX, 69
  SBI, 70–71

SUB, 70–71
SUI, 70–71
ASCII:
  assembler data format, 103
  character strings, 144
  conversion algorithm, 206–22
  data, 37
  entabling of, 232
  sorting of, 253–58
Assembler:
  arithmetic operators, 104
  description of, 16, 22
  error detection, 109–10
  introduction to, 22–23
  language, 99–102
  logic operators, 104
  macro, 110
  pseudo operations, 23, 105–9
  statement, 102–4
  structured programming, 116–32
  types of, 100

B

BASIC, 16, 23
BCD:
  addition and subtraction, 68–69,
    172–97

354 Index

Rotate instructions *(cont.)*
  RLC/RRC, 79
RST, 32
RS-232C testing, 272–73

S

Searching tables, 232–37
Sequence construct, 120
Serial data, 30, 286
SET pseudo operation, 107
Shell, software, 19
Shift instructions:
  ADD A, 80
  DAD H, 80
SID (serial input data), 30, 95
Signed integers, 36–37
Significand, 183
SIM, 94–95
SOD (serial output data), 30, 94–95
Software design of, 20–22
Software development, 14–23
  sytems, 15–17
  task, 17–19
Sorting:
  alphanumeric, 253–58
  bubble-sort, 243–48
  Shell-sort, 249–52
Source code, 22
Source register, 54
SPC (space) pseudo operation, 108–9
Special purpose registers, 31–32
SRAM (static random access memory), 8
Stack instructions:
  PUSH-POP, 58–59
  XTHL, 59
Stack memory operation, 32, 57–59
Stack pointer register, 32
States, machine, 287–88
Static RAM testing, 262–64
STC, 93
Strobe, 295–96
Structured programming, 116–32
  constructs, 119–27
  description of, 20
Subroutine instructions, 89
Subroutines, 88–92
Subtraction:
  BCD, 179
  with borrow, 71–72
  8-bit, 70–71

8-bit binary, 156–58
floating-point, 195–97
multiple-byte, 170–71
Symbols, flowcharting, 117
System:
  design, software, 21
  testing, final, 18, 22

T

Table lookup, 225–37
Temporary register, 28
10's complement, 179
Terminal flowcharting symbol, 118
Testing, programs, 18–19
TEST instruction, 76-77
Texas Instruments TMS1000, 2
Three-byte commands, 41–42
Time delay:
  long, 239
  short, 238
  software, 237–40
Timing:
  read, 287–88
  write, 288–90
TITLE pseudo operation, 108–9
Top-down programming, 19
Trainers, microprocessors (*see*
      Microprocessors)
TTL (transistor-transistor logic), 2
Two-byte commands, 40–41

U

Unconditional jump instructions, 85–86
Unpacking BCD data, 174
Unsigned integers, 34–36

V

VDT (video display terminal), 15–16

W

Walking bit test, 264–67
Wait states, 286
$\overline{WR}$, 30, 281
Write timing, 288–90